HEALTH
SUSTAINABILITY
AND THE BUILT
ENVIRONMENT

HEALTH
SUSTAINABILITY
AND THE
BUILT
ENVIRONMENT

DAK KOPEC, PH.D.

FAIRCHILD BOOKS, INC.

NEW YORK

Director of Sales and Acquisitions: Dana Meltzer-Berkowitz

Executive Editor: Olga T. Kontzias

Acquisitions Editor: Olga T. Kontzias

Senior Development Editor: Jennifer Crane

Art Director: Adam B. Bohannon

Production Director: Ginger Hillman

Associate Production Editor: Jessica Rozler

Associate Art Director: Erin Fitzsimmons

Copyeditor: Roxanne Furlong

Cover Design: Adam B. Bohannon

Text Design: Renato Stanisic

Photo Research: Erin Fitzsimmons and Cathy Cesario-Tardosky

Library of Congress Catalog Card Number: 2007935037

ISBN-13: 978-1-56367-525-6

GST R 133004424

Printed in China

TP17

I would like to dedicate this book to Mitra Kanaani of the NewSchool of Architecture and Design for her continual support and Denise Guerin of the University of Minnesota for being such an inspiration.

Contents

EXTENDED

Contents

Preface

With the emergence of sick building syndrome in the 1970s and the emphasis of Leadership in Energy and Environmental Design (LEED) Standards, many designers are becoming increasingly interested in the topics of health and sustainability.

The average American spends approximately 90 percent of their time indoors, so the quality of the built environment significantly influences human health. A major theme in this book is the application of one of Sir Isaac Newton's laws of motion, which states that **for every action there is an equal and opposite reaction.** As academicians, professionals, and society as a whole, we tend to focus on the intended actions of our inventions and designs. Although the goal has always been a better quality of life for the humans who use our inventions and occupy our designs, every action has an equal or greater reaction—and sometimes this is negative.

In the past we tended to neglect these reactions and this has cost America billions—even trillions—of dollars in health care, workman's compensation benefits, and chronic disabilities. For example, the United States experienced an energy crisis in the 1970s that prompted a trend toward tighter and more energy-efficient buildings. Most of these buildings were constructed with windows that did not open

and, thus, no source of fresh air. The primary air exchange was provided through heating, ventilation, and air-conditioning (HVAC) systems. Also during this time, the ventilation standards for indoor air were lowered from 20 cubic feet per minute per occupant to five cubic feet per occupant. The unintended result was a multitude of unrelated symptoms among the occupants of modern, energy-efficient buildings. These symptoms became known as Sick Building Syndrome (SBS) and Building-Related Illness (BRI). One problem was simply exchanged for another and ultimately resulted in more human cost than before attempts to conserve energy were implemented. The use of asbestos to provide fireproofing is another tragic example of unintended consequences. Today's design professionals must be proactive and strive to identify the potential negative reactions associated with both new construction and environmental modification.

Sustainability is the second major theme of this book. This term originally applied only to the preservation and wise use of natural resources. However, it now defines an area of design practice that encompasses issues of environmental health as well as environmental preservation. The modern-day premise behind sustainability is the ability to meet the needs of the present without compromising the ability of future generations to meet their needs. The concept has been adopted by many disciplines, including economic development, food production, energy, social organization, and human health and welfare.

In this book, sustainability will be examined predominantly from the perspective of sustaining human health, with an emphasis on the use of human- and environmentally friendly products. Planning the height of kitchen counters serves as an example of applying sustainability to the built environment. The standard counter height, at 36 inches, is based on the 5-feet, 10-inch average height of an American male. Individuals above and below this average height may experience back, neck, and arm pain when working for extended periods at a standard counter. Ways to provide counters that are sustainable in terms of human health are to make them adjustable or to provide more than one height in a kitchen. To address the sustainability of the natural environment, the counters could be constructed of either recycled products or those made from a renewable resource.

The two themes, actions-reactions and sustainability, are closely interconnected because actions we take to provide healthy, sustainable built environments require *forethought* and careful consideration of possible unintended consequences. After-the-fact learning is inevitable. Decreasing the number of these unfortunate incidences is the purpose of this book.

One additional note: This book also includes Expert Spotlight boxes, which were written by professionals in the field.

Acknowledgments
I salute all the researchers who dedicate themselves to environmental health and the relationship between sustainability and human health. Without them there would be no knowledge to bring into practice. I also applaud the excellent work of InformeDesign.com, an Internet research tool administered through the University of Minnesota and sponsored by the American Society of Interior Designers. This website provides excellent and easy-to-use information that can benefit all designers.

In addition, I would like to thank the following reviewers, selected by Fairchild Books, for their helpful comments and suggestions during the preparation of the manuscript: Jan Merle, Art Institute of Fort Lauderdale, and Dale Landry, Fanshawe College.

Finally, I would like to thank Ashley Bogajczyk for student testing this book for its readability, and Lee Haroun for her editorial assistance.

Introduction to Environmental Health

CHAPTER **1**

Environmental Health and Sustainability

LEARNING OBJECTIVES

1. **Describe how humans have developed the built environment over history to suit our needs.**
2. **Explain how man-made modifications to land features can harm both humans and the earth.**
3. **Describe the relationship between human health and the built environment.**
4. **Explain the meaning of** *sustainability* **as it relates to the built environment and quality of life.**
5. **Explain the mission and services of LEED and Green Seal.**

Every civilization and culture has modified the built environment in search of human comfort. The desire for comfort is universal, and yet the definition of comfort is variable and depends on numerous factors typically derived from culture and tradition. In developed countries, comfort is often associated with interior spaces and the widespread use of heating, ventilating, and air-conditioning (HVAC) systems in private residences and public buildings. These comfortable interior environments have led to a host of conditions with which we must now contend.

Human health is heavily influenced by all environmental conditions, both exterior and interior. The human body is made up of organs and systems that function as intricate, interacting parts in a global system. This close relationship is sometimes ignored as humans modify and manipulate the environment, with sometimes negative results. Designers who learn from the actions that humans have taken upon the built environment, and the consequences of those actions, will be prepared to address these issues in a sustainable manner.

The purpose of this text is to help interior designers expand their view of their profession and to give them a basis for understanding how they can make positive contributions to the well-being of their clients and the world. This chapter presents a brief overview of the issues and concerns that are addressed in greater detail throughout the text.

CREATING THE BUILT ENVIRONMENT

Since humans have inhabited the planet, we have faced many natural threats to health and well-being. Predators, diseases, inclement weather, and the scarcity of food and water have all threatened human existence. The early humans, who sustained themselves through hunting, fishing, and foraging for food, did not occupy a single piece of land. They were nomads, following food and water sources and migrating to warmer climates as the seasons changed. Significant to life's preservation, this continual movement prevented many diseases from being able to proliferate.

As the civilizations of early humans evolved, they became less nomadic and began to settle in one place. Early settlements ranged from a small group of tepees to larger numbers of relatively simple structures. This shift in human behavior had advantages and disadvantages, but the most important change was the way humans interacted with the environment. No longer part of nature's rhythms, ebbing and flowing with the seasons, weather, and food sources, humans needed to manipulate and modify their environment to survive. They dug water channels to siphon and purposefully direct water from rivers, lakes, and other sources for irrigation and consumption. They built sturdier structures to protect themselves from inclement weather patterns. They developed fortification techniques to protect against invaders.

Underlying this human evolution from living as nomadic hunter-gatherers to living in settlements is a shift in the way humans viewed the world. Their view changed as they gained the intellectual abilities to modify their envi-

ronments to meet their lifestyle needs. Their intellect, in turn, led to a new worldview—and the realization that humans could dominate nature and the land. The results of this domination, through environmental and lifestyle modification, can be seen throughout the centuries and continues today.

ENVIRONMENTAL MODIFICATION

Jericho, one of the world's oldest cities (Jericho Municipality, n.d.), illustrates some of the first environmental modifications to the land by humans. These modifications included clearing a piece of land and placing many buildings onto the site. Because of the region's dry weather patterns and the level of modification to the land, much of the original footprint has remained visible.

Humans also modified the land through the generation of new materials by combining other, separate materials. In the case of Jericho, clay, straw, and water were combined to create sun-dried bricks, as illustrated in Figure 1.1 (Jericho Municipality, n.d.). These longer-lasting and purposefully structured materials allowed the building of safer, more useful human shelter.

Health Risks

As humans continued to evolve, so did the levels of environmental modification. Nevertheless, one constant has remained throughout human civilization with regard to environmental modification: Knowledge is most often gained through trial and error. For example, the first people who occupied Jericho likely contracted a multitude of diseases that originated from inadequate sanitation or food storage. In fact, many cultural and religious traditions practiced today can be traced to health-related concerns. For example, many Middle Eastern religions forbid the consumption of pork. This tradition probably originated from an inability to store or cook the meat properly, which would result in many people contracting **trichinosis,** an infectious disease caused by a roundworm.

As the settling process continued, we see more comforts and luxuries included as part

FIGURE 1.1 Human habitation of the city of Jericho dates back to roughly 7000 B.C. In the photo below, we can see that the structures created by these peoples continue to linger into the present, thus providing evidence of how the earth has been altered to accommodate human habitation.

of the environmental modification process. In ancient Rome, engineers delivered water to and removed sewage from individual homes; many of the pathways through which the water traveled were lined with **lead.** It is widely believed that many ancient Romans, including some of the most notorious emperors, suffered from lead poisoning. Another hazardous material that was harvested by the early humans and used well into the twentieth century is **asbestos.** Prized because of its strength and its resistance to fire, asbestos was found to cause many adverse health effects in humans (MesotheliomaHealth.org, 2007).

More recently, humans have learned how to go beyond simply utilizing and combining materials found in nature to extract and recombine the basic chemical elements that comprise the natural world. The result has been the introduction of synthetic, or fabricated, materials such as nylon, Teflon, and vinyl. These materials have been embraced by humanity for their ease of use, durability, and the many lifestyle-improvement opportunities they afford. For example, nylon is used in clothing, carpeting, string, rope, and many other commonly found items in the modern world. The consequences of these newly formed chemical compounds include low biodegradation rates and **off-gassing,** the production of toxic gases at room temperature. The presence of heat and humidity can exacerbate the level of off-gassing, increasing the degree of toxicity. Also, with the breakdown of the chemical bonds (not to be confused with **decomposition**) of these synthetic materials, particulate matter is generated that can be inadvertently inhaled or consumed. To reduce the levels of off-gassing in the built environment, Goedken (2006) suggests the following:

1. Use only building materials declared to have low volatile organic compound (VOC) levels and avoid, when possible, the use of adhesives and sealants, paints and coatings, carpet systems, composite wood and laminate adhesives, and systems furniture and seating.

2. Follow the proper order of materials installation because Type Two materials absorb the gases from Type One and later release those gases along with their own. Materials categorized as *Type One* (composite wood products, adhesives, sealants, glazing compounds, and paint) off-gas for a short time. *Type Two* (woven, fibrous, or porous) materials off-gas for very long durations.

3. Force large amounts of outdoor air through a recently completed building for a period of 3 to 90 days.

Changing the Landscape

Jericho not only served as the prelude for humans to combine materials to make new or different materials, it also foreshadowed human densification and the complete reconfiguration of a specific place. As we can see from the rendered image of the fortified city of Jericho in Figure 1.2a, humans removed the natural elements completely and reshaped the land. This same pattern can be seen in the model of ancient Rome and again in the aerial photo of Manhattan Island (Figure 1.2b). Through the extreme alteration of the landscape, each of these habitats experienced climate changes. Perhaps the most notable changes were increases in ambient temperatures and air pollution. Trees and other forms of vegetation help cool the air through the release of water vapors, and they also attract dust and other particulate matter from the air onto their leaves and branches. In many of our modern cities, which are filled with skyscrapers, we have created several microclimates. New York City, for example, tends to be warmer year-round than the surrounding areas (Rosenzweig, Solecki, and Slosberg, 2006), and it tends to experience greater periodic wind velocities as a result of funneling between buildings and downdrafts generated by skyscrapers.

Natural Restoration

One result of a man-made environment, in which vegetative growth and naturally occurring elements (water, rocks, and so on) have all

FIGURE 1.2A AND B From Jericho to ancient Rome to the modern city of New York, humans have removed nature and reshaped the land to meet their needs and fulfill their desires.

but been eradicated, is that humans spend most of the day in planned surroundings. According to the Kaplan and Kaplan Attention Restoration Theory (1989), when humans are forced to pay sustained attention to their surroundings, they inevitably experience **attentional fatigue.** To compensate, they should be exposed to a "restorative environment" in which they can function primarily in an involuntary mode. In the built environment, humans are rarely allowed to function in an involuntary mode. They must be constantly alert in order to avoid the many threats to health and well-being: moving cars, other people, and a host of environmental features such as stairs, doors, and escalators. Because we rarely function in an involuntary mode, many of us have

or will have elevated levels of stress. Unfortunately, prolonged levels of stress can lead to high blood pressure and heart disease, as well as depression and anxiety. To illustrate the importance of leaving some areas designated for development in their natural state, consider that the U.S. Department of Health and Human Services declares that as many as one in ten young people may suffer from an anxiety disorder (National Mental Health Association, n.d., "Children's Mental Health") and that a restorative environment may be able to reduce these numbers.

Environmental Hazards

In some situations our successes in environmental modification have led to overconfidence and we have, thus, created hazards that threaten human life. Consider the 1989 Loma Prieta earthquake and subsequent devastation to the Marina District of San Francisco (Figure 1.3). This area originally comprised marshy wetlands; to expand San Francisco's real estate, humans moved soil from other landmasses, along with various debris, to fill in the wetlands and create more dry land on which to build. A fact that should have been considered during

FIGURE 1.3 Wetlands that have been filled in and built on undergo more movement during earthquakes. This increases the potential for damage, such as the collapsing of buildings. This was dramatically illustrated after the San Francisco earthquake of 1989 when the Marina District, built mostly on filled-in land, sustained the greatest damage.

this process was that San Francisco lies within the area known as the Ring of Fire (the basin of the Pacific Ocean), in which earthquakes and volcanoes occur fairly regularly. Although there are no volcanoes in San Francisco, the city is subject to strong earthquakes. Hence, within this region, tremors and ground shaking are part of the natural cycle of the earth. During the 1989 earthquake, the Marina District underwent a process called **liquefaction,** which severely diminished the strength and stiffness of the soil under its buildings. During the shaking of the earth, the water-filled spaces between individual particles of soil were forced together in a manner that squeezed out the water. This action caused amplification of the ground movement and, ultimately, led to the collapse of many structures.

More recently, Dubai, an arid country, has expanded its coastline by importing sand from inner desert regions and dredging the seafloor to raise soil levels so they can be developed as habitable land (Figure 1.4). While many ecologists have expressed concern over the destruction of coral reefs and the potential ramifications of altering sea currents, designers of the built environment are intrigued at the

possibilities, and the population at large finds the notion and aesthetics inviting. The implications of this ambitious attempt to dominate the natural world have yet to be determined, and the projections are nothing more than speculation.

Throughout the world humans have altered their environment and in today's modern

FIGURE 1.4 Dubai is planning to reduce its dependency on oil revenues by attempting to turn itself into a premier vacation destination. One step in achieving this goal is to expand its coastline by creating islands and peninsulas. However, some ecologists fear that the ecological consequences could be devastating.

environment, we have the capability and technology to completely alter the land in ways never before conceived. For example, the island of Manhattan in New York City contains only miniscule vestiges of the natural landscape, topography, or climate. Where once Manhattan was marshy scrubland, today it is a jungle of concrete, glass, and steel. From the perspective of many designers of the built environment, both Manhattan and the newly constructed islands of Dubai stand as a testament to human ingenuity and our ability to dominate the landscape. However, the consequences of environmental modifications such as these are only now starting to be realized.

THE INTERIOR WORLD

In Western society, technological developments and advancements have led to humans spending more time than ever in the built environment. Some experts contend that the average American will spend approximately 90 percent of his or her life inside (Kemp and Baker, 2006). On first glance, 90 percent seems incredibly high, but upon consideration of our daily activities and how these activities change throughout the life span, the number seems more plausible. In 2007, the U.S. Census Bureau stated that the average American spends 9.6 hours a day watching television, using computers, listening to the radio, going to the movies, and/or reading (U.S. Census Bureau, 2006, "2007 Statistical Abstract").

Given that a day only has 24 hours, of which sleep accounts for approximately 8 hours, this leaves us roughly 7 hours (after subtracting our media time) to shower, eat, commute to work or school, and perform the other tasks of daily living.

Health Effects of Indoor Living

The consequences of indoor modern life are numerous. Because we spend much of our time in a sitting position, our caloric expenditure is minimal. At the same time, our immune systems are exposed to myriad chemical off-gassing, our exposure to the full spectrum of ultraviolet (UV) light derived from the

sun is minimized, and our muscle and joint strength declines from lack of activity. Each of these conditions or situations negatively affects health. In addition, the severity of these negatives can be amplified through building trends that promote energy efficiency. For example, paints, carpets, laser printers, and many other materials off-gas. Energy-efficient homes tend to be "tight," meaning that the accidental exchange of interior and exterior air is kept to a minimum. This means that the polluted air from off-gassing lingers within the home and reaches ever greater levels.

Sunlight and Human Health

Children, and people in general, require exposure to the full spectrum of ultraviolet sunlight. For example, in the late nineteenth and early twentieth centuries, it was discovered that young children in Britain had higher incidences of rickets than did children in the tropics. Rickets is a metabolic bone disease resulting from vitamin D deficiency, which causes a host of skeletal disorders (Figure 1.5). Upon further investigation, scientists determined that children need exposure to full-spectrum sunlight in order to photosynthesize vitamin D (Palm, 1890; McCollum, 1957), thereby increasing bone strength and growth.

Exposure to sunlight has also been shown to increase levels of serotonin, a neurotransmitter associated with mood. In short, bright light causes the body to produce serotonin while darkness and overcast days cause serotonin levels to drop. Lowered levels of serotonin can lead to **seasonal affective disorder (SAD),** a form of depression associated with a lack of daylight (Lambert et al., 2002). Furthermore, some recent studies suggest that low serotonin levels and seasonal affective disorder may be causal factors in alcoholism and attention-deficit/hyperactivity disorder (ADHD) (Lurie et al., 2006). Currently, ADHD is the most common psychiatric condition affecting children (Herrerias, Perrin, and Stein, 2001). This means that as potential mitigation for ADHD, we should consider increasing our children's exposure to sunlight.

Melatonin

Lack of sunlight also causes increased carbohydrate cravings because of the imbalanced production and absorption of hormones like **melatonin.** Exposure to sunlight facilitates the absorption of melatonin, a hormone responsible for drowsiness (Kopec, 2006). It has been found that workers doing a third shift, commonly referred to as the graveyard shift, notice moderate to severe weight gain during the first year working this shift. This is because increased melatonin levels within the body can cause a person to become sleepy. In order to stay alert, many employees on the graveyard shift rely on simple sugars and products with caffeine. Levels of melatonin generally increase at about 9:00 P.M. and remain elevated until about 7:00 A.M. The effect of high melatonin levels and the consumption of simple sugars and caffeine results in weight gain.

Although one design remedy is the incorporation of brighter lighting to reduce melatonin production, it should be noted that this decreased production may result in the occurrence of certain types of cancers. This is because melatonin is also an **antioxidant** that has been shown to prevent some types of cancer (Malhotram, Sawhney, and Pandhi, 2004).

Balancing the Need for Sunlight

Unfortunately, media campaigns against premature aging and skin cancer in recent years have led to widespread fear of sunlight. Many people believe that they should avoid the sun altogether. In fact, the old adage "everything in moderation" applies to sun exposure. All people, especially children, should be exposed to sunlight on an average of fifteen to twenty minutes per day. Not only is sunlight needed for the production of vitamin D and to help keep human sleep-wake cycles in balance, it is needed for the regulation of certain hormones and neurotransmitters.

Designers can facilitate exposure to the sun's light by placing parking lots farther from buildings, using multiple smaller buildings as opposed to one large facility for schools, and incorporating outdoor courtyards and terraces in office buildings. Early humans spent the majority of their time outdoors—humans spending so much time indoors is a relatively new phenomenon.

BUILDING SYSTEMS

In the early part of the twentieth century, the amount of time spent indoors was not of great concern. Most buildings had windows that opened, windows were limited to single-paned glazing without UV filtration, and insulation was inferior to what is common today. The result was often drafty buildings that allowed movement and circulation of air even when the windows were closed.

FIGURE 1.5 Rickets is a disease resulting from vitamin D deficiency. Vitamin D can be acquired through foods such as cod liver oil and it can be photosynthesized through exposure to the sun. Ideally, children should be exposed to the full ultra-violet spectrum of the sun each day through activities such as outdoor play and sports and visits to parks with the family.

With increased technology and the energy shortages of the 1970s, developed countries became increasingly concerned with energy conservation. This led to a "tightening up" of our buildings. Better insulation, double- and triple-paned UV-filtering windows, and increased reliance upon mechanical ventilation became the norm. The result was the appearance of **sick building syndrome** (SBS) and building-related illnesses.

Heating, Ventilation, and Air-Conditioning

One of the more notable inventions that led humans indoors was the advent of climate control. In the past, humans relied on fire for warmth; fires had to be constantly maintained, and when they went out, the building would cool. With new technologies and furnaces that use wood, coal, oil, gas, or electricity, heating an interior environment became much easier.

Conversely, the hot desert or humid tropical climates required people to find relief from the heat. In many cultures, the desire to escape the heat led to the cultural tradition of siestas or afternoon breaks. This custom enabled people to avoid heat-related illnesses such as heatstroke or exhaustion. In ancient Rome, wealthy citizens cooled the air through the use of subterranean ponds (LaBauve et al., 2002). As air passed over the water, it would cool before being circulated throughout the home. Although this method of cooling air was functional, it was impractical for the masses.

Many centuries would pass before we would see viable options for cooling interior air. In fact, it was 1902 when the first air-cooling system was used to cool an interior space. One of the first environments to incorporate air-conditioning was the New York Stock Exchange (Cooper, 1998). Within eight years, many movie theaters regularly employed the use of air conditioners (Cooper, 1998) and some schools and office buildings began to install them. The greatest use of air conditioners in the early twentieth century was in textile factories, because they helped control the humidity levels and increased worker performance.

After the personal lifestyle deprivations caused by the Great Depression and World War II from 1929 to 1945, many Americans craved the gadgets and gizmos that promised a more comfortable life. Air-conditioning became available to the masses (Figure 1.6). Advertisers touted the health benefits of air conditioners and claimed that they would help keep homes cleaner and that people would sleep better. These promises, along with the availability of the technology, caused the demand for air conditioners to exceed the supply (Cooper, 1998).

A number of architectural changes that resulted from air-conditioning would lead to unintended consequences. First, architects could design buildings without worrying about issues such as radiant heat. Hence, they designed buildings with more glass. In addition, the use of foliage for shading declined and cross-ventilation was considered unnecessary. At the same time, the private home market exploded in areas such as Florida and Arizona, where high temperatures previously inhibited much human settlement. Because air conditioners resolved issues related to high temperature, many postwar homes along the so-called Sun Belt, the warm-weather states in the southern and southwestern United States, were designed as low, rectangular structures with large windows and sliding glass doors.

Sick Building Syndrome and Building-Related Illness

The advancement of HVAC technologies has experienced setbacks involving negative effects on human health. The most notable case involving HVAC systems leading to an illness is **Legionnaires' disease.** This condition was widely documented in 1976 when an outbreak of pneumonia occurred among the people attending a convention of the American Legion at the Bellevue Stratford Hotel in Philadelphia. While there is some controversy over the number of affected people, it is estimated that as many as 221 people received medical treatment and 34 died. Upon examination of the hotel environment and its mechanical systems,

FIGURE 1.6 Early air-conditioning units were being marketed to the general population by the middle of the 20th century. These units promised a cool, comfortable, and health-promoting environment. However, early models used Freon, which was later discovered to destroy the earth's ozone.

scientists identified a bacterium unknown at that time in the humidification portion of the HVAC system. This bacterium, later named *Legionella pneumophila,* had been distributed through the ventilation system, thus leading to the widespread nature of the illness. Current estimates suggest that between 8,000 and 18,000 people contract Legionnaires' disease in the United States each year (Centers for Disease Control and Prevention, 2005, "Legionellosis").

A building's HVAC system can be a breeding ground for a variety of fungi and bacteria that can lead to contagious illnesses. These illnesses include:

- Legionnaires' disease: A type of pneumonia that predominantly affects the lungs but can also affect the stomach, intestines, kidneys, and central nervous system. Usually requiring hospitalization, the disease is caused by contaminated water in an

HVAC system's cooling towers or evaporative condensers, as well as in whirlpools, showerheads, faucets, and hot water tanks.

- Pontiac fever: A type of flu resulting in fever, chills, headache, achy muscles, cough, nausea, and breathlessness. The flu tends to last for two to five days and is caused by contaminated cooling towers, evaporative condensers, whirlpools, showerheads, faucets, and hot water tanks.

- Histoplasmosis and Cryptococcosis: Fungal infections that result from contaminated bird droppings entering the interior environment and subsequently being circulated by the ventilation system. The symptom manifestation is usually an inflammation of the brain and the membranes covering it. The illness can also affect the lungs, kidneys, prostate gland, bones, and liver. In some instances, the skin may show signs of acne-like lesions, ulcers, or tumor-like masses. The infections are rarely life-threatening.

While most of the illnesses that spread through HVAC systems are generally referred to as SBS, there is also a class of illnesses related to the sensitivity of the human immune system. These illnesses are often referred to as hypersensitivity illnesses or **building-related illnesses** and manifest from a person's exposure to environmental pollutants or antigens found within the environment. Because of recirculated air through mechanical systems, which are often used to conserve energy, many of these environmental pollutants and antigens are recirculated throughout the building, thus increasing human exposure. The more common hypersensitivity illnesses include:

- Allergic rhinitis: A condition that leads to a stuffy, runny, and itchy nose, sneezing, and in some cases swollen and itchy eyes. Airborne fungi such as alternaria, glycoproteins from fungi, ragweed pollen, dust mites, and animal dander cause these symptoms.

- Building-related asthma: Symptoms include chest tightness, wheezing, coughing, and shortness of breath within thirty minutes of exposure or in some cases four to twelve hours after exposure. The causes of building-related asthma are the same as allergic rhinitis but can include bacterial proteases, which are digestive enzymes often found in dried saliva.

- Humidifier fever: Fever, chills, muscle aches, and fatigue within five to ten hours after exposure, lasting about twenty-four hours. Bacteria, endotoxins, and fungi found in humidifier reservoirs, air conditioners, and aquaria are often the cause of this illness.

- Hypersensitivity pneumonitis: A recurring pneumonia accompanied by fever, cough, chest tightness, and fluids entering the lungs. Symptoms can progress to a persistent cough, shortness of breath, fatigue, weight loss, and thickening and scarring of the lungs. The causes of this illness are fungi, bacteria, and protozoa, all of which can be found in poorly maintained air conditioners that circulate them throughout a building.

HEALTH IN THE INTERIOR ENVIRONMENT

Despite the maintenance challenges associated with HVAC systems, the off-gassing associated with many of the materials found within the built environment, and our proven need for regular exposure to sunlight, we continue to spend much of our lives in the built environment. To add to our "confinement," many jobs require multiple hours sitting at a computer, many youth would rather play a video game than play outside, and as a society we look to the built environment to satisfy our recreation and leisure time. Some of the results of these habits are repetitive demands on our skeletal system that lead to carpal tunnel syndrome or damage to the sciatic nerve; loss of muscle mass and joint strength, leading to an increase in joint-related injuries; a slower metabolism

BOX 1.1 EXPERT SPOTLIGHT: Sick Building Syndrome/ Building-Related Illness

Professor Alan Hedge
Cornell University
Department of Design and
Environmental Analysis

A "building-related illness" (BRI) is an illness that originates from exposure to a source that is inside a building or that is associated with the operation of a building, e.g., exposure to contaminated mist from the cooling towers. With a BRI, the affected persons show clinical signs of illness, such as fever, that remain when they are away from the building, that can worsen progressively, and that can be life-threatening. The best known BRI is Legionnaire's disease, caused by contamination of building water or cooling systems by the Legionella bacterium, and this affects up to 18,000 people annually in the USA (Centers for Disease Control, 2005).

The "sick building syndrome" (SBS) is a collection of nonspecific symptoms including eye, nose, and throat irritation, mental fatigue, headaches, nausea, dizziness, and skin irritation, which seem to be linked with occupancy of certain workplaces (WHO, 1983). Symptoms can also include odor or taste complaints (Mølhave, 1989) and eyestrain (Hedge et al., 1995). SBS reports can be temporary, acute outbreaks of symptoms following an identifiable trigger event, e.g., office redecoration, building maintenance, or renovation work, or SBS reports can be "permanent," where symptoms are widespread and chronic among workers in a building. Unlike BRIs, SBS symptoms are experienced when in a particular building but alleviated when away from that building for a period of time (see Hedge, 1990). SBS can be associated with indoor climate problems and poor indoor air quality, but although a number of indoor air pollutants have been suspected, the physical cause or causes of SBS symptoms remains unclear. SBS symptoms also appear to be multifactorial (Hedge, 1990) and symptoms can be influenced by worries about work and the workplace changes, work demands (workload), perceived role conflict at work, and overall workplace satisfaction (Hedge et al., 1995).

Practical Solutions

1) Monitor and maintain good indoor climate and air quality in the building.
2) Keep the building heating, ventilating, and air-conditioning (HVAC) system and also the building interior clean and dry.
3) Use high-efficiency air filters either in the HVAC system or in local personal air cleaners to remove particulates, allergens, etc.
4) Use "green" products, such as low-emissions furniture, furnishings, and finishes, in buildings.
5) Manage and minimize workplace stressors.

References

Centers for Disease Control (2005) Legionellosis: Legionnaires' Disease (LD) and Pontiac Fever (http://www.cdc.gov/ncidod/dbmd/diseaseinfo/legionellosis_g.htm#1) accessed 1/8/07.

Hedge, A. (1990) Sick building syndrome correlates with complex array of factors, *International Facilities Management Journal*, January/February, 52 58.

Hedge, A., Erickson, W.A. and Rubin, G. (1996) Predicting sick building syndrome at the individual and aggregate levels, *Environment International*, 22 (1), 3-19.

Mølhave, L. (1989) The sick buildings and other buildings with indoor climate problems, *Environment International*, 15, 65–74.

W.H.O. (1983) Indoor Air Pollutants: Exposure and Health Effects. EURO Reports and Studies 78, World Health Organization

due to a lack of physical energy demands; and overweight and obesity rates reaching 66 percent in adults and 34 percent in children ages 6 to 19 (White, 2006), leading to an increase in diabetes and heart disease, among other serious conditions. Clearly, the built environment has affected our health and well-being.

SUSTAINABILITY

As humans have developed and adapted to the built environment, we have jeopardized some and destroyed other parts of the natural environment. Through both deliberate and ignorant actions, we have threatened the health of humans and the livability of the earth.

Negative human activities include overlogging, pouring pollutants and greenhouse gases into the atmosphere, and contaminating both land and water. During the past four decades, there has been growing concern about the implications and ramifications of our actions to our very existence. As a result, many designers of the built environment have adopted standards of ethics to promote sustainable design. Nevertheless, the term *sustainable* has never been defined. As a result, the term and subsequent actions are often regarded from a singular and limited rather than a holistic perspective.

To gain a better perspective on **sustainability,** we must look at the built environment in its totality. First, the built environment is a place for human occupation. Therefore, it must be an environment that promotes the physical and psychological health of humans. In 1946, the World Health Organization defined *health* as "the state of complete physical, mental and social well-being and not merely the absence of disease or infirmity" (World Health Organization, 1946).

While this definition has been discussed, criticized, and even modified, the basic premise holds that health includes physical, social, and psychological factors. Hence, when designers consider sustainability, we must consider ways to sustain good health.

Another aspect of sustainability is the relationship between the built environment and the natural world. The microclimates that cities cause were discussed previously in this chapter. What we have learned from places like Manhattan Island, Tokyo, Hong Kong, and large cities around the world is that the increased use of asphalt, concrete, and steel raises temperatures. With increased population will come larger and denser cities. Environmental manipulation such as forming new islands and peninsulas, which could change the water currents in a region, may cause earth imbalance. Sustainability, on a broad scale, needs investigation and assessment of our actions. Humans may dominate the earth to some extent, but the quality of that domination must be examined and even questioned.

Much current thought with regard to sustainability is focused on embodied energy and energy conservation. *Embodied energy* refers to the total amount of energy necessary to construct, maintain, and perhaps later demolish a building. This perspective considers land preparation, the acquisition and transportation of building materials, and the actual construction. For example, machines use fossil fuels to prepare the land. Hence, we have simultaneously polluted the environment and consumed fossil fuels. Next, we may harvest natural resources for building materials. These might come from the other side of the planet, and harvesting and transporting these materials for refinement and then again to the construction location takes energy and creates pollution. Finally, there is a great deal of energy associated with the construction of a building.

Energy conservation once a building is completed is the total amount of energy needed to make that building functional. This includes HVAC systems, glazing, material uses, and so on; other important components of energy conservation include renewable resources and the disposability of resources. For example, it takes decades to replace many of the hardwoods used for flooring and furnishings. Bamboo, on the other hand, has a wood-grain look and texture and grows quickly. Thus, bamboo is often considered a quickly renewable resource. Carpeting has long come under scrutiny because of the vast quantities used each year. Its synthetic qualities limit its ability to biodegrade, and it produces gases known to make humans ill. Many carpet manufacturers offer carpet recycling programs, but other problems, discussed in Chapter 4, remain with its use.

As we become more informed and consider the effects of our actions on the planet, sustainability is a significant first step; *sustainability* must be defined in the broadest terms if it is to make a significant impact on the earth's long-term well-being. For the purposes of this book, sustainability will be considered as the process by which human life and health are promoted through the acknowledgment and integration of the built environment with the natural world, the wise use of resources without waste, and the conservation of energy. Therefore, the working definition of sustainability for this text is: all those elements that comprise the design, development, and construction of the built environment that have the potential of permanently altering the physical environment and/or the human condition.

Sustainable Design

Sustainable design, also referred to as **green design** and sustainable construction, emphasizes energy conservation, healthy indoor environments, and overall structural durability (Figure 1.7). An all-encompassing definition from a designer who is active in supporting the concept is that "sustainable design consists of meeting the needs of the present without compromising the ability of future generations to meet their own needs" (Bonda, 2005). More specifically, in 1994, the Conseil International du Batiment, an international construction research networking organization, defined the goal of sustainable construction as "creating and operating a healthy built environment

---

BOX 1.2   THE SEVEN PRINCIPLES OF SUSTAINABLE CONSTRUCTION

1. Reduce resource consumption.
2. Reuse resources.
3. Use recyclable resources.
4. Protect nature.
5. Eliminate toxics.
6. Apply life-cycle costing.
7. Focus on quality.

Source: Kibert, C. J. (2005). *Sustainable construction: Green building design and delivery.* Hoboken, NJ: John Wiley & Sons.

---

based on resource efficiency and ecological design" (Kibert, 2005). This organization went on to develop seven principles, listed in Box 1.2, to guide sustainable construction.

Sustainable design is a comprehensive building concept and, as such, should be applied in the initial planning stages of construction (Bartlett and Howard, 2000). A systemic, comprehensive set of goals and plans brings better results than deciding to "go green" later in the building process. For example, desiring

FIGURE 1.7 In 2006, the Skyscraper Museum in Battery Park had an exhibit called "Green Towers for New York: From Visionary to Vernacular" to educate visitors about the principles and technologies of green design. It focused on 14 sustainable high-rise buildings already completed or in progress in the city.

to use solar energy to heat a building that has been sited without any southern exposure or wanting to use natural cooling techniques in a home that has large banks of western-facing windows is unlikely to work without major energy-consuming changes to the buildings. And, even then, the needed changes may be structurally impossible.

To successfully achieve sustainable design, we must integrate land use, architecture, construction, and interior and exterior conservation systems (Youngentob and Hostetler, 2005). Land use considerations go beyond the siting of a single building or even a small subdivision of houses. Rather, they must take into account all environmental influences, including the location of retail and other services in a community to decrease the need for driving and increase the likelihood of physical activity and subsequent improved health. (The benefits of walking for health are discussed in Chapter 10.)

Green Building Materials and Products

Green building materials are sustainable, ecologically sound basic materials that may be used as a stand-alone component in the construction of a building or as a component of another product. An example is wood that has been certified by the Forestry Stewardship Council as sourced from sustainable forests. In such forests, trees are planted to replace trees that have been harvested, making such wood a natural, renewable resource (Kibert, 2005). **Green building products,** on the other hand, may not be made of green materials but have characteristics that make them preferable to alternative products. For example, they may save on energy consumption or contain fewer potentially harmful chemicals than other products. Special forms of glass that prevent the passage of heat-producing light waves are an example (Kibert, 2005).

There are various descriptions of the requirements for green building materials and products. *Environmental Building News* has developed five categories to serve as guidelines for making green selections (Box 1.3).

Green building products are a relatively new concept, and many green manufacturers have small markets; therefore, green manufacturers may charge higher prices than the manufacturers of traditional products (Malin, 2000). In many cases, the initial cost of using green building products is offset by long-term savings in energy, replacement costs, and improved human health (Johnson, 2000). For this reason, some cities are requiring that public buildings be constructed to green specifications and some owners of private buildings are recognizing the benefits of green construction. In addition to saving on operational energy costs, green construction can promote higher employee productivity; fewer claims of illnesses related to SBS; and more rentable space if heating and air-conditioning needs are reduced and ducts are made smaller (Johnson, 2000). Thus, it is expected that as the demand for green products accelerates, prices will become more competitive. Informed interior designers, working with other professionals, can help clients calculate projected savings and encourage the use of green materials and products as well as methods such as daylighting and natural ventilation (Bartlett and How-

---

BOX 1.3   FIVE CATEGORIES OF GREEN BUILDING PRODUCTS

1. Made from environmentally attractive materials
   Use materials that are salvaged, recycled, certified wood, etc.
2. Green because of what is not there
   Reduce material use, do not deplete ozone, are not made from PVC and polycarbonate, do not use preservative-treated wood, are not considered hazardous to human health
3. Reduce environmental impacts during construction, renovation, or demolition
4. Reduce environmental impacts of building operation
   Reduce heating and cooling loads, conserve energy, use renewable energy and fuel cell equipment, conserve water, prevent pollution and waste, reduce or eliminate pesticide treatments
5. Contribute to a safe, healthy environment
   Do not release significant pollutants inside building, block indoor contaminants, remove indoor pollutants, warn occupants of health hazards inside building, improve light quality

Adapted from: Kibert, C. J. (2005). *Sustainable construction: Green building design and delivery.* Hoboken, NJ: John Wiley & Sons.

ard, 2000). (See Chapter 5 for information on ventilation and Chapters 6 and 7 for information on daylighting.) Box 1.4 lists some of the factors that designers should consider when making decisions about the cost of sustainable construction. New green materials and products are being constantly developed, and designers should make a priority of keeping up-to-date on them as they become available. The Web sites listed at the end of this chapter are good sources of emerging information.

Environmental certification programs have been developed to help the public make informed decisions about green products. For example, **Green Seal** is an independent non-profit environmental testing program that uses a life-cycle approach. They evaluate a product or service beginning with material extraction, continuing with manufacturing and use, and ending with recycling and disposal (Green Seal, www.greenseal.org).

Green Seal establishes standards for a product and then accepts applications from manufacturers for certification. Testing is performed by third-party laboratories. If a product meets Green Seal's predetermined standards, the manufacturing plant is visited to ensure that future products will be made to the same standards. Finally, once all requirements are met, the product is awarded the Green Seal, which it may use on its packaging and in its advertising. Once certified, products are subject to annual monitoring to ensure that they continue to meet the Green Seal standard. Products can lose the Green Seal for noncompliance (Green Seal, www.greenseal.org). Box 1.5 contains information about product reports prepared by Green Seal.

LEED

LEED, which stands for Leadership in Energy and Environmental Design, was developed by the U.S. Green Building Council. Its principal purposes are to raise awareness of green design and building practices and to encourage sustainability. In an effort to achieve these purposes, LEED created the Green Building Rating System, which awards points for buildings

BOX 1.4   MAKING THE FINANCIAL CASE FOR GREEN CONSTRUCTION

- Beginning the planning process with a green orientation can lower building costs.
- Productivity can be increased if occupants are more comfortable with thermal, lighting, and indoor quality conditions.
- Costs of worker dissatisfaction and illness can be reduced.
- Ongoing energy costs are lower.
- Corporations can attract business and positive public relations if they demonstrate concern for the environment.
- Maintenance, repair, and replacement costs may be lower over the life of the building.
- Companies with better environmental performance tend to achieve superior financial performance.

Adapted from: Bartlett, E., & Howard, N. (2000). Informing the decision makers on the cost and value of green building. *Building Research & Information, 28* (5/6), 315-324.

Bonda, P. (2005). *Creating sustainable interiors.* Washington, DC: National Council for Interior Design Qualification.

BOX 1.5   GREEN SEAL REPORTS

Green Seal has prepared six- to 12-page reports on a variety of topics, many of interest to the interior designer.
- Carpet
- Compact Fluorescent Lighting
- Floor Care Products: Finishers and Strippers
- Lawn Care Equipment
- Luminaires, CFL Downlight
- Luminaires, High Intensity Discharge
- Luminaires, Linear Fluorescent
- Occupancy Sensors
- Office Furniture
- Office Supplies
- Paper, Alternative Fiber
- Paper, Bathroom Tissue and Paper Towels
- Paper, Copy
- Paper, Printing and Writing
- Particleboard and Medium-Density Fiberboard
- Quick-Serve Food Packaging, Rigid
- Room Air-Conditioning
- Tires, Low Rolling Resistance
- Wood Finishes and Stains

Each peer-reviewed report is based on market surveys and includes suggestions for alternate approaches, purchasing criteria based on a life-cycle approach, recommendations for specific brands and models, and sources for the products.

Links to the reports can be accessed at www.greenseal.org/resources/reports.cfm

that meet predetermined criteria in a number of categories. Depending on the number of points earned, new construction can earn a platinum, gold, silver, or certified rating. LEED is recognized by the building industry as setting the standards for green building in the United States.

LEED addresses six categories related to environmental and human health. Each category, listed below, has a list of requisites and specific numbers of points for meeting them:

1. Sustainable sites
2. Water efficiency
3. Energy and atmosphere
4. Materials and resources
5. Indoor environmental quality
6. Innovation and design process

Interior designers have numerous opportunities to meet LEED standards. Examples include selecting sturdy furnishings that are built to last, using paints and finishes that do not off-gas, and encouraging clients to purchase energy-saving appliances. Table 1.1 contains examples of LEED measures for home-building.

LEARNING FROM HISTORY

Yielding to the reality that the actions of humans on our environments will have both intended and unintended reactions, design professionals must be proactive in identifying the consequences associated with environmental modification. Ancient civilizations such as the Romans lacked a sophisticated understanding of the causes of disease. In the example of the Romans and their widespread use of lead, the result was that many Roman citizens suffered from lead poisoning. Human societies have engaged in this kind of after-the-fact learning throughout history and unfortunately, we continue to engage in unhealthy environmental practices, be it through clear-cutting wooded areas, filling in our wetlands, perching homes precariously,

TABLE 1.1 EXAMPLES OF LEED MEASURES FOR HOMES

CATEGORY	MEASURES
Sustainable Sites	• Drought-tolerant plants • Locate and plant trees to shade hardscapes • Select insect and pest control alternatives from list
Water Efficiency	• High or very high efficiency fixtures (toilets, showers, and faucet)
Energy and Atmosphere	• Windows meet or exceed ENERGY STAR • Improved hot-water distribution system • Pipe insulation • Energy-efficient light fixtures and control
Materials and Resources	• Reduce waste sent to landfill by 25 to 100% • Use environmentally preferred products
Indoor Environmental Quality	• Install high-performance fireplace • Timer/automatic controls for bathroom exhaust fan • Permanent walk-off mats OR shoe storage OR central vacuum • Detached garage OR tightly sealed surfaces between home and garage

Source: U.S. Green Building Council. (January 26, 2007). *Project Checklist: LEED for Homes. Version 1.11a.*

along the sides of cliffs, or using inadequately tested chemical compounds in our building and design materials. If we are to believe Sir Isaac Newton's laws of motion, then we must also concede that all of our actions will have opposite and equal reactions. The challenge for our society—and especially for the designers who shape it—is to determine and prevent the reactions that may lead to health problems.

The following chapters expand on the examples presented in this chapter and discuss the many ways by which designers can contribute to the health of their clients, communities, and planet by applying principles based on sustainability and the maintenance of human health. At the same time, designers should understand that these are suggestions to consider; cities, counties, states, and the federal government have rules that must be followed. Therefore, all building owners and built-environment professionals should consult applicable building codes for the most up-to-date regulations.

GLOSSARY TERMS

Antioxidant

Asbestos

Attentional fatigue

Decomposition

Green building materials

Green building products

Green design

Green Seal

Lead

LEED

Legionnaires' disease

Liquefaction

Melatonin

Off-gassing

Seasonal affective disorder

Sick building syndrome

Sustainability

Sustainable design

Trichinosis

LEARNING ACTIVITIES

1. Visit Green Seal's reports at www.green-seal.org/resources/reports.cfm. Select a product report to read and then visit local

---

BOX 1.6 VIEW TO THE FUTURE

Goals for Future Green Building

Three major challenges for advancing sustainable design have been identified by South African research architect Chrissna du Plessis:

1. Taking the next technology leap
2. Reinventing the construction industry
3. Rethinking the products of construction (Kibert, 2005)

Resolving these challenges will require combining creative thought and applied science. Two useful approaches have been suggested:

Historical wisdom to learn from the successes and mistakes of the past

Biomimicry to use nature's designs and processes as the basis for human goods and services (Kibert, 2005)

---

stores or online sources at which you can buy the product. Prepare a report summarizing the potential health consequences of traditional forms of the product; brand recommendations; product availability in your area; and how the price of the green product compares to traditional products.

2. Make a study of the geographic area where you live. Prepare a report in which you describe the original landforms, vegetation, and animal life and answer the following questions: How have these changed as the result of human habitation and manipulation? What have been the probable effects on human health? What can interior designers do within the built environment to mitigate these effects?

3. Choose a specific aspect of the built environment, such as lead or asbestos, that has had a negative impact on human health. Write a report exploring the history of its use, the discovery of its negative consequences, and regulation of the material or product.

4. The World Health Organization's definition of *health* contains three categories: physical, mental, and social. For each of the three, list five aspects of the built environment that have a potentially positive effect and five that have a potentially negative effect (total of 30 effects, 10 for each category). Finally, come up with at least one suggestion for how the interior

designer might counteract each negative aspect (total of 15 suggestions).

5. Research the concept of sustainable design. Then choose a room in a house to design in which you incorporate as many materials, products, and techniques as possible. Describe your project in a written report that includes drawings, product descriptions, and product samples.

SUGGESTED WEB SITES

1. U.S. Green Building Council
www.usgbc.org
This site contains complete information about the council's objectives and the LEED rating system. Even for those not directly involved in new construction, the standards provide ideas for improving the sustainability of all aspects of the built environment.

2. Green Seal
www.greenseal.org
Green Seal's home page is the link to information about its certification procedures, product information reports, and green programs for facilities for all levels of government.

3. U.S. Environmental Protection Agency
www.epa.gov
The EPA home page contains easily accessible links to hundreds of sites covering all aspects of the environment, including the built environment.

4. EPA Environmentally Preferable Purchasing
www.epa.gov/opptintr/epp/
This EPA site deals specifically with products and their effects on the environment. It includes suggestions for green products and contains useful tools, such as a Green Cleaning Pollution Prevention Calculator that quantifies the projected environmental benefits of purchasing and using green janitorial services and products. Although designed for use by federal purchasers, the information and suggestions on this Web site are applicable to the general public.

5. Whole Building Design Guide
www.wbdg.org
This organization espouses "whole building" design with the goals of creating successful high-performance buildings. It explains that to achieve that goal, an integrated design approach and an integrated team approach must be applied during all phases of a project, including the planning and programming phases.

6. U.S. Environmental Protection Agency
Healthy Buildings, Healthy People
www.epa.gov/iaq/hbhp/index.html
The EPA's *Healthy Buildings, Healthy People* report is a vision for indoor environmental quality in the twenty-first century. This Web site contains links to each chapter of the report, which explains the purpose of studying human health indoors, vision and goals, and potential actions.

REFERENCES

Bartlett, E., and N. Howard (2000). "Informing the Decision Makers on the Cost and Value of Green Building," *Building Research and Information* 28 (5/6): 315–24.

Bonda, P. (2005). *Creating Sustainable Interiors.* Washington, D.C.: National Council for Interior Design Qualification.

Centers for Disease Control (updated October 12, 2005, retrieved January 24, 2007). *Legionellosis: Legionnaires' Disease (LD) and Pontiac Fever.* Available online at www.cdc.gov/ncidod/dbmd/diseaseinfo/legionellosis_t.htm.

Cooper, G. (1998). *Air Conditioning America: Engineers and the Controlled Environment, 1900–1960.* Baltimore: The Johns Hopkins University Press.

Goedken, A.K. (December 2006). "Reduce Off-gassing for Better IAQ," *Buildings.* Available online at www.buildings.com/Articles/detailBuildings.asp?ArticleID=3476.

Green Seal. www.greenseal.org.

Herrerias, C.T., J.M. Perrin, and M.T. Stein (2001). "The Child with ADHD: Using the AAP Clinical Practice Guideline," *The American Family Physician* 63 (9): 1803–1810, 1811.

Jericho Municipality (n.d., retrieved January 26, 2007). *History of Jericho.* Available online at www.jericho-city.org/history.html.

Johnson, S.D. (2000). The Economic Case for "High Performance Buildings," *Corporate Environmental Strategy* 7 (4): 350–361.

Kaplan, R., and S. Kaplan (1989). *The Experience of Nature: A Psychological Perspective.* Cambridge: Cambridge University Press.

Kemp, J.M., and K. Baker (2006). *Building Community in Buildings: The Design and Culture of Dynamic Workplaces.* Westport, CT: Praeger Publishers.

Kibert, C.J. (2005). *Sustainable Construction: Green Building Design and Delivery.* Hoboken: John Wiley & Sons.

Klyve, D.M. (n.d., retrieved January 26, 2007). *Pictures from Israel: Jericho, The World's Oldest City.* Available online at www.math .dartmouth.edu/~klyve/travel/israel/jericho/.

Kopec, DAK. (2006). *Environmental Psychology for Design.* New York: Fairchild Books.

LaBauve, K., R. Pachikara, K.V. Pandit, S. Powell, S. Shade, and J. Sivak (2002, retrieved January 26, 2007). *Temperature, Humidity and Worker Productivity Analysis of Constant Air Volume and Variable Air Volume Underfloor Air Conditioning Systems.* Available online at www.rhsmith.umd.edu/quest/ senior%20practicum%20projects/2002/york/ york_final_paper_120402_1211am.doc.

Lambert, G., C. Reid, D. Kaye, G. Jennings, and M. Esler (2002). "Effect of Sunlight and Season on Serotonin Turnover in the Brain," *The Lancet* 360 (9348): 1840–42.

Lurie, S.J., B. Gawinski, D. Pierce, and S.J. Rousseau (2006). "Seasonal Affective Disorder," *American Family Physician* 74 (9): 1,521–24.

Malhotra, S., G. Sawhney, and P. Pandhi (2004). "The Therapeutic Potential of Melato-

nin: A Review of the Science," *Medscape General Medicine* 6 (2): 46.

Malin, N. (2000). The cost of Green Materials. *Building Research and Information* 28 (5/6): 408–412.

McCollum, E.V. (1957). *A History of Nutrition.* Cambridge, MA: Riverside Press.

MesotheliomaHealth.org (2007, retrieved January 26, 2007). *History of the Uses of Asbestos.* Available online at www.mesotheliomahealth. org/asbestos/history.php.

Milne, G., and C. Readon (modified March 1, 2004, retrieved February 23, 2007). *Your Home Technical Manual: Embodied Energy.* Available online at www.greenhouse.gov.au/ yourhome/technical/fs31.htm.

National Mental Health Association (n.d., retrieved January 29, 2007). Children's Mental Health Statistics. Available online at www1 .nmha.org/children/prevent/stats.cfm.

Palm, T. (1890). "The geographical Distribution and Aetiology of Rickets," *Practitioner* 45: 270, 279, 321–42.

Rosenzweig, C., W.D. Solecki, and R.B. Slosberg (June 2006). *Mitigating New York City's Heat Island with Urban Forestry, Living Roofs, and Light Surfaces* (Report). Albany: New York State Energy Research and Development Authority.

U.S. Census Bureau (updated December 22, 2006, retrieved January 27, 2007). *2007 Statistical Abstract.* Available online at www.census .gov/prod/www/statistical-abstract.html.

White, G. (October 19, 2006). "The Obesity Fight," *The Atlanta Journal–Constitution,* A-1.

WHO (1946). Constitution of the World Health Organization, Geneva.

Youngentob, D., and M. Hostetler (2005). "Is a New Urban Development Model Building Greener Communities? *Environment and Behavior* 37 (6): 731–59.

CHAPTER **2**

Overview of the Human Body

LEARNING OBJECTIVES

1. **Describe the cause-and-effect relationship between the human body and the built environment.**
2. **Explain the relationship between human cells and off-gassing.**
3. **Provide examples of how each of the body systems can be affected by factors in the built environment.**
4. **Give examples of how designers of the built environment can contribute to protecting and maintaining the health of the various body systems.**

Interior designers who have a rudimentary understanding of basic human anatomy and physiology can better appreciate the interactions between humans and the built environment. Both anatomy and physiology are complex, and they interact in a variety of ways. **Anatomy** is the study of the structure and form of the human body. For example, studying the shape, size, and composition of bones is part of anatomy. From an anatomical perspective, the human body might be regarded as a machine with design limitations. It must function within certain movement parameters while maintaining proper alignment. Ergonomics and industrial design are two of the design sciences that specialize in creating

spaces and products that take into account the relationship between design and human anatomy. Just as ergonomics has become an important part of interior design, so too will the principles of industrial design be applied to our knowledge of the body. For example, excessive vibration caused by noise can damage the very fine hairlike cells in the ear canal that pick up sound waves. Industrial designers who work on the design of cockpits for fighter jets understand this and make provisions to protect the hearing of pilots. In today's media-rich environment, home theaters are becoming popular, complete with surround sound. Designers are being asked to create such rooms, so understanding how the ear works is useful when selecting the type and positioning of acoustical equipment to function in a way that does not damage hearing.

Physiology, on the other hand, is the study of how the body functions, or how and why the various parts of the body work. For example, the action of chemicals on foods as they are digested and converted into forms of energy the body can use is explained by physiology. This knowledge further informs the designer about why and how something might be harmful, such as certain chemicals that interfere with body functions. Interior designers need to understand physiology, because it is at this level where we see the effects on the body when chemicals off-gassed from certain carpets, draperies, and other fabric upholstery items are inhaled by occupants. These gases are composed of chemicals that, once inhaled into the lungs, permeate the cells of different organs, leading to a physiological reaction. The result could be any one of a host of diseases, including cancer. Interior designers often select materials, and may even design materials, so it is important for them to understand the possible effects of their choices on the physiology of the individuals who will live with these materials.

CELLS

Cells are the smallest units of life and serve as the basic building blocks of the body. As small as they are, cells are complex structures that perform all the functions necessary for maintaining life: reproduction, growth, and self-repair. Most of the harm done to the body by environmental factors occurs at the cellular level and involves an environmental factor's interference with these three vital activities. This is because, although cells are amazingly capable of adjusting to adverse conditions, sometimes the adaptations are permanent and harmful. For example, lung cancer is a condition in which an environmental agent, such as cigarette smoke, causes the cells to **mutate** (change) and grow abnormally.

The majority of cells found in the human body contain the following major components:

1. Cell membrane: outer covering that controls the passing of substances in and out of the cell. This membrane has a special feature called semipermeability that, under normal conditions, allows needed substances to enter and exit the cell; damage can occur when contaminants break through the cell wall. Benzo(a)pyrene, which results from incomplete combustion of organic (derived from living matter) materials, is an example of a toxic substance that can permeate cell membranes. The EPA has determined that even with relatively short exposure, benzo(a)pyrene may cause red blood cell damage, leading to anemia (reduced delivery of oxygen to the tissues) and suppression of the immune system (U.S. Environmental Protection Agency, 2006, "Consumer Factsheet").

2. Cytoplasm: thick, sticky fluid found between the nucleus and the cell membrane containing water, proteins, carbohydrates, lipids (fats), and salts.

3. Organelles: structures within the cell that perform certain tasks. The most prominent of these is the nucleus, which controls the activities of the cell and facilitates cell reproduction. This is the level at which pollutants do their harm by disrupting the normal activity of the nucleus. For example, a pollutant may cause the cell to die or reproduce in a mutated form. Although mutation can produce a stronger cell that has adapted to its environment, it frequently produces an abnormality such as the fast-growing, invasive cancer cells.

Cells come in a variety of forms, each suited to a different part of the body. Examples include muscle, bone, skin, and nerve cells.

Cell Reproduction and Mutation

Cells reproduce through a process called **mitosis** in which they split to create exact duplicates of themselves. Cell reproduction is important for sustaining life because individual cells, like whole organisms, die from disease, damage, and old age. Cell death can result from a variety of conditions, including:

- Trauma caused by accidents, such as bumping into furnishings or tripping over items that are either placed within or protrude into areas of high traffic.
- Lack of oxygen and nutrients that can occur as a result of recirculating poor-quality air within buildings. When too many people are breathing the same air over and over, the level of oxygen

decreases and carbon dioxide increases. Air can also carry inhalable contaminants, such as asbestos fibers, bacteria, and lead dust, which damage cells in the lungs.

- Pollutants that enter the body and kill the cells. Benzo(a)pyrene, for example, is inhaled into the lungs and passed along to the blood, which carries it to every part of the body. As it is passed along, benzo(a)pyrene has the capability and opportunity to enter cells, including their nuclei.
- Natural aging, which happens to everyone. The results of the death of and changes in cells can be witnessed by comparing photographs of an individual taken in ten-year increments.

While cell division is essential to maintain life, it also presents an opportunity for significant damage to occur with exposure to certain conditions in the built environment. Excessive sunlight, for example, has been shown to damage **deoxyribonucleic acid (DNA),** the molecules inside cells that pass genetic information to the next generation of cells. When damaged, the DNA may be unable to produce an identical copy of itself. This results in a change, or mutation. (Mutations are not always negative; they sometimes enable species to survive environmental changes that would otherwise kill

them off.) To prevent this particular damage, designers may want to promote covered decks, patios, and porches to reduce their clients' direct exposure to the sun's rays (Figure 2.1).

Another example of a substance found in the built environment that interferes with normal cell reproduction is **arsenic.** Until 2003, this chemical was used to treat lumber used in decks and fences. Designers should consider having older structures of this type tested for toxic chemicals and possibly replacing them as part of remodeling projects. At the very least, because the chemical leaches into the soil, it is recommended that play areas, vegetable gardens, and other areas created for human activities not be located under or close to deck perimeters. These precautions are needed because, for example, young children who are still crawling and putting their hands in their mouths should not be allowed to play on or around treated decks (Building Green, 1997).

Specialized Cells

Nerve cells transmit messages between the brain and every other part of the body. They are distinguished by the inability to reproduce, so that injuries to nerve cells can be permanent. This is why spinal cord injuries can result in lifelong paralysis.

Nerve cells are also susceptible to certain toxins (poisons). You may have heard the term *nerve gas,* a contaminant that contains **organophosphates.** These compounds are present in a variety of insecticides, which, once they enter the body, interfere with the transmission of messages via neurotransmitters along the nerve cells. This is why it is important to use safe methods for destroying pests around the home or, if chemical pesticides are used, to take precautions to prevent their being tracked into the interior. Individuals exposed to very high doses of organophosphates can suffer permanent nerve damage and even death.

Two unique types of cells responsible for creating new human life are the female ovum (egg) and male spermatozoa (sperm). When united, they form the zygote, a fertilized egg that will reproduce millions of times within

FIGURE 2.1 Shaded areas, such as covered decks, allow access to the outdoors without exposure to the damaging rays of the sun.

a relatively short period of time. This normal cell division can be disrupted by a multitude of environmental agents, which is why the first few months of pregnancy are crucial to the health of the developing fetus. The exact causes of up to 70 percent of birth defects are unknown, but genetics, elements in the environment, and a combination of the two, can be causal factors (March of Dimes, 2006, "Birth Defects"). Known causes related to the built environment include lead and arsenic. Major birth defects have also been linked to exposure to certain organic solvents during the first trimester, including alcohols, degreasers, paint thinners, and varnish removers.

Implications for Designers

Clearly, it is important that designers understand the potential seriousness of damage and changes to the body's cells. Some types of cellular damage can result in permanent disability or death. Therefore, learning about potentially harmful materials and products, discussed in Chapter 4, will enable designers to take a more proactive role in the preservation of their clients' health.

As designers, it is important to provide healthy environments for expectant mothers. In addition to providing adequate ventilation to clear environments with poor indoor air quality, steps should be taken to protect against specific dangers:

- Pregnant women should not be on the premises during projects that involve scraping or sanding old paint that might contain lead.
- Older water pipes should be checked for lead, which can leach into drinking water.
- Brass (metal containing copper and zinc) faucets should be checked, as this metal can also leach into water.
- Construction areas in which arsenic-treated wood is used should be avoided.
- Nonchemical pesticides and cleaning products should be substituted for products containing potentially harmful components (see Chapter 9 for a list of recommendations).

- Secondhand smoke should be avoided by creating separate rooms with their own ventilation outlets or, even better, through the prohibition of smoking in buildings used or inhabited by pregnant women.
- Kitchens should be well designed for ease of hygienic food preparation and thorough cleaning because of the risk of foodborne contaminants, such as bacteria, that are especially harmful to pregnant women.

Newborns and young children are also developing at the cellular level as they grow, so homes and schools should be checked for possible contaminants. Young children are especially vulnerable to contaminants tracked into houses because of the time they spend crawling on the floor. Creating ways to keep floors clean, such as locating sturdy mats both outside and inside exterior doors, can be helpful. Chapter 8 discusses designing safe environments for children.

TISSUES

Most of the trillions of cells in the human body are combined by similarity in shape, size, structure, and intercellular material to form the body's **tissues.** The tissues, in turn, are grouped into four main categories that are organized by the specialized functions they perform:

1. Epithelial tissue provides internal and external covering. The skin is composed of epithelial tissue, so this is the type of tissue that has the most direct contact with the built environment and is subject to a multitude of reactions. Examples include dryness and itchiness when the humidity is low and rashes caused by fungal infections when the humidity is high. The skin is also exposed to the chemicals, such as formaldehyde, used to treat fabrics. These can cause allergic contact dermatitis, an inflammation resulting from direct contact with an irritant. A common problem for people with sensitive skin is contact with fabrics treated with fire retardants, such as compounds containing phosphorous.

FIGURE 2.2 Wooden blinds make an attractive alternative for clients who may be sensitive to the chemicals used to treat the fabrics in draperies, curtains, and some blinds.

For individuals who suffer from allergies related to phosphorous, designers should consider using leather or vinyl furnishings along with non-fabric-based window treatments (Figure 2.2).

2. Connective tissue supports and connects other tissue and the organs. Tendons and ligaments that connect bones and muscles are types of connective tissue. These tissues can be stretched or torn as a result of sudden jarring, falls, or improper body movements such as lifting heavy objects. Sprains, slipped discs, and pulled tendons fall into this category. Many of these common injuries can be prevented through good design and space planning. For example, designers should work to avoid trip hazards and apply good ergonomic principles. (See Chapter 7.) Designers should also anticipate how spaces will be used and take appropriate measures to limit potential hazards. For example, many offices accumulate an overflow of files that make their way into boxes stored around the workspace, often in major pathways. The preferable solution in this case is to provide adequate file space for the employees. If overflow situations develop, file boxes should slide easily under or between other pieces of furniture so that they don't become trip hazards.

3. Muscle tissue enables the body to move. This is another soft tissue that can be damaged by tearing, overextending, or overexertion. In the workplace environment, muscles can be strained or torn when individuals are required to carry heavy loads over extended distances. For example, medical and legal personnel are often asked to transport large numbers of files from one area of a building to another. Designers should ensure that file cabinets are not too high or that safe steps are available; that some form of transportation device is readily and easily accessible; and that flooring materials allow for the smooth transport of heavy carts.

4. Nerve tissue reacts to stimuli and conducts impulses so that messages can be sent from one part of the body to another. Nerves can be damaged by sudden trauma or repetitive movements. Perhaps the most publicized repetitive nerve damage is carpal tunnel syndrome, which occurs from improper positioning of one's wrists while spending many hours repeating similar movements, as happens when using a computer keyboard. (See Chapter 3 for information about injuries caused by repetitive movements.)

Table 2.1 contains a summary of the four major types of tissue.

Implications for Designers

In order to plan interiors that support the health of occupants and best protect them from injury, designers must understand the types of individuals who will inhabit an interior and the activities that will likely take place. This is especially important in workplace environments and areas in the home where physical activity is likely to take place, such as kitchens, laundry rooms, workshops, playrooms, and exercise rooms. It is also important that designers are aware of special conditions, such as allergies, sensitivities, and personal preferences.

TABLE 2.1 TYPES OF TISSUE

TYPE OF TISSUE	FUNCTIONS	EXAMPLES OF LOCATION
Epithelial	1. Provide a protective covering for body surfaces 2. Produce secretions such as digestive juices, hormones, and perspiration 3. Regulate the passage of substances	• Skin • Linings of organs • Glands
Connective	1. Store fat 2. Cushion and support 3. Insulate 4. Join body parts, such as muscles and bones 5. Transport oxygen, nutrients, waste, and other materials	• Fat tissue • Ligaments • Tendons • Cartilage • Bone • Blood
Muscle	1. Enable heart to contract 2. Allow voluntary movement 3. Provide involuntary movement	• Heart • Skeletal muscles • Smooth muscles in digestive tract and blood vessels
Nerve	1. Respond to changes in their environment 2. Carry nerve impulses	• Brain • Spinal cord • Nerves

ORGANS AND SYSTEMS

Various types of tissues combine to form **organs,** structures that perform specific functions. The stomach, for example, is an organ made of four types of tissue and performs a major function of digestion.

The organs, in turn, are organized into **systems** that perform necessary bodily functions, such as the digestive system, which converts food to fuel, and the circulatory system, which carries oxygen throughout the body. (See Table 2.2 for a list of the body systems.) Designers should understand how the body systems interact with one another, because a causal agent derived from the environment, such as a chemical used as a fire retardant, can affect multiple organ systems. This explains why damage to the heart can result from inhaling toxic fumes: The fumes enter the lungs, the contaminants are passed into the blood, and the circulatory system moves the blood to the heart. Likewise, a condition such as an allergic reaction to dust mite droppings harbored by a giant stuffed toy placed on a child's bed (Figure 2.3) can affect various systems:

- Immune system: becomes hyperresponsive (overreacts) and sends signals for the body to respond to the dust mite droppings
- Respiratory system: lining of bronchial tubes produces excessive mucus and the smooth muscles contract, making breathing difficult
- Integumentary (skin) system: responds with itching and rashes

FIGURE 2.3 This room may look inviting, but the many sources of soft materials, most notably the large stuffed toy, provide excellent opportunities for the proliferation of dust mites.

An environmental agent known to affect multiple symptoms is formaldehyde. The off-gassing related to this chemical often yields symptoms that include irritation of the upper airway and skin; **chronic** (long-lasting or permanent) bronchitis and shortness of breath; and burning of the eyes and nasal passages. Prolonged exposure to formaldehyde can result in depression, headache, nausea, irritability, and memory dysfunction (Morgan, 2003). (Chapter 4 contains more detailed information about formaldehyde and other contaminants.)

Ironically, this systemic effect of many contaminants is one reason why Western medicine is sometimes quick to dismiss such illnesses as multiple chemical sensitivity and chronic fatigue syndrome. Many medical practitioners are trained to identify illnesses within specific cells, tissues, organs, or a single system. As such, people who have a variety of symptoms, as happens with building-related illnesses, are often dismissed or simply treated for their symptoms without diagnosis of the underlying cause (Bower, 2001; Oberg, n.d.).

INTEGUMENTARY SYSTEM

The integumentary system consists of the epithelial tissue (skin) and its appendages, which include the hair, nails, and sudoriferous (sweat) and sebaceous (oil) glands and their ducts (passages for secretions). This system often provides us with our first clues of health problems related to the environment. For example, arsenic and lead are both substances used in paint. If they are present in the body, this can be determined by sampling hair and fingernails. Also, rashes and hives on the skin can indicate trouble elsewhere in the body.

The integumentary system has four major functions, all of which are related to its exposure to the external world: (1) protect the deeper tissues from dehydration, injury, and invasion by microorganisms, such as viruses and bacteria; (2) assist in the regulation of body temperature by controlling the amount of heat loss; (3) help manufacture vitamin D; and (4) enable sensory input, such as temperature and pressure, through numerous nerve endings and receptors. Design can support these functions in a number of ways: preventing hazards that might compromise the integrity of the skin; providing for optimum climate control (temperature and humidity); enabling access to natural sunlight (needed to synthesize vitamin D); and providing for a variety of sensory stimuli.

The skin is composed of two layers, the epidermis and dermis, which contain a number of components (Figure 2.4). The epidermis is composed of dead, flat, scaly cells that flake away at the rate of approximately 500,000 per day. These cells accumulate in carpeting, bedding, and other fabrics, where they provide an abundant food source for dust mites, a major cause of allergies.

The layer that lies under the dermis, called the subcutaneous, is not a true part of the integumentary system but is often described along with it because of its proximity. It is important to be aware of this layer, because the built environment is the source of many contaminants, such as **persistent organic pollutants (POPs),** that accumulate in the fat cells located here. Because of the storage capacity of

TABLE 2.2 ORGAN SYSTEMS

BODY SYSTEMS	ORGANS IN THE SYSTEM	BODY SYSTEMS	ORGANS IN THE SYSTEM
Cardiovascular	Heart Blood vessels (arteries, capillaries, veins)	Blood	Blood cells and platelets Plasma (the liquid part of blood) Bone marrow (where blood cells are produced) Spleen Thymus
Respiratory	Nose Mouth Pharynx Larynx Trachea Bronchi Lungs	Digestive	Mouth Esophagus Stomach Small intestine Large intestine Rectum Anus Liver Gallbladder Pancreas (the part that produces enzymes) Appendix
Nervous	Brain Spinal cord Nerves (both those that carry impulses to the brain and those that carry impulses from the brain to muscles and organs)		
Integumentary (Skin)	Epidermis (surface skin) Dermis ("true skin") Connective tissues, including fat, glands, and blood vessels Hair Nails	Urinary	Kidneys Ureters Bladder Urethra

		Reproductive	Male
			  Penis
			  Prostate gland
			  Seminal vesicles
			  Vasa deferentia
			  Testes
			Female
			  Vagina
			  Cervix
			  Uterus
			  Fallopian tubes
			  Ovaries

Musculoskeletal	Muscles Tendons and ligaments Bones Joints		
Endocrine	Thyroid gland Parathyroid gland Adrenal glands Pituitary gland Pancreas (the part that produces insulin) Stomach (the cells that produce gastrin) Pineal gland Ovaries Testes	Lymphatic	Lymph fluid Lymph vessels Lymph nodes Tonsils Spleen Thymus gland

FIGURE 2.4 The various layers and components of the skin enable it to carry out a variety of protective functions, such as sweating to maintain body temperature and secreting oil to keep the skin from drying out.

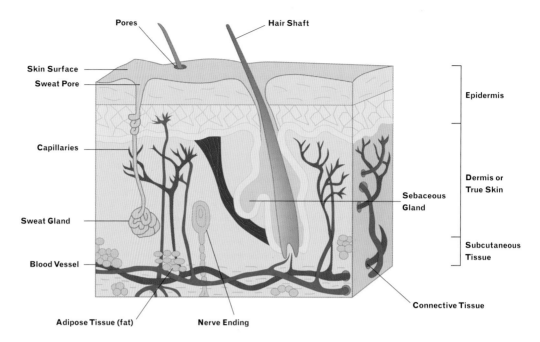

fat tissue, various contaminants can accumulate over time, a process called **bioaccumulation,** and reach harmful levels. Some of the best known POPs are PCBs (mixtures of chemicals), DDT, and dioxins. For the most part, these are intentionally produced chemicals that are currently or were once used in agriculture, disease control, manufacturing, and industrial processes. DDT, for example, is extremely effective in killing the mosquitoes that carry malaria, a disease that continues to kill millions of people each year. This potential lifesaver might cause other health problems when it bioaccumulates in the body fat of living creatures. Another example is polybrominated diphenyl ethers (PBDEs), which were originally developed as a fire retardant in fabrics such as furniture upholstery, carpeting, and clothing. It turned out that these chemicals off-gas toxins that can accumulate in the body and harm the developing brains of infants (Cone, 2003). Other potentially harmful pollutants are by-products of industrial processes and combustion. These include **dioxins,** which are among the most toxic, cancer-causing chemicals in the environment (U.S. Environmental Protection Agency, 2006, "Consumer Factsheet"). A common source of dioxins is backyard burning of plant material and household waste, so finding alternate means of disposing of such wastes or,

at least, ensuring that the smoke does not enter interior spaces is important. Another important thing to understand about dioxins is that they derive from plastics, materials widely used in the built environment for manufacturing computer and television cases, appliances, and synthetic fibers. In natural and accidental disasters such as fires, these plastics melt and dioxins are released into the air and soil. Therefore, designers need to consider the possible chemical releases and environmental contamination that might result from such events as tornados, hurricanes, earthquakes, flooding, and fires. They should be aware of possible chemical emissions and proper recycling techniques. For example, many carpet and rug manufacturers offer a recycling option in an effort to encourage sustainable practices; carpeting that is ruined as a result of a natural disaster is often not recycled and leads to further environmental contamination.

Implications for Designers

The examples in the previous section are excellent illustrations of unintended consequences. Some products developed for good purposes have turned out to be harmful to human health. Because we can't always know the outcomes of new products, designers should strive to stay informed about chemicals and products related to the built environment so that if early warning signs of potential harm are reported, they can pass this information along to their clients.

There are specific steps that designers can take to help clients who suffer from allergies. When the culprit is dust mites, designers can recommend bedding and other fabrics that are labeled hypoallergenic. Materials that are hypoallergenic provide limited surface spaces for dead skin cells to accumulate, thus, they do not attract dust mites. Designers should inform their clients that buying hypoallergenic pillows does not negate the need to clean those pillows regularly. The majority of dead skin cells may not cling to the pillow, but they will fall to the next surface, such as the bedding or the floor. This provides us with an example of why designers must understand their clients' lifestyles. Asking how often clients wash their sheets may seem a bit personal, but knowing that a young male is starting his own business and does not have time to change his sheets frequently can lead a designer to make healthy recommendations. In this case, the designer might suggest the use of sheets and pillowcases with high thread counts. Like hypoallergenic fabrics, fabrics with high thread counts have tight weaves that limit the frequency and depth of spaces in the fabric's surface where dead skin cells can accumulate, thereby providing fewer spaces for dust mites and their droppings to accumulate. Additional recommendations for safeguarding the health of the skin are discussed in Chapter 3.

SKELETAL SYSTEM

The skeletal system consists of 206 bones, half of which are in the hands and feet. The multitude of bones in these areas allows for a wide range of maneuverability. With more moving parts comes a greater probability of injury. Some of these injuries we encourage through the choices we make, such as styles of shoes and clothing. High heels, which regularly become a trendy style, can get stuck in the open grates of staircase treads and cause twisted ankles (Figure 2.5). They can also get caught in carpeting with high pile or very soft

FIGURE 2.5 Many designs have great visual appeal and practical use, as in the case of these stairs on which water does not accumulate. However, grated steps create unintended safety issues. Many women have twisted, sprained, or broken their ankles on designs like this when the heels of their shoes become lodged in the grate openings.

backing and cause the wearer to lose her balance and fall.

The long bones are found in the arms and legs. At the ends of each of these bones is an area called the epiphysis, where there is a thin layer called the growth line, or growth plate, where bone growth takes place during childhood and adolescence. What is important for designers to understand about this area is that it must be stimulated through physical activity in order for the bone to grow and strengthen. During childhood two things happen to the bones. The first is that the repeated pressure from running and jumping placed on the bones helps them to become stronger, and second is that running and jumping facilitate growth. In addition, it is important to understand that even after growth is completed, the bones continue to respond positively to physical stress. Without continual pressure the bones will become brittle and easily breakable. (See Box 2.1.) Designers, therefore, must consider the need for exercise throughout the life span. This might mean the incorporation of treadmills, stair-climbers, and exercise space into a residential or workplace environment (Figure 2.6).

BOX 2.1 STRESS IS ESSENTIAL TO BONES: THE CASE OF THE ASTRONAUTS

Space travel has offered many opportunities for scientists to study the human body under various conditions. As it turns out, astronauts face a number of health challenges. One of these is the lack of gravity in space that decreases the stress on bones needed to maintain their strength. In spite of their physical training, astronauts have an increased risk of broken bones and osteoporosis later in life. Recent Russian data shows that in space, hip and lower spine mass decreases at a rate of one percent a month. This is ten times faster than the loss that occurs on Earth during the average individual's aging process. Under normal gravitational conditions, new bone formation and the destruction of old bone tissue is balanced. Experiments on rats have been conducted to confirm these observations, and demonstrated that, indeed, when stress on the skeleton decreases, bone growth also decreases.

Adapted from: Keeping life sciences alive in Russia. *Airspace America.* March, 1997. Retrieved August 17, 2006, from www.imbp.ru/webpages/engl/Articles/artic3_e.html

Also of importance to the designer are the 26 irregularly shaped bones, called vertebrae, that comprise the spinal column. This important component of the skeletal system houses and protects the delicate spinal cord,

FIGURE 2.6 An erroneous belief held by some is that elderly people are frail and incapable of many everyday activities. While this might be true for a small segment of the population, most older adults prefer to stay active and should be encouraged to do so.

which carries messages from the brain to the nerves that branch out to the rest of the body. The vertebrae are separated by disks of thick, bundled cartilage, which act as shock absorbers and give the spine flexibility.

One of the problems that affects many tall individuals is curvature of the spine caused by the need to hunch over to adjust to the standardized built environment, which has been designed for people of average height. Another concern for designers is damage to the intervertebral disks, such as ruptures, that can result from uneven surfaces. For example, many people incur damage to their disks as a result of the gyration caused to the body when they suddenly step down onto an elevation that is lower than their current walking surface. This commonly happens when a person is forced to quickly—and sometimes unexpectedly—step down from a curb at an intersection; this sudden change in elevation can also occur within the built environment when a clear change in elevation is not apparent, such as a shallow sunken portion of a room. Although the intervertebral disks are designed to act as shock absorbers to prevent the hard surfaces of the vertebrae from colliding into one another during actions such as walking and jumping, during unanticipated changes in elevations they can be damaged. Any type of wrenching, twisting, or improper lifting can result in damage to the disks and back pain.

The bones are connected to each other at the joints. With a few exceptions, the body's joints are movable, enabling the body to bend and turn but also making it vulnerable to injuries caused by overmovement, as in the previous example of the twisted ankle. In fact, the tissues that hold the muscles and bones together are susceptible to injury because they are prone to stretching and tearing.

Implications for Designers

Because the skeletal system's primary responsibility is to support the body's structures, designers need to ensure that furnishings, and the environment as a whole, support the skeletal system. This includes proper ergonomics to fit the body size, as described in Chapter 7.

It also means providing ways for individuals to engage in the physical activity needed to maintain the strength of their bones. Ideally, this would be done in the planning phase of an office building, in which a health or fitness center and walking track could be included in the initial plans; such features can be incorporated during remodeling or retrofitting projects when coordinated with space planners who can work to find the appropriate space for such facilities. Exercise rooms in homes are becoming popular, and incorporating them into new construction or existing residences can contribute to bone health as well as overall fitness (Figure 2.7).

When working on private residences, designers will want to conduct a quick visual survey of the surrounding neighborhood. If a child lives in a home that lacks play areas or parks in the immediate vicinity, designers should incorporate areas for active play in either the child's bedroom or a separate rumpus room.

The bones need a continual supply of calcium to retain their density. Vitamin D is needed to convert calcium into bone matter, and it is for this reason that opportunities to spend time in the sun, which supplies vitamin D, should be emphasized.

Much of the joint and back pain we experience is a result of the continual wear and tear on cartilage, the material that prevents bones from grinding against each other. Lack of ample cartilage cushioning leads to pain, swelling, and the deformation of joints when the bone creates extra cells as it attempts to protect itself. A problem designers face is the multitude of hard surfaces that are part of modern living. To illustrate this point, consider the hardest surfaces that our hunter-gatherer ancestors were forced to walk or stand upon—probably compressed dirt. Today, the environment is covered with hard concrete surfaces. This means that, in some respects, our bodies are subjected to more hostile conditions than were the bodies of our distant ancestors. Hence, designers will want to consider the use of pressure-absorbing flooring materials such

as cork in environments that require lots of walking, including hospitals, malls, and airports. On the other hand, caution should be exercised against the incorporation of surfaces that are too soft, such as deep pile carpeting in public places, because these surfaces can pose trip hazards for women who wear high heels or people who use walkers.

Healthy spines are encouraged by correct posture, so designers should provide furniture selections that encourage sitting up straight rather than slouching. (See Chapter 7.)

MUSCULAR SYSTEM

There are more than six hundred muscles in the body, and, when combined, those muscles make up about 50 percent of the body's total weight. The cells that form muscle tissue have special characteristics that enable them to produce body movement. To do this, they receive and respond to stimuli, shorten, stretch, and return to their original position. Because of the specialized nature of muscle cells, we are able to react to dangerous situations, such as moving away from a bookcase that is toppling over, reacting quickly to rescue a pet from being crushed by the bookcase, and lifting the bookcase off someone who gets trapped underneath.

FIGURE 2.7 Home gyms can be dedicated rooms, like the basement gym shown, or may consist of one or two pieces of exercise equipment tucked into the corner of a room that has other uses.

All of the muscles in the human body are categorized into four groups based on their function:

1. Sphincter, or dilator, muscles are circular in shape and have the ability to control the passage of substances or light from entering or exiting the body. There are several sphincter muscles in the body, with the main ones being in the digestive system and the eyes. As we age, sphincter/dilator muscles lose their strength, resulting in problems such as incontinence and impaired vision. Designers, therefore, will want to decrease the use of materials that absorb bodily fluids and provide greater transition zones between areas of bright and dim light in facilities in which older adults reside.

2. Cardiac muscle is an involuntary muscle, which means that it acts without our awareness or control. It makes up the heart and can be strengthened through exercise. Designers can encourage exercise by incorporating easily identifiable, attractive, and safe staircases that can be used instead of elevators in corporate buildings, malls, and other large-scale environments. Also, walking tracks can be included as part of a building's design so that workers can break away from their daily routines to walk a lap or two.

3. Smooth muscle lines the walls of body organs such as the stomach, intestines, bladder, and blood vessels. These muscles are involuntary and controlled by the autonomic nervous system (again, without our control). Just as with the cardiac muscle, exercise can contribute to healthy smooth muscle action such as digestion and breathing (Shore and Fredberg, 2005). Designers can encourage exercise by placing resident rooms in long-term care facilities away from primary dining areas. This way, residents will be required to walk farther distances. At the same time, provisions must be made to deliver food to nonambulatory residents or transport them to the dining room.

4. Skeletal muscles enable movements under our control. Because these muscles require conscious effort to move them, they are classified as voluntary. These muscles must be used and continually stretched in order to maintain strength and flexibility. This is especially important for elderly and other populations who tend to live sedentary lives because without use, muscles will weaken and decrease in size, thus increasing the chances of falls and other accidents.

RESPIRATORY SYSTEM

The body needs a continual supply of nutrients to survive, and it is oxygen that enables the release of energy from these nutrients so it can be used to carry on vital bodily functions. The waste product of this process is carbon dioxide. The respiratory system fulfills the dual purpose of delivering oxygen, necessary for cells to survive, and removing carbon dioxide, a waste product. It accomplishes this by bringing air into the body and delivering it to sites where these two gases can be exchanged in the blood.

While it is well planned for taking in air under ideal circumstances, the respiratory system's opening to the external world makes it vulnerable to the many pollutants in indoor and outdoor air. These pollutants can cause problems before they even reach the lungs, the large spongy organs filled with tiny air sacs. This can happen because, as the pollutants pass through the airways that extend from the nose to the lungs, they can irritate the linings and cause them to produce excess mucous and to contract. These two actions, which interfere with normal breathing, are symptoms of an allergic reaction or asthma attack. You can see why these conditions are frequently related to airborne substances present in the built environment. Once certain harmful substances are inhaled deep into the lungs, they are passed into the blood through capillaries, very tiny blood vessels through which oxygen and carbon dioxide are exchanged. From this point, the harmful substances can be distributed throughout the body.

Tobacco smoke is an example of a particularly dangerous respiratory pollutant: When inhaled, it paralyzes the cilia, the tiny hairlike structures in the airways to the lungs that capture and sweep dust particles upward so they can be breathed or coughed out; it damages the lung cells, in some individuals leading to lung cancer; and its chemical components, such as nicotine, are carried to the brain, where they cause changes in the cells that result in dependency (addiction). Chapter 4 contains other examples of airborne contaminants that can lead to lung damage.

Implications for Designers

In the past, designers accommodated the desires of smokers and nonsmokers through **behavior zoning** initiatives. This meant that there were smoking and nonsmoking sections in buildings, restaurants, airplanes, and other public places. Yet cigarette smoke can drift into the nonsmoking section, where it is inhaled by nonsmokers, who can suffer some of the same harmful effects as the smokers themselves. Today, designers usually separate smoking areas from the general facility. If smokers have a designated indoor area, it is ventilated directly outdoors.

Modern office machinery, such as laser printers and copiers, has contributed to the contamination of air quality in workplaces that previously did not experience such problems. This is because they produce high levels of ozone, which can cause headaches and scratchy throats, among other symptoms. (See Chapter 4 for more information about ozone.) Hence, designers need to plan separate dedicated rooms for such equipment. As in rooms with tobacco smoke, the air in equipment rooms should have separate ventilation systems so the contaminants can be vented directly outside and not recirculated throughout the entire facility.

Learning about common airborne contaminants found in both new construction and maintenance products can help designers make healthy choices as well as informed suggestions when working with clients. Common contaminants and indoor air quality are covered in more detail in Chapters 4 and 5.

CARDIOVASCULAR SYSTEM

The cardiovascular system works with the respiratory system to deliver oxygen to and remove carbon dioxide from the body; transport nutrients and water; carry away waste products; and transport other body fluids and materials, such as hormones, as needed. To accomplish these tasks, the system consists of the heart, which is basically a pump comprised of cardiac muscle, and the arteries, veins, and capillaries through which the blood is pumped. As the cardiac muscle contracts, it pushes the blood throughout the entire body. These contractions are initiated and regulated by electrical impulses sent out by special cells known collectively as the **pacemaker.** These impulses can be interrupted through the inhalation of high concentrations of certain chemicals, such as those contained in many household cleaners. This is why the directions on such products state that they should only be used in well-ventilated areas. Therefore, designers should identify areas where the use of cleaning fluids is greatest, such as bathrooms and kitchens, and ensure ample ventilation. This can be done with windows that open and exhaust fans that pull air to the outside.

Implications for Designers

Heart disease is the leading cause of death in the United States. Many of these deaths are preventable through good nutrition and adequate exercise. Therefore, installing exercise facilities, as mentioned in previous sections and discussed more fully in Chapter 10, may contribute to reducing this death rate.

Another environment-related heart condition involves people who rely on artificial pacemakers to maintain and regulate heartbeat; these devices use electrical currents that can receive interference from a host of environmental equipment, including:

FIGURE 2.8 Architects and developers should be aware of transformers, wiring, and other electrical devices located in the areas that surround commercial and residential buildings.

- Power plants
- Large generators
- Arc welding equipment
- Large magnets
- Dielectric heaters
- TV or radio transmitting towers
- Electrical power lines

While many of these items are found in industrial work environments, such as auto mechanic shops that often use arc welders, architects and developers should be aware of potential hazards in the surrounding environment when planning residential, office, and health-care facilities. When selecting building sites, caution should be exercised to locate buildings away from high-tension (electrical) lines and to ensure ample distance from energy-producing sites such as hydro, nuclear, and fossil fuel plants, because these devices can interfere with pacemakers (Figure 2.8).

Another growing concern for architects is the use of antennas on top of highrise buildings. The Sears Tower in Chicago contains an array of television- and radio-transmitting antennas. For the most part these are safe; with the advent of cellular technology, it is becoming more common for building rooftops to be used for wireless base-station antennas. The increased number of these antennas means the cumulative and aggregate effects could reach potentially harmful levels of electromagnetic energy output, which could interfere with pacemakers and negatively affect the neurophysiology of humans.

For the architect, the best way to help mitigate the exposure levels of these electromagnetic fields on the building's occupants is to increase the distance between the rooftop and the inhabitants of the top floor. Architects may want to consider the proximity of these antennas to rooftop gardens and recreational spaces as well.

Unfortunately, there is little the interior designer can do to prevent or reduce these electromagnetic fields aside from being aware of the sources. For example, many homes in the southeastern United States have backup generators for use during power failures caused by hurricanes and tornados. These generators can interfere with pacemakers and should be placed far from areas, such as bedrooms, where occupants will be spending long periods of time. Designers should also be aware of New Age magnetic therapies that suggest that magnetic mattress pads can be used to promote good health. This type of mattress pad can interfere with the functioning of a pacemaker and, therefore, should not be suggested for a client who uses one. Designers need to understand that, as technology advances, they must keep abreast of current trends in the mainstream market as well as the alternative markets in order to best serve their clients.

NERVOUS SYSTEM

The nervous system is one of the most complex systems; it oversees the functions of the systems discussed thus far. Because of its importance and its limited healing capabilities (nerve cells cannot regenerate), damage to this system can be catastrophic and often permanent. The nervous system is made up of two major divisions: the central nervous system, which consists of the brain and spinal cord; and the peripheral nervous system, which consists of nerves that extend out from the brain and spinal cord to send messages to all parts of the body.

The central nervous system functions as the communication and coordination system for the body. It receives messages from internal and external stimuli; interprets the meaning of the stimuli; and then sends an appropriate response to the body parts involved, via the nerves in the spinal cord and peripheral nervous system. Suppose that a person is walking through the interior of a mall and sees a window display of attractive furnishings. The images of the display enter the eyes as light waves, which are converted to electrical impulses; these impulses are then sent to the brain via sensory nerves, beginning with the optic nerve at the back of the eye. The neural impulses travel from the axon of one nerve cell to the dendrite of the next across a small gap, called the synapse, by means of a chemical intermediary called a **neurotransmitter.** Once inside the brain, the impulses are decoded. In this example, the brain interprets the images as something desirable and sends out numerous messages, including feelings of pleasure and interest. It also sends instructions to the motor neurons to tell the skeletal muscles how to respond with appropriate actions, such as approaching the store, opening the door, and entering. These are simple actions like those we

---

BOX 2.2 LONGITUDINAL STUDIES

Longitudinal studies require years of data gathering and analysis. When we consider longitudinal studies of humans, this generally means throughout one or more human life spans. Because much of modern technology, and the high use of modern technology, is relatively new, there are limited longitudinal studies to confirm or dispute the effects of that technology on humans. Those results are still 20 to 40 years into the future when we see the children who grew up with cell phones, computers, numerous televisions, and other electronic devices, reach their 60s and 70s. Only then can we start to make deductions about the safety or harm of our technological advancements.

---

perform many times each day. In fact, they are accomplished by millions of nerve impulses, much brain activity, and hundreds of muscles. Concurrently, and without the person's awareness, the brain is sending continuous signals to the involuntary muscles with instructions to breathe, move blood throughout the body, and digest the contents of the latest meal. Whether it's sight, sound, touch, taste, smell, or a combination of senses, the process is the same: Stimuli are converted into electrical impulses that travel to the brain, via vast networks of nerves, to be decoded and responded to with instructions for appropriate actions.

Knowing the basics of this process is significant for designers because certain chemicals, used in products such as pesticides, household and personal care products, and building materials, can interact with neurotransmitters, impairing their ability to send communications along the nerve cells. For example, organophosphate pesticides, such as chlorpyrifos, interfere with the transmission process of certain neurotransmitters by inhibiting the action of a necessary enzyme, a protein that speeds up the body's natural chemical process (EXTOXNET, 1993).

Brain

The brain acts as the master controller of the body, directing every function, from the beating of the heart to hiccups to the movement of muscles. In addition, the brain enables us to experience emotions and makes it possible for us to learn and recall information. This is why

FIGURE 2.9 Bunk beds are great space-saving pieces of furniture for children's rooms or even studio apartments. However, the elevation of the upper bed, if not properly fitted with safety mechanisms, can be very dangerous, leading to head injuries and even death.

enter the body through other means, such as the mouth, nose, and eyes. For example, inhalation of certain concentrated fumes, such as those emitted by gasoline, glue, and paint thinner, not only kill brain cells but can also lead to convulsions (involuntary contractions of normally voluntary muscles). Some of the minor symptoms resulting from exposure to noxious gases, headaches and dizziness, are commonly experienced by occupants of office buildings. Another example is the pathway from eye to brain. Vision is initiated as light enters the pupil and on reaching the optic nerve is converted to neural impulses, which are sent to the brain. Erratic light patterns such as strobe lights and similar types of flickering light can set off a chain reaction of chaotic neural firings that may prompt an epileptic seizure.

Implications for Designers

Designers must be prepared to help prevent many of the hazards that can damage the nervous system. Being aware of chemicals that affect the system is especially important, because these chemicals are typically present in the built environment. All aspects of interiors should be continually surveyed for the possible presence of harmful substances. Even "solutions" to other environmental concerns should be reviewed carefully for their potential to cause yet other problems—that is, for unintended consequences. For example, as we continue to learn about how green spaces and natural views promote healing and a positive attitude, many office buildings are bringing more plants inside. New buildings are incorporating atriums and courtyards. Indoor plants are sometimes treated with organophosphate pesticides that, as noted previously, can be harmful to the nervous system (Figure 2.10). This is important for designers to know so they can make appropriate accommodations. For example, proper care should be provided for plants to prevent the need for excessive amounts of pesticides. Containers should hold the soil so that it cannot spill out and be tracked onto carpeted floors. If children will be present, the plants should be inaccessible to the touch of small hands.

brain injury, which can interfere with physical and mental abilities, can be so devastating. In an effort to avoid such injuries, the brain is well protected. The first layer of protection is the hard layer of bone called the skull, which protects the brain from blunt force trauma such as being hit on the head by falling debris. The second, inner layer is made up of a series of tissue layers called meninges and a layer of liquid called cerebral fluid. These two substances provide the brain with stability within the skull and a soft cushion between the brain tissue and the hard surface of the skull. In spite of this protection, the brain is subject to injury from trauma; over a million Americans each year suffer brain injuries from various types of accidents, such as falling down the stairs or falling off the top bunk of bunk beds (Figure 2.9).

And although the structure of the brain is protected from physical contact, its inner workings can be affected by substances that

Other potentially harmful pollutants that can be generated by positive activities are those associated with arts and crafts at schools, recreation centers, and senior facilities. These spaces should be designed to disperse and vent out the off-gassing caused by glues, markers, and paints, because exposure can result in damage to the brain cells.

STRESS

The section of the nervous system that controls bodily functions such as digestion, heartbeat, and breathing, all without our awareness, is called the autonomic nervous system. It is divided, in turn, into two systems, the sympathetic and parasympathetic, which perform mutually antagonistic (opposing) functions. Under normal conditions, the two systems are in balance. When the body reacts to stress, the functions of the sympathetic system automatically go into action and put the body in a state of physical high alert so that it can handle anticipated danger. A cascading series of hormone releases takes place. These hormones cause a variety of bodily changes that help focus concentration, speed up physical reactions, and increase strength (Mayo Clinic, 2006, "Stress"). Some specific examples include increasing the heart rate to speed oxygen throughout the body; dilating the pupils to allow more light to enter; slowing digestion so more blood can be sent to the brain; and opening the respiratory passages so more air can be inhaled.

These physical responses to stress, often referred to as the fight or flight response, function to safeguard humans from physical threats by enabling them to think quickly, see better, and run faster. In the modern world, stress is more likely to be mental. The physiological responses are the same for mental stress and physical danger. This is important to understand, because it explains why everyday worries and anxieties can signal the sympathetic system to continually send out messages to which the body responds physically. Over time these reactions, such as heightened blood pressure, literally wear the body out. Responses to stress are also believed to suppress the immune

system, which defends us against infection. Table 2.3 shows how widespread stress responses can be in the body.

Implications for Designers

Designers should incorporate ways to alleviate stress and encourage relaxation into the design of the built environment. For example, disorganization and overwork have been identified as two major causes of stress (American Psychological Association, n.d., "The Different"). To help prevent these problems, designers can create interiors with efficient work areas to save time, easy-to-use storage to encourage good organization, and easy-to-clean surfaces and

FIGURE 2.10 Indoor plants and atriums have become a common element in many public and workplace environments. While the benefits of plants are numerous, some of the chemicals used to maintain the health of the plants can be harmful to humans. For this reason, designers must be proactive to ensure that such green spaces are incorporated into the design as safely as possible.

TABLE 2.3 EFFECTS OF CHRONIC STRESS ON THE BODY

SYSTEM	EFFECTS	CAUSED BY:
Digestive	Stomachache, diarrhea	Release of stomach acid and emptying of stomach are slowed. Colon is stimulated, speeding the release of contents.
Nervous	Feelings of anxiety, helplessness, and impending doom. Depression. Sleep disturbances, loss of sex drive, and loss of appetite.	Constant stream of stress hormones
Cardiovascular	Increased heart rate, blood pressure, and cholesterol and triglyceride levels, all factors that increase the risk of heart disease.	High levels of cortisol
Integumentary	Worsening of psoriasis, eczema, hives, and acne	Increased hormonal activity. Increase in the inflammatory response.
Respiratory	Trigger for asthma attacks	Emotions associated with stress may cause the brain to release chemicals that cause smooth muscle constriction and the inflammatory response.

Adapted from: Mayo Clinic. (Last updated September 12, 2006). *Stress: Unhealthy Response to The Pressures of Life.* Retrieved September 16, 2006, from www.mayoclinic.com/print/stress/SR00001/METHOD=print

National Library of Medicine. National Center for Biotechnology Information. PubMed. Sandberg, S., Paton, J. Y., Ahola, S., McCann, D. C., McGuiness, D., Hillary, C. R., Oja, H. "The role of acute and chronic stress in asthma attacks in children."
www.ncbi.nlm.nih.gov/entrez/query.fcgi?cmd=Retrieve&db=PubMed&list_uids=11041399&dopt=
Citation

furnishings. Logical floor plans can eliminate extra steps, and items needed for similar activities can be clustered in one area. For example, in many modern homes, laundry facilities are located near bedrooms and bathrooms, where most dirty laundry is generated. Additionally, these facilities contain counters and cabinets to eliminate the hauling of laundry to another room for sorting and folding.

Floor plans and room design can also promote relaxation and reflection. Designers can provide quiet areas away from the main traffic flow and activity areas: bedrooms with comfortable chairs for reading, outdoor spaces such as Zen gardens, and rooms for hobbies and music-making. (See Chapter 10 for more about eliminating stress.) Another consideration is that humans do not move at right angles; hence, when space planning, designers should allow for smooth-flowing movement.

SPECIAL SENSES

The special senses include vision, hearing, smell, taste, and touch. The sensation of touch has a variety of functions that include balance and the detection of pressure, pain, and temperature. To enable sensory input, the body has receptor cells that are stimulated in different ways: vision by light; hearing by sound waves;

smell and taste by chemicals; touch by temperature, pressure, and motion. The ability to detect sensation from the built environment protects and preserves our body. Consider the barefoot person who steps on a carpet tack protruding from the floor. The sensation travels to the brain, which decodes the information as pain and commands the skeletal muscles to lift the foot quickly. Understanding human sensation is important when studying design, because it is through sensation that we can appreciate as well as be harmed by our environment.

Eye

The eyes are relatively small, averaging only about one inch in diameter, but they are extremely complex. The eyes are protected in a number of ways: the orbital socket of the skull protects them from blows and resulting injuries; the eyebrows and eyelashes catch moisture and particles that might enter the eye; the eyelids distribute moisture over its surface; and the lacrimal glands produce tears to clean and moisturize. In spite of this protection, the eye is vulnerable to items that protrude into space or are suspended in the air, such as mobiles or other forms of art; the eye tends to focus on objects in the distance and often misses those that are close by.

The following steps, which follow the pathway of vision illustrated in Figure 2.11, are initiated when light enters the eye:

1. Light rays enter the eye through the cornea, a circular clear area in the sclera.
2. Light passes through the pupil, an opening in the choroid coat. The iris, a muscular layer surrounding the pupil, controls the amount of light that enters.
3. The lens, located behind the iris and pupil, refracts (bends) the light rays.
4. The rays are reflected on the retina, at the back of the eye, which contains specialized cells called rods and cones. Rods pick up stimuli from dim light, while cones are sensitive to bright light and enable color vision.

5. Sensations are transmitted along the optic nerve to the brain for interpretation.

Implications for Designers

Because light is the means by which the eye receives messages from the outside world, adequate interior and exterior lighting is essential for optimum vision. In addition, the internal workings of the eye are subject to a number of problems, such as a misshapen eyeball, leading to vision problems. Nearsightedness is an example of a problem designers can address; clocks with large numerals can be read from a distance, and computer screens can be placed close enough for the operator to see.

As with so many of the body systems, a variety of fumes can irritate the eyes' delicate membranes. Care should be taken to avoid these fumes or, when this is not possible, to provide adequate ventilation. This is especially

---

BOX 2.3 STRESS AND THE IMMUNE SYSTEM

Research is beginning to reveal how stress affects the immune system. Dr. Esther Sternberg, director of the Integrative Neural Immune Program at the National Institute of Mental Health, suggests that cortisol suppresses the functioning of the immune system and decreases the inflammatory response. Under normal circumstances, release of cortisol is the brain's way of letting the immune system know when it is no longer needed. However, during times of stress, cortisol is decreased whether immune functions are needed or not. Studies of people experiencing high-level acute or long-term chronic stress, such as Army Rangers undergoing extreme physical stress, caregivers of family members with Alzheimer's, or couples with serious marital problems, show a longer-than-normal healing time to wounds and response to vaccinations and an increased susceptibility to viral infections.

An opposite reaction is also possible. That is, the production of too few stress hormones, possibly caused by a lack of cytokines, the molecules from the immune system that monitor the body to ensure against immune system overreactions, can result in above-normal immune system activity. This may be at least one cause of autoimmune diseases such as rheumatoid arthritis and lupus. The interrelationships between the brain and immune system are complex and depend on a number of factors, but the brain's hormonal stress response appears to affect the proper functioning of the immune system.

Adapted from: Wein, H. (October, 2000). *Stress and disease: New perspectives.* Word on Health [Newsletter]. Bethesda, MD: National Institutes of Health, Office of Communications.

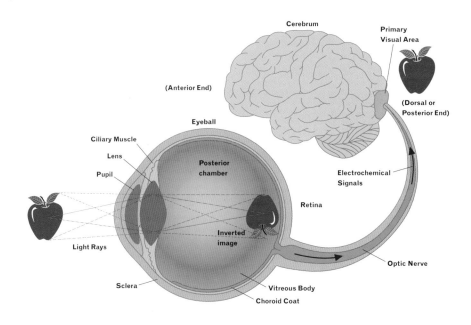

FIGURE 2.12A AND B A: If this mobile were hung at eye level, the points from the tail could easily poke and injure the eye of a passing person. It is best to hang items like this close to walls and out of walking pathways. B: This eye injury demonstrates the danger of sharp, protruding, or hanging objects. Many pieces of hanging art have such pieces that protrude into the path where people walk.

important if clients wear contact lenses, which can trap particulates. These clients should be forewarned, for example, of the particulates emitted from fireplaces and woodstoves so they can consider other heat sources. (Chapter 4 has more information about harmful contaminants.)

Finally, consideration should always be given to creating safe areas that prevent falls, collisions, and puncture wounds that can damage the eye. Play areas, in particular, are of concern because children run when playing and often fail to pay attention to where they are going. Obstacles that protrude at a child's eye level should be avoided (Figure 2.12A and B).

Ear

The ear contains three parts, each with an essential role in collecting or transporting sound waves:

1. Outer ear: collects sound waves and directs them into the auditory canal, which ends at the tympanic membrane (eardrum).
2. Middle ear: a cavity containing three tiny bones whose movement transmits sound waves from the eardrum to the inner ear.
3. Inner ear: several membrane-lined channels. The cochlea contains a tube filled with fluid and lined with hairlike cells

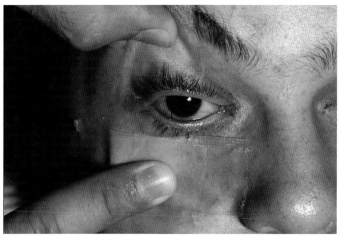

that pick up vibrations made by sound waves moving within the fluid. These sensations are sent to the brain via the auditory nerve.

In addition to hearing, the ear also plays an important role in maintaining balance and equilibrium.

Implications for Designers

The very delicate nature of the ear's structures makes them susceptible to injury, including from factors present in the built environment. Very loud noise, for example, causes strong vibrations that damage the extremely delicate structures of the inner ear. Exposure to loud music is one reason why hearing loss is becoming more prevalent among young people. Unfortunately, noise-induced hearing loss is usually permanent because the damaged ear components do not regenerate. To help eliminate noise from the home and workplace, designers can include double-glazed windows, shields, or soundproof walls around loud machinery and introduce fabrics to muffle sounds. (See Chapter 7 for more information about noise and its abatement.) Residential spaces in urban environments need to incorporate as much sound-blocking material as possible, because the urban clamor often penetrates the home and occupants often respond by playing a television or stereo louder in order to compensate for the outside noise.

As with the eyes, the delicate inner structures of the ear can become damaged if hit, as in a fall. If an impact is hard enough, it can rupture the eardrum, causing pain and even hearing loss. Thus, it is important to design environments that will prevent such accidents.

IMMUNE SYSTEM

The **immune system** is actually a combination of mechanisms and actions performed by various components of the other body systems. The immune system protects the body against infection by detecting, identifying, and killing bacteria, viruses, tumor cells, and other patho-gens (agents that cause disease) that manage to enter the body. The key activities of this system take place at the cellular level, and its capabilities are quite amazing. For example, once a pathogen is identified, antibodies are created to fight and kill that specific pathogen by surrounding it with their own bodies, eating it, or releasing toxic chemicals. In addition, certain cells act as immune memories, so that if the same pathogen returns, it can be immediately attacked. Certain cells in the immune system migrate into various organs, such as the lungs, kidneys, brain, and liver, to help rid the body of debris, such as worn-out cells that have sloughed-off tissue.

The immune system is vital to maintaining health. To illustrate, consider why HIV is almost always eventually fatal: The virus attacks and kills T cells, which are major components of the immune system's line of defense. With an inadequate number of T cells, the body cannot protect itself against infections that the immune system often detects and takes care of before they make a non-HIV individual ill.

Implications for Designers

Designers should be aware that conditions that suppress or damage the immune system are extremely serious. One such condition is quite common in the United States: attaching a garage to a house. This is serious, because benzene is produced when cars are running and is part of the exhaust that can enter through doors that connect the garage to the house and through leaks in the wall that separates the garage from the living space. Benzene interferes with the bone marrow's ability to produce red and white blood cells, and the white cells are essential components of the immune system because they fight infection. Designers should take the placement of garages seriously and, if a garage is already attached to an occupied home or building, ensure that the adjoining walls are built as tightly as possible. In addition, designers should ensure that ventilation is adequate to clear the air of exhaust, in both the garage and the living space. Finally, designers should be aware that intakes for "fresh" air are

BOX 2.4 THE SUSTAINABILITY CONNECTION

A major principle of sustainability in the built environment is the sustainability of human health. Having a very basic understanding of the workings of the human body will help designers understand why certain components of the environment are helpful, while others are harmful.

Human health and sustainability of the environment are interrelated. For example, finding alternatives to limited (nonsustainable) fossil fuel supplies, a topic in Chapter 6, also contributes to good respiratory health. This is because burning fossil fuels releases harmful pollutants into the air we breathe. Another example is the retention of forests of natural areas near our cities. Not only does this benefit the earth, it preserves resources that create the oxygen we breathe.

These are only two of many examples of how our bodies are part of a larger system that, when sustained and working together, improves the life of everything on the planet.

GLOSSARY TERMS

Anatomy

Arsenic

Behavior zoning

Bioaccumulation

Cell

Chronic

Deoxyribonucleic acid (DNA)

Dioxins

Immune system

Mitosis

Mutate

Neurotransmitter

Organophosphates

Organs (body)

Pacemaker

Persistent organic pollutants (POPs)

Physiology

Systems (body)

Tissues

sometimes inadvertently placed near garages and parking areas and, thus, can create indoor pollution rather than prevent it. Designers also should ensure that in car dealerships, auto shops, and smog-check businesses, the waiting areas are well separated from the work areas. Other sources of benzene include cigarette smoke, glues, paints, furniture wax, and detergents. For this reason, indoor benzene levels can become quite high.

Lead is another indoor contaminant that research is showing may lower the body's ability to fight bacterial and viral infections. Lead and its abatement are discussed in more detail in Chapter 4.

For clients who have suppressed or impaired immune systems and patients in health and long-term care facilities, it is essential designers suggest measures that will protect the indoor environment from contaminants. Surfaces should be easy to clean and disinfect; components should be washable; and measures should be taken to reduce the entry of pollutants from outside. Leaks should be sealed and floor mats, shoe racks, and other receptacles should be provided to avoid the tracking in of contaminated materials.

LEARNING ACTIVITIES

1. Choose a home or other residential facility and look for hazards that might result in the following types of injuries: sprains, broken bones, brain injury, eye damage, and hearing loss. List the hazards and develop a plan for removing them and replacing them, if necessary, with safer options.

2. Designing based on fulfilling the needs of people rather than applying the latest trends is a healthier approach to the profession. Develop a list of questions you could use to politely interview clients to learn about their preferences, activities, and any health issues that would influence how you would create an interior that would safely support their lifestyle. Then work with a classmate, taking turns in the roles of interior designer and client, using the questions you have developed.

3. For each of the following body systems, describe three ways you could, as a designer, prevent harm to the system from elements in the built environment. Use examples other than those given in the text.

- Integumentary
- Skeletal
- Muscular
- Respiratory
- Nervous

4. Design a living space for an individual with poor vision. Some questions to consider:
   - What would be the most important factors in the overall design?
   - What types of products are available to make the interior more user-friendly?
   - How can the space support daily activities, such as cooking and personal care?
   - What safety features should be included?

5. Conduct an Internet search to find indoor contaminants that can be harmful to unborn babies. What are the potential consequences of each? How might they be avoided without hindering the lifestyle of the mother?

6. Think about buildings you have visited recently (or choose a few to explore now). What, in your opinion, are the five most notable design flaws that are potentially harmful to human health? Explain and support each of your selections.

SUGGESTED WEB SITES

1. Plants for People
www.plants-for-people.org/eng/faq/f.htm
This Web site contains a lot of information about indoor plants as they relate to human health.

2. Understanding the Immune System: How It Works
www.niaid.nih.gov/Publications/immune/the_immune_system.pdf
This interesting, well-illustrated booklet, prepared by the Department of Human Health and Services, is written for the layperson who wants a basic understanding of how the immune system works.

3. Medline Plus
www.nlm.nih.gov/medlineplus/tutorial.html
Medline Plus is a service from the National Library of Medicine. It contains information for the general public on thousands of health topics. This Web page lists the tutorials available on a variety of topics. The one on dust mites includes general information on allergies as well as ideas for reducing dust mite exposure.

4. Mayo Clinic
www.Mayoclinic.com
The Mayo Clinic in Minnesota maintains a Web site with user-friendly information about all types of health conditions, including many that are related to the built environment.

5. Canadian Centre for Occupational Health and Safety
www.ccohs.ca/oshanswers
This Web site has information about dozens of topics related to human health and the built environment. Although focused on the workplace, the illustrated materials are applicable to all types of indoor environments.

6. Centers for Disease Control and Prevention
www.cdc.gov
The CDC's home page is your link to hundreds of articles written for the general public about all aspects of health and safety. Categories of topics most applicable to the work of interior designers are "Environmental Health," "Healthy Living," and "Workplace Safety and Health."

REFERENCES

Airspace America (March, 1997, retrieved August 17, 2006). *Keeping Life Sciences Alive in Russia*. Available online at www.imbp.ru/webpages/engl/Articles/artic3_e.html.

American Psychological Association (n.d., retrieved July 16, 2006). *The Different Kinds of Stress*. Available online at www.apahelpcenter.org/articles/article.php?id=21.

Bower, J. (2001). *The Healthy House.* Bloomington, IN: The Healthy House Institute.

Building Green (March 1997). "Disposal: The Achilles' Heel of CCA-Treated Wood," *Environmental Building News* 6, 3, 1.

Cone, M. (April 20, 2003). "Cause for Alarm over Chemicals," *Los Angeles Times,* A1.

EXTOXNET (updated September 1993, retrieved August 24, 2006). *Cholinesterase Inhibition.* Available online at extoxnet.orst.edu/tibs/cholines.htm.

March of Dimes (retrieved July 2, 2007). "Quick Reference and Fact Sheets," *Birth Defects.* Available online at www.marchofdimes .com/professionals/14332_1206.asp.

Mayo Clinic (updated September 12, 2006, retrieved September 16, 2006). *Stress: Unhealthy Response to the Pressures of Life.* Available online at www.mayoclinic.com/print/stress/SR00001/METHOD=print.

Morgan, M.T. (2003). *Environmental Health,* 3rd ed. Belmont, CA: Wadsworth Publishing.

Oberg, G.R. (n.d.). *An Overview of Environmental Medicine.* Wichita, KS: American Academy of Environmental Medicine.

Shore, S.A., and J. J. Fredberg (2005). "Obesity, Smooth Muscle, and Airway Hyperresponsiveness," *Journal of Allergy and Clinical Immunology* 115 (5): 925–27.

U.S. Environmental Protection Agency. (updated November 28, 2006, retrieved July 4, 2007). "Consumer Factsheet on Benzo(a)pyrene." Available online at www.epa .gov/safewater/contaminants/dw_contamfs/benzopyr.html.

U.S. Environmental Protection Agency (updated July 26, 2006, retrieved August 20, 2006). "Persistent Organic Pollutants: A Global Issue, A Global Response." Available online at www.epa.gov/international/toxics/pop .htm#pops.

When you consider the number of hours spent indoors, it only makes sense to build a healthy house rather than an unhealthy one.

—John Bower

CHAPTER 3

Common Environmentally Related Diseases and Conditions

LEARNING OBJECTIVES

1. **Explain the influence of the built environment in both causing and preventing various diseases and injuries.**
2. **Provide examples of how good design can help prevent various diseases and injuries.**
3. **Describe how a well-planned built environment can support the needs of individuals who have various health conditions.**

Chapter 2 contained an overview of the structures and functions of the human body and included suggestions for how designers can use this understanding to inform their work to develop health-promoting environments. We saw that good design can promote human health in two major ways. The first is by reducing risks to health through careful selection of materials and attention to details in the interior design of structures. The second is by creating environments that promote wellness lifestyles, such as by providing inviting spaces for physical exercise and designing efficient cooking areas. Although it is not the responsibility of designers to impose their ideas of good lifestyle habits on clients, designers can incorporate elements that encourage wellness and prevent injury.

In this chapter, we will look at some of the diseases and injuries that are related to the built environment. Specific suggestions are included about how good design can contribute to the prevention of some of these conditions, as well as ideas for providing better quality of life for people who already have certain conditions, such as vision impairment. When working with clients, residential designers should strive to become aware of that person's individual physical and mental conditions (and those of family members sharing the home), which may be the result of genetics, illness, or aging, so they can provide designs that are most suitable for their needs.

DISEASES AND DISORDERS OF THE CELLS

Cancer, the second-leading cause of death in the United States, directly or indirectly affects millions of Americans every year. (See Box 3.1.) The disease is caused by a malfunction of cells when they are reproducing. Normal cells have built-in signals that indicate when and how many new cells should be reproduced and for what purpose. As described in Chapter 2, cells reproduce by creating exact replicas of themselves. Cancer cells, on the other hand, lack the structure and function of the cells

BOX 3.1 CANCER FACTS AND FIGURES

- Cancer is the second-leading cause of death in the United States and is the cause of one of every four deaths (Cancer Facts & Figures 2005).
- Estimated new cases diagnosed in 2005: 1,372,910
- Estimated deaths in 2005: 570,280 deaths
- Estimated deaths per day in 2005: 1,500
- Overall costs in 2004: $189.8 billion
  - $69.4 billion for direct medical costs
  - $16.9 billion for lost productivity due to illness
  - $103.5 billion for lost productivity due to premature death
- About 76% of all cancers are diagnosed in persons 55 and older

Source of statistics: American Cancer Society (2005). *Cancers facts and figures 2005.* Atlanta: Author.

they originated from and have no constructive purpose (Neighbors, 1999). Their uncontrolled growth results in malignant (cancerous) tumors that can harm the body by depriving normal cells of needed nutrients and oxygen, blocking blood supplies to normal tissues and organs, and disrupting the normal functions of the invaded organs.

Skin Cancer

Not one disease, but actually a group of diseases, cancer can affect almost any part of the body. In the United States, skin cancer is the most common form (National Cancer Insti-

tute, 2007, "Common Cancer Types"). Although the most common type of skin cancer is not fatal, incidences of the most deadly form, **malignant melanoma**, are increasing rapidly, with over 62,000 cases expected to be diagnosed and almost 8,000 deaths from the disease in 2006 (American Cancer Society. (American Cancer Society, 2006, "Overview: Skin Cancer").

Implications for Designers

The most common cause of skin cancer is excessive sun exposure. Designers can consider ways to shield people from the harmful effects of the sun's rays, which are growing increasingly stronger as the atmosphere's ozone layer is being damaged. At the same time, some exposure is beneficial because (among other things) the skin uses sunlight to manufacture vitamin D. A good compromise is to create outdoor areas that provide access to both filtered sunlight and shade, such as that provided by a generous array of trees. Other methods include using roof extensions, awnings, vine-covered trellises, glassed-in sunrooms with mini-blinds, covered patios, and gazebos (Figure 3.1a and b). Features that tend to encourage excessive exposure to the sun (sunbathing), such as swimming pools, should include shaded areas for relaxing without overexposing the skin.

FIGURE 3.1A AND B Gazebos that offer sun protection come in a variety of styles and prices. Their purpose is to protect the skin against excessive ultraviolet rays while providing access to fresh air and the outdoors.

Lung Cancer

Lung cancer is very often fatal because it is rarely diagnosed before it reaches an advanced stage. In addition to damaging the lungs, this type of cancer tends to spread to other parts of the body, frequently the brain, because of the large number of blood vessels that come into close contact with the lungs. Lung cancer has been directly tied to tobacco use—not a surprise, considering that cigarette smoke contains more than 4,000 chemicals, many of which are known **carcinogens** (cancer-causing substances). People have the right to decide whether or not to smoke, but second-hand smoke, also called environmental tobacco smoke (ETS), causes about 3,000 deaths from lung cancer in nonsmoking adults in the United States each year. In addition to cancer, ETS also causes an estimated 35,000 to 40,000 deaths from heart disease in noncurrent smokers; 150,000 to 300,000 lower respiratory infections in children younger than 18 months; and increases in the number and severity of asthma attacks in 200,000 to 1 million children (American Cancer Society, 2005, "Cancer Facts and Figures").

Radon, a gas discussed in Chapter 4, is believed to be the second-leading cause of lung cancer in the United States. Other causes of lung cancer that are related to the built environment include asbestos, arsenic, uranium, and certain petroleum products. Any inhaled particulates (small granular or powderlike substances, often referred to as particulate matter) that irritate the lining of the respiratory system or that lodge in the lungs' delicate air sacs can increase the risk of cancer. These particulates can be present in substances such as heavy outdoor air pollution, wood dust, and diesel fumes.

Implications for Designers

The damage done by environmental smoke to the health of nonsmokers is a public health concern. Designers can help protect nonsmokers, as discussed in Chapters 2 and 4, by providing all-season smoking areas that go beyond simply providing behavioral zoning (designated smoking and nonsmoking sections).

Smoking areas should be adequately separated from those occupied by nonsmokers, and the smoke should be vented directly to the outside into nonpopulated areas. General ventilation systems cannot protect nonsmokers against ETS if it is present in the same area.

Obviously, designers should avoid the use of chemicals and building materials linked to cancer, such as asbestos. Arsenic is another dangerous substance that is found throughout the environment, both natural and manmade. Designers should be aware that arsenic is principally used in the United States as a wood preservative. Although the EPA withdrew approval in December 2003 for the use of chromated copper arsenate (CCA) to pressure-treat wood, thousands of existing structures still pose a risk. These include outdoor decks, arbors, swing sets, and playground equipment (Orndoff & Ramirez, 2005). The fact that children commonly play on these structures may account for part of the increase in cancer among children, up 20 percent between 1975 and 1995 (Orndoff & Ramirez, 2005). Designers may want to recommend that clients replace treated wood or make it inaccessible to children. Some building professionals are recommending the use of composites made of recycled plastics and sawdust or pressure-treated woods treated with alkaline copper quaternary or copper boron azole, both of which are nontoxic to humans (Orndoff & Ramirez, 2005). At the very least, designers should suggest that deck sealant be applied to exposed surfaces. Although this process can increase protection, ultraviolet exposure triples the release of arsenic from the wood (Orndoff & Ramirez, 2005).

Common symptoms of lung cancer include shortness of breath and fatigue. Environments inhabited or used by people with lung cancer should be easy to navigate, with minimal inclines and stairs. When walking some distance is necessary, seating areas should be provided for frequent resting. For example, long hallways in health-care facilities should have benches located every few yards. Walkways to parking areas should also have rest spots. At the same time, designers should take care that seating

FIGURE 3.2 Long hallways and walkways should have seating to accommodate individuals whose health conditions cause fatigue. This is especially important in health-care and residential facilities.

does not protrude into pathways in ways that present obstacles for wheelchairs or hazards for the visually impaired. (See Figure 3.2.)

Other considerations for individuals suffering from fatigue caused by cancer, as well as other health conditions, include quiet, darkened areas for resting or napping during the day; shower stools to enable bathing while

FIGURE 3.3 Lift chairs can improve the mobility and life quality of people who have difficulty lifting themselves from a seated position.

seated; and chairs that are high enough to get out of easily. Lift chairs, such as the one illustrated in Figure 3.3, are helpful for people who lack strength in their lower limbs or who suffer from fatigue.

Cancer and Chemicals

Although the exact causes of most cancers are unknown, environmental factors are believed to cause at least 75 percent of all cancers in the United States. The group that may be most affected by these risk factors is children. The age-adjusted annual incidence of cancer in children increased from 129 to 166 cases per million children between 1975 and 2002. (Cancer mortality did decrease from 51 to 28 deaths per million children during the same period, probably due to more effective treatment.) There is evidence that the increase in some childhood cancers is the result of the increased use of pesticides and other common chemicals (U.S. Environmental Protection Agency, 2007, "America's Children").

The rates of reproductive cancers are also increasing; this trend is believed to be due to exposures to chemicals such as DDT, PCBs, dioxin, bisphenol-A (heavily used in the linings of plastic bottles and metal cans), and phthalates. Phthalates are chemical compounds added to plastics to increase their flexibility. They are also used in adhesives, caulk, and paint pigments. The chemicals used as stain repellents on fabrics include PFO (perfluorooctanoic), which has been linked to increased tumors in the liver and pancreas. PFOs have generated concern because of their widespread use and presence in the blood of most Americans, indicating that they tend to build up in the body over time, the phenomenon known as bioaccumulation (discussed in Chapter 2).

Implications for Designers

Obviously, sound advice for designers includes avoiding the use of known carcinogens, such as the chemicals and building materials discussed in this chapter and Chapter 4. However, a problem for interior designers is that it is becoming increasingly difficult to avoid potentially harmful chemicals because of their huge numbers and extensive use in the modern world. As of 2005, there were more than 85,000 synthetic chemicals registered for use in the United States, but fewer than 10 percent of these had been tested for their effects on human health (Orndoff & Ramirez, 2005). Thus, we find ourselves confronted with choices for products with purported benefits and unknown consequences. It is suggested that designers keep current by periodically reviewing resources such as the following:

- EPA's Integrated Risk Information System at www.epa.gov/iris/intro.htm. This is an electronic database containing information on human health effects that may result from exposure to various chemicals in the environment.
- EXTOXNET at http://extoxnet.orst.edu. Science-based information about pesticides written for the nonexpert.
- Department of Health and Human Services Agency for Toxic Substances and Disease Registry at www.atsdr.cdc.gov. This agency provides health information to prevent harmful exposures and diseases related to toxic substances.

The workplace is a common source of dangerous chemical exposure. Fetuses are especially susceptible to chemicals. Benzene, for example, a chemical found in plastics, resins, and dyes, has been found to shorten pregnancy, thus depriving the infant of needed time to develop fully. For pregnant women who must work with chemicals such as solvents, adequate ventilation is critical, and eating areas should be well separated from work areas where the chemicals are present. (See Chapter 5 for more information about ventilation.)

Lifestyle Habits and Cancer

In addition to the environment, significant cancer risk factors include poor diet and lack of physical activity, perhaps being related to about one-third of all cancer deaths (American Cancer Society, n.d., "What Are the Risk Factors?"). Foods that appear to decrease cancer risk include fruits, vegetables, and grains. Fresh fruits and vegetables contain antioxidants, substances that reduce the damage to molecules caused by the action of oxygen. Studies have shown that whole grains protect against certain types of cancer, such as stomach, colon, breast, and prostate, because of a variety of chemical reactions they cause in the digestive tract (Slavin, 2000). In addition, they are a low-fat source of protein in the diet—this is important because high-fat diets have been linked to increased cancer risk.

It is believed that exercise helps reduce cancer risk in several ways. Examples include accelerating the movement of food through the intestines, thereby reducing the time the bowel is exposed to potential carcinogens that cause colon cancer; increasing blood circulation to reduce lingering levels of estrogen that have been linked to breast cancer; improving energy metabolism; and decreasing circulating concentrations of insulin (American Cancer Society, 2005, "Cancer Facts and Figures").

Implications for Designers

Because certain lifestyle habits are shown to help prevent some cancers, interior designers might consider how they could promote the practice of these habits. An important consideration, for example, is the design of kitchens and cooking areas that make the preparation of meals from fresh ingredients easier and more efficient. This means that ample counter space is needed, along with nonporous and scratch-resistant cutting boards. To help make cleaning and preparing fresh foods easier and safer, a large cutting board can be incorporated into the sink area. This cutting board, as illustrated in Figure 3.4, could have a drop drain so that an extended faucet could freely and liberally rinse the board while the excess water runs down and into the drain.

In regard to physical activity, designers can ensure there are ample spaces for exercise. These might include walking space in workplaces, dedicated areas in homes for exercise equipment or a mat, floor space for children to run and play, and areas in long-term care facilities where residents can walk. Other features include hallways and covered walkways that

FIGURE 3.4 This cutting board is especially easy to clean and sanitize. Food scraps can be pushed into the sink and the board washed with the nearby faucet.

can be incorporated into the overall design of a structure. (See Figure 3.5.) Therefore, when considering design initiatives, designers should develop ideas and concepts that facilitate and promote movement.

A common treatment for various types of cancer is chemotherapy, which involves administering strong drugs to the patient. Common side effects include loss of energy, fatigue, and susceptibility to infection. Therefore, when designing homes and facilities for people with cancer, it is important to create environments that can be easily cleaned. Surfaces of furnishings, for example, should be as smooth as possible to avoid catching dirt and moisture. Bedding should be easy to wash and clean, with sheets able to withstand hot water. Because cancer patients may be somewhat restricted to their homes for long periods of time as they receive treatment, it is especially important to make the living environment as pleasant as possible. This requires learning about the interests of clients. For example, readers should have a comfortable chair with good lighting; people who watch television frequently should have a comfortable viewing area without glare on the screen; and clients with indoor hobbies should have easy-to-access areas provided, such as desks or worktables.

Experiencing a serious health condition is stressful. Stress is a condition that causes discomfort in itself as well as interfering with healing. Thus, creating a calming, relaxing environment in the home and in health-care facilities can be health-promoting. This might mean using the client's favorite colors, displaying treasured objects, providing sunlight and views of nature, and ensuring quiet for rest. (See Chapter 10 for more ideas about creating stress-reducing environments.)

DISEASES AND DISORDERS OF THE INTEGUMENTARY SYSTEM

Although our skin is designed to be tough and protective, it is nonetheless vulnerable to a variety of harmful conditions. Athlete's foot, for example, is a fungal infection of the upper skin layer between the toes and sometimes the fingers. It is characterized by cracking and scaling of the skin and is quite contagious. This microscopic fungus is commonly found in damp areas such as showers and wet floors.

Dermatitis is a good example of the skin's vulnerability to the external world because it is often caused by contact with irritating chemicals, including those commonly found in the built environment. The skin becomes red, inflamed, and swollen, often taking the form of a rash, red blotches, or skin eruptions. It may also cause itching and discomfort. Both natural and man-made chemicals can cause dermatitis. Among the estimated 3,000 artificial chemicals that can irritate the skin, many are found in strong soaps, cleaning solutions and fluids, pesticides, adhesives, and substances found in the fabrication of building materials and furnishings. A specific example is the chemical phenol, a manufactured substance used in a variety of common consumer products, such as disinfectants, resins, and adhesives. The use of these, along with highly processed personal products (such as deodorants and fragrances), is on the rise, which might explain why the prevalence of atopic (caused by allergies) dermatitis is increasing and now occurs in 9 to 30 percent of the population (National Institute of Allergy and Infectious Diseases, n.d., "Facts and Figures").

Implications for Designers

Locker rooms are known to be breeding grounds for the fungus that causes athlete's foot, which is how the infection got its name. To help minimize the presence of this fungus, designers should avoid using porous flooring materials, such as grout lines between ceramic tiles, because the fungus can hide in the pores. Instead, flooring materials should be composed of continuous and durable materials that are able to withstand frequent cleaning with bleach. Another feature designers should consider is the placement of air-stream vents in the walls and along the floor. The continual blowing of air helps to keep places like locker-room floors dry. It is advisable, however, to use warm air in these streams as opposed to hot or cold air. (See Chapter 5 for more information about ventilation systems.)

Although designers cannot always control which chemicals are used or how they are applied (sprayed versus swabbed), they can make recommendations and offer cautions, as well as ensure adequate ventilation systems that vent more interior air to the outside and bring in greater quantities of clean air from the outside. Unfortunately, this latter solution is often forsaken because it tends to lack energy efficiency.

Burns

A common injury to the skin comes from burns, which can be caused by heat, chemicals, and electricity. Burns are classified according to their severity. A first-degree burn affects only the epidermis and results in redness of the skin; second-degree burns also involve the dermis and cause blisters; and third-degree burns destroy the two layers of skin and the subcutaneous layers. A serious consequence of burns, in addition to pain and possible disfigurement, is the body's loss of its natural barrier against infection. Between one and two million Americans seek medical attention for

FIGURE 3.5 Design elements such as covered walkways can encourage walking even in inclement weather.

burns each year, with 50,000 to 70,000 being hospitalized (University of Maryland Medical Center, 2001).

Implications for Designers

The high number of burn injuries suffered each year means that designers should be proactive in analyzing environments and designs to eliminate the potential for burns. Most burns occur in the home, at work, or as a result of motor vehicle accidents (University of Maryland Medical Center). Common causes of burns in the home, especially with children, are hot liquids, stovetops, scalding water from the tap, and accidents involving candles and fireplaces. Designers can select and place heat-producing appliances in ways to help prevent burns, such as oven ranges that are chest height. Other preventive measures include conveniently located heat-resistant surfaces for placing hot pans off the stove, safety doors on fireplaces and wood-stoves, and child-resistant hot-water dispensers. (More safety features to prevent burns are discussed in Chapters 9 and 10.)

Cuts, Punctures, and Abrasions

The skin can also be damaged by cuts, punctures, and abrasions. Each of these traumas involves breaks in the skin that provide an entryway for pathogens that lead to infection. Cuts are often caused by a sharp object slicing the skin's surface. Knives, razors, metal edges, and even paper can all cut the skin.

Puncture wounds are often the most difficult to clean and thus a source of infection. They can result from carpet tacks protruding up from the floor, nails sticking out from the wall, or staples caught in carpeting (something commonly seen in the workplace environment). Both cuts and puncture wounds, if deep enough and in the right place, can also cause nerve damage.

Abrasions are another type of wound that often leads to infection. These wounds typically cover larger areas and only affect the skin's surface layers. Sources of abrasions include unfinished surfaces such as concrete, sandstone, and wood.

Implications for Designers

Carpet tacks and staples lodged in carpeting are a significant source of puncture wounds. Thus, designers may want to consider alternative flooring materials. Another measure to prevent cuts is to ensure that the edges of walls are rounded off to avoid the potential for cuts. Other sources of sharp edges that designers can eliminate include particleboard cabinetry and furnishings and improperly stored knives, sharp utensils, and tools. (See Figure 3.6.)

A source of abrasions is the rustic edges that come into style from time to time. With populations who may be prone to come into contact with edges, such as children and the elderly, it is best to use smooth finish materials to decrease the potential for abrasions.

DISEASES AND DISORDERS OF THE SKELETAL SYSTEM

A prevalent skeletal disorder in the United States is osteoporosis, a condition in which the bones lose minerals, such as calcium, resulting in the loss of density and strength. An estimated 44 million Americans are at risk for this condition and 10 million (8 million women and 2 million men) already have osteoporosis (National Institute of Arthritis and Musculoskeletal

FIGURE 3.6 Knives can be stored in a number of convenient ways that prevent the need to reach into a drawer and chance a cut.

and Skin Diseases, 2006, "Once Is Enough"). In many respects, osteoporosis is analogous to the wooden framework of a structure after it has been infested with termites. Just as support beams lose their strength from the damage inflicted by termites, so too do the bones lose their strength. The most serious, as well as most common, result of osteoporosis is a broken bone, with one in two women and one in four men incurring at least one osteoporosis-related fracture in their lifetime. The most common break sites are the hips and spine. Broken bones are generally quite painful, and broken hips can be especially devastating and debilitating injuries. For older adults who break a hip, one in five will end up in a nursing home within a year. It is further estimated that 10 million people in the United States over the age of 50 have osteoporosis of the hip, with 1.5 million suffering bone fractures each year (U.S. Department of Health and Human Services, 2004, "Surgeon General's Report").

Implications for Designers

The best preventive measures for broken bones from a design perspective include 60 minutes of exposure to early morning or late afternoon sunlight. (See Figure 3.7.) Also, opportunities for low levels of weight-bearing exercise should be available for people as they age. Physical activity involving direct impact, such as the foot hitting the ground when walking, initiates signals to the body to create new bone cells and is important throughout the life span. The following are examples of appropriate activities for different age groups:

- Children: running, jumping rope, active games
- Teens: running, skateboarding, sports, dancing
- Adults: walking, dancing, weight lifting
- Older adults: walking, dancing, gardening

As designers, we need to ensure ample space for these types of activities. In more temperate climates such as Southern California, this might mean the design of outdoor spaces; for climates with more severe temperatures such

FIGURE 3.7 Sunrooms provide opportunities to benefit from daylight all year round.

as Phoenix and Minneapolis, this might mean making adequate provisions within interior spaces. In many modern hotels, for example, walking tracks have been incorporated into the design; likewise, many retirement communities and condominium complexes include workout rooms, and many municipal recreation departments have dance studios. Regardless of the climate, a mix of both indoor and outdoor activity areas should be included in the overall design.

Osteoarthritis

Another common disease condition is called **osteoarthritis,** which is a degenerative disease of the joints that involves the cartilage between the ends of bones wearing away and

FIGURE 3.8 Flooring designed for exercise and sports comes in a variety of types. In this example, large cushions act as shock absorbers to relieve the joints from receiving the full impact of jumping and running.

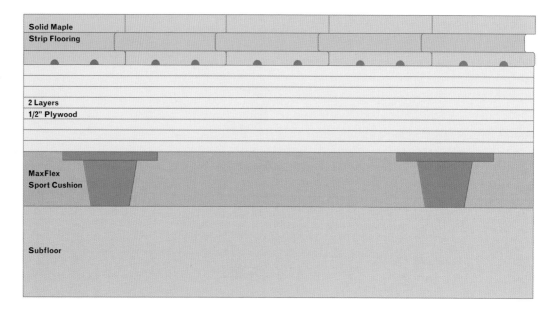

Solid Maple
Strip Flooring

2 Layers
1/2" Plywood

MaxFlex
Sport Cushion

Subfloor

leaving them exposed. Without this protective cartilage, the bones grind painfully against each other. In an effort to protect themselves, the bones grow new cells and this is what leads to the lumps and deformed appearance commonly seen in the joints (especially the fingers) of older people.

Although aging and lifetime use of the joints are the most common causes of this disorder, excessive body weight, joint injuries, and stress from work and sports activities contribute to the onset of the disease.

Implications for Designers

Interior designers can create conditions that help prevent osteoarthritis by looking for ways to reduce joint stress while at the same time keeping them flexible. As with osteoporosis, the best method to prevent and cope with osteoarthritis is physical exercise. It is also important to reduce the stress exerted on the joints. An example of good design to reduce stress on the knees, ankles, and feet is the use of **floor suspension systems** in fitness and exercise areas. Some examples of floor suspension systems include:

- Rubber-dot system: One-inch rubber disks are placed every 12 inches between sheets of plywood. Resilience is provided by both the rubber disks and the air between them.

- Sleeper system and foam pad: rubber strips are attached to 2-by-4s placed about 16 inches apart from one another.

- Rubber pad: a foam rubber pad, such as 3/8-inch cell, is placed beneath the floor.

In many health clubs, fitness centers, gyms, and dance studios, **spring-load floors** are used in which a hardwood floor floats atop a bed of springs. The springs, rather than the body's joints, absorb much of the impact on landing. Other types of floors, as illustrated in Figure 3.8, use cushions to absorb impact. Unfortunately, many fitness centers, particularly in hotels and condominium complexes, use carpeting because of the lower cost and better sound absorption. While this material will absorb some of the impact from exercise, the drawbacks are odors, bacterial growth, and the higher probability of tripping because carpeting wears out more quickly. Carpeting, therefore, is an undesirable and unsustainable solution.

In addition to preventive measures like proper flooring, therapeutic features can be incorporated into designs to benefit people who have osteoarthritis and osteoporosis. Water therapy, for example, can be helpful in relieving the pain and stiffness associated with osteoarthritis. Heated pools, hot tubs, and whirlpool bathtubs have been shown to provide this relief as well as providing buoyancy that takes much of the pressure off the skeletal system during physical exercise. Hence, designers should consider installing these features in facilities such as retirement communities, condominiums, and even the private homes of clients who would benefit.

Sprains and Fractures

In addition to diseases, the skeletal system is subject to a host of injuries, including sprains, fractures, and damage to the cartilage. The least traumatic of these injuries is a sprain. A **sprain** is the result of a joint being twisted, which stretches or tears the ligaments. Symptoms include rapid swelling and acute pain. In some instances, a joint is twisted or impacted so severely that one of the bones is dislocated.

Another common injury to the skeletal system is a fracture, or breakage of a bone. A compound fracture, in which a broken edge of the bone protrudes through the skin, is the most serious type. Fractures that are not the result of bones being weakened by osteoporosis are usually caused by a sudden blow to or twisting of the bone. Falls are common causes of fractures, especially among older people. In fact, falls are so prevalent, they are considered a serious public health problem among older adults (National Center for Injury Prevention and Control, 2006), frequently resulting in life-altering fractures. These falls are commonly caused by tripping over obstacles or walking on uneven terrain or flooring.

Implications for Designers

Designers have opportunities to contribute toward good health and safety by incorporating important details such as adequate lighting systems, even floor grades, and the placement of furnishings and decorative objects out of pathways. In situations that require changes in elevations, designers should provide warnings. Examples include using a different texture, color, or pattern prior to a step or ramp. Other flooring safety measures are securing area rugs to the floor and installing nonslip tile in kitchens and bathrooms where water might be present. Depending on the ages and needs

---

BOX 3.3 ECONOMIC IMPACT OF BACK PAIN

A comprehensive analysis of 1998 medical data carried out by a team of Duke University Medical Center researchers revealed that back pain, defined as pain in any part of the back and caused by injuries, herniated disks, or other spinal disorders, cost more than $90 billion in health-care expenses. This amount represented 1 percent of the U.S. Gross Domestic Product that year and thus represents a significant economic impact.

The 25.9 million Americans who reported back pain had the following characteristics:
1. 55 percent female
2. 88.3 percent white
3. 61 percent married
4. Average age: 48

Back pain is the most common reason for visits to the physician's office next to the common cold. After headaches, it is the second-most common pain complaint. Three out of four Americans are predicted to suffer a disabling bout of back pain some time in their lives.

Adapted from: Economic Impact of Back Pain Substantial. *DukeMed News.* Retrieved July 14, 2006, from www.dukemednews.org/news/article.php?in=7312

---

of their clients, designers might also suggest installing grab bars in showers, tubs, and next to toilets.

Back Injuries

Back pain is a common health problem in the United States, experienced at least once by about 85 percent of adults under the age of 50. It is the second-most common health-related reason for missing work and the most common cause of disability among adults (Neurology Channel, 2000). See Box 3.3 for a summary of the economic impact of all types of back pain.

Skeletal injuries that are the cause of back pain for many people are torn cartilage and a **herniated disk,** also known as a slipped or ruptured disk. When this happens, the soft, gelatinous central portion of the disk puts pressure on the spinal nerve. This can impair movement, hamper the detection of sensation, and cause severe pain.

Implications for Designers

As with fractures, back injuries can result from a fall. They can also be caused by lifting heavy objects or experiencing sudden jarring, such as when stepping down quickly onto a hard surface. Good design can help prevent back injuries. For example, methods can be incorporated to prevent the need to lift and carry heavy objects in the home. Many families buy items in bulk, which can mean carrying boxes containing thirty-two cans of soda or large containers of liquid detergent. Installing shelving in garages to store these items prevents people from having to carry them into the house—especially problematic when there are stairs. This allows smaller quantities to be brought into the living space as needed. When planning storage, provide space at mid-body height for heavy items so they don't have to be lowered and lifted. The space should also be designed so that turning is not necessary while placing or lifting heavy items.

A common household appliance that can contribute to back injury is the typical oven, which often requires that the cook lean forward and bend at the waist. Lifting foods like turkeys and roasts, while avoiding the swing-down door, is awkward. Chest-high ovens are less apt to cause injuries. When fitted with a door that swings open to one side, they are even better. Even bending and lifting that does not involve heavy objects can cause backs to "go out." Providing a rolling cart for performing household chores, such as moving laundry, can be helpful.

DISEASES AND DISORDERS OF THE MUSCULAR SYSTEM

You might think that most muscular injuries happen to athletes, but this is not true. In fact, many of these injuries commonly happen to people you might not expect, such as computer operators and office workers. This is due to the increased number of **cumulative trauma disorders (CTDs)** or repetitive motion disorders. As the name implies, these injuries are caused by repetitive tasks or motions, common in today's computerized office. Forceful exertions, pressure against hard surfaces, and sustained or awkward positions of the affected body parts can also be

responsible. These injuries affect the tendons (fibrous tissue that attaches muscles to bones). Because tendon injuries generally heal slowly, they are responsible for many hours of lost productivity.

One of the most common CTDs is **carpal tunnel syndrome.** This happens when there is pressure on the median nerve in the wrist, caused by swelling and irritation of the tendons and tendon sheaths (coverings) that pass through the narrow carpal tunnel along with the nerve. This pressure on the nerve causes tingling and numbness in the hand, pain, and muscle weakness. The condition seems to be on the increase, especially among people who spend long hours working at computers.

Implications for Designers

The proper design of workstations, especially those involving computer or other machine use, is one way these painful disorders can be prevented. Chapter 7, which focuses on the topic of ergonomics, contains more detailed information and suggestions about preventing these types of injuries. Designers should be aware that certain physical characteristics appear to put individuals at greater risk for CTDs. These include diabetes, being overweight, thyroid conditions, rheumatoid arthritis, and previous injuries to the stressed body parts. Although designers would never take a client's "medical history," they could endeavor to gain a sense of a client's overall health to ensure that any medical conditions are considered in the design process. This could include learning about a client's existing CTD or a client requesting that special attention be given to preventing CTDs. Although CTDs are typically associated with work activities, they can happen with any repeated activity, such as sewing or playing a musical instrument. Hobby furnishings, such as height-adjustable ergonomic sewing tables, are available for use in the home.

Contractures, Strains, and Tetanus

Other common muscle afflictions include muscle contractures and strains. Muscle contractures occur when muscles remain in a shortened position and restrict the body part from moving freely. An example is when a woman wears high-heeled shoes more often than flat-soled shoes. The calf muscle shortens so that there is discomfort when the woman does wear flat-soled shoes. A more common example is shortening of the hamstring resulting from sitting for long periods each day. **Muscle strain,** a different condition, results from tearing or stretching a muscle or a tendon.

Tetanus, also called lockjaw, is caused by a bacterial toxin that attacks the central nervous system and voluntary muscles, causing them to contract continuously until the body becomes rigid. This bacterium typically enters the body through a cut or puncture wound.

Implications for Designers

As with the skeletal system, the health of the muscular system relies heavily on the ability to move in a safe and consistent manner. As such, walkways should not only be provided but also maintained to avoid tripping and possibly tearing a tendon or muscle. Also, through the incorporation of swimming pools and walking tracks, people not only condition their skeletal muscles but also strengthen their cardiac muscle. (Diseases of the cardiovascular system are addressed later in this chapter.) While the former helps to protect the body from injury and retain its strength, the later helps to prevent heart attacks.

Fibromyalgia

A chronic (long-term) disorder, **fibromyalgia** is characterized by widespread muscle pain, fatigue, and tender points in specific places (National Institute of Arthritis and Musculoskeletal and Skin Diseases, 2004, "Fibromyalgia"). In addition to these symptoms, many people with fibromyalgia also experience headaches, irritable bowel syndrome, irritable bladder, cognitive and memory problems, pelvic pain, restless leg syndrome, sensitivity to noise and temperature, and anxiety and depression. Some sources estimate that fibromyalgia affects 2 to 4 percent of the population, the majority of them women (Clauw & Taylor-Moon, 2006).

Implications for Designers

No cure has been discovered for fibromyalgia, so people with this condition are encouraged to adapt their lifestyles to live as best they can. Designers can help clients with fibromyalgia create surroundings that are pleasing and supportive. As with many other health conditions, research has shown physical exercise to be one of the most effective treatments (National Institute of Arthritis and Musculoskeletal and Skin Diseases, 2004, "Fibromyalgia"). Therefore, creating space for exercise in the home is helpful.

A common experience of people with fibromyalgia is difficulty sleeping or benefiting from the time spent sleeping. Therefore, providing a comfortable, rest-inducing bedroom is important. A major symptom is pain throughout the body, particularly at various pressure points. Therefore, when selecting mattresses and chairs, be sure to take into account the individual's pressure-pain points.

DISEASES AND DISORDERS OF THE RESPIRATORY SYSTEM

Asthma is a chronic condition in which the airways of the lungs become restricted, often in response to an allergen that enters through the airways. This restriction is caused by an inflammatory response in which the muscles around the airways tighten, the membranes lining the airways swell, and excessive mucous is produced, all of which make it difficult for air to both enter and leave the lungs. (See Figure 3.9.) During an asthma attack, people can experience wheezing, breathlessness, tightness in the chest, and coughing. Secondary symptoms include increased sensitivity to a variety of allergens, cold and dry air, smoke, and viruses.

Occupational asthma, as the name suggests, is caused by agents found in work environments. In most cases, it is caused by an agent that a worker has become sensitized to. In others, it is the result of a strong respiratory irritant (National Academy of Sciences 2006). Examples of allergens include laboratory rats (Hollander et al., 1996); storage mites, which

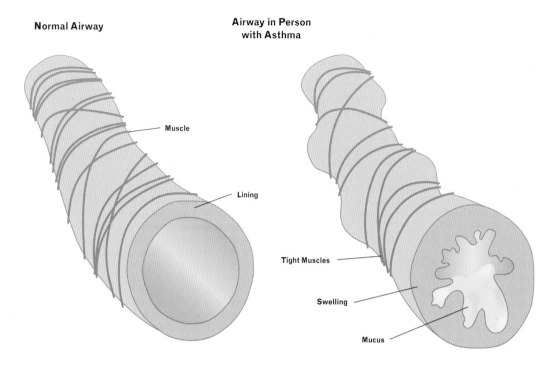

tend to infest foods and stored grains, in agricultural settings; and biocides used in humidifiers in office buildings (National Academy of Sciences, 2006).

With some allergens, such as animals, only a few workers develop sensitivities. In other situations, large numbers of people are affected in what is called epidemic asthma. A well-documented case occurred in a Denver county social services building in which employees reported physician-diagnosed asthma at nearly three times the rate of employees in a comparable building, in addition to other lung diseases. The suspected cause was bioaerosols (airborne biological particles) associated with moisture in a wall built into an earthen bank (Hoffman et al., 1993).

More information about indoor air quality, along with suggestions for designers about preventing the types of health problems discussed in this chapter, is discussed in Chapter 5.

Implications for Designers

The causes of initial allergy attacks are not known. Evidence has been found, however, to conclude a causal relationship between episodes and exposure to the allergens produced by cats, cockroaches, and house dust mites. In preschool-age children, secondhand smoke has been shown to have a causal relationship. Possible associations have also been found for mold and various chemical irritants, such as formaldehyde, used in hundreds of common products, and nitrogen dioxide, a common pollutant produced by gas and kerosene appliances (National Academy of Sciences, 2006). Outgassing of a variety of chemicals from carpets may also be a culprit (Asthma and Allergy Foundation of America, n.d., "Asthma Overview").

Although designers cannot control what kinds of pets their clients choose, they can investigate flooring alternatives to carpeting, make suggestions for the removal of mold (see Chapter 4), point out the potential problems of the use of certain chemicals (also discussed in Chapter 4), and suggest cleaning systems such as central vacuums. These efforts are certainly called for, as an estimated 14 million adults and 6 million children in the United States have asthma (Mayo Clinic, 2004, "Asthma").

It is the most common chronic illness in children and accounts for the largest number of school absences (Mayo Clinic, Asthma,

BOX 3.4   EXPERT SPOTLIGHT: Environmental Asthma

Susan Butler, MEd, EdD, CHES
Research Assistant Professor
Rollins School of Public Health
Emory University

The Problem

The primary issue related to environmental asthma is air quality. Poor air quality can trigger asthma. An asthma trigger is any substance that irritates the lungs and causes an allergic reaction. Asthma triggers come from indoor, occupational, and outdoor sources. Indoor triggers include secondhand cigarette smoke, dust mites, mold, cockroaches and other pests, household pets, and improperly used or malfunctioning heating devices, such as gas ranges and improperly vented fireplaces and gas space heaters. Occupational asthma triggers include daily exposure to certain workplace industrial and manufacturing substances, especially among tobacco smokers. Occupational asthma is the most common occupational respiratory disease, claiming approximately 20 percent of asthmatic adults whose symptoms improve when away from work and worsen while at work. Outdoor triggers include sulfur dioxide, ozone, and particulate matter (PM). High levels of outdoor air pollution have been associated with short-term increases in asthma morbidity and mortality. Sulfur dioxide, which primarily irritates the upper airway, is the only regulated outdoor air pollutant that has a dose-response association with bronchoconstriction that may present problems in people with asthma who exercise outdoors. Ozone is the product of photochemical reactions between nitrogen oxides and volatile organic chemicals from automobiles, and exerts its effect on the trachea and bronchi. Particulate matter (PM) is composed of tiny particles of smoke, soot, metals, and other chemical compounds emitted from sources such as power plants, factories, and diesel trucks. The American Lung Association calls PM one of the most common and dangerous air pollutants because it can travel deep into the lungs. Epidemiological studies have shown that when PM air concentrations were below the National Ambient Air Quality Standards, medication use, hospital admissions, and number of emergency room visits increased, especially among the elderly and individuals with cardiopulmonary disease. Long-term exposure to PM is linked to an increase in hospitalization for asthma attacks for children living within 200 yards of roads with heavy truck traffic.

A Practical Solution

A practical solution to environmental asthma is to reduce or eliminate asthma triggers. Studies have shown that in utero exposure to tobacco smoke is a predictor of wheezing within the first year of life. Physicians should insist that pregnant women stop smoking. Parents and caregivers should conduct strict allergen control in the home. Cigarette smoking should not be allowed anywhere in the home. All sleeping surfaces, such as pillows and mattresses, should be covered with zippered plastic cases. Humidity levels in the home should be reduced to 30 to 50 percent with a central air conditioner and/or dehumidifier. Regularly clean mold from walls and ceilings and vacuum the house on a regular basis. In the workplace, adult-onset asthma can be prevented by not smoking, because this enhances the sensitivity to workplace allergens. People with existing asthma should avoid seasonal outdoor allergens and schedule outdoor activities for times when ozone levels are the lowest. The American Lung Association, American Medical Association, American Thoracic Society, and American Academy of Pediatrics all urge the strengthening of national public health standards for particulate matter by the Environmental Protection Agency. The American Lung Association–recommended standards would protect 3.4 million children and 9.7 million adults with asthma. To reduce the prevalence of environmental asthma in the United States, preventive measures, standards, and laws that are consistent with science and that protect the public's health should be implemented and followed.

section 4) and nearly 500,000 hospital stays annually (Asthma and Allergy Foundation of America, n.d., "Asthma Overview").

Of particular concern to health officials is the fact that asthma is on the increase, nearly doubling from 6.8 million cases in 1980 to 14.6 million cases in 1996 (Public Health Policy Health Advisory Board, 2002, "Asthma").

Because most people spend the majority of their time indoors, research is now focusing on how the indoor environment may be playing a role in this trend. It is recommended that designers keep current on this research as it becomes available in order to be of most benefit to their clients.

Chronic Obstructive Pulmonary Disease

The ability to efficiently move air in and out of the lungs is compromised by a group of diseases collectively called **chronic obstructive pulmonary disease,** or **COPD.** The two most common forms of COPD are chronic bronchitis and emphysema. About 90 percent of the time, these diseases are caused by cigarette smoking (Neighbors, 1999).

Bronchitis is inflammation of the bronchi that causes the mucus membranes to swell and produce excessive mucous, and impairs the cilia so they can't sweep irritants out of the airways. In addition to smoking, bronchitis can be caused by viral or bacterial infection and exposure to irritants such as ammonia, chlorine, sulfuric acid ("Formula for Disaster?", 2005), and smoke, including environmental tobacco smoke.

The second major COPD is **emphysema,** a condition in which the walls of the lungs' tiny air sacs lose their elasticity, are weakened, and break. When this happens, the air sacs combine with their neighbors and become larger structures with less surface area for the exchange of oxygen and carbon dioxide to take place. This decreased surface area and decreased elasticity mean that the lungs cannot expel air efficiently and so it becomes trapped, along with the carbon dioxide it contains. Progressively degenerative, there is no cure for emphysema and it usually leads to respiratory failure and death.

All COPDs combined comprise the fourth-leading cause of death in the United States (American Lung Association, 2004, "Emphysema").

Implications for Designers

As mentioned previously, protecting non-smokers from ETS has become a major public health concern. Designers can contribute to the efforts to eliminate this hazard by ensuring that ventilation systems don't draw in smoke-polluted air from the outside (i.e., smoke from wood-burning stoves and fireplaces) or areas that have been designated for smoking. In fact, fireplaces and other combustion appliances should be discouraged in the homes of individuals with lung conditions because of the chance of inhaling particulates. Another preventive measure is creating easy-to-clean spaces that discourage the passing of viruses and bacteria that cause bronchitis.

Individuals with COPD, especially emphysema, need places to rest because their breathing is compromised. This becomes even more necessary as these diseases progress and intermediate seating may need to be provided in the home to enable the person to move from one room to another and outdoors or to the garage or parking area. Another possibility is installing handrails in halls, entryways, and large rooms. Chairs or stools can be included in places where seating is not normally provided (such as in the bathroom to use when grooming). In the kitchen, a stool on wheels provides support and mobility. If telephones are corded, they should be placed near some type of seating.

Pulmonary Fibrosis

A serious, often fatal lung condition is pulmonary fibrosis. In this disease, hard, nonelastic tissue replaces the soft lung tissue that expands when filled with air. This causes the person to gradually lose the ability to breathe.

The main cause of pulmonary fibrosis is excessive exposure to asbestos, silica (quartz, a hard, glassy mineral), or coal dust. Asbestos was once used extensively as insulation and in many building materials because of its strength and fire-resistant qualities. As such, asbestos can still be found in many homes and buildings. It should be noted, however, that left intact, asbestos is harmless; it is only when the fibers are released, such as during remodeling projects, that it can be harmful to health. (Chapter 4 contains more extensive information about asbestos, including suggestions for designers.)

DISEASES AND DISORDERS OF THE CARDIOVASCULAR SYSTEM

"Heart disease" is a general term that includes several different conditions that damage the heart muscle and impair its ability to efficiently pump blood. Collectively, these conditions constitute the leading cause of death in the United States, accounting for just over 652,000 deaths in 2004 (National Center for Health Statistics, 2007). Heart disease is also a significant cause of disability among adults. Heart disease is a major health problem for both men and women. In fact, females account for about 50 percent of heart-related deaths.

The most common type of heart disease in the United States is **coronary artery disease,** in which the arteries that supply oxygen and nutrients to the heart muscle become reduced in size or completely blocked (Centers for Disease Control and Prevention, 2006, "Heart Disease").

Starved of these essential elements, the cardiac muscle cells die. Extensive muscle damage results in heart attack. Risk factors for heart disease include family history, high blood pressure, diabetes, diets high in saturated fats and cholesterol, lack of physical exercise, obesity, smoking, and excessive alcohol use (CDC. Heart Disease. www.cdc.gov/HeartDisease). Thus, heart disease, like many other health problems, can largely be prevented by adopting a healthy lifestyle.

Hypertension (high blood pressure) is not a disease but rather a condition that leads to heart disease and stroke. Higher than normal pressure on the walls of the arteries damages the blood vessels themselves, requiring the heart to pump harder to move the blood. Medical professionals suggest lifestyle changes, such as a better diet and exercise, for mild hypertension; more serious cases are usually treated with medication.

Implications for Designers

Many cases of heart disease can be prevented through diet and exercise, topics discussed throughout this text. For clients with heart disease, residential designers can incorporate helpful features. Outdoor stairs might be replaced with ramps that replace climbing with a more gradual ascent. Steep stairs can be divided into sections with seating provided on landings (Figure 3.10). If the home has bedrooms upstairs, the designer might suggest creating a sleeping area on the main floor to prevent having to use stairs. Individuals with heart disease can suffer from weakness, fatigue, and depression. Falling or fainting can also occur as a result of their condition; the following suggestions are made in light of this possibility:

- Place telephones and/or intercom devices throughout the home, including the bathroom, so that help can be summoned.
- Remove locks from bathroom and bedroom doors so that persons trying to help won't be locked out.

FIGURE 3.10 Many homes in resort-type settings, such as beaches and mountains, feature reverse-living arrangements with living and eating areas on the second floor. Adding landings and seating, as pictured here, makes them more accessible to individuals who have various health conditions that make climbing stairs difficult.

- If the doors to bathrooms open in, change them to open out so that if a person falls against them, the door can still be opened.
- Replace glass tub and shower doors with curtains, which are safer if fallen against and also make it easier to exit the tub or enclosure.

Blood Disorders

The blood is also susceptible to problems. Contaminants are especially dangerous when they enter the blood. For example, when excessive carbon monoxide (CO) is inhaled, its molecules crowd out the oxygen in the red blood cells, thus depriving the body of necessary oxygen. In severe cases it results in death. Carbon monoxide is produced from burning, whether tobacco or logs in the fireplace. This is why properly maintaining stoves and fireplaces is extremely important. These appliances must be vented properly and checked periodically. (See Chapter 4 for more information about carbon monoxide poisoning.)

Septicemia, commonly called blood poisoning, is the presence of harmful bacteria in the blood. It is frequently caused by a break in the skin that allows bacteria to enter the body. The blood then carries the infection throughout the body. If not treated promptly, septicemia can be fatal and, in fact, was the eleventh-leading cause of death in the United States in 2002 (Anderson & Smith, 2005).

Another serious blood disorder is **leukemia,** cancer of the body's blood-forming tissues. Recall from Chapter 2 that white blood cells are essential pathogen-fighters that protect the body against infection and disease. In leukemia, the white blood cells no longer divide normally, but instead create abnormal cells that don't function properly. Not only do these abnormal cells fail to fight infection, they eventually interfere with the normal production of white and red blood cells, so that both infection-fighting and oxygen-carrying capabilities are decreased. Certain environmental chemicals have been shown to cause leukemia, including the solvent benzene and the pesticide pentachlorophenol (PCP) (Roberts, 1990).

Implications for Designers

Interior designers should consider ways to prevent conditions that cause cuts and scratches. This is especially important when there are children who play and run about; people with vision and balance difficulties (frequently the elderly); and those prone to infection. Providing accessible hand-washing facilities for people of all ages and abilities is an important step in the fight against infection.

Consider the needs of people with infections who frequent places such as health-care facilities. Waiting areas, for example, should be easy to clean and disinfect. Furnishings might be covered with the new performance fabrics that are durable and cleanable, even able to repel blood and urine.

DISEASES AND DISORDERS OF THE NERVOUS SYSTEM

In spite of its protective layers, as described in Chapter 2, the brain is nonetheless subject to a variety of injuries from blows to the head. Collectively, these are called **traumatic brain injury (TBI)** and range from a mild bump on the head to penetration of the skull and brain. A surprisingly high number of people suffer TBIs each year: 1.4 million in the United States, of which 230,000 are hospitalized and 50,000 die. In addition to the human cost, the financial cost of these injuries is high, estimated at $56 billion a year (Office of Communications and Public Liaison, 2002, "Traumatic Brain Injury"). Although half of all TBIs suffered by people under the age of 75 are caused by accidents involving transportation, the majority suffered by adults over age 75 are caused by falls (Office of Communications and Public Liaison, 2002, "Traumatic Brain Injury").

The degree of damage to the brain influences the symptoms experienced. Some brain injuries heal rather quickly, with the worst symptom being a headache. More serious injuries can result in coma; paralysis; permanent changes in the ability to learn, reason, think, and monitor one's social behavior; and post-traumatic epilepsy (recurrent seizures).

Implications for Designers

The implication for designers is twofold. First, safety considerations to prevent accidents such as falls should be a top priority when creating the built environment. Second, the number of people surviving serious accidents is increasing, along with a growing population of older Americans. The need for appropriately and humanely designed living spaces, including private homes and assisted-living facilities, will increase and will provide interesting challenges for architects and designers. (Chapters 8 and 9 contain more detailed information about safe environments and special populations.)

Stroke

Another devastating and widespread condition that affects the brain is cerebrovascular accident, commonly called a **stroke.** This occurs when the blood supply to the brain is blocked, cutting off oxygen and nutrients and causing the death of affected brain tissue. Common results of stroke are paralysis on one side of the body, cognitive deficits, the inability to communicate, and depression. Stroke is the third-leading cause of death and the primary cause of serious adult disability in the United States (Office of Communications and Public Liaison, 2004, "Stroke"). Risk factors for stroke, in order of importance, include hypertension, heart disease, blood cholesterol levels, and diabetes.

Implications for Designers

Interior designers who create environments for people who have had a stroke must consider the specific condition and needs of the client. Changes in the home might be necessary to accommodate changed conditions. For example, a right-handed person who has lost function of the right side may have to reorganize various elements of the environment. These may include changing the bedroom furniture so that the lamp and telephone are located on the left; changing the wall from which the showerhead is plumbed to allow a grab bar for the left hand; and reorganizing the desk so that space is available on the left side for writing and performing other tasks.

For clients who have any condition that weakens the body, such as stroke and heart disease, there are many designer details that can be beneficial. The bedroom, for example, should be arranged to make self-care as easy as possible, as demonstrated by the following suggestions:

- Provide a lamp switch that is easy to reach and operate.
- Select clocks with large digital numbers that can be read without turning on the light.
- Place a phone where it can be reached without getting out of bed.
- Lower the bed, if necessary. New beds with pillow-top mattresses can be too high for sitting and turning to get into bed.
- Use a quilted comforter with a duvet to eliminate the need to pull up both sheets and blankets.
- Place a padded bench near the bed—perhaps at the foot—for laying out clothes and sitting while dressing.
- Allow space near the bed for a walker or cane.

Dementia

A condition whose causes are less well understood than stroke is **dementia,** a general term for a collection of symptoms. Medical professionals define dementia as the loss of at least two areas of complex behavior, such as language, memory, visual and spatial abilities, and the use of judgment, which significantly interferes with a person's daily life. Other symptoms include losing emotional control, experiencing personality changes, and demonstrating behavioral problems such as agitation, delusions, and hallucinations. These changes are the result of damage to or loss of brain cells, although the initiating cause of this destruction is unknown.

Alzheimer's disease is the most common cause of dementia in people age 65 and older. A progressively degenerative disease in which persons lose their sense of self and reality, it also causes the loss of motor skills during the later phases. It is believed that up to 4 million people in the United States currently have the disease, with at least 360,000 new cases diagnosed each year and 50,000 people dying from the disease (Office of Communications and Public Liaison, 2006, "Dementia").

Incidences of Alzheimer's have risen dramatically over the last 20 years and many health-care professionals believe this might be due to our increased exposure to pollutants and chemicals, including those found in common products such as household detergents. Many researchers believe that the interaction of various chemicals is a likely cause of increasing cases and deaths (Orndoff & Ramirez, 2005).

Implications for Designers

Although the causes of Alzheimer's remain a mystery, research has shown that engaging in intellectually stimulating activities, such as reading, puzzles, and games, may significantly lower the risks of developing dementia (Office of Communications and Public Liaison, 2006, "Dementia"; Verghese, et al., 2004).

Providing areas that encourage these kinds of activities, such as comfortable, well-lighted nooks for reading, is therefore important in private homes, nursing homes, assisted-living, and other health-care facilities.

FIGURE 3.11 Designs can be beautiful, such as this room, unsuitable for Alzheimer's patients. In this example, there are too many shadows; not enough contrast between walls; flooring, and furnishings; and too many changes in the floor pattern which may cause confusion.

For people who suffer from Alzheimer's, safety is a primary concern. Interior designers can incorporate many beneficial features into existing private home or residential facilities, including:

- Provide access to bright light, especially natural light, which may help restore Alzheimer's patients' natural body rhythms and improve their sleep patterns (Boyce, Hunter, and Howlett, 2003).
- Limit access to exits, as patients might wander away and be unable to find their way back.
- Install locks on doors to the garage and any storage spaces that contain chemicals, cleaners, and medications.
- Provide consistent lighting throughout, including hallways, to prevent shadowed areas and contrast that can cause confusion and fear (Figure 3.11).
- Take steps to reduce glare, which can produce confusion, anger, and agitation (See Chapter 7 for more information about glare and contrast).
- Paint rooms in different colors to help the person distinguish one from another.
- Avoid highly patterned floor and wall coverings and furnishings, as they can be confusing and contribute to unsteadiness in persons with impaired depth perception.
- Select easy-to-clean flooring; spills are common occurrences.
- Remove mirrors if they cause confusion for people who no longer recognize themselves.
- Install handheld showerheads to give a sense of control to those who might have a fear of water.
- Install anti-scalding devices on all faucets (Ahmadi, 2000).

Parkinson's Disease

The second-most prevalent chronic degenerative neurological disease is **Parkinson's disease** (PD) (National Institute of Environmental Health Sciences. N.D., "The Role of Environment"). In this condition, the cells in the brain that produce dopamine, essential for the proper functioning of the central nervous system, die or become impaired. Dopamine is responsible for transmitting signals between portions of the brain that enable smooth, purposeful movement. The resulting major symptoms include trembling in the hands, arms, legs, jaw, and face; stiffness of the limbs and trunk; slow movement; and impaired balance and coordination (Office of Communications and Public Liaison, 2004, "Parkinson's Disease"). As the disease progresses, patients may have difficulty walking, talking, and performing self-care tasks.

The exact cause of Parkinson's is unknown, although researchers have discovered increased incidence associated with pesticide use, consumption of well water, exposure to herbicides, and proximity to certain types of industrial plants, printing facilities, and quarries (Hubble et al., 1993).

Genetic predisposition may also play a part and, as with many diseases, current theories point to combinations of genetic and environmental factors as probable causes.

Implications for Designers

Because Parkinson's impairs balance, coordination, and motor skills, it is important to incorporate safety features into the environment: grab bars, safe walking surfaces, and adequate seating. Any furnishings or objects that a person might lean against should be heavy enough to support human weight. If not, those items should be removed from the environment. This might mean giving away or storing items such as freestanding decorative pieces, lightweight hall tables, and lightweight dining chairs. Chairs should have adequate support, with arms sturdy enough to use when getting up. People with Parkinson's are susceptible to falls, thus, the prevention strategies discussed in Chapter 8 are important to incorporate when designing environments used by those with this disease.

Spinal Cord Injuries

The spinal cord links the brain to the rest of the body. When either the cord itself or the nerves between the vertebrae are torn or severed, the result can range from some loss of sensation and movement in parts of the body to paralysis of the body below the site where the cord is cut. For example, if the cord is severed at the neck, the trunk and all four limbs will be paralyzed. Typical causes of spinal cord injuries are falls, auto accidents, and gunshot or knife wounds. In most incidences, the spinal cord is not completely severed.

Spinal cord injuries affect an estimated 10,000 to 12,000 people a year in the United States; 80 percent of these patients are male and 55 percent are between 16 and 30 years old. A quarter of a million Americans are currently living with spinal cord injuries (Spinal Cord Injury Information Network, 2006, "Facts and Figures").

Implications for Designers

Disabled individuals can benefit from appropriately designed living facilities. When injuries require the use of a wheelchair, adaptations such as those discussed in Chapter 8 will be necessary. As with brain injuries and other conditions, care should be taken to determine the specific needs of the individual so that designs can be created to best increase the person's independence and quality of life.

DISEASES AND DISORDERS OF THE EYE

Vision problems are widespread, affecting approximately 60 percent of Americans (Healthy People 2010, n.d., "Healthy Vision"). These problems, called **refractive errors,** are caused by misshapen eyeballs, which prevent light rays from being refracted (bent) so they hit the retina properly to create a clear image. There are four common refractive errors:

1. Myopia (nearsightedness): the eye is longer than normal
2. Hyperopia (farsightedness): the eye is shorter than normal
3. Astigmatism (distorted vision): the cornea is misshapen and unevenly bends light rays

4. Presbyopia (aging eyes): the lens becomes increasingly rigid and cannot change shape easily. This is what causes difficulty in reading for most people after about age 40. (American Academy of Ophthalmology, n.d., "Refractive Errors").

Fortunately, most refractive errors can be corrected with glasses, contact lenses, or surgery.

Cataract

In addition to refractive errors, there are a number of common eyesight problems caused by the natural aging process. **Cataract,** for example, is the irregular clumping of the protein that makes up the eye's lens; this causes it to become cloudy and produce blurry vision. It is estimated that approximately half of Americans will have developed some degree of cataracts by age 80 (National Eye Institute, 2006, "Cataract"). In addition to aging, cataracts can be the result of surgery for other eye problems, an injury to the eye, exposure to some types of radiation, and a congenital (present at birth) defect. Removal of cataracts is one of the most common surgeries performed in the United States, with approximately 1.5 million done annually (National Eye Institute, "Cataract").

Glaucoma

Another common condition (especially in people over age 40) is **glaucoma,** in which excessive fluid in the eye creates pressure that eventually damages the optic nerve and results in blindness. According to the Glaucoma Research Association, of the approximately 3 million Americans who have glaucoma, only 50 percent of these people know it because it progresses without symptoms (Glaucoma Research Foundation, n.d., "Funding Innovative Research"). Once diagnosed, glaucoma can be stopped or slowed with medications, but damage to the optic nerve cannot be repaired, nor loss of vision restored.

Macular Degeneration

A third condition that robs the eyesight is **macular degeneration,** the breakdown of the area of the retina responsible for providing central vision and seeing fine detail. Because peripheral vision is not lost, it does not result in total blindness. However, as it advances, it significantly affects the ability of the individual to perform everyday tasks such as reading and driving a car. This is the leading cause of severe vision loss in people age 60 and older, with more than 1.6 million American adults having the advanced form of age-related macular degeneration. Although the damage cannot be reversed in most cases, early detection can help reduce the extent of vision loss (Mayo Clinic, 2006, "Macular Degeneration").

Implications for Designers

With so many Americans having conditions that reduce optimal vision, designers should consider enhancing vision a priority in all types of built environments. These include providing adequate lighting, especially for reading and doing tasks that require good close vision. A common problem in homes is that lamps are chosen for style rather than utility. Even in public places, such as restaurants, the lighting is often insufficient for reading menus and bills. In the home and other residential facilities, the installation of night-lights can help compensate for decreased night vision. In addition to providing proper lighting, designers can select materials with high-contrasting colors. This will help the individual with cataracts and other vision impairments discern between where one object begins and another ends.

For many people, accessing the contents of pill bottles with childproof safety caps is a problem. This is especially true with older people and made worse by impaired vision. Designers should therefore consider incorporating spaces into both kitchen and bathrooms where pharmaceuticals can be stored. The storage space should have a safety mechanism to prevent children from accessing medicines, and the location should be away from direct sunlight and possible sources of moisture.

People with glaucoma tend to be hypersensitive to light and experience difficulty coping with glare. Therefore, windows that receive direct sunlight should be tinted with either yellow, amber, or brown films—these are the best colors to help eliminate glare. It is also advisable to reduce dependence on fluorescent lighting in long-term care facilities and other health-care environments where many people who are vision-impaired are likely to reside.

Individuals in the early stages of macular degeneration require bright lighting and need longer transition zones between gradients of light, such as moving from the outdoors on a sunny day into a more dimly lighted building. Hence, entry spaces should not be as bright as the outside, but brighter than the areas located deeper in the building. Another problem for people with macular degeneration is that they experience visual distortions so that straight lines appear wavy or crooked. Therefore, the use of wavy patterns in the flooring or along the walls in hallways should be avoided; this could amplify the visual distortions and lead to falls. Additional methods to help those who are vision impaired include providing logical floor plans, good directional signs, and easy-to-see indications of grade changes on floors.

Color Blindness

Color blindness is a genetic disorder carried by females, but transmitted only to male children. The cone cells in the retina are unable to distinguish colors, especially red, green, blue, or mixtures of these colors. Figure 3.12 shows how the world looks to people with different types of color blindness.

The yellowing of the eye's lens is a condition that occurs with aging. This makes it more difficult for a person to distinguish between blues, purples, and greens.

Implications for Designers

Color is often used to convey symbolic meanings. For example, green means go, red means stop or danger, and yellow means slow or caution. For a person who is color blind, some of these colors may not be recognized, depending on the type of disorder. The symbolic use of color should therefore be accompanied by words and perhaps shape. The hexagon, for example is often equated with stop signs, a circle with a diagonal line through it usually means

no, and a skull and crossbones often signals danger. Safeguards should also be provided on items that include color to indicate their operation, such as knobs and buttons on appliances. Chapter 8 includes additional suggestions for designing environments for the visually impaired.

Eye Infections

Infections caused by environmental elements, such as bacteria and irritants, include conjunctivitis, an inflammation of the membrane that lines the inner eyelids. Symptoms include redness, pain, swelling, and the discharge of mucous. It is caused by irritants or pathogens; the bacterial form is highly contagious. Blepharitis is the inflammation of the edge of the eyelid, caused by bacterial infection or allergic reactions to smoke, dust, or chemicals. Two other common conditions are keratitis, an inflammation of the cornea, usually caused by trauma or infections; and sty, a bacterial infection of an oil gland in the eyelid.

Implications for Designers

Eye infections are highly contagious and can be spread through contaminated towels, napkins, and other cloth-based materials. Designers will therefore want to avoid fabric-covered furniture in doctor's offices because children could rub their faces on the furniture, leaving pathogens that can be picked up by others. Vinyl is a good alternative because it can be easily wiped down with a disinfectant. Also, care should be taken in health clubs and spas to limit the possible spread of bacteria from used towels and robes. One solution is a laundry shoot for members to discard used materials. The shoot deposits the items into a laundry bag accessed from the outside (where it could then be picked up and the contents laundered). Another effective way to prevent the spread of eye infections is providing proper hand-washing facilities, including sinks of appropriate height for children.

Irritations can be prevented by eliminating, or at least limiting, the use of substances known to hurt the eyes, or at the very least, making provisions for proper ventilation

FIGURE 3.12A, B, C, AND D These maps demonstrate how the world looks to persons with normal vision and those who have the three types of color blindness. (Figure continued on page 71.)

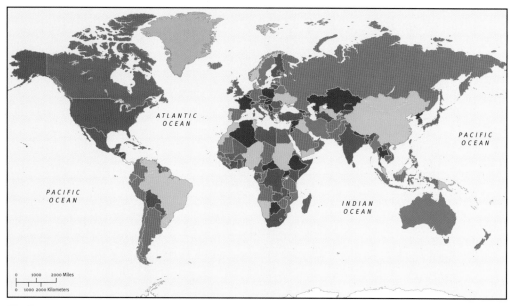

(A) Normal World

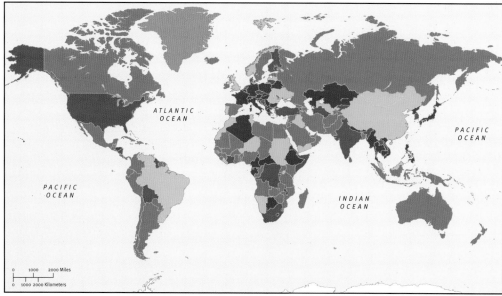

(B) Protanope

during building and remodeling projects. There are some locations where high-energy activities routinely take place, thus increasing the potential for eye-irritating dust and chemicals to waft through the air. Common examples include day-care centers, aerobics rooms, and playrooms. A good solution is to include air-purification systems in the design of such rooms to continually remove as many of the harmful materials from the environment as possible.

Retinal Detachment

A serious condition caused by trauma to the eye is retinal detachment, the pulling away of the retina from its normal position. This can

happen as the result of other eye disorders, cataract surgery, or from an injury to the eye. Untreated, it can lead to blindness. With prompt treatment, which may include surgery, there is a 90 percent rate of successful recovery (National Eye Institute, 2006, "Retinal Detachment").

Implications for Designers

Design suggestions to help reduce instances of retinal detachment include safety considerations to prevent falls and bumping into objects at eye level, specifically eliminating objects that protrude from walls and limiting items that hang from ceilings (particularly at eye level). Examples of items used for

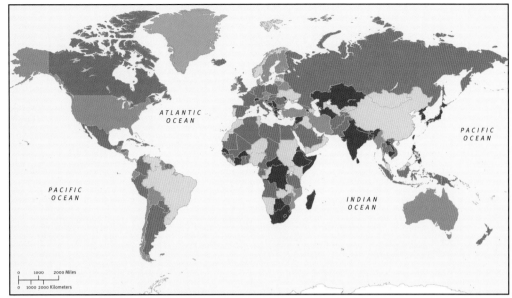

(C) Tritanope

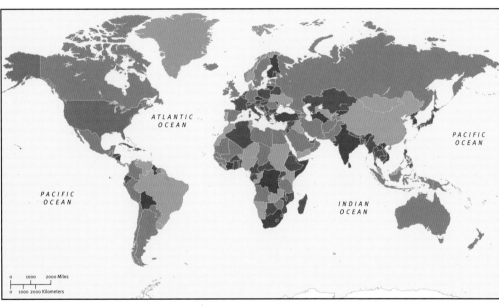

(D) Deuteranope

decorative purposes that can harm the eye include dried tree branches, low-hanging mobiles, and lamps that have sharp pieces. Another consideration is the design of play and recreation areas to be free of hazards that can cause tripping, falling, and colliding with obstacles, all of which can result in injury to the eye.

DISEASES AND DISORDERS OF THE EAR

The most prevalent, as well as preventable, environmentally related hearing problem is **noise-induced hearing loss (NIHL).** As its name implies, it is caused by exposure to loud noise, either a onetime very loud sound or continuous high-level noise. Loud sounds cause relatively violent vibrations that damage the sensitive hairlike cells of the inner ear as well as the auditory nerve. More than 30 million Americans are exposed to hazardous sound levels on a regular basis and of the 28 million who have some degree of hearing loss, about one-third can attribute all or part of the loss to excessive noise (National Institute on Deafness and Other Communication Disorders, 2006, "Noise Induced Hearing Loss"), making noise the most common cause of hearing loss in the United States (American Hearing Research Foundation, n.d., "Noise-Induced"). Recent studies show a significant increase in hearing loss in young people, with evidence suggesting that loud music, along with increased use of portable listening devices with earphones may be responsible (American Hearing Research Foundation, n.d., "Noise-Induced").

Age-related hearing loss is the progressive loss of hearing; this condition affects a large number of older people: about 25 percent of those aged 65 to 75 and 70 percent to 80 percent of those over age 75 have some degree of hearing loss (Medline Plus, 2006, "Age-Related"). The first sounds lost are high-frequency sounds such as speech.

Implications for Designers

People with hearing loss and hearing-related disorders often use a hearing aid. However, hearing aids amplify *all* sounds, not just the sounds the person wants to hear. Suppose someone with a hearing aid eats with a friend in a restaurant. The hearing aid amplifies all the conversations at nearby tables, not just the friend's words. This reverberation and other background noise can be frustrating. Designers can help by identifying ways to reduce reverberation and incorporate sound barriers, particularly in restaurants, health clubs, and other public places. Whether it is in the home or workplace environment, designers should identify ways to reduce environmental noise. Suggestions are included in Table 3.1. (Chapter 7 includes more information about the effects and control of noise.)

Tinnitus

Tinnitus is the sensation of ringing or buzzing in the ears. It has various causes, including loud noise. In some cases, it is a permanent condition. It follows that noise reduction, discussed more fully in Chapter 7, is an important consideration when planning the built environment. For people with tinnitus, complete silence can make the ringing noise unbearable. To help reduce the discomfort, introduce other sounds into the environment either through a central sound system or through the introduction of "white noise." Sources of white noise might be a water fountain, fish tank, or fan.

DISEASES AND DISORDERS OF THE IMMUNE SYSTEM

While the immune system safeguards our bodies from harmful pathogens, it can also create problems if it is oversensitive and responds inappropriately to substances that are generally harmless. The result of this overreaction is an **allergy.** During the first exposure to a substance, such as to a certain food or plant, the oversensitive immune system is triggered to recognize it as an **allergen** for the affected individual. This means that later exposures to the substance will cause the release of histamines from specialized cells in the immune system. Histamines cause the symptoms commonly associated with allergies, such as swelling, redness, rashes, hives, and itching; increased mucus production; and muscle spasms. Repeated exposures to the allergen tend to cause more severe symptoms, including breathing difficulty and a life-threatening condition called anaphylactic shock.

The most common allergens are those that come into direct contact with the body: skin, nasal passages, eyes, or mouth. Reported allergies have been on the increase in recent years. In the United States, for example, rhinitis (irritation and running of the nose), the most common symptom of allergy, increased by 31 percent from 1985 to 1995; pediatric peanut allergies doubled from 1997 to 2002; and asthma increased from 35 cases per 1,000 in 1982 to 56 cases per 1,000 in 1994 (Zanni, 2005). The result of these increases is that allergies have a high impact on both individual Americans and the economy, as seen in the following statistics:

- More than 50 million Americans suffer from allergies.
- Allergies are the sixth-leading chronic disease in the United States.
- Allergies cost the health-care system $18 million annually.
- Chronic sinusitis (infected or inflamed sinuses) is the most commonly reported chronic disease, affecting almost 32 million people in the United States.

TABLE 3.1 REDUCING ENVIRONMENTAL NOISE

SOURCES	REMEDIES
Noisy appliances	Install vibration mounts; isolate source in sound-insulating enclosure.
Ventilation noise	Reduce blower speed; install acoustic lining and flexible connectors in ducts.
Reverberant noise	Install sound-absorbing materials, e.g., carpets and pads, drapery, upholstered furniture, acoustical wall padding, ceiling. Total surface area of absorbent material should be at least one-fourth of total room surface area.
High-pitched sounds from ventilators, heating and refrigerant systems, high-velocity gas flow through furnaces and burners, or wornout or defective washers	Reduce pressure in plumbing system and isolate pipes and valves from supporting wall and floor structures with resilient sleeves or collars. Replace worn or defective faucet washers or valve seals. Wrap pipes.
Excessive noise from conversations (above 70 db at 3–5 feet)	Install barriers and/or a prefabricated, sound-insulated booth or field office enclosure.
Neighboring conversations (sounds transmitted through a partition, ductwork, or ventilation ducts)	Caulk or seal all visible cracks at ceiling and floor edges of party wall. Remove cover plates of all electrical outlets in party walls to check for back-to-back installation; in such cases, pack cavities with foam mat or jute fiber wadding and seal with a resilient caulk.
Noise from upper floors	Install a gypsum-board ceiling mounted on resilient hangers, place foam mat blanket in void between ceilings. In some cases, wall paneling with foam backing mounted on resilient furring members may also be required.
Outdoor noise	Install window "plugs." Install gaskets around existing windows and doors; install storm windows and doors; replace hollow-core or paneled entrance doors with solid-core doors.

Source: Adapted from: www.soundproofing.org/infopages/solutions.htm

- Hives affect 10 to 20 percent of the population at some time in their lives (American Academy of Allergy, Asthma and Immunology, 2001, "The Allergy Report").

The mechanism and cause of allergic reactions is not well understood, nor are the reasons for the spike in reported cases. Two theories have been advanced to explain the increase. The "allergen exposure hypothesis" suggests that increased exposure to allergens present in modern life leads to higher allergy rates. Examples include artificial additives and preservatives in foods; increased time spent

BOX 3.5 CENTRAL VACUUM SYSTEMS

Central vacuum systems have a power unit located in a closet, basement, utility room, or garage that includes the motor and a large dirt collector. Wall outlets are installed throughout the house for attaching a flexible hose and attachment. The motors on central vacuums are larger than the ones on mobile cleaners and, therefore, generally more powerful. Dirt is gathered into a receptacle rather than a mobile bag so that dust and other fine particles do not escape back into the room.

indoors exposed to dust, synthetic materials, and household chemicals; pets living indoors in the same environment as people; and higher levels of outdoor pollution.

The "hygiene hypothesis" suggests that inadequate exposure to genuinely harmful agents leads to immune dysfunction. Today's emphasis on cleanliness and germ avoidance, along with the increased use of antibiotics, have decreased exposures that could help the immune system ready itself to attack pathogens (Zanni, 2005). There is evidence that infants exposed to certain allergens, such as dust mites and cat dander, are less likely to develop related allergies later in life. Observations have also shown that infants on farms tend to have fewer allergies than children raised in more sterile environments (Medline Plus, 2007, "Allergies").

The research is not conclusive, however, and allergies are most likely the result of an interaction of several factors, including genetic predisposition.

BOX 3.6 VIEW TO THE FUTURE

RNAi

RNA, which stands for ribonucleic acid, is a genetic chemical messaging system that enables communication among cells. In addition to enabling normal body functions, RNA also allows communication between the body's cells and other organisms, such as bacteria and viruses. When this happens, the body's cells can mutate and cause disease.

Scientists believe that understanding how RNA works may one day provide us with a powerful tool for combating certain diseases. This is because it can be duplicated as a mirror image of mutated RNA. This fabricated RNA is called RNAi because it has the capacity to interfere with the functioning of the targeted, disease-causing RNA.

Implications for Designers

With the prevalence of allergies, many of which are caused by elements in the built environment, it is appropriate for designers to ask their clients about possible concerns or sensitivities. For example, increasing numbers of people are becoming sensitive to the outgassing of carpets and plastics, formaldehyde, chemicals contained in paint and other construction products, and household cleaning products. One Swedish study showed that household dust containing phthalates, found in some types of flooring as well as the products previously mentioned, was linked to childhood asthma, as well as eczema (inflammation of the epidermis) and rhinitis (Orndoff & Ramirez, 2005). Designers can provide substitutions, when possible, or take precautions such as airing out carpets before installation. (See Chapter 4 for more information about potential contaminants.) In addition, design considerations can contribute to relieving existing allergy problems. For example, clients with dust-mite allergies should have minimal carpet, fabric, and upholstery, especially in sleeping areas. Other recommendations include the use of vacuum cleaners with HEPA (high efficiency particulate air) filters or the installation of central vacuum systems. (See Box 3.5.)

Immune Deficiency Disorders

Immune deficiency disorders refer to the inability of the immune system to respond appropriately and protect the body. Primary immune deficiency is a genetic disorder and can result in repeated and sometimes fatal infections in infants and children. Acquired disorders are the most common and may be the result of drugs, such as those used in chemotherapy and organ transplants, that suppress the immune system; or from diseases, the most common of which is acquired immunodeficiency syndrome (AIDS). In this disease, the human immunodeficiency virus (HIV) destroys the primary cells that fight pathogens, leaving the body unable to protect itself against infections that would normally not be serious and certain types of cancer. First reported in the United States in 1981, AIDS has become a worldwide epidemic (National Institute of Allergy and Infectious Diseases, 2005, "HIV Infection").

Implications for Designers

Designs of environments for people with immune deficiency conditions must incorporate hygienic principles to reduce the chance of contact with infectious material and infection. These include air-cleaning systems; the use of flooring, wall, and furnishing materials that can be disinfected; sufficient hand-washing facilities that are easily accessible; and adequate garbage control.

GLOSSARY TERMS

Abrasion

Allergen

Allergy

Alzheimer's disease

Asthma

Carcinogen

Carpal tunnel syndrome

Cataract

Chronic obstructive pulmonary disease

Coronary artery disease

Cumulative trauma disorder

Dementia

Dermatitis

Emphysema

Fibromyalgia

Floor suspension system

Glaucoma

Herniated disk

Hypertension leukemia

Immune deficiency disorders

Macular degeneration

Malignant melanoma

Muscle strain

Noise-induced hearing loss

Osteoarthritis

Osteoporosis

Parkinson's disease

Refractive errors

Septicemia

Sprain

Spring-load floor

Stroke

Tetanus

Traumatic brain injury

BOX 3.7 THE SUSTAINABILITY CONNECTION

When creating designs and selecting furnishings to address specific health conditions, it is wise to consider the future needs of the household or facility. Look for furnishings that fit with the overall decor of the home so they can be used indefinitely. For example, when purchasing a lift chair, find one that matches the color and style of the house so it can remain in use.

Another sustainable practice is to look for furnishings that are adaptable for various uses and come with replaceable components. Many manufacturers of health-care furnishings, for example, design them so that arm caps, seats, backs, and cushions can be replaced without having to buy a complete new chair.

Source: www.abledata.com/abledata.cfm?pageid=19327&ksectionid=19327&top=11723

LEARNING ACTIVITIES

1. Understanding the needs of people with health problems or conditions can help you better create designs that will benefit them. This exercise can help increase your understanding and empathy. Choose at least one of the following activities to simulate a health condition for a few hours:
   - Spend a day, or at least a few hours, using a wheelchair or a walker.
   - Smear petroleum jelly on eyeglasses or wear a blindfold around your eyes and conduct your daily routine in your living quarters.
   - Wear earplugs.
   - Navigate the day with the idea that you must frequently stop and rest—every 25 feet or so.

   When you have completed the exercise, write a description of your experiences. What design elements presented obstacles? What did you learn that might help you working with clients who have the condition you simulated? Can you apply what you learned to other conditions?

2. Design a living space appropriate for someone with Alzheimer's that has progressed to the point of significant loss of memory and perception of reality. Include a floor plan and illustrations of the flooring, wall colors,

and furnishings. Write a description of the safety features you would include.

3. Visit health-care and/or long-term care facilities. If this is impractical, find photos of such facilities on the Web. Critique them for how well they fulfill the needs of people with the following health conditions or requirements:
   - Fatigue and weakness, as with Parkinson's and some cancers
   - Alzheimer's
   - Depression
   - Opportunities for light physical exercise
   - Partial paralysis, as with stroke

4. Conduct an Internet search to learn more about asthma and its triggers. Create a list of known and suspected causes that relate to the built environment. Then suggest ways that interior designers can eliminate these substances in homes and schools.

5. Sometimes the needs of clients can create contradictions. For example, individuals with compromised immune systems are susceptible to infection and need clean environments. At the same time, some strong cleaning agents can cause allergic reactions, irritation of the lungs and mucous membranes, and so on. Research ways to incorporate safe, easy-to-clean components into interiors.

6. Explore the three Web chemical information sites listed in the chapter:
   - www.epa.gov/iris/intro.htm
   - http://extoxnet.orst.edu
   - www.atsdr.cdc.gov

   Which did you find easiest to use? Which had the most accessible information? Which seemed the most useful for interior designers?

SUGGESTED WEB SITES

1. Vision Australia. Accessible Design for Homes.
"Recommendations for People Who Are Blind or Vision Impaired"
www.visionaustralia.org.au/%5Cinfo.aspx?page=724

2. Vision Australia. Accessible Design for Public Buildings.
"Recommendations for People Who Are Blind or Vision Impaired"
www.visionaustralia.org.au/%5Cinfo.aspx?page=721

3. Alzhome: The Way to Stay at Home
www.bsu.edu/web/nursing/alzhome
This Web site has dozens of practical suggestions for creating a safe and appropriate home environment for people with Alzheimer's disease.

4. American Cancer Society
www.cancer.org
This organization provides information about all types of cancer, its prevention, current research, and support services.

5. American Heart Association
www.americanheart.org
This organization provides information about heart disease, its prevention, current research, and support services.

6. Mayo Clinic
www.mayoclinic.com
The Mayo Clinic in Minnesota maintains this informational Web site to provide information about all types of health conditions.

REFERENCES

Ahmadi, R. (Last updated March 26, 2000). Alzhome: The way to stay at home. Retrieved August 12, 2007, from www.bsu.edu/web/nursing/alzhome. Muncie, IN: Ball State University.

American Academy of Allergy, Asthma and Immunology. (2001). *The allergy report: Science based findings on the diagnosis & treatment of allergic disorders, 1996–2001.* Milwaukee, WI: American Academy of Allergy, Asthma and Immunology.

American Academy of Ophthalmology. (n.d.). *Refractive errors.* Retrieved July 30, 2006, from www.medem.com/medlb/article_detaillb.cfm?article_ID=ZZZYXB80Z9C&sub_cat=2017

American Cancer Society (2005). *Cancer facts and figures* 2005. Atlanta, GA: American Cancer Society.

American Cancer Society (Last updated April 24, 2006). Overview: *Skin cancer–melanoma.* Retrieved August 23, 2006, from www.cancer.org/docroot/CRI/content/CRI_2_2_1X_How_many_people_get_melanoma_skin_cancer_50.asp?sitearea

American Cancer Society. (n.d.). *What are the risk factors for cancer?* Retrieved August 6, 2006, from www.cancer.org/docroot/CRI/content/CRI_2_4_2x_What_are_the_risk_factors_for_cancer_72.asp?sitearea

American Hearing Research Foundation. (n.d.). *Noise-induced hearing loss.* Retrieved July 31, 2006, from www.american-hearing.org/disorders/hearing/noise_induced.html

American Lung Association. (November 2004). *Emphysema.* Retrieved August 9, 2006, from www.lungusa.org/site/apps/s/content.asp?c=dvLUK9O0E&b=34706&ct=67284

Anderson, R.N. and Smith, B.L. (2005). *Deaths: Leading causes for 2002.* National Vital Statistics Reports 2002, 53, 17, 1–90.

Asthma and Allergy Foundation of America. (n.d.). *Asthma overview.* Retrieved July 25, 2006, from www.aafa.org

Boyce, P., Hunter, C., & Howlett, O. (2003). *The benefits of daylight through windows.* Troy, NY: Rensselaer Polytechnic Institute.

Centers for Disease Control and Prevention. (Last updated November 14, 2006). *Heart disease.* Retrieved November 27, 2006, from www.cdc.gov/HeartDisease

Clauw, D.J. and Taylor-Moon, D. (Last updated June 2006). *Fibromyalgia.* Retrieved August 8, 2006, from the American College of Rheumatology at: www.rheumatology.org/public/factsheets/fibromya_new.asp

Duke University Medical Center. (January 1, 2004). *Economic impact of back pain substantial.* Raleigh NC: DukeMed News Office.

Formula for disaster? (July 15, 2005). Retrieved August 22, 2006, from www.pbs.org/now/science/chemsafenotes.html.

Glaucoma Research Foundation. (n.d.). *Funding innovative research to find a cure for glaucoma.* Retrieved July 30, 2006, from www.glaucoma.org

Healthy People 2010. (n.d.). *Healthy vision 2010: Examination and prevention.* Retrieved July 30, 2006, from www.healthyvision2010.org/exams/errors.asp#data

Hoffman, R. E., Wood, R. C., and Kreiss, K. (1993). Building-related asthma in Denver office workers. *American Journal of Public Health* 83, 1, 89–93.

Hollander, A., Doekes, G., and Heederick, D. Cat and dog allergy and total IgE as risk factors of laboratory animal allergy. *Journal of Allergy and Clinical Immunology* 98, 3, 545–554.

Hubble, J. P., Cao, T., Hassanein, R. E., Neuberger, J. S., and Koller, W. C. (1993) Risk factors for Parkinson's disease. *Neurology,* 43, 9, 1693–1697.

Mayo Clinic. (June 1, 2006). *Asthma.* Retrieved July 25, 2006, from www.mayoclinic.com/ health/asthma/DS00021/DSECTION=4

Mayo Clinic. (August 14, 2006). *Macular degeneration.* Retrieved July 30, 2006, from www.mayoclinic.com/health/macular-degeneration/DS00284.

Medline Plus. (Last updated November 6, 2006). *Age-related hearing loss.* Retrieved July 31, 2006, from www.nlm.nih.gov/medlineplus/ency/article/001045.htm

Med Line Plus. (Last update February 15, 2007). *Allergies.* Retrieved November 28, 2007, from www.nlm.nih.gov/medlineplus/ency/article/000812.htm

National Academy of Sciences. (2006). Clearing the air: Asthma and indoor air quality. Electronic book available at www.nap.edu/catalog/9610.html

National Cancer Institute. (Last updated January 18, 2007). *Common cancer types.* Retrieved November 28, 2007, from www.cancer.gov/cancertopics/commoncancers

National Center for Health Statistics. (Last updated October 10, 2007). *Deaths-leading causes.* Retrieved October 22, 2006, from www.cdc.gov/nchs/fastats/lcod.htm

National Center for Injury Prevention and Control. (Last updated January 16, 2006). *A tool kit to prevent senior falls: The cost of fall injuries among older adults.* Retrieved August 17, 2006, from www.cdc.gov/ncipc/factsheets/fallcost.htm

National Eye Institute. (Last updated April 2006). *Cataract.* Retrieved July 30, 2006, from www.nei.nih.gov/health/cataract/cataract_facts.asp

National Eye Institute. (Last updated December 2006). *Retinal detachment.* Retrieved July 31, 2006, from www.nei.nih.gov/health/retinaldetach/index.asp#2

National Institute of Allergy and Infectious Diseases. (n.d.). *Facts and figures.* Retrieved August 4, 2005, from www.niaid.nih.gov/factsheets/allergystat.htm

National Institute of Allergy and Infectious Diseases. (March 2005). *HIV infection and AIDS: An overview.* Retrieved August 3, 2006, from www.niaid.nih.gov/factsheets/hivinf.htm

National Institute of Arthritis and Musculoskeletal and Skin Diseases/National Institutes of Health. (Last revised June, 2004). *Fibromyalgia.* Retrieved November 28, 2007, from www.niams.nih.gov/Health_Info/Fibromyalgia/default.asp

National Institute of Arthritis and Musculoskeletal and Skin Diseases. (Last updated May, 2006). *Once is enough: A guide to preventing future fractures.* Retrieved November 28, 2007, from http://www.niams.nih.gov/Health_Info/Bone/Osteoporosis/Fracture/default.asp

National Institute of Environmental Health Sciences. (n.d.). *The role of the environment in Parkinson's disease.* [Information Sheet] Research Triangle Park, NC: National Institute of Environmental Health Sciences.

National Institute on Deafness and Other Communication Disorders/National Institutes of Health. (Last updated August 24, 2006). *Noise-induced hearing loss.* Retrieved July 31, 2006, from www.nidcd.nih.gov/health/hearing/noise.asp

Neighbors, M. and Tannehille-Jones, R. (1999). *Human diseases.* Clifton Park, NY: Thomson Delmar Learning.

Neurology Channel. (January 1, 2000). *Back pain.* Retrieved August 12, 2007, from http://www.neurologychannel.com/backpain

Office of Communications and Public Liaison/National Institute of Neurological Disorders and Stroke. (December 2006). *Dementia: Hope through research.* [Booklet] Bethesda, MD: National Institute of Neurological Disorders and Stroke.

Office of Communications and Public Liaison/National Institute of Neurological Disorders and Stroke. (January 2006). *Parkinson's disease: Hope through research.* [Booklet] Bethesda, MD: National Institute of Neurological Disorders and Stroke.

Office of Communications and Public Liaison/National Institute of Neurological Disorders and Stroke, (July 2004). *Stroke: Hope through research.* [Booklet] Bethesda, MD: National Institute of Neurological Disorders and Stroke.

Office of Communications and Public Liaison/National Institute of Neurological Disorders and Stroke. (February 2002). *Traumatic brain injury: Hope through Research.* [Booklet]. Bethesda, MD: National Institute of Neurological Disorders and Stroke.

Orndoff, D., & Ramirez, K. Strategic 2005 *environmental report.* Prepared for ASID by Future Impact Education. Retrieved August 8, 2007, fromhttps://asid.org/NR/rdonlyres/0B876389-DF1B-43F5-BCDE-E221F5DAB511/177/Environmental_scan.pdf

Public Health Policy Advisory Board, (March 2002). A*sthma: Epidemic increase, cause unknown.* Washington, DC: Public Health Policy Advisory Board.

Roberts, H. J. (1990). Pentachlorophenol-associated aplastic anemia, red cell aplastia, leukemia and other blood disorders. *Journal of the Florida Medical Association* 77, 2, 86–90.

Slavin, J. L. (2000). Mechanisms for the impact of whole grain foods on cancer risk. *Journal of the American College of Nutrition, 19,* No. 90003, 300S–307S.

Spinal Cord Injury Information Network. (2006). *Facts & figures at a glance–June 2006.* Retrieved November 28, 2007, from http://www.spinalcord.uab.edu/show.asp?durki=21446

U.S. Department of Health and Human Services. (2004). *The 2004 Surgeon General's report on bone health and osteoporosis: What it means to you.* Washington, DC: U.S. Department of Health and Human Services, Office of the Surgeon General.

U.S. Environmental Protection Agency. (Last updated July 2, 2007). *America's children and the environment. Measure D5: Cancer incidence and mortality.* Retrieved August 11, 2007, from www.epa.gov/envirohealth/children/child_illness/d5.htm

University of Maryland Medical Center. (2001). *Burns.* Retrieved August 16, 2006, from www.umm.edu/altmed/ConsConditions/Burnscc.html

Verghese, J.; Lipton, R. B.; Katz, M. J.; Hall, C. B; Derby, C. A.; Kuslansky, G.; Ambrose, A. F.; Sliwinski, M.; and Buschke, H. (2003). Leisure activities and the risk of dementia in the elderly. *New England Journal of Medicine* 348, 24, 2508–2516.

Zanni, G.R. (April 2005). Are allergies on the rise? [Newsletter] Jamesburg, NJ: *Pharmacy Times.*

The Built Environment and Health Threats

*Our interiors, once our chief refuge from urban
terrors, are now themselves seen as sources
of danger.*
—Stanley Abercrombie

CHAPTER **4**

Common Contaminants in the Built Environment

LEARNING OBJECTIVES

1. **Describe the following contaminants in the built environment, including how they affect human health:**
   a. asbestos
   b. lead
   c. biological contaminants
   d. chemical pollutants
   e. gases
2. **Provide examples of contaminants that are the result of actions once thought to have positive effects.**
3. **Explain ways the designer can help reduce the negative effects of each type of contaminant.**

Contaminants in the built environment can cause many health problems, some of which are even fatal, as we saw in Chapter 3. They provide us with numerous examples of actions that result in unintended negative consequences. Many substances, used for their positive—even "miraculous"—properties, are now known to be harmful to human health. Before the development of scientific methods, people had no way of proving the effects of substances, even when they suspected they might be causing problems. Today we have more analytical tools and easier access to information to reduce the number of errors we

make when choosing what to include in our environment. Learning about common contaminants can help architects and designers make good choices.

Contaminants come in various forms, including:

1. Mist: a mass of fine droplets of liquid
2. Vapor: gaseous form of substances that are solids or liquids at room temperature
3. Gas: at room temperature, they are neither solid nor liquid
4. Smoke: small particles of carbon and other materials that do not burn completely
5. Dust: fine, dry, solid particles
6. Fume: gas, smoke, or vapor
7. Aerosol: liquid droplets or solid particles that remain dispersed in the air for a prolonged period of time
8. Live organisms: animals, insects, and microorganisms such as mold and bacteria

Contaminants are measured and reported as concentrations in air, water, or other media, such as soil and food. Knowing these units and how they are used can help in identifying the contents of products used in the built environment. Table 4.1 contains examples of commonly used measuring units.

TABLE 4.1 REPORTING CONCENTRATIONS OF CONTAMINANTS

UNITS OF MEASUREMENT	ABBREVIATION
milligrams per liter	mg/L
milligrams per cubic meter	mg/m^3
milligrams per kilogram	mg/k
parts-per-million	Ppm
parts-per-billion	Ppb
parts-per-trillion	Ppt

ASBESTOS

Asbestos is the general name given to a group of naturally occurring minerals found in deposits throughout the world. Its main component, silicon, is one of the most common elements in the earth's crust, second in mass only to oxygen. What makes asbestos different from other minerals is its crystal development, which forms long, thin fibers much like cotton (Asbestos Resource Center, n.d., "What is"). When ore that contains asbestos is broken up or disturbed in other ways, the fibers divide and redivide until they are microscopic in size and invisible to the human eye. (See Figure 4.1.)

The three most common types of asbestos are (1) chrysotile, (2) amosite, and (3) crocidolite. Chrysotile, also known as white asbestos, is the most commonly used and makes up approximately 90 to 95 percent of the asbestos contained in buildings in the United States (U.S. Environmental Protection Agency, 2006, "Asbestos"). Amosite is the second-most commonly used in construction, and crocidolite, or blue asbestos, is most often used in high-temperature applications.

All asbestos mines ceased operation as of 2001 in the United States (Virta, 2003) and other materials are being substituted for

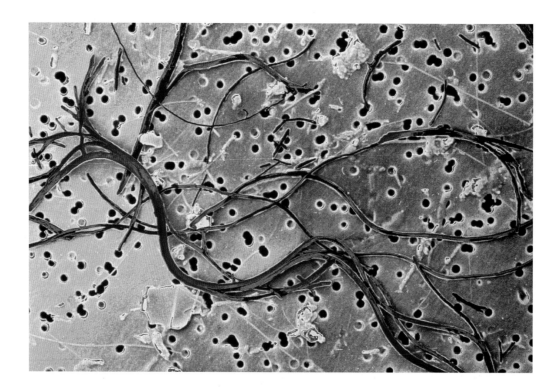

FIGURE 4.1 When they become embedded in the lungs, microscopic asbestos fibers can result in serious, even fatal, lung conditions.

asbestos in the manufacture of many products. Examples include calcium silicate, ceramic fiber, glass fiber, steel fiber, and polypropylene, although no one substance is as versatile as asbestos (Virta, 2003).

Historical Uses of Asbestos

The discovery and use of asbestos present us with an excellent example of actions initially thought to be beneficial to humans that subsequently proved to be harmful—even fatal. More than 2,000 years ago, the Greeks discovered that asbestos fibers were extremely heat resistant and resilient to wear. Naming the mineral asbestos, which means "inextinguishable," they made extensive use of the fibers to weave cloth for articles such as napkins and funeral shrouds (Asbestos Resource Center, n.d., "History"). The Romans also used asbestos, but its use declined during the Middle Ages. It appeared sporadically throughout history until the Industrial Revolution in the late 1800s, when its ability to insulate and prevent the conduction of electricity made it the "perfect product" for insulating steam pipes, turbines, boilers, and other high-temperature equipment.

In the twentieth century, asbestos was used extensively as a fire retardant in houses and buildings of all kinds and as a binding component in many common building materials, including cement, floor tiles, millboard, textured paint, shingles, and acoustical materials (U.S. Environmental Protection Agency, 2006, "Asbestos"). The most prominent use of asbestos occurred between the 1920s and 1980s. Box 4.1 contains a list of where asbestos is most commonly found in homes.

Effects of Asbestos on Humans

When the microscopic fibers of asbestos are inhaled, they can become trapped in lung tissue. Although some of the particles are expelled in mucus, those that remain become embedded and stay permanently in the lungs. Susceptibility to health problems is linked to the concentration, frequency, and duration of exposure, combined with an individual's health characteristics.

Three diseases comprise the majority of asbestos-related health problems:

BOX 4.1   ASBESTOS IN THE HOME

- Vinyl and linoleum flooring and adhesives
- Ceilings, including sprayed-on soundproofing, patching compounds, and textured paints
- Insulation for walls, pipes, and furnace ducts
- Gaskets in appliances, including furnaces
- Roofing and siding shingles

Adapted from: Schoemaker, J. M. & Vitale, C.Y. (1991). *Healthy homes, healthy kids: Protecting your children from everyday environmental hazards.* Washington, D.C.: Island Press.

---

1. Asbestosis: chronic breathing disorder caused by scarring of lung tissue. The body, using its natural defense mechanisms to reject foreign bodies, releases acids to dissolve the fibers. Instead of completely dissolving the fibers, which are relatively long, the acid instead scars the delicate lung tissue. This leads to impairment of the lungs' ability to efficiently exchange oxygen and carbon dioxide. Major symptoms include shortness of breath and coughing. Although rarely fatal itself, asbestosis puts people at a higher risk for developing lung cancer.

2. Lung cancer: malignant tumors invade and block the air passages. The main symptoms include shortness of breath, wheezing, unexplained weight loss, coughing up blood, and labored breathing. The period between initial exposure to asbestos and the appearance of symptoms is 15 to 40 years. Lung cancer is often not diagnosed until it has reached advanced stages and by then it is usually fatal. Lung cancer is discussed in detail in Chapter 3.

3. Mesothelioma: cancer of the lining of the lungs, chest cavity, or abdominal wall. There is evidence that exposure to asbestos is the only cause of this type of cancer (University of Alberta, n.d.), a fairly rare form with about 2,000 to 3,000 new cases each year in the United States. As with other forms of lung cancer, it is usually not diagnosed until the disease is in its advanced terminal stages (Asbestos Resource Center, n.d., "Mesothelioma").

Exposure to asbestos does not cause immediate symptoms, such as headaches or sore muscles, so a victim may not be aware of the danger until many years later. Results of studies seeking a link between asbestos exposure and cancers other than lung cancer have been inconclusive (Agency for Toxic Substances & Disease Registry, 2007).

Regulation and Prevention

Ill effects from asbestos have been observed from the beginning of its use. The Greeks and Romans noticed that many of the slaves who wove asbestos into cloth suffered from lung ailments. The usefulness of asbestos triumphed over concern for human health (Asbestos Resource Center). Unfortunately, reactions were similar in the twentieth century after studies in 1917 and 1918 revealed unnaturally young deaths among asbestos workers. A confirmed asbestos-related death in 1924 in England brought attention to the problem, but asbestos companies covered up the health effects on workers so they could retain profits (Asbestos Resource Center, n.d., "History").

The U.S. Environmental Protection Agency (EPA) has been working for many years to ban most asbestos-containing products. A final ruling it issued in 1989 was overturned by a court of appeals in 1991. To date, flooring felt, rollboard, and corrugated, commercial, or specialty paper are banned, but other products are not. More information can be found on the EPA's Web site, www.epa.gov.

The EPA has established regulations that require school systems to inspect their facilities for damaged asbestos. If found, it must be removed or covered to prevent the fibers from escaping into the air. The release of asbestos from manufacturing facilities during building renovation and demolition is also regulated by the EPA, as well as the disposal of asbestos waste products, which can be placed only in approved locations (Department of Public Health, San Francisco, 2007).

Implications for Designers

Asbestos can be relatively harmless if it is left undisturbed. It is the release of airborne fibers, caused by activities such as moving, cutting, or sanding, that makes asbestos dangerous. The term "friable" is used to describe asbestos that can be reduced to dust by hand pressure (U.S. Environmental Protection Agency, 2006, "Asbestos"). "Nonfriable" refers to asbestos that is hard enough to resist hand pressure; this form is not considered dangerous. In general, many interior asbestos materials are friable, and most exterior materials are not.

If asbestos is not deteriorating or crumbling, it is usually best to leave it alone (U.S. Environmental Protection Agency, 2006, "Asbestos"). Moving products such as old insulation can result in the fibers crumbling and becoming airborne. Any suspicious materials that require handling, moving, or removing during demolitions and renovations, for example, should be done by a professional. In some states, asbestos is classified as a hazardous waste and only licensed individuals can legally remove it.

LEAD

Lead is an element occurring naturally in the ore scattered throughout the earth's crust. A soft, easily worked metal, it is durable and very resistant to corrosion. Used for thousands of years, it was the Romans who made the most extensive application of lead in the construction of their vast water storage and aqueduct systems. They also favored it for lining food storage vessels, making utensils, and glazing pottery.

In the twentieth century, lead was added to household paints to extend their protective properties and to gasoline to increase its fuel efficiency. As in Roman times, it was also used until relatively recently to make water pipes and as solder for joining or patching pipes. About two-thirds of the houses in the United States built before 1940, half of the houses built between 1940 and 1960, and a lesser number built between 1960 and 1978 contained lead paint. Today, it is estimated to be present in 24 million U.S. homes (Mayo Clinic, 2005).

Effects of Lead on Humans

Lead is highly toxic (poisonous) to humans. When lead accumulates in the body, as a result of either inhalation or ingestion (eating), it results in lead poisoning. Although some lead is excreted in the urine, most of it goes into the red blood cells, where it can interfere with the production of hemoglobin, the component of blood that carries oxygen from the lungs to the tissues. This results in a condition called anemia, in which inadequate oxygen is delivered to the body's tissues (Centers for Disease Control and Prevention, 2005, "Spotlight"; National Institute of Environmental Health Sciences, 2005). Lead also damages the body tissues that absorb it. No safe level of lead in the blood has been identified, although the higher the level, the more likely and significant the damage (Centers for Disease Control and Prevention, 2005, "Spotlight"; National Institute of Environmental Health Sciences, 2005).

Lead poisoning is particularly damaging in children younger than 6 years of age because their brains and nervous systems are still developing and their tissues are more likely to absorb lead than those of an older child or adult. Lead accumulation in their bodies can result in lower intelligence; kidney damage; speech, language, and behavior problems; poor muscle coordination; decreased muscle and bone growth; and hearing damage (Mayo Clinic, 2005). It is estimated that between 400,000 and 500,000 children under the age of 5 in the United States have high enough levels of lead in their bodies to cause concern (Centers for Disease Control and Prevention, n.d., "Lead").

Lead poisoning in children is not always detected in a timely way for a number of reasons: (1) children with high levels of lead can appear healthy; (2) accumulation is so gradual that symptoms may not appear until dangerous levels are reached; or (3) the symptoms are unspecific and can be indicative of many other conditions. These symptoms include irritability, loss of appetite, weight loss, sluggishness, abdominal pain, vomiting, constipation, and unnatural paleness (Consumer Product Safety Commission, n.d., "What you"). Very high levels of lead can cause seizures, unconsciousness, and, although rarely, death. Symptoms of lead poisoning in adults include high blood pressure, digestive problems, nerve disorders, memory and concentration problems, muscle and joint pain, damage to the male sperm-producing organs, and cataracts (National Institute of Environmental Health Sciences, 2005).

The most common ways of taking in lead are inhaling lead dust; eating paint, which happens when children chew on painted surfaces, such as windowsills and toys; and putting the hands in the mouth after playing in contaminated soil. The primary treatment for lead poisoning is to stop the exposure. Thus, lead abatement techniques involve removing the sources of lead from the environment; this is the most common treatment for childhood lead poisoning (Rich et al., 2001). Very high levels in the body can be treated by chelation, a treatment using drugs that bind to the lead so that it can be excreted from the body. There are no known medical means to reverse the damage already done by lead poisoning.

Regulation and Prevention

Ailments and death from lead exposure were observed as early as 370 B.C. by Hippocrates, the Greek "father of medicine." The Roman architect Vitruvius noted the symptoms among lead metalworkers and in his book, *De Architectura,* he referred to the dangers of the metal in the water system and suggested that water not be transported in lead pipes (United Nations of Roma Victrix, n.d.). As with asbestos, the warnings were largely ignored. Over 2,000 years later, in 1910, the U.S. House of Representatives reviewed but did not pass a bill to ban lead-based paints. Another bill presented later that year to regulate the manufacture, sale, and use of products containing white lead (lead carbonate) was not passed either (Lead411, 2005).

Manufacturers were aware that lead was toxic as early as the nineteenth century, but ignored mounting evidence throughout the twentieth century about the danger of lead paint to children. In fact, the Lead Industries

Association, which represented the paint pigment manufacturers, carried out extensive advertising campaigns to reassure the public that lead paint was not only safe but healthful for interior use (Cincinnati Children's Hospital Medical Center, n.d.). They were successful in their efforts and from 1910 through 1977, over 4,000 tons of lead pigments were used in homes and in products throughout the United States (Lead411, 2005). In 1978, after years of accumulating medical evidence and the efforts of concerned citizens, both public and private, the Consumer Product Safety Commission (CPSC) banned the sale of lead-based paint for use in residences and on children's toys and household furniture. In the 1980s, the Safe Drinking Water Act was changed to restrict the use of lead in pipes, solder, and other components used in public water systems. These measures have led to a substantial decline in the numbers of children suffering from lead poisoning: from 3 to 4 million in 1978 to fewer than 500,000 today.

The Lead Contamination Control Act of 1988 authorized the Centers for Disease Control and Prevention (CDC) to initiate efforts to eliminate childhood lead poisoning in the United States by 2010, a goal of Healthy People 2010 (a national health-promotion and disease-prevention initiative). The Department of Housing and Urban Development (HUD) and the Environmental Protection Agency (EPA) have joined efforts with the CDC to provide and support public education, funding, grants, and research (CDC Lead Poisoning Prevention Program). In 1992, the Residential Lead-Based Reduction Act of 1992, commonly referred to as Title X, became law. This legislation affects almost everyone involved with owning, selling, or working on residential property, including home remodelers. Local HUD offices provide information about the requirements of this law (American Industrial Hygiene Association, 2006, "Is Lead").

Testing for Lead

Lead is not biodegradable and therefore can remain a health threat if not properly removed or contained (Mayo Clinic, 2005). Any building

or house built before 1978 may contain leaded paint. Although home testing kits are available, these have not been recommended by the U.S. Consumer Product Safety Commission because it is easy to misinterpret the results, and false positives are sometimes caused by the presence of other metals (Consumer Product Safety Commission, n.d., "What you"). Tests conducted by certified professionals or testing laboratories are more reliable. One method, done on the premises, uses X-ray fluorescence to determine if paint contains lead. Another method requires the concerned person to collect samples and send them to a testing laboratory. HUD recommends that action be taken if either of the following results is obtained:

1. X-ray fluorescence shows more than 1.0 milligram per square centimeter
2. Lab testing shows the lead in the paint to be greater than 0.5 percent

Taking action is especially important when the paint is deteriorating or there are young children or pregnant women living on the premises (Consumer Product Safety Commission, n.d., "What you"). State and local health departments have information about testing labs and certified contractors who can safely remove lead. The disposal of lead-based paint and contaminated materials is regulated by state and local guidelines.

Implications for Designers

The EPA has created publications for home owners and professionals involved in remodeling and renovation projects. When planning such projects, it is important to determine the age of the home or building. If it was built before 1978, take steps to check for the presence of lead paint. Simply breaking through a wall that contains lead-based paint, even if it is covered with non-lead paint, can release dangerous levels of lead dust. Box 4.2 lists guidelines for small jobs involving lead paint.

Removing lead paint or painted structures requires specialized techniques, such as sealing off work areas from the rest of the building, removing all rugs and furnishings, wearing a respirator, using a HEPA-filter-equipped vacuum cleaner for daily clean up, and changing shoes and clothes before leaving the work area (U.S. Environmental Protection Agency, 1997, "Reducing Lead"). (See Figure 4.2.) Designers should be aware of what is involved in projects involving lead so they can properly advise clients and calculate these costs into the remodeling budget.

MERCURY

Some of the paints developed to replace lead-based paints have been discovered to have problems of their own: the inclusion of mercury, a metallic element liquid at room temperature and poisonous to people. Elevated levels of mercury are being reported in people who have been exposed to interior latex (water-based) paints that contain phenylmercuric acetate (PMA), a preservative added to prolong the paint's shelf life (Agocs et al., 1990). In 1991, the Environmental Protection Agency prohibited the use of PMA in the manufacture of paints. Care should be taken to avoid using older stocks of paint that could contain mercury.

Mercury has also been discovered in antique mirrors in which the reflecting layer was made of a combination of tin and mercury. Designers might recommend that if clients own or are considering buying these items that they be tested to ensure they are not emitting mercury vapors.

BIOLOGICAL CONTAMINANTS

Biological contaminants are living things that can harm human health. These fall into a number of categories that range in size from microscopic bacteria to large rodents, such as rats. Human beings coexist with millions of kinds of microorganisms, most of which are harmless or even helpful, such as bacteria in the intestines that help us digest food. Microorganisms that are harmful or disease-causing are called pathogens. Bacteria, viruses, fungi, and protozoa are pathogens that can be problems in the built environment.

BOX 4.2   DOS AND DON'TS WHEN DEALING WITH LEAD-BASED PAINT

- Do not sand, as this creates lead dust that can be inhaled.
- Do not use an open-flame torch to remove paint. This produces lead particles small enough to inhale.
- Do not use the highest setting on a heat gun when softening the paint for removal.
- Use caution when painting over old lead paint.

Bacteria

Bacteria are one-celled plants that are able to reproduce approximately every 20 minutes, thus producing millions in just a few hours. Some bacteria can form spores that go into a dormant stage until favorable living conditions exist. Examples of diseases caused by bacteria include strep throat, tuberculosis, botulism (a severe form of food poisoning), urinary tract

FIGURE 4.2 This photograph shows a worker using a power sander with a high-efficiency particulate air filter exhaust system that collected paint particulates, demonstrating an exterior renovation method that was used on residences where lead-based paint was present. This was a low-exposure method.

infections, and tetanus. Most bacteria can be destroyed by antibiotics, although some types have developed that resist medication.

Viruses

Viruses are the smallest pathogens, consisting of fragments of cells that depend on other cells to live and reproduce. Viral infections are challenging to treat because they cannot be killed by antibiotics, are resistant to disinfectants, and multiply very quickly. Examples of diseases caused by viruses include the common cold, influenza (flu), hepatitis B, measles, acquired immune deficiency syndrome (AIDS), and herpes.

Fungi

Fungi comprise a large group of organisms, including mushrooms and yeasts, that are neither plants nor animals, but have characteristics of each. Fungi perform the function of breaking down dead organic material and thus are an important part of the natural cycle of life. Without fungi, we would be overwhelmed by huge amounts of dead plant matter. As with other microorganisms, not all fungi are pathogenic, although fungal infections are quite common and include ringworm, athlete's foot, and nail infections. Mold, a common problem in the built environment, is a fungus that is discussed in detail later in this chapter.

Protozoa

Protozoa are one-celled animals found throughout the environment and the body. For example, thousands are present in the intestines, on the skin, and in the mucus membranes of the nose and throat. Pathogenic protozoa can cause dysentery, malaria, and trichomonas (a sexually transmitted genital infection).

Vermin

Vermin are small animals or insects, such as rats or cockroaches, that are destructive, annoying, and/or injurious to health. Rats and mice destroy property and rats can transmit infectious diseases such as salmonella, trichinosis, and leptospirosis.

In some cases, the animals themselves carry disease. For example, mosquitoes carry malaria, which kills millions of people each year, most notably in Africa. In the United States, the threat from mosquito bites is encephalitis, an inflammation of the brain (Illinois Department of Public Health, n.d.).

Other animals, called vectors, carry yet another creature that actually transmits disease. This is the case with rats and the bubonic plaque that has killed millions of people over the centuries, sometimes up to 75 percent of a city's population. The rats carried fleas that bit people and infected them with the deadly bacteria.

Implications for Designers

The best general way to prevent problems with biological contaminants is to maintain a clean environment that discourages their presence and reproduction. Thus, designing spaces that are easy to clean, especially in cooking areas and bathrooms, is an important and effective way to help eliminate all types of harmful biological organisms. (See Figure 4.3.)

This can be done in a number of ways:

1. Provide convenient and appropriate means of garbage disposal, including containers that close tightly to discourage flies, rats, and other pests. Garbage containers should be located away from primary food preparation areas. This is especially important in restaurants, cafeterias, and other large-scale food establishments.
2. Make recycling easy so that papers and damp cans and bottles do not accumulate in corners or other areas that could be inviting to pests. Bins should be small enough to encourage frequent emptying, but not so large as to be unwieldy to handle.
3. Select easy-to-clean flooring and furnishings.
4. Limit the amount of porous materials, such as natural stone and unfinished woods.

5. Create easy-to-access and clean storage spaces to discourage nesting areas for rats and other animals (see Figure 4.4).

6. Design kitchens and bathrooms that are easy to clean and sanitize to prevent the growth of viruses and bacteria. Surface areas should be able to withstand frequent washing with bleach or other disinfectant solutions.

7. Seal grout lines to prevent porous hiding places for bacteria. This is important not only in kitchens and bathrooms but also in hospitals, gyms, and health spas.

8. Place screens on doors and windows to allow ventilation while preventing insects and other pests from entering.

9. Close holes and cracks in structures that enable pests to enter the interior.

10. Use sheet metal, hardware cloth, or steel wool to close the gaps around pipes, cables, and other openings from the outside or crawl spaces.

11. Provide hand-washing facilities to encourage frequent use. Hand washing is the most effective way to prevent the transmission of germs. In structures with children, such as day-care centers and

schools, provide hand-washing facilities, including soap and towels, at child level.

12. Do not allow unnecessary standing water to accumulate near structures; this can quickly become a breeding ground for insects such as mosquitoes.

FIGURE 4.3 Rooms that have smooth surfaces and a minimum of clutter are the easiest to clean and keep free of biological contaminants.

FIGURE 4.4 Storage areas, especially in the garage and basement, should be well organized so that piles of items do not become nesting places for vermin.

Preventing Food Poisoning

Food poisoning is a serious condition caused by bacteria. The Centers for Disease Control and Prevention estimates that 76 million Americans get sick, more than 300,000 are hospitalized, and 5,000 people die from food-borne illnesses each year (Centers for Disease Control and Prevention, 2003, "Food-Related"). Because of the dangers of food spoilage and working with raw food products that could carry such bacteria as salmonella, food preparation areas should be carefully designed. Salmonella, for example, can live in materials that are not well sealed, such as granite. Adequate work space, near a sink, should be provided so that raw foods, such as meats and chicken, can be prepared in separate areas from other foods. (See Figure 4.5 for an example.)

Temperature may be the most important variable in preventing food-borne illnesses (Morgan, 2003), so the major criterion when selecting refrigerators should be their ability to keep food sufficiently cold to prevent spoilage (40°F in the refrigerator, 0°F in the freezer), especially during the summer months in hot climates.

Preventing Problems with Hot Tubs

As previously mentioned, standing pools of water can be breeding grounds for insects and bacteria. Hot tubs, popular in many parts of the country, must be monitored and treated with chlorine to prevent contamination and the spread of disease. Two conditions have been associated with hot tub use. The most serious is nontuberculous mycobacterial disease, a lung infection that can be difficult to treat and cure (Mangione et al., 2001). The second, "hot tub rash," is an itchy skin condition caused by a bacteria (Centers for Disease Control and Prevention, 2005, "Hot Tub"). Tubs must have proper levels of disinfectant and controlled pH levels (pH refers to acidity or alkalinity). Convenient storage for testing and maintenance materials should be located near the hot tub, and the means to change water as needed should be available and convenient. At the same time, chemicals should be kept out of the reach of children. Locating hot tubs inside indoor enclosures is discouraged because this prevents air contaminated with bacteria from being dispersed quickly; it therefore tends to accumulate (Mangione et al., 2001).

DUST MITES

Dust mites are related to spiders and ticks and are commonly found living in house dust. Mites themselves do not bite and are generally harmless; their fecal matter and skeletal parts adhere to dust and can cause allergic reactions such as sneezing, itching, watery eyes, and wheezing and may be a trigger for 50 to 80 percent of asthmatics (Lyon, 2006).

Mites are difficult to eradicate because their primary food is human skin flakes, which we produce in abundance as we continually shed our outer layer of skin. Mites prefer warm environments, such as that found in our beds when we are occupying them. Along with their droppings, they become trapped in mattresses, bedding, upholstery, and carpeting. They make up much of the dust you see in the air when sunlight streams through a window.

FIGURE 4.5 It is important to provide adequate, easy-to-clean work space near kitchen sinks so there is space for preparing raw foods such as chicken, which may contain bacteria.

Implications for Designers

Bedrooms are the most susceptible areas for the accumulation of mites. Prevention involves eliminating materials that trap mites, such as carpets, fabric window coverings, and upholstery. (See Figure 4.6.) Select beds and mattresses for which it easy to change the linens. Encase mattresses in plastic covers that can be wiped off frequently. Areas near sleeping quarters should have floors and surfaces that are easy to clean and dust. Central vacuum cleaners are helpful in controlling dust levels, because the air is ducted to the outdoors. Air purifiers, either portable or attached to the central air return, can reduce the amount of dust in the air. Dehumidifiers can be helpful, too, when relative humidity levels exceed 50 percent, because moisture promotes the growth of mites as well as other living organisms that contaminate the environment (U.S. Environmental Protection Agency, 1994, "Indoor Air Pollution").

MOLD

Molds, as mentioned previously, are members of the fungi kingdom. There are over 20,000 species of molds that all reproduce by making microscopic **spores,** single-celled bodies that are the equivalent of seeds in plants. Released into the air, spores are naturally present in all indoor and outdoor environments, but do not become mold until they land on a moist surface. If undisturbed, they begin growing within 48 hours and eat whatever they are growing on. Spores that do not find moisture right away, necessary for them to grow, can survive for many years until damp conditions exist.

The term "toxic mold" has become popular in the media, but according to the CDC, the term is inaccurate. Although common molds can produce **mycotoxins,** or poisonous substances, molds themselves are not poisonous (Centers for Disease Control and Prevention, 2004, "Questions"). More than 200 mycotoxins have been identified and some are known to affect human health; little is known about most mycotoxins (U.S. Environmental Protec-

tion Agency, 2001, "Mold Remediation"). One of the most dangerous mycotoxins is aflatoxin B1, which has been found on contaminated food and plants; it is not commonly found on building materials (U.S. Environmental Protection Agency, 2001, "Mold Remediation"). Some of the compounds produced by molds are volatile, meaning they evaporate and enter the air quickly. Once in the air, they are known as **microbial volatile organic compounds (mVOCs)** and often have the strong, sometimes unpleasant odors that we associate with mold.

Effects of Mold on Humans

Most individuals do not have reactions when exposed to mold (Mayo Clinic, 2004, "Mold"). However, an increasing number of people who occupy homes and buildings containing mold are reporting negative health effects, including headaches, breathing difficulties, skin irritation, allergic reactions, and aggravation of asthma symptoms. These may be associated with mold exposure (Mayo Clinic, 2004, "Mold").

All molds, whether alive or dead, can negatively affect health because they produce allergens, irritants, and toxins (EPA, 2001, Mold

FIGURE 4.6 Mites are less likely to accumulate in easy-to-clean bedrooms that use a minimum of fabrics, upholstery, and carpeting.

Remediation in Schools). The type and severity of symptoms experienced depend on several factors: (1) type of mold, (2) extent of exposure, (3) age of the person, (4) existing sensitivities or allergies, and (5) health condition, such as a weak immune system or history of asthma (EPA, 2001, Mold Remediation in Schools).

Reactions to mold include the following:

1. Allergic: inhaling mold spores can cause sneezing, runny nose, red eyes, and a skin rash (See Box 4.3 for a list of the specific molds the Asthma and Allergy Foundation of America suggests are the major causes of allergic reactions.)
2. Asthma: mold can trigger asthma attacks
3. Hypersensitivity pneumonitis: a serious but uncommon condition similar to bacterial pneumonia
4. Irritant effects: irritation or burning sensation in the eyes, skin, nose, throat, and lungs
5. Opportunistic infections: infections that do not usually occur in healthy people, but take hold in those with weakened immune systems (EPA, 2001, Mold Remediation in Schools)

Recent studies have shown a positive correlation between dampness and mold exposure in the home and the rising incidence of asthma.

The health and economic impacts are reportedly very large, with one study concluding that, of the 21.8 million people with asthma in the United States, about 4.6 million cases may be attributable to dampness and mold exposure in the home (Lawrence Berkeley Lab, 2007).

Childhood asthma, in particular, is on the increase and investigations around the world have shown a relationship between the disease and living in houses that contain mold growth (Etzel and Rylander, 1999). A more recent study reported that childhood asthma risks were more than double if the home smelled of mold, although no connection was found between the incidence of asthma and visible mold (Jaakkola, 2005). Cases have been reported in which adults, apparently in good health, have suffered onsets of asthma after being exposed to certain molds (Laport, 2001). Excessive exposures to mold are reported to increase the risk for hemorraghic pneumonia and death among infants (Etzel and Rylander, 1999).

Many health problems resulting from mycotoxins have been reported, including central nervous–system damage and liver cancer. However, the sources for this information consist mainly of workplace reports and case studies. More scientific research is needed to understand the effects of mycotoxins on the human body. The EPA advises that until we learn more about these effects, we should avoid exposure to molds and mycotoxins (U.S. Environmental Protection Agency, 2001, "Mold Remediation"). (Note: More is known about the reactions caused by eating certain molds; these include liver and nervous system damage and immunological effects.)

Exposure to the mVOCs released by molds has been associated with the following symptoms: headaches, nasal irritation, dizziness, fatigue, and nausea (U.S. Environmental Protection Agency, 2001, "Mold Remediation"). Research on the effects of mVOCs on humans is in the early stages. Another concern is glucan, a component of mold cell walls that may cause reactions in the airways and lungs and cause a flulike illness called Organic Dust Toxic Syndrome (ODTS). This is most

BOX 4.3   MOLDS MOST LIKELY TO CAUSE ALLERGIC REACTIONS

- Altenaria
- Cladosporium (Hormodendrum)
- Aspergillus
- Penicillium
- Helminthosporium
- Epicoccum
- Fusarium
- Mucor
- Rhizopus
- Aureobasidium (Pullularia)

Adapted from: Asthma and Allergy Foundation of America. *Mold allergy*. Retrieved March 5, 2006, from www.aafa.org/display.cfm?id=9&sub=18&cont=234

commonly observed in agriculture and manufacturing environments (U.S. Environmental Protection Agency, 2001, "Mold Remediation").

Regulations and Standards

There are currently no federal regulations or standards for airborne mold contaminants. According to the American Industrial Hygiene Association, the available science is incomplete and sometimes contradictory (American Industrial Hygiene Association, 2006, "Facts About"). For example, no clear standard values of mold levels have been definitely linked to health problems. One problem is the number of variables involved. For example, not everyone is susceptible to mold and those who are can be affected by various levels of the contaminant. Government agency committees and research teams are studying indoor air quality issues, including mold, and the EPA, AIHA, and CDC have all published guidelines and recommendations for addressing mold problems.

Dealing with Mold

Moisture control is the key to mold control (U.S. Environmental Protection Agency, 2001, "Mold Remediation"). Any unresolved moisture problem can—and likely will—become a mold problem. Because there are always mold spores in the air and the only ingredients a spore needs to begin a mold colony are moisture and oxygen, the chances are very high that a constantly damp wall from a leaky faucet will become infested with mold. See Box 4.4 for common sources of indoor mold problems and Figure 4.7 for an example of mold growing on an interior wall and ceiling.

Starting in the 1970s, construction practices were to tightly seal buildings to save energy costs. Many of these buildings lacked adequate ventilation and this led to moisture buildup and mold infestations, giving us another example of an action that was meant to solve one problem actually creating another. The cost of energy saved was, in many cases, negated by the expense of mold

---

BOX 4.4 COMMON SOURCES OF INDOOR MOLD PROBLEMS

- Roof leaks
- Deferred maintenance
- Condensation from high humidity or cold spots
- Localized flooding from plumbing or heavy rains
- Slow leaks in plumbing fixtures
- Malfunction or poor design of humidification system
- Uncontrolled humidity in hot, humid climates
- Gutters directing water under a structure
- Unvented combustion appliances
- Inadequate ventilation

Adapted from: Environmental Protection Agency. (March, 2001). *Mold remediation in schools and commercial buildings.* (EPA Publication No. 402-K-01-001). Washington, DC: Author.

---

damage. Adding to the problem is that some popular building materials, such as drywall, do not allow moisture to escape (U.S. Environmental Protection Agency, 2001, "Mold Remediation").

Sampling to determine the presence or type of mold is usually not recommended (U.S. Environmental Protection Agency, 2001, "Mold Remediation"). Because mold spores

FIGURE 4.7 Mold can do serious structural damage in addition to presenting a human health hazard.

BOX 4.5   MOLD PREVENTION TIPS

- Fix leaky plumbing and leaks in the exterior surfaces of the building.
- Watch for condensation and wet spots; dry within 48 hours.
- Keep heating, ventilation, refrigerator, and air-conditioning drip pans clean.
- Maintain low indoor humidity; 30 to 50 percent is ideal. Use a dehumidifier if needed. (But do not let it become a new source of molds.)
- Inspect and maintain HVAC equipment regularly.
- Provide proper drainage so foundations do not stay wet.

Adapted from: Environmental Protection Agency. (March, 2001). *Mold remediation in schools and commercial buildings.* (EPA Publication No. 402-K-01-001). Washington, DC: Author.
Centers for Disease Control and Prevention. (n.d.) *Molds in the environment.* Retrieved March 5, 2006, from www.cdc.gov/mold/pdfs/faqs.pdf.

are always in the air, an air sample only provides information about the level of spores present at the time the sampling occurs; in addition, results are difficult to interpret. The human nose is actually one of the best tools for detecting mold, even hidden mold, because of the odors emitted. Any mold, regardless of type, should be removed. For this reason, the EPA and AIHA recommend spending resources on cleaning rather than on testing. Minor mold problems can be cleaned with a bleach solution. Extensive mold or hidden mold, such as under wallpaper and inside walls, should be handled by an experienced professional. Moldy items should be bagged and sealed with duct tape before being discarded. It is important to check for local ordinances that may be in effect for the disposal of mold-contaminated materials. Once mold has been removed, a permanent solution requires solving the moisture problem. If the moisture

problem is not solved, mold will almost certainly return. See Box 4.5 for ways to prevent mold from getting out of control.

Implications for Designers

If mold is a problem in a structure, it should be resolved before remodeling or redecorating projects begin. Box 4.6 contains information on how to determine if mold might be present. Be sure that cleanup and/or removal is done before such activities as rebuilding, painting, and applying wallpaper. If mold has been present for a long time, it can weaken structures, cause hazards, and require repair or reconstruction.

In new construction, it is important that building materials be allowed to dry. For example, moisture can be trapped between two vapor barriers, resulting in a constant mold problem. When possible, bathrooms should have at least one window to provide good ventilation. At a minimum, an exhaust fan should be installed. Carpeting in areas where moisture can accumulate, such as bathrooms, kitchens, and laundry rooms is not recommended. If carpeting is to be installed in rooms with a concrete foundation, it is important that there be a moisture barrier between the concrete and the carpeting. This is because concrete is porous and moisture can pass through to the carpeting and create an ideal climate for mold growth.

In humid climates where moisture is a continual problem, air conditioners and dehumidifiers are recommended because they not only cool the interior environment, they extract moisture from the air.

CHEMICALS

The word "chemical" has acquired a negative meaning for many people because of the widespread belief that chemicals are unnatural and inferior to "natural" substances. In fact, chemicals exist in nature and are the building blocks of the physical world, including our own bodies. Human digestive systems, for example, depend on chemical actions to process food and convert it into the substances needed to maintain

BOX 4.6   IS MOLD PRESENT?

- Were there moisture problems in the past?
- Are there musty or moldy odors?
- Does it appear that general maintenance has been neglected?
- Are there signs of mold, such as stains or damage to building materials and furnishings?
- Is the indoor humidity higher than 50 percent?
- Are the home or building occupants reporting health problems?

Adapted from: Environmental Protection Agency. (March, 2001). *Mold remediation in schools and commercial buildings.* (EPA Publication No. 402-K-01-001). Washington, DC: Author.

life. By understanding chemical elements and interactions, scientists and engineers can apply their knowledge to solving human problems such as curing diseases and making the building materials we use every day stronger, longer lasting, more economical, and more healthy for humans and the environment. When speaking of problematic chemicals, a better word to use is **"pollutant,"** which is defined as a harmful chemical or waste material that is released into the air, soil, or water.

The use of chemicals presents us with many more instances of actions intended to solve one problem but that lead to unexpected negative consequences. Using chemicals to make products flame resistant is one example. In an effort to prevent fire deaths, especially among children, polybrominated diphenyl ethers (PBDEs) were used in a variety of plastic and foam products for homes and offices. It has since been shown that PBDE compounds accumulate in the body as well as harming the brains of developing infants (Cone, 2003).

Even when chemicals are suspected of causing serious injury to humans, it sometimes takes years for tests to be completed and products to be banned. PBDEs were banned by the European Union several years ago. Although the U.S. Environmental Protection Agency continues to study their effects and some local governments have recommended limiting their use, they have not been banned in the United States. For several years, the Consumer Product Safety Commission has been investigating the effectiveness of safer chemicals to use as flame retardants (CPSC, 1998, "Flame Retardant"). In 2000, the National Academies' National Research Council identified eight chemicals that appear to be free of health risks (National Academies, 2000).

In addition to flame retardants, chemical compounds have been developed for many other applications in the built environment. As you can see from the list in Box 4.8, chemical applications are intended to achieve positive results, ranging from reducing building costs to controlling harmful insects. Unfortunately, many have been discovered to negatively affect human health. In other

---

BOX 4.7 THE SUSTAINABILITY CONNECTION

Protecting the interior from the damage of biological contaminants prevents having to replace furnishings and possessions. For example, mice and rats can chew through electrical cords, build nests in furniture, and create other havoc that requires discarding the items they contaminate or destroy.

Molds are especially destructive because they destroy whatever they grow on: walls, ceilings, structural supports, and furniture. Therefore, eliminating mold growth saves both resources that must be replaced as well as money.

Another way to prevent waste is to carefully assess clients' needs to reduce the chances that the materials and products chosen contain irritating or allergy-causing components that will require the items to be discarded and replaced.

---

words, they are actually pollutants. Most indoor environments contain hundreds, if not thousands, of potential pollutants.

Volatile Organic Compounds

Of particular concern to built-environment professionals are **volatile organic compounds,** commonly referred to as **VOCs,** compounds that release chemicals into the air. (A compound consists of two or more chemical elements in specific proportions.) The term for this release is **outgassing.** The odors associated with a new car, for example, are caused by the release of VOCs from the plastics used in

---

BOX 4.8 APPLICATIONS OF CHEMICALS IN THE BUILT ENVIRONMENT

- Synthetic materials for carpet, wall coverings, and fabrics for upholstery and window coverings
- Treatments to repel stains
- Paints and varnishes
- Glues used in particleboard, a wood product created to reduce building costs
- Insecticides and poisons to control rodents and other pests
- Treatments to prevent and kill mold
- Chemicals to make materials flame resistant
- Caulking substances
- Insulation materials
- Equipment such as photocopiers, personal computers, and laser printers
- Household cleaning and disinfecting products

BOX 4.9 COMMON SOURCES OF VOCS

- Adhesives
- Aerosol products
- Air freshener
- Art and hobby materials
- Body care products
- Carpets and carpet pads
- Cleaning products
- Dry-cleaned garments
- Finishes
- Insecticides
- Insulation
- Mothballs
- Paints
- Particleboard
- Plastic furniture; casings for televisions, computers, and other electronic equipment
- Plywood
- Polyester padding
- Solvents
- Synthetic fabrics
- Urethane foam
- Wood paneling

---

car interiors. VOCs are also released from new carpeting and synthetic upholstery materials. The air in a typical house contains between 30 and 100 different VOCs (Bower, 2001). It is important to note that, as with any chemicals, not all VOCs are potentially toxic. See Box 4.9 for a list of common sources of VOCs.

Decay refers to the speed at which VOCs are released into the air. In fast decay, most chemicals are released within minutes, although some can continue to be released over time. In slow decay, there is an initial blast, and then emissions decrease slowly over a period of time. With some materials, VOCs are released over many years.

A reaction called the **sink effect** takes place when materials that may not outgas VOCs themselves absorb the chemicals outgassed by other materials and then release them later. This is why VOCs can still be present in a building even after the offending materials have been removed. In one reported case, carpeting and drywall were reported to have absorbed the VOCs from latex paint (U.S.

Environmental Protection Agency, 1993, "Predicting"); in another, gypsum (a mineral used in the manufacture of wallboard) was found to be a strong sink for formaldehyde (U.S. Environmental Protection Agency, 1993, "Absorption"). **Synergism** describes what happens when substances that combine are many times more toxic than the individual substances. A common household example is the creation of poisonous chlorine gas that results when ammonia and bleach are accidentally combined, as can happen when cleaning a bathroom.

Effects of Chemical Pollutants on Humans

Not all people react to all pollutants, although there are some chemicals, such as chlorine gas, that are likely to cause negative reactions in everyone. Potentially harmful chemicals cause problems by either their mass or their ability to take part in chemical reactions with the molecules of the body (Morgan, 2003).

Toxicity refers to the ability of a substance to cause an undesirable or harmful effect. Whether a substance is toxic or not often depends on the **dose** (amount in the body), the route of exposure, and the duration and frequency of exposure (Morgan, 2003). Chemicals generally enter the body in one of three ways:

1. Inhalation: breathed into the lungs, transferred to the bloodstream, and then delivered throughout the body.
2. Absorption: absorbed through the skin.
3. Ingestion: taken in through the mouth by eating, drinking, or smoking.

It should be noted that even necessary substances, such as water, can be toxic if taken in too-large doses. The National Institute for Occupational Safety and Health has listed more than 12,000 toxic materials, and new potentially toxic substances are continually created. **Threshold limit values (TLVs),** prepared by the American Conference of Governmental Industrial Hygienists, Inc. (ACGIH), are the levels of exposure an individual can experience without an unreasonable risk of disease or injury. The Occupational Health and Safety

Administration (OSHA) establishes permission standards of potentially toxic substances in the workplace. For some individuals, a very low level of a pollutant causes immediate health problems. For others, a higher level causes no noticeable effects. Some experts believe that long-term exposure to even low levels of pollutants can cause many people to eventually suffer ailments such as heart disease, cancer, and chronic bronchitis (Bower, 2001).

People react to different chemicals; people also can react differently to the same chemicals. This is because susceptibility is influenced by factors such as genetics and general health (Morgan, 2003). As Box 4.10 shows, reactions include many nonspecific symptoms that can be caused by many conditions and diseases other than chemical exposure. This is why many people are unaware that they are reacting to chemicals in their environment and can suffer for many years without relief.

As was discussed in Chapter 3, the number of people in the United States with allergies has steadily increased over the years; it is now estimated that between 25 and 75 percent of the population has allergies (Laport, 2001; Bower, 2001). According to the Centers for Disease Control and Prevention (CDC), asthma cases nearly doubled from 3 to 5.5 percent of the population between 1980 and 1996. Although it is possible that some of the increase is due to better diagnosing and reporting, many experts believe that these rising percentages are related to increased exposure to chemicals.

Implications for Designers

It is important to determine whether clients are sensitive to certain chemicals by asking questions and listening carefully. Always respect clients' opinions and stated needs. Some individuals believe that chemical sensitivity is "all in the head," but often this belief does not serve the best interests of clients. Family history of allergies and/or asthma can signal a potential for problems with chemicals.

One major source of information on the chemical contents of products is the Material Safety Data Sheet (MSDS). Developed as a result of OSHA's right-to-know regulations, the

---

BOX 4.10 POTENTIAL EFFECTS OF CHEMICALS ON THE BODY

Nonspecific Symptoms
- Abdominal discomfort
- Blurred vision
- Cough
- Drowsiness
- Fatigue
- Headache
- Joint and muscle pain
- Malaise (an indefinite feeling of being sick or uneasy)
- Ringing in the ears
- Swelling

Specific Conditions
- Allergies
- Asthma
- Birth defects
- Cancer
- Multiple chemical sensitivity
- Mutation: DNA in cells is damaged or changed
- Neurological problems: confusion, loss of memory, dizziness, depression, anxiety, mood swings, hallucinations, apathy, lethargy, insomnia

---

sheets contain information about a product's content, characteristics, and potential health hazards (Figure 4.8). The sheets do have certain limitations. For example, they do not list substances that make up less than 1 percent of the product. While small, this amount can still cause problems for sensitive individuals. Another hindrance is that trade laws protect companies from having to list "secret ingredients" as well as the nonactive components. Because the disclosure requirements are related to exposures in the workplace, tests are based on eight hours of exposure for a healthy person. Twenty-four-hour exposure, as can happen in the home, can pose more danger for infants, the elderly, and the chemically sensitive than is indicated on the data sheets (Bower 2001). Some manufacturers are converting to environmentally friendly products that designers can suggest for clients. For example, Steelcase, Inc., a producer of office divider panels and other furnishings, announced in February 2006 that it would no longer use polyvinyl chloride (PVC), a common VOC. These types of products are becoming increasingly available.

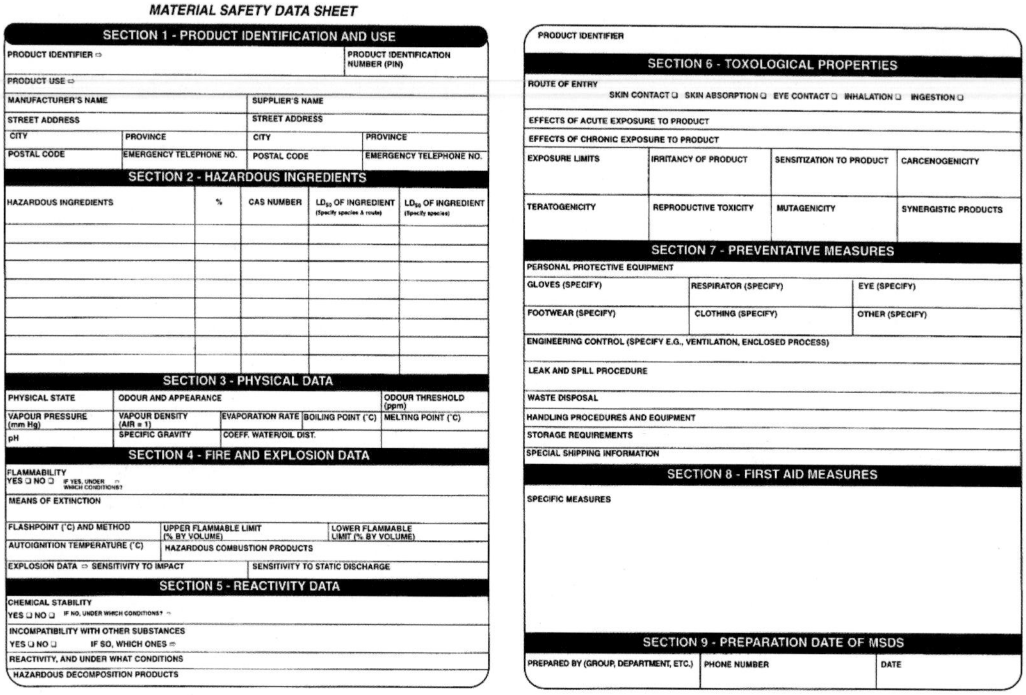

FIGURE 4.8 Material Safety Data Sheets can help designers identify products that might cause problems for chemically sensitive clients.

MATERIAL SAFETY DATA SHEET

SECTION 1 - PRODUCT IDENTIFICATION AND USE

PRODUCT IDENTIFIER ⇨
PRODUCT IDENTIFICATION NUMBER (PIN)
PRODUCT USE ⇨
MANUFACTURER'S NAME | SUPPLIER'S NAME
STREET ADDRESS | STREET ADDRESS
CITY | PROVINCE | CITY | PROVINCE
POSTAL CODE | EMERGENCY TELEPHONE NO. | POSTAL CODE | EMERGENCY TELEPHONE NO.

SECTION 2 - HAZARDOUS INGREDIENTS

HAZARDOUS INGREDIENTS | % | CAS NUMBER | LD_{50} OF INGREDIENT (Specify species & route) | LD_{50} OF INGREDIENT (Specify species)

SECTION 3 - PHYSICAL DATA

PHYSICAL STATE | ODOUR AND APPEARANCE | ODOUR THRESHOLD (ppm)
VAPOUR PRESSURE (mm Hg) | VAPOUR DENSITY (AIR = 1) | EVAPORATION RATE | BOILING POINT (°C) | MELTING POINT (°C)
pH | SPECIFIC GRAVITY | COEFF. WATER/OIL DIST.

SECTION 4 - FIRE AND EXPLOSION DATA

FLAMMABILITY YES ☐ NO ☐ IF YES, UNDER WHICH CONDITIONS?
MEANS OF EXTINCTION
FLASHPOINT (°C) AND METHOD | UPPER FLAMMABLE LIMIT (% BY VOLUME) | LOWER FLAMMABLE LIMIT (% BY VOLUME)
AUTOIGNITION TEMPERATURE (°C) | HAZARDOUS COMBUSTION PRODUCTS
EXPLOSION DATA ⇨ SENSITIVITY TO IMPACT | SENSITIVITY TO STATIC DISCHARGE

SECTION 5 - REACTIVITY DATA

CHEMICAL STABILITY YES ☐ NO ☐ IF NO, UNDER WHICH CONDITIONS?
INCOMPATIBILITY WITH OTHER SUBSTANCES YES ☐ NO ☐ IF SO, WHICH ONES ⇨
REACTIVITY, AND UNDER WHAT CONDITIONS
HAZARDOUS DECOMPOSITION PRODUCTS

PRODUCT IDENTIFIER

SECTION 6 - TOXOLOGICAL PROPERTIES

ROUTE OF ENTRY SKIN CONTACT ☐ SKIN ABSORPTION ☐ EYE CONTACT ☐ INHALATION ☐ INGESTION ☐
EFFECTS OF ACUTE EXPOSURE TO PRODUCT
EFFECTS OF CHRONIC EXPOSURE TO PRODUCT
EXPOSURE LIMITS | IRRITANCY OF PRODUCT | SENSITIZATION TO PRODUCT | CARCENOGENICITY
TERATOGENICITY | REPRODUCTIVE TOXICITY | MUTAGENICITY | SYNERGISTIC PRODUCTS

SECTION 7 - PREVENTATIVE MEASURES

PERSONAL PROTECTIVE EQUIPMENT
GLOVES (SPECIFY) | RESPIRATOR (SPECIFY) | EYE (SPECIFY)
FOOTWEAR (SPECIFY) | CLOTHING (SPECIFY) | OTHER (SPECIFY)
ENGINEERING CONTROL (SPECIFY E.G., VENTILATION, ENCLOSED PROCESS)
LEAK AND SPILL PROCEDURE
WASTE DISPOSAL
HANDLING PROCEDURES AND EQUIPMENT
STORAGE REQUIREMENTS
SPECIAL SHIPPING INFORMATION

SECTION 8 - FIRST AID MEASURES

SPECIFIC MEASURES

SECTION 9 - PREPARATION DATE OF MSDS

PREPARED BY (GROUP, DEPARTMENT, ETC.) | PHONE NUMBER | DATE

Because built environments are systems, it is important to consider the overall effects when planning ways to eliminate chemical problems in a structure or to avoid them in the first place (Bower, 2001). At the building stage of construction or remodeling, ensure that there is a job site plan to deal with dust, chemicals, fumes, odor, outgassing materials, and moisture. For example, if kitchen cabinets, a common source of chemicals, are ordered ahead of time, they can be unpacked and allowed to air out in a garage or other storage area before being installed.

There is some evidence that many common houseplants absorb certain chemicals through photosynthesis or by absorbing and depositing them into the soil. Soil and roots have also been found to remove pollutants because they are a food source for microorganisms in the soil. The U.S. National Aeronautic and Space Agency (NASA) and the Associated Landscape Contractors of America (ALCA) are conducting research on the potential use of houseplants in resolving indoor air pollution (John C. Stennis Space Center, n.d.). NASA has constructed an experimental BioHome at the Stennis Space Center in which common houseplants are being used as living air puri-fiers (John C. Stennis Space Center, n.d.). The hope is that plants may become an effective means of curing "sick building syndrome," a condition in which indoor air is polluted and negatively affects the health of occupants. (This condition is discussed in Chapter 5.)

Overall, adequate ventilation is much more important and effective in the removal of pollutants from indoor air (U.S. Environmental Protection Agency, 1994, "Indoor Air Pollution"). Because plants are an attractive feature in the built environment, the fact that they might aid in removing pollution is a good reason to incorporate them into the design of all types of interiors. Table 4.2 contains a list of the plants tested and found to be potentially effective. At the same time, care must be taken to avoid overly damp soil, which can become a breeding ground for microorganisms (U.S. Environmental Protection Agency, 1994, "Indoor Air Pollution").

FORMALDEHYDE

Formaldehyde is found in many products because it is inexpensive to make and has a variety of useful applications. For example, it is a component of particleboard and medium

TABLE 4.2 HOUSEPLANTS THAT MAY ASSIST IN REMOVING POLLUTANTS

SCIENTIFIC NAME	COMMON NAME
Hedera helix	English ivy
Chlorophytum comosum	Spider plant
Epipiremnum aureum	Golden pothos
Spathiphyllum "Mauna Loa"	Peace lily
Chamaedorea sefritzii	Bamboo or reed palm
Sansevieria trifasciata	Snake plant
Philodendron scandens oxycardium	Heartleaf philodendron
Philodendron selloum	Selloum philodendron
Philodendron domesticum	Elephant ear philodendron
Dracaena marginata	Red-edged dracaena
Dracaena fragrans "Massangeana"	Cornstalk dracaena
Dracaena dermensis "Janet Craig"	Janet Craig dracaena
Dracaena deremensis "Warneckii"	Warneck dracaena
Ficus benjamina	Weeping fig

density fiberboard (MDF), which are used in making kitchen and bathroom cabinets, shelving, and subfloors. In fact, almost all manufactured wood products are held together with formaldehyde-based glue. Common interior components such as wall paneling and cabinetry are made with the most potent glues and tend to cause the highest emissions. Even thin wood veneers that cover particleboard allow enough emissions to pass through to bother some people. Although the wood industry is reducing the amounts of formaldehyde used in particleboard and plywood, many products continue to be potentially harmful to health (Bower, 2001). For chemically sensitive individuals, solid wood cabinetry, while more expensive, may be the best choice. (See Figure 4.9.) Other sources of formaldehyde, at levels that might bother sensitive individuals, include paints and certain coatings used on fabrics and paper products.

Because of its extensive use, formaldehyde is present in the air of many homes. A survey of houses conducted in southern Louisiana revealed that 74 percent contained detectable levels of formaldehyde and 60 percent had concentrations above recom-mended guidelines. Some had amounts that were five times higher than recommended levels (Lemus et al., 1998). More recently in the same region, elevated levels of formaldehyde were found in trailers provided by FEMA to Gulf Coast residents left homeless by Hurricane Katrina in 2005. Occupants are frequently unaware of its presence because formaldehyde is odorless except at very high concentrations.

Effects of Formaldehyde on Humans

Common reactions to formaldehyde include burning eyes, respiratory tract irritation with impaired mucous membranes, tightness in the chest, headaches, depression, and asthma attacks. Exposure to high levels can cause death. Because some symptoms are the same as for the common cold, it can take a long time to detect the source of the problem. Although not everyone reacts negatively to formaldehyde, studies have suggested that a significant percentage of the population is susceptible to even low concentrations. The American Lung Association recommends that formaldehyde levels not exceed 0.1 parts per million (Laport, 2001). For comparison, when FEMA tested

BOX 4.11 EXPERT SPOTLIGHT: Airborne Particulates and Interior Finish Materials

Debra D. Harris, Ph.D., AAHID
Principal, IDR Studio, Inc.

Well-being and productivity are affected by the quality of the indoor environment (Samet & Spengler, 2003). The federal government, business community, and design professionals are interested in the relationship between environments and health. Productivity, worker satisfaction, and related costs are incentives for employers to provide safe and healthy indoor environments (Samet & Spengler, 2003). One result is placing greater emphasis on prevention and creating a holistic approach to design and maintenance to provide health benefits, as well as merely sustaining the health status of the environment and its occupants.

Airborne particulates are defined by the U.S. Environmental Protection Agency (2007) as suspended matter found in the atmosphere as solid particles or liquid droplets. Sources of indoor airborne particulates include dust, emissions from combustion products (fireplaces, stoves, tobacco smoke, and vehicle exhaust), and biological and chemical contaminants. Indoor finish materials also contribute to the overall indoor air quality problems.

Biological contaminants are agents derived from, or are, living organisms. Biological particulates include dust mites, fungi (including mold), and bacteria that can be inhaled and cause allergic reactions, respiratory disorders, environmental sensitivities, and infectious diseases. Normal building materials and interior furnishings provide ample nutrition for many species of mold, although molds can grow and amplify only when there is an adequate supply of moisture (ACOEM, 2003). If an indoor location is identified to be supporting mold growth, then the source of water must be removed before remediation of the mold colonization can succeed. Bacteria grow in appropriate hosts, which include people and water. They can be spread through person-to-person contact, secondary transference through an intermediate host, and through the ventilation system. Interior finish materials are potential temporary hosts; recent studies have shown that bacteria may live a few hours to a few days on typical indoor materials such as laminates, textiles, carpets, and vinyl products.

Volatile organic compounds (VOCs) are compounds that become a gas at room temperature. Common sources of VOCs include: 1) Formaldehyde (furniture, millwork, pressed wood products, textiles); 2) Styrene (printers and copiers); 3) Pinene (wood furniture and millwork); and 4) Phenylcyclohexene, typically found in carpeting. Health effects attributed to exposure to VOCs include eye, nose, and throat irritation, headaches, allergic reactions, breathing difficulties, fatigue, and loss of coordination. Greenguard Environmental Institute (GEI), an industry-independent organization with a certification program recognized by the USGBC LEED program, is an excellent source where designers can find information, as well as certified furniture, materials, and products so as to exercise a source-control strategy for minimizing total volatile organic compounds (TVOCs). The GEI resource is located at www.greenguard.org. A second strategy is to flush out the indoor space by operating the mechanical system for a specified period of time at 100 percent outside air at the end of construction and prior to occupancy.

Strategies for minimizing interior finish material impact on the indoor air quality include specifying low-VOC materials and cleaning agents; flushing out the building prior to occupancy; maintaining levels of humidity between 30 percent and 60 percent; and using mitigate water intrusions to prevent the moisture that promotes biological contaminant growth. These strategies will provide a base for limiting airborne particulates that affect the health and well-being of the building and its occupants.

American College of Occupational and Environmental Medicine (ACOEM) (2003). Adverse human health effects associated with molds in the indoor environment. *Journal of Occupational and Environmental Medicine, 45*(5), 470–478.

Environmental Protection Agency (2007). Terminology Reference System. Retrieved January 14, 2007 from http://iaspub.epa.gov/trs/trs_proc_qry.navigate_term?p_term_id=15518&p_term_cd=TERMDIS

Samet, J. M., & Spengler, J. D. (2003). Indoor environments and health: moving into the 21st century. *American Journal of Public Health, 93*(9), 1489–1493.

closed-up trailers intended for Katrina victims, formaldehyde levels averaged 1.04 parts per million, significantly exceeding all recommended levels (Lohr, 2007).

Formaldehyde is an example of an **immune-system sensitizer,** meaning that exposure to it can result in sensitivities to a variety of unrelated chemicals. Known as the "spreading phenomena," this is one of the most serious consequences because identifying and removing sources of irritation, which can grow in number, become more difficult. Individuals who are repeatedly exposed to high levels have the greatest risk.

Implications for Designers

To avoid or reduce exposure to formaldehyde, designers should be aware of standards and labeling. For example, on particleboard flooring, look for American National Standards Institute (ANSI) grades "PBU," "D2," or "D3" stamped on the panel. These standards specify lower formaldehyde emission levels (Consumer Product Safety Commission, 1997, "An Update"). When formaldehyde-containing products cannot be avoided, a number of actions can be taken to at least limit the degree of exposure to the chemical. Products made of pressed wood can be sealed on the raw edges. Plywood can be aired out before use and then sealed with several coats of polyurethane or lacquer, although the efficiency of this method has not been widely documented (Schoemaker & Vitale, 1991). Some builders recommend using wood products designed for exterior use in interiors because they are made in a way that outgasses less than products designed for use inside (Schoemaker & Vitale, 1991). For highly sensitive individuals, the designer can suggest alternative materials such as steel and hardwoods.

Designers should make sure the construction/renovation team avoids using foamed-in-place insulation containing formaldehyde, especially urea-formaldehyde foam insulation (Consumer Product Safety Commission, 1997, "An Update"). Because it is difficult to avoid formaldehyde completely, good ventilation should always be provided through windows that open, screened doors, and efficient exhaust fans.

CARPETING

Carpeting is popular for its warmth, soundproofing ability, cost, appearance, and for helping prevent injuries from falls. In spite of these advantages, many healthy-home proponents believe it to be an unhealthy choice for flooring. There are several reasons for this opinion. Carpeting has a high chemical content, including formaldehyde, benzene, styrene, toluene, and xylene. The Carpet and Rug Institute (CRI) has conducted tests to identify respiratory irritants in carpet chemicals, working with the U.S. Consumer Product Safety Commission (CPSC) to set investigation standards

and data review (Consumer Product Safety Commission, 1995, "Respiratory Irritation"). Controversy exists because some health proponents believe the problem is not being adequately addressed. Tests at Anderson Labs, for example, have shown that many "safe" carpets are actually highly toxic (Bower, 2001). One problem is that outgassing may result from a combination of chemicals, so identifying the specific culprit and then finding carpeting without that particular combination is difficult, if not impossible (Anderson in Bower, 2001). In a study sponsored by the Carpet and Rug Institute, 58 chemicals were chosen for sensory irritation testing, an indication of just how many chemicals comprise synthetic

FIGURE 4.9 Installing solid wood kitchen cabinets avoids the offgassing of formaldehyde that is used in manufacturing particleboard cabinetry.

carpeting. In addition, outgassing can be caused by carpet pads and adhesives.

Another serious problem with wall-to-wall carpeting is the difficulty of keeping it clean. Small particles and food crumbs provide a breeding ground for biological contaminants, such as mites, spores, and bacteria (Bower, 2001), discussed earlier in this chapter. Carpeting also serves as a trap for the skin we all continually shed, the primary food for dust mites. There are products to control dust mites, but these contain chemicals that can cause other problems for chemically sensitive individuals (Bower, 2001). Because most people do not remove their shoes when entering a house, any contaminants present outside can be deposited onto the carpeting (see Figure 4.10). Examples include the dust from flaking exterior lead-containing paint and pesticides used on lawns.

When young children crawl on carpets and then put their hands in their mouths, they ingest these pollutants.

Carpeting can also serve as a sink, catching particles and then releasing them when they are stepped on. When tiny particles, such as carpet fibers, are released and get absorbed into the heating system and burn on hot surfaces, they produce a toxic substance called "fried dust," which then recirculates throughout the indoor environment. Synthetic carpets tend to hold dust better than wool carpets, but they outgas, so the choice can be between dust and VOCs. Although wool carpeting does not outgas, it can attract moths. And if any type of carpeting is installed directly over a concrete floor that has not been treated properly to prevent absorbing moisture from the soil beneath it, the moisture can rise up through the concrete and into the carpet (Bower, 2001).

Effects of Carpeting on Humans

A number of problems have been attributed to carpets, including eye irritation, asthma, and neurological problems. Some people suffer a wide variety of symptoms, including headaches, muscle and joint pain, fatigue, inability to concentrate, and multiple chemical sensitivity. Cases of severe seizures have even been reported. Because children play on floors, the widespread use of carpeting may be one cause for the increase in childhood asthma. Some schools have eliminated carpeting after health problems were discovered among their students.

Implications for Designers

Clients should be informed about the variety of numerous floor covering options available today. Chemically sensitive clients should be encouraged to seriously consider flooring other than carpeting. These types of people can do well with hardwood floors, or by using cotton scatter rugs (but beware of slipping and tripping) or old Oriental carpets (Anderson in Bower, 2001). Bamboo and cork are other natural materials designers can suggest that clients consider for flooring.

BOX 4.12 EXPERT SPOTLIGHT: The Use of Carpeting in Low-Income Housing

Pamela Thorsch
Executive Director
Rebuilding Together San Diego

The individuals served by Rebuilding Together San Diego are low income and often socially disadvantaged. These people are considered the "sheltered poor" of our community. They have limited financial resources and are literally choosing between food, medicine, and making a home repair, let alone considering an upgrade. A common problem our charity runs into when helping low-income residents is old wall-to-wall carpeting that should have been replaced years ago. In these cases, people are forced to live with old carpeting that either emits mal-odor from particle accumulation or from the growth of mold. In some cases, the carpet is tattered and poses a trip hazard. Some people even pull up the old carpeting and live with unfinished flooring.

Carpeting is often used in low-income housing because it is inexpensive at the time of installation; however, over time, durable flooring materials, such as stone or tile, would be more cost effective and sustain quality and beauty for a greater length of time.

In one home we worked on, our beneficiary reported an increased ability to breathe and fewer allergy problems once the carpeting was removed and replaced with tile, a much more durable material that had been donated to the charity. We only wish we could provide more recipients with the opportunity to replace their flooring with tile or stone. Poverty shouldn't mean substandard living conditions. We believe we should be concerned about the health and well-being of all people.

For those who still prefer carpeting, some manufacturers specialize in carpets made exclusively from nonsynthetic components, which are biodegradable and contain no added chemicals. The backing and glues should also be chemical-free, or carpets can be secured with tack-strips instead of adhesives. For clients who do decide to use synthetic carpeting, designers should choose one with as little odor as possible, as this is an indication of the extent of outgassing from the product. The new carpeting should be unrolled and thoroughly aired out before it is installed, for two to four weeks if possible. Good ventilation with open windows and fans should be provided when new carpeting is installed.

Designers can also suggest the installation of central vacuuming systems, which blow collected dust outdoors rather than storing it in a bag that often simply reintroduces small particles into the air. At the least, designers can suggest clients use higher-quality vacuum cleaners with HEPA filters. Some models come with a light that indicates when the carpet is clean.

Mudrooms and shoe storage spaces can be included near a home's exterior doors so people can easily remove and store their shoes or boots (Figure 4.10). Designers can select a permeable, rugged outdoor mat that collects gritty materials and allows them to fall through as well as a sturdy indoor mat for wiping feet.

GASES

There are a number of gases that present health hazards in the built environment. Because they are inhalable, and therefore enter the blood quickly, the content of gases can be circulated throughout the body in seconds. This makes them particularly dangerous, especially because many gases have no odor or color and, therefore, may be undetectable.

CARBON MONOXIDE

Carbon monoxide (CO) is an odorless, colorless gas that is a by-product of the incomplete burning of fuels containing carbon. Sources of indoor carbon monoxide include unvented or

FIGURE 4.10 Adding a mudroom near an entrance makes it easy for occupants to remove dirty boots and shoes that would otherwise track soil and pollutants onto interior floors. This is especially important in homes that are carpeted.

leaking combustion appliances such as space heaters, water heaters, and kitchen stoves; leaking or poorly maintained chimneys, furnaces, and boilers; back drafting from furnaces, woodstoves, and fireplaces; car exhaust from attached garages; and mainstream cigarette smoke (exhaled directly from the smoker). Poor ventilation, in part due to tightly sealed, energy-efficient buildings, contributes to the buildup of carbon monoxide. The fact that windows in many modern buildings do not open contributes to the problem of inadequate air exchange (Morgan, 2003).

No standards for safe levels of CO have been agreed upon for indoor air, although the U.S. National Ambient Air Quality Standards for outdoor air are 9 ppm, 40,000 micrograms per cubic meter for 8 hours, or 35 ppm for 1 hour (U.S. Environmental Protection Agency, 2007, "Carbon Monoxide").

Effects of Carbon Monoxide on Humans

Carbon monoxide is an asphyxiant, meaning that it reduces the level of oxygen in the body to dangerous levels. It does this by attaching to the hemoglobin in the blood and preventing it from transporting oxygen throughout the body. Carbon monoxide poisoning may cause more than 50 percent of the fatal poisonings reported in many countries, although it is suspected that the number is actually higher because of underreporting (U.S. Environmental Agency, 2006, "Carbon Monoxide Poisoning"). People who are especially sensitive to high levels of carbon monoxide include fetuses, the elderly, and individuals with cardiovascular and pulmonary (lung) diseases (U.S. Environmental Agency, 1994, "Indoor Air Pollution").

Symptoms of carbon monoxide poisoning include fatigue; headache; dizziness; nausea and vomiting; impairment of perception, memory, and judgment; and an abnormally fast heart rate. The severity of the symptoms depends on the level of the concentration of the gas. At very high concentrations, carbon monoxide poisoning is fatal. It is often difficult for health-care providers to diagnose carbon monoxide poisoning because many of the less severe symptoms are similar to those of the flu. Two clues that can indicate that carbon monoxide poisoning is the problem are that (1) a group of people who share the same indoor environment suffer the symptoms at the start of the heating season, when carbon monoxide is produced, and (2) the symptoms persist

even when those people have received medical treatment (U.S. Environmental Agency, 1994, "Indoor Air Pollution"). These clues can also lead to the mistaken conclusion that the flu—not carbon monoxide poisoning—is the culprit, given that the flu season occurs during the winter, when more heating is used.

Implications for Designers

When remodeling kitchens and/or replacing appliances, designers could suggest that electric stoves might be a better choice than gas. If gas stoves are installed, they should have electric starters, rather than pilot lights, because about one-third of the stove's carbon monoxide emissions are from the pilot lights (Tate, 1994). Efficient exhaust fans should always be installed over gas stoves. (See Figure 4.11.) Adequate venting for space heaters and other appliances must be provided. Surprisingly, 520,000 unvented gas heaters and fireplaces were sold in the United States in 1995 (Bower, 2001). When possible, designers should make sure to isolate gas furnaces and hot water heaters in a separate closed room or outside the living area. If clients request woodstoves, designers can choose models that are appropriate for the size of the living area and are certified to meet EPA standards, as discussed in Chapter 6 (U.S. Environmental Protection Agency, 1995, "The Inside Story"). The walls between garages and the interior living spaces should be sealed and ventilated so that vehicle exhaust does not enter the living space. Particular care should be taken when building second-story living spaces over garages, as with the popular "bonus rooms" that are added as offices or guest rooms.

Carbon monoxide sensors and alarms are recommended for all homes that have combustion fireplaces, woodstoves, and gas appliances. They are also recommended for people who burn candles frequently (Bower, 2001). The Consumer Product Safety Commission recommends installing a CO detector/alarm that meets the requirements of the current UL standard 2034 or the requirements of the IAS 6-96 standard (Consumer Product Safety Commission, n.d., "Carbon Monoxide"). Since 1993, Chicago and

FIGURE 4.11 Gas stoves should have adequate exhaust fans to prevent the buildup of carbon monoxide in the living space.

several other cities have adopted ordinances requiring the installation of CO detectors/alarms in all new single-family homes and in existing single-family residences that have new oil or gas furnaces (Consumer Product Safety Commission, n.d., "Carbon Monoxide").

NITROGEN DIOXIDE

Nitrogen dioxide is a toxic gas produced by kerosene heaters, unvented gas stoves, heaters, and tobacco smoke. It causes eye, nose, and throat irritation and can cause impaired lung function and increased respiratory infections in young children (U.S. Environmental Protection Agency, 2006, "Indoor Air Quality"). Prevention involves providing proper vents and, in the case of cigarette smoke, creating well-ventilated spaces for smokers that are away from the spaces used by nonsmokers.

RADON

Radon is a naturally occurring radioactive gas that results as part of the cycle of uranium decay (breakdown): uranium breaks down into radium, which in turn breaks down into radon. Found in the soil in most parts of the country, radon is odorless, colorless, and tasteless, so there can be exposure without detection. In addition to soil, well water can be contaminated. Certain building products, such as stone, can contain very small amounts of uranium and radium, which then release radon. Radon can also be emitted as a by-product of combustion.

Radon enters living spaces through holes in the foundation of structures and diffusion through concrete. (See Figure 4.12.) The most concentrated source results when air pressure is lower in the living space, caused by leaks such as chimneys, exhaust fans, and central heating, than in the outside. That pressure moves from high to low, so the radon is pulled into the structure (Bower, 2001). It is estimated that nearly one out of every fifteen homes in the United States has elevated radon levels (U.S. Environmental Protection Agency, 2005, "A Citizen's Guide"). Stated another way, the EPA

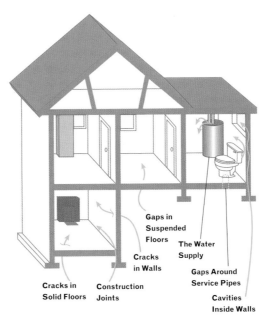

FIGURE 4.12 Radon is present in many parts of the U.S. and can enter the interior at many points in the structure. This is why the EPA recommends that homeowners test for the presence of radon.

estimates that as many as 6 million homes in the United States have elevated levels of radon (U.S. Environmental Protection Agency, 1994, "Indoor Air Pollution"). Radon can be a problem in any type of built structure, including schools, day-care facilities, and workplaces.

Effects of Radon on Humans

Outdoors, radon is diluted in the air and does not usually pose a problem. When it becomes concentrated indoors, tiny alpha particles are inhaled and penetrate the lining of the lungs. The energy released by these particles as they continue to break down is what damages the lungs. The EPA estimates that 21,000 lung cancer deaths per year are caused by radon,

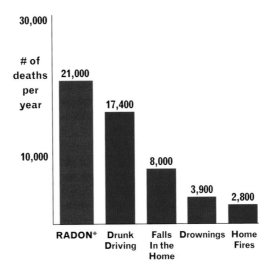

FIGURE 4.13 Lung cancer caused by radon is a major cause of death in the U.S. Exposure to radon in the home can be prevented by performing a simple test and taking steps to prevent its entry.

making it the second leading cause of lung cancer, as shown in Figure 4.13 (U.S. Environmental Protection Agency, 2005, "A Citizen's Guide"). Smokers who are exposed to radon have an especially high risk of developing lung cancer.

Implications for Designers

Any home can have a radon problem; it is not confined to older, drafty homes. Even new houses, built to be radon-resistant, can have unacceptably high levels (EPA, 9/05. Citizen's Guide to Radon). The presence of radon can be detected only by testing, therefore, the EPA and the Surgeon General recommend testing below the third level for all homes and residential facilities. It is especially important to test if a basement is to be finished or remodeled and used as a living space, because this area is where radon concentrations are likely to be highest.

The EPA also recommends testing in schools. Although testing is easy and inexpensive, state-certified measurement devices should be used. Kits from the National Safety Council can be ordered for as little as $10. Amounts of radon vary, so the testing should be done over an extended period of time.

The EPA recommends taking remedial action if radon measures at 4 picoCuries per liter (a picoCurie is a measurement of radioactivity) or higher. If there are problems, professionals should be hired to seal cracks and holes in the foundation and install a vent pipe system and fan under the house to pull the gas out of the structure. Radon contractors can advise on the best approach to eliminate radon, using criteria such as the entry points of the gas, the pressure inside the structure, and the climate. There are also companies that sell specialized products, such as fans and sealants. In living spaces, ventilation through open windows and/or exhaust fans can be used to move the gas to the outdoors.

OZONE

Ozone is an interesting gas because it can be either "good" or "bad." Good ozone exits in the stratosphere, the atmospheric layer that ex-

tends upward from about 6 to 30 miles above the earth's surface, where it protects life from the ultraviolet rays of the sun. When ozone accumulates near the earth's surface it is considered bad because of its negative effects on human health. Formed from chemical reactions between nitrogen oxide and volatile organic compounds, ozone causes a number of respiratory problems whose severity depends on the concentration of ozone and the length of exposure.

Sources of the components of ozone are from everyday activities:

- Nitrogen oxides
  - 56 percent motor vehicles
  - 22 percent utilities
  - 17 percent industrial, commercial, and residential combustion
  - 5 percent other
- Volatile organic compounds
  - 50 percent industrial and commercial processes
  - 45 percent motor vehicles
  - 5 percent consumer solvents (U.S. Environmental Protection Agency, 2006, "Ozone")

High temperatures, such as those occurring during the summer months, increase the levels of ozone concentrations in the air. Because ozone can be carried long distances by the wind, many areas of the United States, both urban and rural, experience unhealthy levels of ozone.

Effects of Ozone on Humans

Exposure to even small amounts of ozone can result in serious respiratory irritation and even death. At exposures of 0.25 to 0.75 ppm, otherwise healthy individuals can experience coughing, shortness of breath, tightness of the chest, a feeling of inability to breathe, dry throat, wheezing, headache, and nausea. When the levels of concentration are over 1.0 ppm, the symptoms are more severe and include reduced lung function, extreme fatigue, dizziness, inability to sleep and concentrate, and a bluish discoloration of the skin (Canadian Centre for Occupational Health & Safety, 1998). Repeated exposure can result in permanent lung damage, and extremely high levels can result in accumulation of fluid in the lungs, a condition that can be fatal.

In addition to the symptoms listed above, exposure to ozone seems to cause bronchial hyperresponsiveness, which means the airways become more reactive to other irritating substances. This is why breathing ozone is especially serious for people, especially children, with asthma.

Implications for Designers

It is possible to determine regional levels of ozone by checking the Web site www.airnow.gov. Many newspapers and local weather reports also list their area's ozone levels. If clients live in regions with high ozone levels, it is important that they limit heavy outdoor physical activity. For those with existing respiratory problems, they should avoid exposure as much as possible. In these cases, designers can create indoor spaces for exercise and play to be used during ozone alerts. They can also advise clients about ways to lower their energy consumption to prevent the introduction of components that create the "bad" type of ozone. (Chapter 6 discusses many energy-saving strategies.) Finally, designers can suggest the use of low-VOC paints and solvents. In areas with very high summer ozone levels, the use of electric, rather than gas-powered lawn mowers and gardening equipment, could also be a wise choice.

GLOSSARY TERMS

Asbestos
Bacteria
Carbon monoxide
Contaminant
Decay
Dose
Formaldehyde
Fungi
Immune-system sensitizer
Lead
Microbial volatile organic compound (mVOC)
Mold
Mycotoxin

Outgassing
Ozone
Pollutant
Radon
Sink effect
Spores
Synergism
Threshold limit values
Toxicity
Viruses
Volatile organic compounds

LEARNING ACTIVITIES

1. Collect resources listing professionals and products available in your area that help with the following interior contaminant problems: asbestos, lead, and mold removal; radon and carbon monoxide testing; and rodent and insect extermination. What kind of certifications and training do the professionals have? What type(s) of methods do they use? Are there products available that will not result in other health problems, as in the case of certain pesticides?

2. Design a bedroom for a woman who is allergic to dust mite droppings. Include illustrations or photos of appropriate furnishings, decorative items, and a written description of the flooring, window coverings, and bedding you have chosen.

3. Develop a list of criteria for garbage, recycling, and storage areas that will deter rodents, the growth of bacteria, and so on, for the kitchen, garage, and basement. Find appropriate products that can be purchased or constructed to meet your criteria.

4. Research companies that manufacture low-VOC emitting products, such as cabinets without particleboard made with formaldehyde and low-VOC paints. Are these items available at common big-box stores or must they be special ordered? How wide is the selection of products? How do the prices compare with more traditional products?

5. Design a play/exercise area suitable for a family of two adults and three young children. Include space for age-

appropriate physical activities the family can enjoy indoors when pollution levels make it dangerous to perform them outdoors. Include space for storing toys and equipment and a description of how the space can be sustainably modified as the children grow older.

6. Collect ideas for flooring that can be used instead of carpeting. Create an information sheet for each that includes illustrations; rooms in which each would be most appropriate; advantages and disadvantages; caring for the floor; and price ranges for the product, installation, and maintenance.

SUGGESTED WEB SITES

1. Asbestos Resource Center
www.asbestosresource.com
This site contains general information about asbestos, including its history and related diseases, plus links to many other asbestos resources.

2. U.S. Environmental Protection Agency
www.epa.gov
The home page for the EPA has links to Web pages with information about many contaminants related to the built environment, including asbestos, hazardous waste, lead, mercury, mold, ozone, and pesticides, as well as news reports and current information about environmental issues.

3. U.S. Environmental Protection Agency
Guide to Chemical, Pesticide and Toxicology Web Sites.
www.epa.gov/oppt/library/pubs/
publicpaths/toxsites/toxsites.htm
This site contains links to dozens of informative Web sites specific to chemical contaminants and includes self-guided tutorials about environmental health.

4. U.S. Environmental Protection Agency
Indoor Air Pollution: An Introduction for Health Professionals

www.epa.gov/iaq/pubs/hpguide.html
Although written for health professionals, this is a reader-friendly publication featuring recommendations for remedial actions for removing pollutants that are applicable for interior designers.

5. U.S. Environmental Protection Agency
A Citizen's Guide to Radon: The Guide to Protecting Yourself and Your Family From Radon
www.epa.gov/radon/pubs/citguide.html

6. Mayo Clinic
www.mayoclinic.com
The Clinic's Web site has articles on a wide variety of medical conditions, including those related to contaminants.

7. National Lead Information Center
U.S. Environmental Protection Agency
www.eap.gov/lead/pubs/nlic.htm
This Web page provides contacts for requesting information about lead hazards and their prevention.

8. American Industrial Hygiene Association (AIHA)
www.aiha.org
This site contains information about industrial hygiene and indoor air quality issues including mold hazards and legal issues related to contaminants.

9. American Lung Association
www.healthhouse.org/index.asp
This site contains information about healthy houses, including a room-by-room identification of health hazards and suggested home maintenance schedules.

10. American Lung Association
www.lungusa.org/site/pp.asp?c=
dvLUK9O0E&b=23033
Online booklet available: "How to Read a Material Safety Data Sheet."

11. National Institute for Occupational Safety and Health
www.cdc.gov/niosh/npg
This site contains the NIOSA Pocket Guide to Chemical Hazards, which has key information on several hundred chemicals as well as classifications of chemicals found in the work environment.

12. National Institute for Occupational Safety and Health
www.cdc.gov/niosh/topics/hazards.html
Browse the Occupational Safety and Health Topics for links to information about dozens of topics such as asbestos, pesticides, and allergies.

13. East Carolina University
www.ecu.edu/oehs/LabSafety/ReadMSDS.htm
Learn to read a Material Safety Data Sheet on this site.

14. National Library of Medicine
http://householdproducts.nlm.nih.gov/index.htm
The Household Products Database includes health information and warnings about thousands of commonly used products.

REFERENCES

Agocs, M. M.; Etzel, R. A.; Parrish, R. G.; Paschal, D. C.; Campagna, P. R.; Cohen, D. S.; Kilbourne, E. M.; and Hesse, J. L. (1990). Mercury exposure from latex interior paint. *The New England Journal of Medicine, 323*, 1096–11011.

American Industrial Hygiene Association. (Last updated February 14, 2006). *Is Lead a Problem in My Home?* Retrieved March 3, 2006, from www.aiha.org/Content/AccessInfo/consumer/IsLeadaProbleminMyHome.htm.

American Industrial Hygiene Association. (Last updated October 20, 2006). *The Facts About Mold*. Retrieved March 16, 2006, from www.aiha.org/Content/AccessInfo/consumer/factsaboutmold.htm.

Asbestos Resource Center. (2003–2006.) *What is asbestos?* Retrieved March 2, 2006, from www.asbestosresource.com/asbestos.

Asbestos Resource Center. (2003–2006.) *History of asbestos.* Retrieved March 2, 2006, from www.asbestosresource.com/history.

Asbestos Resource Center. (2003–2006). *Mesothelioma cancer.* Retrieved March 2, 2006, from www.asbestosresource.com/mesothelioma.

Bower, J, (2001). *The Healthy House: How to Buy One, How to Build One, How to Cure a Sick One (4th ed).* Bloomington, IN: The Healthy House Institute.

Canadian Center for Occupational Health and Safety. (January 15, 1998). *Health effects of ozone.* Retrieved June 10, 2007, from www.ccohs.ca/oshanswers/chemicals/chem_profiles/ozone/health_ozo.html.

Centers for Disease Control and Prevention. (n.d.). *About the Childhood Lead Poisoning Prevention Program.* Retrieved March 4, 2006, from www.cdc.gov/nceh/lead/about/program.htm.

Centers for Disease Control and Prevention. (Last updated December 5, 2003). *Food-Related Diseases.* Retrieved May 28, 2006, from www.cdc.gov/ncidod/diseases/food/index.htm.

Centers for Disease Control and Prevention. (n.d.). *Lead.* Retrieved March 4, 2006, from www.cdc.gov/lead.

Centers for Disease Control and Prevention. (July 2005). *Spotlight on Lead.* CDC's Third National Report on Human Exposure to Environmental Chemicals, NCEH Pub 05-0664.

Centers for Disease Control and Prevention. (Last reviewed September 7, 2005). *Questions and Answers on Stachybotrys Chartarum and Other Molds.* Retrieved March 5, 2006, from www.cdc.gov/nceh/airpollution/mold/stacy.htm.

Centers for Disease Control and Prevention, Division of Parasitic Diseases. (Last updated August 19, 2005). *Hot Tub Rash: Pseudomonas Dermatitis.* Retrieved May 28, 2006, from www.cdc.gov/healthyswimming/derm.htm.

Cincinnati Children's Hospital Medical Center. (n.d.). *History of lead advertising: The role of the lead industry in a public health tragedy.* Retrieved March 4, 2006, from www.cincinnatichildrens.org/research/project/enviro/hazard/lead/lead-advertising/industry-role.htm.

Commission on Life Sciences. (2000). *Toxicological Risks of Selected Flame-Retardant Chemicals.* Washington, DC: National Academy Press.

Cone, M. (April 20, 2003). Cause for alarm over chemicals. *Los Angeles Times,* A1, 30, 31.

Consumer Product Safety Commission. (n.d.). *What you should know about lead based paint in your home. Safety alert.* [CPSC Document # 5054] Retrieved March 3, 2006, from www.cpsc.gov/cpscpub/pubs/5054.html.

Consumer Product Safety Commission. (December 15, 1995). *Respiratory Irritation of Carpet Chemicals. Agenda for Meeting on Respiratory Carpet Chemicals* [pdf]. Retrieved July 17, 2006, from www.cpsc.gov/LIBRARY/FOIA/meetings/mtg96/CarpetChem.pdf.

Consumer Product Safety Commission. (April 14, 1998). Flame Retardant Chemicals that May Be Suitable for Use in Upholstered Furniture: Extension of Comment Period. *Federal Register,* 63, 71.

Consumer Product Safety Commission. (n.d.). *An Update on Formaldehyde: 1997 Revision.* Retrieved March 29, 2006, from www.cpsc.gov/cpscpub/pubs/725.html.

Consumer Product Safety Commission. (n.d.). *Carbon Monoxide Questions and Answers.* Retrieved May 18, 2006, from www.cpsc.gov/CPSCPUB/PUBS/466.html.

Consumer Product Safety Commission. (n.d.). *What you should know about lead based paint in your home: Safety alert.* Document # 5054, Bethesda, MD: Consumer Product Safety Commission.

Department of Public Health, City and County of San Francisco. (January 9, 2007). *What has the government done about the hazards of asbestos?* Retrieved January 18, 2007, from www.sfdph.org/eh/asbestos/9Gov_laws.htm.

Etzel, R. and Rylander, R. (June 1999). Indoor mold and children's health, *Journal of Environmental Health Perspectives,* 107, S3, 463.

Illinois Department of Public Health, Prevention and Control. (n.d.). *Mosquitoes and Disease.* Retrieved May 28, 2006, from www.idph.state.il.us/envhealth/pcmosquitoes.htm.

Jaakkola, J. J., Hwang, B. F., and Jaakkola, N. (2005). Home dampness and molds, parental atopy, and asthma in childhood: A six-year population-based cohort study. *Environmental Health Perspectives,* 113 (3), 357–361.

John C. Stennis Space Center. (n.d.). *Environmental Assurance Program.* Retrieved May 5, 2006, from www.ssc.nasa.gov/environmental/docforms/water_research/water_research.html.

Kids Health. (2004). *Blood.* Retrieved March 4, 2006, from www.kidshealth.org/parent/general/body_basics/blood.html.

Laporte, P. B., Elliot, E., and Banta, J. (2001). *Prescriptions for a Healthy House: A Practical Guide for Architects, Builders & Homeowners (2nd ed.).* Gabriola Island, British Columbia, Canada: New Society Publishers.

Lawrence Berkeley Laboratory. (May 24, 2007). Berkeley Lab, EPA studies confirm large public health and economic impact of dampness and mold. *Research News.* [Electronic version]. Retrieved June 6, 2007, from www.lbl.gov/Science-Articles/Archive/EETD-mold-risk.html.

Lead411.org. (n.d.). *Manufacture of white lead pigment.* Retrieved on March, 4, 2006, from www.lead411.org/Templates/history/white_lead_white_pigment.htm.

Lemus, R.; Abdelghani, A. A.; Akers, T. G.; and Horner, W. E. (January–June 1998). Potential health risks from exposure to indoor formaldehyde. *Reviews of Environmental Health,* 13, 91–98.

Lyon, W. E. (May 15, 2006). *Entomology: House Dust Mites.* Fact Sheet, HYG-2157-97, Columbus, OH: Ohio State University Extension.

Mangione, E. J.; Huitt, G.; Lenaway, D.; Beebe, J.; Bailey, A.; Figoski, M.; Rau, M. P.; Albrecht, K. D.; and Yakrus, M. A. (Nov-Dec

2001). Nontuberculous mycobacterial disease following hot tub exposure. *Emerging Infectious Diseases,* 7, 6, 1039–1042.

Mayo Clinic. (May 15, 2005). *Lead Poisoning.* Retrieved March 4, 2006, from www.mayoclinic.com/health/lead-poisoning/FL00068/DSECTION=2.

Mayo Clinic. (November 5, 2004). *Mold Allergy.* Retrieved March 5, 2006, from www.mayoclinic.com/health/mold-allergy/AN00411

Morgan, M. T. (2003). *Environmental Health (3rd ed.).* Belmont, CA: Thomson Wadsworth Learning.

National Academies. (April 27, 2000). *Eight Flame Retardant Chemicals Can Safely Be Used on Upholstered Furniture.* [News Release]. Washington, DC: Author.

National Institute of Environmental Health Sciences. (April 2005). *Lead and Your Health.* [Brochure] Research Triangle Park, NC: National Institute of Environmental Health Sciences.

Rich, D. Q.; Rhodes, G. G.; Wartenberg, D.; and Sweatlock, J. (2001). The effects of home lead abatements on childhood blood lead levels: A retrospective follow-up study. *Journal of Environmental Health,* 63 (10), 9–15.

Schoemaker, J. M., and Vitale, C. Y. (1991). *Healthy Homes, Healthy Kids: Protecting Your Children From Everyday Environmental Hazards.* Washington, DC: Island Press.

Tate, N. (1994). *Sick Building Syndrome: How Indoor Air Pollution Is Poisoning Your Life — And What You Can Do.* Far Hills, NJ: New Horizon Press.

United Nations of Roma Victrix. (n.d.). *Lead.* Retrieved March 4, 2006, from www.unrv.com/economy/lead.php.

U.S. Department of Health and Human Services. (n.d.). *Health Effects of Asbestos.* Retrieved March 3, 2006, from www.atsdr.cdc.gov/asbestos/asbestos/health_effects.

U.S. Environmental Protection Agency. (Summer/Spring1993). Absorption and re-emission of formaldehyde by gypsum wallboard. *Inside IAQ,* #EPA/600/N-93-010.

U.S. Environmental Protection Agency. (Last updated January 11, 2006). *Asbestos.* Re-

trieved March 1, 2006, from www.epa.gov/asbestos/pubs/asbe.pdf.

U.S. Environmental Protection Agency. (n.d.). *Carbon Monoxide.* Retrieved May 25, 2006, from www.epa.gov/iaq/co.html.

U.S. Environmental Protection Agency. (Last updated March 2, 2006). *Indoor Air Quality: Sources of Indoor Air Pollution-Nitrogen Dioxide.* Retrieved May 28, 2006, from www.epa.gov/iaq/no2.html.

U.S. Environmental Protection Agency. (1994). *Indoor air pollution: An introduction for health professionals.* U.S. Government Printing Office Publication, No. 1994-523-217/81322, EPA 402-R-94-007.

U.S. Environmental Protection Agency. (September 1997). *Reducing Lead Hazards When Remodeling Your Home.* EPA Brochure, 747-K-97-001. Washington, DC: U.S. Environmental Protection Agency.

U.S. Environmental Protection Agency. (Spring/Summer 1993). Predicting the behavior of indoor sinks. *Inside IAQ,* 8. #EPA/600/N-93-010.

U.S. Environmental Protection Agency, Indoor Environments Division. (September 2005). *A Citizen's Guide to Radon: The Guide to Protecting Yourself and Your Family From Radon.* [Booklet] Washington, D.C.: U.S. Environmental Protection Agency.

U.S. Environmental Protection Agency Office of Air and Radiation. (October 4, 2006). *Ozone — Good Up High, Bad Nearby.* Washington, D.C.: Author.

U.S. Environmental Protection Agency Office of Air and Radiation Indoor Environments Division. (June 25, 2001). *Mold Remediation in Schools and Commercial Buildings.* Washington, DC: Author.

U.S. Environmental Protection Agency. (September 25, 2006). *Carbon Monoxide Poisoning (sic)—a Public Health Perspective.* Retrieved November 5, 2006, from cfpub2.epa.gov/ncea/cfm/recordisplay.cfm?PrintVersion=True&deid=65703.

U.S. Environmental Protection Agency Region 9: Children's Health. (Last updated November 15, 2006). *Children's Health and*

Polybrominated Diphenyl Ether (PBDE). Retrieved May 5, 2006, from www.epa.gov/docs/region09/cross_pr/childhealth/pbde.html

U.S. Environmental Protection Agency and the United States Consumer Product Safety Commission, Office of Radiation and Indoor Air. (April 1995). *The Inside Story: A Guide to Indoor Air Quality.* EPA Document # 402-K-93-007, (6604J).

University of Alberta, Division of Occupational Health and Chemical Safety (n.d.). *Asbestos Fact Sheet.* Retrieved March 3, 2006, from www.ehs.ualberta.ca/OHCS.

Virta, R. L. (January 2003). *Mineral Commodity Summaries.* Reston, VA: U.S. Geological Survey.

CHAPTER **5**

Indoor Climate

LEARNING OBJECTIVES

1. **Describe the following elements of indoor climate, including how they affect human health and performance:**
   a. **Temperature**
   b. **Air movement**
   c. **Air velocity**
   d. **Relative humidity**
2. **Explain the relationship between indoor air quality and human health.**
3. **List examples of indoor air quality problems, including common pollutants.**
4. **Explain the meaning of building-related illness and sick building syndrome.**
5. **Describe actions interior designers can take to help mitigate indoor air quality problems.**

Good indoor air quality and climate are perhaps the most important elements of the built environment in terms of occupant comfort and health. This is true for two reasons. The first is that factors such as room temperature and the presence of drafts are among the most noticed and, therefore, potentially bothersome, of all indoor environmental factors. People's impressions of the overall comfort of an indoor environment are highly influenced by its climate.

The second reason is that the air we breathe has direct access to nearly all parts of our bodies. Thus the presence of airborne pollutants has an especially high potential for negatively impacting health. The deterioration of indoor air quality in the last few decades provides us with an example of unintended consequences. What began as a positive action—the tightening of buildings and houses to reduce the energy needed to heat and cool them—has resulted in structures lacking the fresh air needed to prevent indoor pollution from reaching unacceptable levels. As stated previously, many experts believe this is contributing to the rising number of cases of allergies and asthma in the United States.

In this chapter we will discuss what factors make up the indoor climate, their effects on human health, and methods of mitigating indoor air quality problems. Designers have an opportunity to help improve indoor climate and air quality and thus make a contribution to improving the health of people of all ages.

TEMPERATURE AND THERMAL COMFORT

People's impressions of thermal conditions in the indoor environment are among the most important in determining their physical comfort. This is because thermal discomfort is stressful and affects both performance and safety (Canadian Centre for Occupational Health and Safety, 2006. OSH Answers: Thermal Comfort for Office Work). Understanding the basics of human body temperature and **thermal regulation**—how the body functions to maintain an optimal temperature—will help designers appreciate the importance of temperature control in the built environment.

The body is divided into two temperature zones: the core and the peripheral. The core consists of the brain's interior, heart, and abdominal organs and its temperature fluctuates a bit around 98.6°F (37°C), which must remain constant for normal body functioning. The muscles, limbs, and the skin, in particular, the peripheral zone, vary in temperature (known as the shell temperature) as the body takes in or gives off heat in order to maintain the core temperature.

Thermoregulatory Activities

The body uses a number of temperature-regulating, or **thermoregulatory** activities. One is based on the principle that energy always flows from the warmer to the colder. You may have noticed that when you are exposed to cold temperatures, your skin feels cold to the touch. This is not because of the transfer of cold from the air onto the skin, but because blood circulation is decreased to the skin's surface in an attempt to maintain heat that would otherwise flow outward from the body. Another body-warming technique is shivering, involuntary, rapid muscular movements that convert muscle energy into heat.

The principle of warm to cool also applies on a hot day, but in the opposite direction: warm blood flows to the surface of the body so that heat can be given off and the core temperature cooled. This additional blood explains why a person's face turns red when exercising on a hot day. The body's most important cooling method is the production of sweat. The purpose of sweat is to place moisture on the skin so that it can be evaporated, a process that requires energy. This energy is supplied in the form of heat that is drawn away from the

body, thus the cooling effect. All of these thermoregulatory mechanisms are controlled by a heat-control center in the brain that receives temperature information from throughout the body (Kroemer & Grandjean, 1997). This control system works continually to maintain a healthy, life-preserving body temperature.

The human body is able to function efficiently within a relatively narrow temperature range, outside of which, several physiological changes take place. The following, for example, occur with a rise in ambient temperature:

1. Slight increase in core temperature and sharp increase in shell temperature
2. Increase in heart rate
3. Increase of blood pressure
4. Reduced activity of the digestive organs
5. Massive increase in blood flow through the skin
6. Increased production of sweat
7. Fatigue (Kroemer & Grandjean, 1997)

The purpose of these physiological activities is to transport heat away from the body's core to the skin. Higher-than-normal amounts of blood move away from the muscles and organs, which explains the feelings of tiredness and nausea, as the stomach refuses food. This leads to reduced physical performance and increased chance of making errors. On the other hand, overcooling can cause restlessness and reduced alertness and concentration, especially on mental tasks. Research has revealed specific examples of the effects of temperature on performance. For example, schoolchildren's performance on reading and comprehension tests was optimum at around 80°F (27°C) (Wyon, 1970). Other studies show that if environments lack air-conditioning, performance is lower on complex task assignments among students (Schoer and Shaffran, 1973). When conditions are too warm, output is reduced among all types of workers.

Temperature not only affects physical comfort and performance but also influences social behavior. Studies have found that people tend to be more irritable and less cooperative and helpful on very hot days (Baron, 1976). Even

violent crime in a select city (Indianapolis) was found to increase with higher temperatures (Cotton, 1986).

Thermal Comfort

Thermal comfort, meaning a person does not feel too warm or too cold, is achieved when body heat exchanges are in a state of balance (Kroemer & Grandjean, 1997). Ideal temperatures that lead to thermal comfort are influenced by people's age, physical condition, metabolic rate (rate of energy used by the body to maintain itself), personal preferences, clothing, and level of activity. Because of these variances, even researchers rely on subjective evaluations (people's opinions) to determine effective temperatures (Kroemer & Grandjean, 1997). A general rule for an office in which light work is performed is a constant temperature between about 69 and 73°F (21–23°C), with slightly higher temperatures advised in warmer seasons to lessen the difference between indoor and outdoor temperatures (Canadian Centre for Occupational Health and Safety, 2006. OSH Answers: Thermal Comfort for Office Work).

Implications for Designers

Although determining thermal comfort can be quite challenging because temperature preferences vary greatly among individuals and there is no one temperature that satisfies everyone (CCOHS, 2006. OSH Answers: Thermal Comfort for Office Work), it is a fact that higher activity levels require lower temperatures to maintain comfort. Muscles produce heat during strenuous effort, becoming several degrees warmer than when they are at rest. The heat produced moves from the muscles into the cooler areas of the body. Thus, the air temperature in an exercise facility such as a gym must be lower than in an office where workers sit at desks most of the day. Even within one

FIGURE 5.1A, B, AND C Many buildings have different zones, which each require a different temperature for optimal human comfort and health. In a health club, for example, the exercise rooms need to be cooler than those in which people are sitting or dressing.

TABLE 5.1 TYPICAL BODILY RESPONSES TO VARIOUS TEMPERATURES

78°F (25.5°C)	Optimal for bathing, showering. Sleep is disturbed.
75°F (23.9°C)	People feel warm, lethargic, and sleepy. Optimal for unclothed people.
72°F (22.2°C)	Most comfortable year-round indoor temperature for sedentary people.
70°F (21.6°C)	Optimal for performance of mental work. Appropriate for children playing on the floor.
65°F (18.3°C)	Sleeping.
64°F (17.8°C)	Physically inactive people begin to shiver. Active people are comfortable.

Adapted from: Canadian Centre for Occupational Health and Safety. (January 9, 2006). OSH answers: *Thermal comfort for office work*. Retrieved January 7, 2007, from www.ccohs.ca/oshanswers/phys_agents/thermal_comfort.html

Morgan, M.T. (2003). *Environmental health* (3rd ed.), Belmont, CA: Thomson Wadsworth.

facility, temperatures might need to be varied. In the gym example, locker rooms should be warmer than the areas in which people use weight machines or take aerobics classes. (See Figure 5.1 a, b, and c.) Table 5.1 lists typical body responses to various temperatures.

Ideally, people within the built structure should be able to adjust temperatures to their own needs. In work environments, having control over the temperature in one's work area is deemed to be an important contributor to work satisfaction. Of course, this can be impractical in buildings in which many people work in the same area. One way to help alleviate this problem is to group people who perform tasks of equal physical effort in a room or area that has its own temperature control (Dul and Weerdmeester, 1993). Within each work area, the preferences of the majority of workers should be considered. That is, if more than half believe that the environment is too warm or too cool, the temperature should be adjusted accordingly.

In a residence, the occupants are likely to be of a variety of ages and physical conditions. Likewise, they will probably engage in different activities and hobbies. For maximum thermal comfort, designers might consider suggesting individual room temperature controls. This is especially helpful when there are residents with special needs. These include infants, who are unable to move about or add and remove

clothing as needed; the elderly, who tend to chill more easily because of decreased blood circulation; and those who are bedridden or severely disabled. Indoor play areas and home gyms may be kept cooler than other rooms in a house or school. Thus, it is important for designers to learn about the intended occupants and the types of activities that will be performed in an environment so that heating and cooling can be planned for accordingly.

Factors That Affect Temperature

The temperature of indoor air, along with perceived comfort levels, are determined by several interrelated factors:

1. Temperature of the air itself
2. Temperature of adjacent surfaces (radiation temperature)
3. Air movement and velocity
4. Relative humidity (Dul & Weerdmeester, 1993; Kroemer & Grandjean, 1997)

Temperatures of Adjacent Surfaces

The initiating temperature of air depends on its source, whether it comes directly from the outdoors through openings such as windows or is warmed or cooled by heating and air-conditioning equipment. The **effective (perceived) temperature** of a room is the average between the air and the adjoining surfaces. These surfaces, such as walls and windows, often are considerably colder or warmer than the ambient indoor air. The heat or cold they give off is called radiation. The difference in temperature between ambient air and radiant surfaces should be small, not more than 2 to 3°C higher or lower (Kroemer & Grandjean, 1997).

Implications for Designers The inner surfaces of glass can be several degrees cooler (or warmer) than the desired temperature of a room. Therefore, it is important in new construction and remodeling projects to carefully plan the type and placement of large windows so that people are not subjected to the radiant effects of hot and cold surfaces. Large windows, as shown in Figure 5.2, are frequently the reason for large amounts of heat loss; when this is a problem in existing buildings, thermal insulation is recommended (Kroemer and Grandjean, 1997). Another measure is to use coverings that admit light but block the cold.

Uninsulated walls can also be culprits in turning a room with a normally appropriate temperature into one that its occupants perceive as uncomfortable. Thus, adequate insulation is an important way to prevent unwanted radiation. As with windows, a good strategy is to locate workstations and furnishings so they are not close to surfaces whose temperatures, especially cold ones, cannot be controlled. In extreme cases, cold surfaces can be screened off from the main work or living area.

An outside surface that can significantly affect indoor temperatures is the roof. White and light-colored roofs reflect heat, while dark ones absorb heat. Another consideration is the ground surfaces that surround a structure. The use of blacktop, for example, will have a warming effect as heat is absorbed during the day, providing very warm adjacent surfaces. When used close to buildings, it can be a source of uncomfortably high temperatures. (See Figure 5.3.)

A different but significant source of radiant heat is the human body, which is exothermic (it gives off heat). In addition, the body emits electromagnetic waves that are absorbed by other objects and converted into heat that is then released into the air. This explains why a room filled with people is warmer and stuffier than an empty room. Therefore, an important consideration for designers is the number of people that will typically be using a space. Without this information, it is difficult to correctly calculate the heating and cooling requirements. Proper planning is essential for work environments, especially when remodeling projects will change the overall needs of the system.

Thermal Conduction

Thermal conduction, the flow of heat through a substance from a warm to a cooler region, is another important design consideration. Metal, for example, is a good conductor, so when touched, it pulls heat away from the body. This is why it feels cold. Wood, on the other hand, has less conductivity so it feels warmer to the touch.

Implications for Designers Designers must consider the conductivity of materials used in furnishings, flooring, and any other items that come into contact with the body. Although sleek metal tables and chairs might look fashionable, they can also cause thermal discomfort by either becoming too hot (if sitting in the sun), or too cold (if sitting in room

FIGURE 5.2 Windows are desirable for natural views and daylighting, but they can be major sources of heat gain and loss of room air temperature.

FIGURE 5.3 This Canadian business park building uses a combination of trees and light outdoor surfaces to prevent overheating. This is especially important in modern structures that employ large surfaces of glass.

temperature or cooler). This is especially true in settings such as restaurants or waiting areas in which customers will spend prolonged periods of time seated.

Air Movement and Velocity

Air movement affects perceived temperature because of convection, the exchange of body heat with the surrounding air. Under normal conditions, convection accounts for about 30 percent of total heat exchange of the body. When air moves across the skin, it increases the speed at which heat leaves the body. This is why moving air, such as from a fan, feels pleasant when temperatures are uncomfortably high. It follows that the greater the air's velocity, the more the cooling effect. In addition to affecting the temperature of a room, moving air can also be perceived as providing freshness and pleasantness to the breathing air (Fountain and Arens, 1993).

In addition to being moved mechanically, such as by fans, air circulation throughout a structure is affected by air pressure. (See Figure 5.4.) For example, if a clothes dryer vent pulls air from a room, the overall air pressure in that room will be lowered. When this happens, there will be a difference in pressure between the laundry room and the adjoining rooms. Air will move naturally into areas of lower pressure, in this case the laundry room. You may have had the experience of opening a door to a room and having the door on the opposite side slam shut. This is because of a change in air pressure: air leaves through the door you open, thus lowering the pressure. The pressure in the room on the opposite side of the second door is higher, so it pushes on that door.

Implications for Designers Moving air can also create discomfort. Examples include when the ambient temperature is "just right" and moving air lowers the temperature at the skin's surface; when the ambient air is already on the cool side; and when the air currents themselves are too cool. This is why cold drafts are uncomfortable and why weatherization techniques, such as seals around doors and windows, add to the comfort of homes and buildings in cold climates. The heating, ventilation, and air-conditioning (HVAC) systems in buildings will cause some air movement as air is removed and added to rooms through ducts. This is why it is important to locate air ducts so that air is not blown directly onto people. If ducts have already been installed, designers should arrange furnishings so they're out of the line of air movement. An important thing to remember is that seated people, such as those who are doing precise tasks or mental work, tend to be more uncomfortable with drafts. Therefore, the locations of vents and furnishings in offices should be carefully designed to

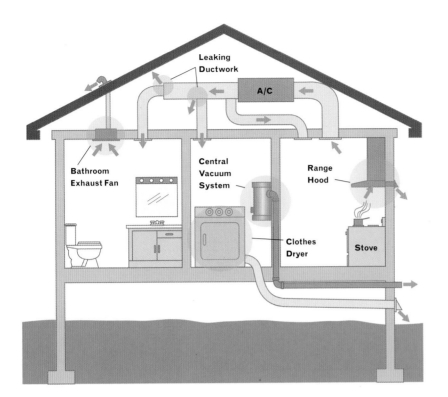

prevent even low-speed drafts (Kroemer and Grandjean, 1997).

Air circulation can be helpful in preventing air from becoming stale and overheated. But it can also create drafts and move undesirable smells throughout a building. This is why exhaust fans placed at the origin of odor- and pollutant-producing activities are important.

It is not only the speed of airflow but also its direction and the parts of the body affected that influence how it is perceived. One researcher studying this issue discovered that currents from the back are more unpleasant than those coming from the front, and the neck and feet are particularly sensitive to drafts (Fanger, 1972).

Air Movement Standards

Setting standards for acceptable levels of air movement in office environments started in the early 1900s; drafts were reported as the most frequent cause of complaints about heating systems (Fountain and Arens, 1993). Current standards, even those set by the American Society of Heating, Refrigerating, and Air-Conditioning Engineers, Inc. (ASHRAE) (see Box 5.1), might not always be appropriate

for specific situations. Researchers have found a wide range of results when comparing the comfort achieved when combining different air speeds with various temperatures (Fountain and Arens, 1993). For example, while one source suggests that air moving more than 10 inches per second will usually be perceived as unpleasant (Kroemer and Grandjean, 1997), another source states that this speed can be twice that at 20 inches per second (Fanger, 1972).

BOX 5.1   ASHRAE STANDARDS

The American Society of Heating, Refrigeration, and Air-Conditioning Engineers, Inc., is a professional organization that develops and updates standards related to indoor climate. The standards are only enforceable if a local or state entity adopts them in their building codes, but they often are used voluntarily.

Standard #	Title
55	Thermal Environmental Conditions for Human Occupancy
A90	Energy Management
62	Ventilation for Acceptable Air Indoor Air Quality
111	Measurement, Testing, Adjusting, and Balancing of Heating, Ventilation, and Air-conditioning Systems

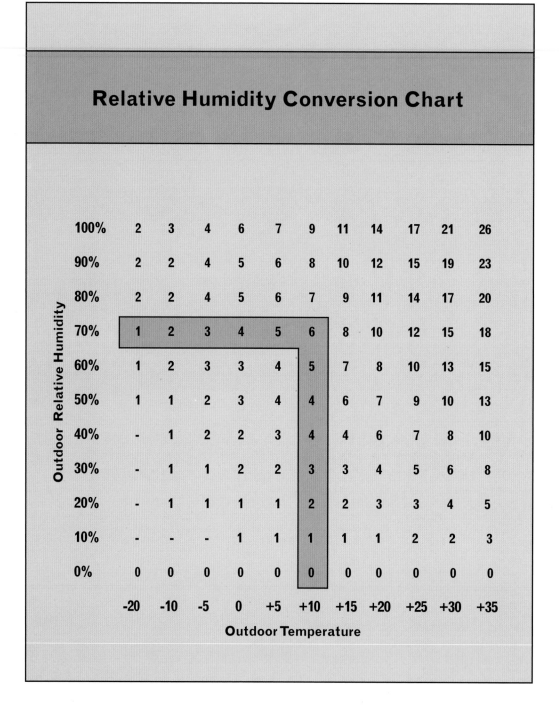

Relative Humidity Conversion Chart

Outdoor Relative Humidity	-20	-10	-5	0	+5	+10	+15	+20	+25	+30	+35
100%	2	3	4	6	7	9	11	14	17	21	26
90%	2	2	4	5	6	8	10	12	15	19	23
80%	2	2	4	5	6	7	9	11	14	17	20
70%	1	2	3	4	5	6	8	10	12	15	18
60%	1	2	3	3	4	5	7	8	10	13	15
50%	1	1	2	3	4	4	6	7	9	10	13
40%	-	1	2	2	3	4	4	6	7	8	10
30%	-	1	1	2	2	3	3	4	5	6	8
20%	-	1	1	1	1	2	2	3	3	4	5
10%	-	-	-	1	1	1	1	1	2	2	3
0%	0	0	0	0	0	0	0	0	0	0	0

Outdoor Temperature

In other studies, the disparities are even larger between recommended conditions (Fountain and Arens, 1993).

Relative Humidity

When water is in a gaseous state, called vapor, it spreads out through the air, a process that results in **humidity.** The amount of moisture that air can hold depends on its temperature: the higher its temperature, the more moisture it can hold. (See Figure 5.5.) **Relative humidity** (RH) is the ratio of the amount of water vapor in the air at a specific temperature to the maximum amount that the air can hold at that temperature. Relative humidity is expressed as a percentage. For example, if the humidity is 80 percent, this means that the air is 80 percent "full" of moisture; once it reaches 100 percent, the moisture "falls out" of the air as rain or fog. Recommended indoor humidity levels range from 30 to 70 percent. Because temperature and humidity levels are related, the relative humidity levels that cause perceptions of room "stuffiness" vary with air temperature. For example, at 64°F, a relative humidity of 80 percent will have the same effect as a relative humidity of 60 percent at 75°F.

The effect of humidity on humans is related to the body's most important method of cooling itself: perspiration. This moisture is not designed to cool the body; it is to enable the cooling effects of evaporation. Under normal circumstances, the average person releases about one quart of moisture each day, a natural process called **insensible perspiration** (Kroemer and Grandjean, 1997). This perspiration accounts for about one-third of the body's daily loss of heat (Kroemer and Grandjean, 1997). **Reflex sweating,** the body's response to uncomfortably high temperatures, happens in addition to insensible perspiration. The effectiveness of sweat in cooling is related to relative humidity in this way: if the air is already highly saturated with moisture, it cannot take on more moisture through evaporation. Even if it can, the process is much slower than it would be at a lower relative humidity. In a sense, it is already "full up." This is why high temperatures in humid climates are especially uncomfortable: not only is it hot but the body's main line of defense against excessive heat is impaired.

In addition to making high temperatures feel uncomfortable, humidity levels have other effects on the body. When levels are very low, for example, the mucous membranes in the nasal passages and bronchi become dry. The condition of these mucus membranes is important because they are part of the body's first line of defense against infection. Mucus traps not only pathogens but also inhaled particles that can irritate the lungs. When there is too little mucus to perform these functions, the results can be coughing, increased allergic reactions, and respiratory infections. Adding to the problem, very dry air also decreases the effectiveness of the cilia, making them less able to sweep dust and other particulates out of the lungs. Finally,

very low humidity can cause the eyes to become dry and irritated; the skin (especially on the hands) to crack; and static electricity to increase, resulting in small but irritating crackles and shocks when energy is discharged. Indoor relative humidity is obviously affected by the humidity of the outdoor air that is brought inside during ventilation. It is also influenced by heating systems that, by their very nature, tend to dry the air. This is why indoor dryness tends to be more of a problem in winter than in summer.

Humidifiers

Humidifiers are devices that add moisture to the air. There are several types; each works in a different way:

1. Ultrasonic: creates a cool mist by means of ultrasonic (too high for humans to hear) sound waves.
2. Impeller: creates a cool mist by means of a high-speed rotating disk (often referred to as "cool-mist humidifiers").
3. Evaporative: uses a fan to blow air through a moistened absorbent material.
4. Steam vaporizer: creates steam by heating water, then cooling the steam before it leaves the machine (U.S. Environmental Protection Agency, 2006. "Indoor Air Facts").
5. Flow-through evaporative cooler: blows air across metal or fiberglass plates through which water runs (Bower, 2001).

Humidifiers can present problems more serious than those posed by low relative humidity. The standing water in most types can become a breeding ground for biological contaminants (U.S. Environmental Protection Agency, 1995, "The Inside Story"), which are then blown into the air. Another problem is that water typically contains minerals and, as is the case with microorganisms, they become airborne and inhaled into the lungs. In addition to reaching the breathing zones, minerals settle in the humidifiers themselves and form scale, crusty deposits that can harbor microorganisms.

Several illnesses have been linked to the use of humidifiers. Hypersensitivity pneumonitis, for example, is an inflammation of the lungs caused by exposure to an allergen. Humidifier fever is a specific type of hypersensitivity pneumonitis. As its name implies, it is caused by the inhalation of contaminants, including mold, fungus, and bacteria, released by stagnant water in humidifiers. Symptoms include cough, fever, chills, shortness of breath, and malaise (feeling ill). This condition can become chronic and result in scarring of the lungs if exposure continues over a long period of time. The bacteria that causes Legionnaires' disease has also been associated with cool-mist vaporizers, including those found in grocery store produce areas.

Implications for Designers   The health risks associated with humidifiers have prompted some building experts to recommend that measures such as sealing a structure against incoming air, a common cause of low humidity, be tried before using a humidifier (Bower, 2001). If a decision is made to use a humidifier, the following information can be used to help prevent the introduction of biological pollutants into the air:

1. Ultrasonic and impeller types appear to produce the greatest dispersions of microorganisms and minerals (U.S. Environmental Agency, 2006, "Indoor Air Facts"),

so consideration might be given to avoiding them.
2. Systems based on recirculated air are not recommended (Baechler et al., 1991).
3. Installing drains to take away runoff water can prevent problems presented by standing water.
4. Steam is a good source of moisture because the heat kills microorganisms.
5. Equipment, especially drip pans, must be properly cleaned, disinfected, and maintained. If ultrasonic or cool-mist humidifiers are used, it is especially important that they are cleaned according to the manufacturer's recommendations and refilled with fresh water daily (U.S. Environmental Protection Agency, 1995, "The Inside Story").

When indoor humidity becomes too high for comfort, there are several possible remedies. For example, air-conditioning often alleviates the problem because the resulting cool air holds less water vapor than warm air. Fans can also provide some relief because the moving air carries heat away from the body's surface and also increases the rate of evaporation of moisture on the skin. If these methods do not solve the problem, a **dehumidifier** can be used to remove moisture from the air by means of a refrigeration system. The water removed from the air is transferred into a tank that must be emptied periodically, unless it has an automatic drain system. (See Figure 5.6.) Most dehumidifiers work within an approximate range of 64 to 90°F (18 to 32°C) and 40 to 95 percent relative humidity. Some models are made to function at lower temperatures, making them suitable for use in basements.

Portable dehumidifiers are available, as well as central types that can be used either as a stand-alone unit in one room or installed as part of an overall heating/cooling system to dehumidify the entire house or building. Dehumidifiers are generally healthier to use than humidifiers because they don't blow potentially contaminated moisture or air into the environment. Because they do contain reservoirs of water collected from the air, they can be the source of molds and other microorganisms. As mentioned previously, they must be emptied regularly (for larger or central units, a drain can be installed) and kept clean.

Implications for Designers

Interior designers are not expected to have the knowledge base of heating and air-conditioning engineers. They should be aware of the various interrelated conditions that contribute to a comfortable indoor climate. For example, it may be helpful to be aware of the following recommendations for sedentary office workers:

- Summer air temperatures between 68 and 75.2°F (20 and 24°C)
- Winter air temperatures between 68 and 69.8°F (20 and 21°C)
- Surface and air temperature differences between 3.6 and 5.4°F and no more than 7.2°F (2 or 3°C, no more than 4°C)
- Relative humidity in summer between 40 and 60 percent
- Relative humidity in winter not below 30 percent
- Air movement between head and knees not more than 8 inches per second (Dul and Weerdmeester, 1993)

It is important to remember that the perception of indoor climate is largely a matter of individual preferences. In spite of the many studies done, along with the development of measurements, equations, and charts, the stated needs of clients should be given the most weight when planning the various aspects of indoor climate. And because there will rarely be consensus about the "right temperature," "right airflow," and "right humidity," designers should look for ways to accommodate the needs of as many people as possible. Such strategies might include personal fans, operable windows, and in the workplace, allowing employees to choose the location of their workspaces in positions that they find most comfortable.

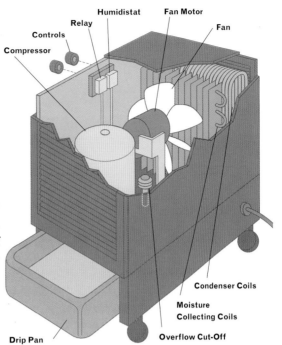

Controls · Compressor · Relay · Humidistat · Fan Motor · Fan · Condenser Coils · Moisture Collecting Coils · Overflow Cut-Off · Drip Pan

FIGURE 5.6 Dehumidifiers use a fan to pull moist air onto condenser coils. Here moisture deposits just as it does on the outside of a cold glass of water set out on a warm day. The resulting water drips into a holding container. The best systems have automatic drains to prevent the problems associated with standing water.

INDOOR AIR QUALITY

In recent decades, outdoor air quality and pollution have received a great deal of attention. Indoor air quality (IAQ), also called indoor environmental quality (IEQ), may well have an even greater influence on human health because most people spend a much larger percentage of their time indoors than out (U.S. Environmental Protection Agency, 1995, "The Inside Story"). The fact is that IAQ may be the single most important aspect of the indoor environment in terms of our well-being. This is because breathing is our most significant interaction with the environment (Tate, 1994). Everything we inhale has a direct path from the outside of the body to the deepest respiratory recesses in the lungs, making the respiratory system the most common entryway for the pathogens that cause 80 percent of all infections (Neighbors, 1999). Examples of the diseases transmitted via indoor air are listed in Table 5.2. Even worse, tens of thousands of deaths each year are attributable to indoor air pollutants. For example, radon is responsible for about 21,000 lung cancer deaths each year and secondhand smoke kills about 3,000 people (U.S. Environmental Protection Agency, 2007, "Health Risks").

TABLE 5.2 INFECTIOUS DISEASES TRANSMITTED VIA INDOOR AIR

ORGANISM	DISEASES
Bacterial	Anthrax Brucellosis (undulant fever) Streptococcal pneumonia Tuberculosis
Viral	Common cold Chicken pox Influenza Measles (rubella)
Fungal	Blastomycosis (refers to infection with any yeast) Coccidioidomycosis (respiratory infection caused by spores of a specific fungus) Histoplasmosis (systemic disease caused by a specific fungus)
Protozoal	Cryptosporidiosis (infection caused by a specific protozoa) Pneumonia

The lungs contain about 500 million or so tiny air sacs made of single-layer tissue, through which oxygen and carbon dioxide are exchanged between the lungs and the blood. This means that inhaled molecules of gases and microscopic particles, such as bacteria and viruses, can easily be transferred to the blood, which then carries them throughout the body. This is why inhaled substances, such as toxic gases, can do serious damage even with short-term exposures (Dul and Weerdmeester, 1993).

In addition to causing infections and illnesses, polluted air can irritate and permanently damage the lungs. For example, asbestos fibers, discussed in Chapter 4, can damage the lungs through their very presence. Other pollutants, such as pet dander, can cause asthma attacks. The average person, doing moderate activity, breathes close to 20,000 liters of air each day; this large amount of air provides many opportunities for inhaling pollutants. (See Table 5.3 for breathing rates at different activities.) As the table indicates, jogging near a busy highway may be more harmful than helpful to a person's health because runners could inhale large quantities of auto exhaust containing carbon monoxide. Thus, designers for urban clients who want to exercise should look for ways to provide indoor areas, free from harmful air pollutants, that are suitable for physical activities.

The interior components chosen by the designer greatly influence indoor air quality. These include flooring, wall coverings, paints and finishes, and furnishings. Many manufacturers are now offering products with minimal levels of VOCs and using substitutes for materials with proven health risks such as formaldehyde. It is therefore important that designers learn about potential pollutants, such as those discussed here and in Chapter 4, and check the contents, usually listed on the label, of the products they recommend for clients. Organizations like Green Seal and LEED have established standards for maximum VOC rates for all types of building components and provide guidelines for choosing healthy products.

Implications for Designers

It is important to understand that people respond differently to various concentrations of air pollutants, ranging from no symptoms to violently ill. Therefore, if one person has no reaction to a substance, this does not mean that

TABLE 5.3 AVERAGE AMOUNT OF AIR BREATHED DURING TYPICAL ACTIVITIES

CHILDREN

ACTIVITY	LITERS OF AIR BREATHED PER MINUTE
Playing outdoors	16–17
Running at 4 miles per hour	32
Walking at 2 miles per hour	16
Standing	8
Sitting	7

ADULT FEMALES

Housework	19
Driving car	9
Running at 4 miles per hour	45
Walking at 2.5 miles per hour	20
Sitting	8

ADULT MALES

Mowing lawn	38
Car maintenance	23
Running at 5 miles per hour	59
Walking at 2.5 miles per hour	24
Sitting	9

Adapted from: Holmes, J. R. (1994). *How much air do we breathe?* (Research Notes: Brief Reports to the Scientific and Technical Community. No. 94-11). Sacramento, CA: California Environmental Protection Agency, Air Resources Board.

there are no indoor air problems. It should also be noted that reactions may be almost immediate, or it may take years for the effects to become apparent. Some of the most damaging materials, such as asbestos and cigarette smoke, for example, usually take years to do their harm; by the time symptoms are noted, the damage is irreparable or even fatal.

Some populations are at increased risk of harm from indoor air pollution. For example, children are at particular risk because they are growing and therefore inhale significantly more air than adults relative to their body surface area (Holmes, 1994). Also, their lungs are still developing and more prone to damage. Other especially vulnerable populations are those who spend the most time indoors, such as infants, the elderly, and the chronically

ill (U.S. Environmental Agency, 1995, "The Inside Story"). It is important that designers working on projects involving occupants who are members of any of these groups, or who are asthmatic or hypersensitive to inhaled substances, pay particular attention to the quality of the project's indoor air.

INDOOR AIR POLLUTANTS

Indoor air pollutants include a wide variety of substances, as shown in Box 5.3. Various concentrations and combinations are present in most buildings, including homes. Even when there is not a high enough level of any one type of substance to cause health problems, several low-level pollutants may combine to cause problems. Also, if they are present at low

BOX 5.3 COMMON INDOOR AIR POLLUTANTS

- Tobacco smoke
- Volatile organic compounds
- Formaldehyde
- Pesticides
- Nitrogen oxides
- Carbon monoxide
- Carbon dioxide
- Biologics
- Radon
- Lead
- Dust
- Dust mites
- Asbestos
- Mold spores

Adapted from: O'Reilly, J., Hagan, P., Gots, R., & Hedge, A. (1998). *Keeping buildings healthy: How to monitor and prevent indoor environmental problems.* New York: Wiley-Interscience.

U.S. Environmental Protection Agency. (1995). *The inside story: A guide to indoor air quality.* (EPA Document No. 402-K-93-007). Washington, DC: Author.

levels for long periods of time, they can accumulate in the body until they reach dangerous levels (U.S. Environmental Agency, 1995, "The Inside Story").

Many contributors to poor air quality are the result of common daily activities. Cooking can increase indoor air pollution levels, due to the buildup of cooking odors and health-threatening carbon monoxide emissions from gas stoves.

Another common but often overlooked cause of indoor air quality problems is the human body itself. In fact, the body contributes to the degeneration of indoor air in a number of ways:

- Releases odors from the skin, some of them very unpleasant
- Emits water vapor through breathing and perspiration, thus adding to the level of humidity
- Gives off heat so that room temperature is raised
- Produces carbon dioxide through breathing (Kroemer and Grandjean, 1997; Morgan, 2003)

- Is a source of bacteria and dust mites through breathing and the shedding of skin cells (Baechler et al., 1991)

The amount of an airborne pollutant that can be present in the air without causing harm to the average person is called a threshold limit value. The actual dose of a pollutant inhaled depends on three factors:

1. Concentration of the pollutant in the air
2. Length of time the person spends in the polluted environment
3. Quantity of air breathed while in the environment (Holmes, 1994)

Although many harmful substances, such as lead and carbon monoxide, are well understood, there is considerable uncertainty about what concentrations and exposure times lead to health problems for thousands of suspected pollutants. In other words, safe levels have not been determined. It is also not known how many pollutants work in combination or even synergistically (meaning the combined effect of two or more agents is greater than the sum of their individual effects) to threaten health (American Lung Association, 1994). Because of these unknowns, a sophisticated form of "better safe than sorry" has been proposed called the **Precautionary Principle.** It states, "When an activity (or product) raises threats of harm to human health or the environment, precautionary measures should be taken, even if some cause and effect relationships are not fully established scientifically" (Thompson, 2004).

Implications for Designers

Identifying health problems related to poor air quality is not always easy because, as mentioned previously, people rarely respond in the same way. And some people in the same environment will have no symptoms. When certain events are followed by the appearance of symptoms in at least some occupants of a space, the possibility of air quality problems should be considered. These events may include the following:

BOX 5.4 EXPERT SPOTLIGHT: The Importance of Understanding Multiple-Chemical Sensitivity in Interior Design

Linda Nussbaumer, Ph.D., ASID, IDEC, CID
Professor
South Dakota State University

Multiple-chemical sensitivity (MCS) is an illness in which the individual becomes sensitive to numerous chemicals and other irritants at very low levels of concentration. The condition affects multiple organ systems in the body (EPA, 2003). The major cause of the illness is poor *indoor air quality.* Indoor Air Quality is defined as the condition of the air inside buildings, including the extent of pollution caused by smoking, dust mites, mold spores, radon, and gases and chemicals from materials and appliances (EPA, 1994; EPA1995).

Exposure to chemicals such as volatile organic compounds (VOC) and petrochemical fuels are particularly strong triggers for symptoms of MCS. VOCs are compounds that become a gas or vaporize at room temperature (EPA, 2003). Petrochemical fuels that emit VOCs include diesel, gasoline, and kerosene (EPA, 1994). These chemicals may be found in a variety of household products (waxes, detergents, and cleaning products), latex, tobacco smoke, personal care products (perfumes and fragrances), and chemical dyes. Additionally, many products used in construction, interior finishes, and interior furnishings contain harmful chemicals (EPA 1994; Gist, 1999; Thivierge, 1999; Wittenberg, 1996).

What may happen to the individual who becomes ill with MCS is that exposure to these chemicals becomes a synergistic reaction. This means that one chemical mixing with another chemical creates a volatile reaction with the body. It is like mixing two dangerous chemicals (e.g., alcohol and barbiturates, or tobacco smoke and radon gas) (Bower, 2000).

To improve conditions for individuals with MCS, materials and products must be carefully researched before specifying. To assist in this research, the following Web sites may be helpful: Green Seal at www.greenseal.org, www.greenguard.org, and www.usgbc.org. After determining the appropriate material, it is essential to properly install and maintain it to preserve good indoor air quality.

Bower, J. (2000). *The healthy house: How to buy one, how to build one, how to cure a sick one* (4th ed.). New York: Healthy House Institute.

Environmental Protection Agency (EPA). (1994). *Indoor Air Pollution: An Introduction for Health Professionals.* Retrieved March 3, 2003, from http://www.epa.gov/iaq/pubs/hpguide.html#faq1

Environmental Protection Agency (EPA). (1994). *Indoor Air Pollution: An Introduction for Health Professionals.* Retrieved March 3, 2003, from http://www.epa.gov/iaq/pubs/hpguide.html#faq1

Environmental Protection Agency (EPA). (1995). *The inside story: A guide to indoor air quality.* Retrieved March 3, 2003, from http://www.epa.gov/iaq/pubs/insidest.html.

Environmental Protection Agency (EPA). (2003) *Indoor air quality: Glossary of Terms.* Retrieved March 3, 2003, from http://www.epa.gov/iaq/glossary.html

Gist, G. (1999). Multiple-chemical sensitivity: The role of environmental health professionals. *Journal of Environmental Health, 61*(6), 4–6. Retrieved April 8, 2003, from InfoTRAC database.

Godish, T. (2001). *Indoor environmental quality.* New York: Lewis Publishers. Thivierge, B. (1999). Multiple-chemical sensitivity. *In Gale Encyclopedia of Medicine, 1st Ed.* (pp. 1953). Toronto: Gale Research. Retrieved, April 20, 2003, from InfoTRAC database.

Wittenberg, J. S. (1996). *The rebellious body: Reclaim your life from environmental illness or chronic fatigue syndrome.* New York: Insight Books.

- A move to a different home or workplace
- Remodeling, redecorating, or refurnishing
- The use of pesticides
- Weatherization measures
- The presence of unusual odors
- The discovery of mold
- New pollutants, such as environmental smoke from a visitor

If symptoms disappear when an individual leaves a specific building and then return when the person reenters the building, that can be considered an additional clue indicating that indoor air quality could be the cause of the problem.

It is important to understand that although the quality of the air we breathe has more impact on our health, it is often less notice-able than other less damaging factors such as air temperature. For example, workers may complain about drafts while, at the same time, unknowingly breathe air that's contaminated with chemicals or carbon monoxide. Design-ers must understand that perceived comfort or the absence of complaints does not necessar-ily correspond to healthy conditions (O'Reilly et al., 1998). Determining indoor air quality, therefore, is not as subjective as other indoor climate factors such as temperature and hu-midity. Notice that in the American Society of Heating, Refrigeration, and Air-Conditioning Engineers, Inc. (ASHRAE) definition of ac-ceptable air quality shown below, only part of the statement concerns the opinion of build-ing occupants.

"Air in which there are no known con-taminants at harmful concentrations as determined by cognizant authorities and with which a substantial majority (80% or more) of the people do not express dissat-isfaction."
(The American Society of Heating, Re-frigerating, and Air-Conditioning Engi-neers, Inc., Standard 62–89)

Therefore, in order to best help their clients, designers need to be aware of common types of air contaminants and methods of mitigation, discussed in this chapter and in Chapter 4.

BUILDING-RELATED ILLNESSES AND SICK BUILDING SYNDROME

The workplace has always harbored health hazards, especially for inherently dangerous occupations, such as mining, and those that involve the heavy use of chemicals, such as agriculture. In recent decades, there has been an increase in health complaints from work-ers in occupations traditionally considered as being performed in safe places, such as office buildings. It is in these very buildings that air quality has come into question. For example, the National Institute for Occupational Safety and Health (NIOSH) responds to requests for

workplace evaluations. In 1980, the number of requests related to air quality problems was 8 percent of the total. By 1990, this number had grown to 52 percent of all requests (National Institute for Occupational Safety and Health, 1997). The extent of this problem is confirmed by World Health Organization experts who estimate that as many as 30 percent of new or remodeled commercial buildings cause com-plaints about indoor air quality (U.S. Environ-mental Protection Agency, 1995, "The Inside Story"). Other sources describe surveys of of-fice workers in the United States in which 24 percent perceived the existence of air quality problems in their workplaces, with 20 percent believing that the air quality negatively affected their work performance (American Lung As-sociation, 1994).

Two conditions have become associated with indoor air quality problems, primarily in office buildings. The first, building-related illness (BRI), refers to a well-defined illness with a recognizable set of symptoms. BRIs are caused by specific, identifiable air problems in buildings, such as the presence of disease-causing bacteria. In addition to the well-pub-licized Legionnaires' disease, these illnesses include hypersensitivity pneumonitis and hu-midifier fever, described earlier in this chapter. The second condition is sick building syn-drome (SBS), in which building occupants report a variety of symptoms that do not fit a specific medical diagnosis. Contrary to the condition's name, the building itself is not sick, but has environmental problems, usually with air quality, that negatively affect the health of at least some of its occupants. Although some people become quite ill in cases of SBS, it is rare that all occupants experience symptoms.

Sick building syndrome has been the source of much scientific controversy regarding both its existence and its cause. For example, there are conflicting reports about the role played by ventilation problems. NIOSH studies report that about 50 percent of sick building prob-lems are attributable to inadequate ventilation (Morgan, 2003), due in part to the construc-tion of tighter buildings in an effort to save energy costs. Other sources claim that studies

TABLE 5.4 VOCS DETECTED IN NEW BUILDINGS

CHEMICAL	POSSIBLE EFFECTS ON HEALTH
Benzene	• Short-term inhalation may cause drowsiness, dizziness, headaches, as well as eye, skin, and respiratory tract irritation, and, at high levels, unconsciousness. • Long-term inhalation exposure has caused various disorders in the blood, including reduced numbers of red blood cells, aplastic anemia, and increased incidence of leukemia. (Adapted from: EPA. Technology Transfer Network. Air Toxics Web Site. Retrieved August 14, 2007, from www.epa.gov/ttn/atw/hlthef/benzene.html)
Toluene	• May affect the nervous system and kidneys. • Low to moderate levels can cause tiredness, confusion, weakness, drunken-type actions, memory loss, nausea, loss of appetite, and hearing and color vision loss. These symptoms usually disappear when exposure is stopped. • Inhaling high levels in a short time can cause light-headedness, dizziness, or sleepiness. It can also cause unconsciousness and even death. Adapted from: CDC. Agency for Toxic Substances and Disease Registry. Retrieved August 14, 2007, from www.atsdr.cdc.gov/tfacts56.html#bookmark05
Chloroform	• Short-term inhalation exposure to chloroform causes central nervous system depression. • Long-term exposure by inhalation can affect the liver, including hepatitis and jaundice; depression and irritability. • Oral exposure increases kidney and liver tumors. Adapted from: EPA. Technology Transfer Network. Air Toxics Web Site. Retrieved August 14, 2007, from http://epa.gov/ttn/atw/hlthef/chlorofo.html
Acetone	• At levels between 100 ppm and 12,000 ppm, people experienced irritation of the nose, throat, lungs, and eyes. • At levels over 12,000 ppm, symptoms included headache, light-headedness, dizziness, unsteadiness, and confusion, depending on length of exposure. Adapted from: Agency for Toxic Substances and Disease Registry. Retrieved August 14, 2007, from www.atsdr.cdc.gov/toxprofiles/phs21.html
Styrene	• Short-term inhalation of high levels is likely to cause nervous system symptoms that include depression, concentration problems, muscle weakness, tiredness, and nausea. Other possibilities are eye, nose, and throat irritation. • Long-term inhalation may cause leukemia. Adapted from: Agency for Toxic Substances and Disease Registry. Retrieved August 14, 2007, from www.atsdr.cdc.gov/tfacts53.html
Ethylene oxide	• Short-term effects consist mainly of central nervous system depression and irritation of the eyes and mucous membranes. • Long-term exposure can cause irritation of the eyes, skin, and mucous membranes, and problems in brain and nerve function. Limited and inconclusive data link it with increase in incidence of leukemia, stomach cancer, cancer of the pancreas, and Hodgkin's disease. Adapted from: EPA: Technology Transfer Network. Retrieved August 14, 2007, from www.epa.gov/ttn/atw/hlthef/ethylene.html

show little conclusive evidence that ventilation alone can explain most cases (O'Reilly et al., 1998).

It is known that the air in office buildings contains a wide range of pollutants that can contribute to sick building syndrome. This seems to be especially true for new buildings. In fact, some estimates are that various volatile organic compounds (VOCs) are 100 times greater in new buildings than in the outdoors and can remain elevated for six months after construction is completed (Morgan, 2003). The most commonly detected VOCs identified in an EPA study were benzene, toluene, chloroform, acetone, styrene, and ethylene oxide (Morgan, 2003). The effects of these chemicals can be serious, as shown in Table 5.4.

Pollutants can also be the result of the day-to-day activities in office buildings. For example, commercial cleaning products tend to be stronger than those used in the home; restroom fresheners are commonly used; and office machines, such as copiers and printers, emit pollutants such as ozone. A 2007 study showed high levels of particulates, equivalent to that of cigarette smoke, were emitted from certain models of laser jet printers. Although limited in scope, the study does raise questions about the need for further research on the effects of common office equipment on human health.

The difficulty in determining exact sources of air pollutants is illustrated by a study that found a direct correlation between the presence of open shelving and fleecy materials in the environment and the number of people reporting symptoms (O'Reilly et al., 1998). To complicate matters further, factors other than air quality have been identified that may cause or contribute to sick building syndrome. These include poor lighting, noise, vibration, thermal discomfort, and psychological stress (U.S. Environmental Protection Agency, 1995, "The Inside Story").

In spite of the controversies and unknowns, health complaints among building inhabitants are numerous and widespread. The possibility of factors other than air quality contributing to health problems does not eliminate responsibility, nor remove the need to address the issues. On the contrary, these types of situations prove that a systemic approach must be taken to establish and maintain healthy workplaces. They also demonstrate how important it is to incorporate all types of appropriate wellness-promoting strategies in the built environment.

BOX 5.5

Common Airborne Pollutants We Cannot Detect with Our Senses
- Carbon monoxide
- Radon, thoron (different form of radon)
- Asbestos, mineral fibers
- Viruses, some bacteria
- Pollen
- Dust mites, dust feces
- Nonaromatic (odorless) volatile organic compounds

Common Airborne Contaminants We Can Detect with Our Senses
- Formaldehyde (irritation)
- Aromatic VOCs (odors, irritation)
- Ozone (irritation)
- Some bacteria (odors)
- Environmental tobacco smoke (odors, irritation, sight)

Adapted from O'Reilly, J.T., Hagan, P., Gots, R., & Hedge, A. (1998). *Keeping buildings healthy: How to monitor and prevent indoor environmental problems.* New York: Wiley-Interscience. Pages 141–142.

ODORS

Odors are reportedly among the major causes of health complaints in the work environment because people associate them with chemicals they perceive to be dangerous and unhealthy (O'Reilly et al., 1998). Bad smells can have strong psychological effects, sometimes making people feel sick and believing they are being poisoned, even when this is not the case (O'Reilly et al., 1998). In fact, an unpleasant odor does not necessarily mean that the air is harmful. On the other hand, some of the most toxic substances—such as carbon monoxide—are odorless. Box 5.5 provides examples of other common airborne contaminants that are not detected by the senses, along with a list of those that are.

At the same time, some odors that are indicators of potentially harmful substances in the air are considered by many people to be pleasant, even desirable. Consider, for example, the odors given off by new products, such as cars and carpets. The positive perception of these odors is probably due to their association with the purchase of something of value. There are even spray products available that replicate the odor of new cars. These smells are the result of potentially harmful chemicals being emitted from plastics, adhesives, and other substances.

As with other aspects of the indoor climate, then, tolerance of odors is highly subjective and not everyone will be of the same opinion about the odors present. Simply stated, every environment contains some odors. And actually, a certain level is desirable. If a space is truly odor free, the occupants' sensitivity and ability to detect odors become enhanced. When this happens, any new odor, regardless of how low-level, will seem very strong (O'Reilly et al., 1998).

Standards for acceptable nuisance (nonharmful) odors are based on the reactions of the occupants of a space. For example, the World Health Organization describes a threshold value as that at which less than 5 percent of a population finds the odor annoying less than 2 percent of the time. The American Society of Heating, Refrigeration, and Air-Conditioning Engineers has a less stringent standard: an odor is acceptable if 80 percent of an untrained panel of observers considers the air to be "not objectionable" when they first enter a space (O'Reilly et al., 1998).

Implications for Designers

Designers should avoid making assumptions about what their clients will and won't find objectionable regarding nuisance odors. If products are used that could emit even a slight smell, it is important to secure the opinions of clients before making purchases.

Designers should be aware that the fragrance and freshening products sold to improve or enhance indoor air quality might have negative health consequences. These products are potentially dangerous for at least two reasons. The first is that they could mask odors that are indicators of problems that

should be addressed, such as mold and the urine of rodents. Second, there is evidence that the chemicals in some of these sprays, powders, scented candles, and scented oils contain respiratory irritants. For example, a VOC called 1,4 dichlorobenzene (1,4 DCB), used in some air fresheners and urinal blocks in public restrooms, has been associated with reduced lung function (National Institutes of Health, 2006). Another possibly dangerous chemical used in moth repellents and recommended by manufacturers as an air freshener is paradichlorobenzene (U.S. Environmental Protection Agency, 1995, "The Inside Story"). Avoiding products that contain these compounds is especially important for people who already have respiratory problems, such as those who have asthma, or who have children with this condition.

It should also be noted that some candle wicks contain lead that, when burned, release the lead into the air. In addition, the chemicals that provide the scent in candles can deliver harmful pollutants into the air as well as soot, whose very fine particles can be inhaled into the deepest areas of the lungs (Alabama Cooperative Extension System, 2000).

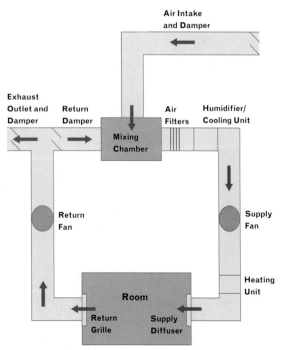

FIGURE 5.7 HVAC systems must be carefully designed and maintained to prevent them from becoming sources of air quality problems.

TABLE 5.5 HVAC COMPONENTS AND POTENTIAL PROBLEMS

COMPONENT	PURPOSE	POTENTIAL PROBLEMS
Outdoor air intakes	Provide entryway for outdoor air into building	If poorly located, they pull in outdoor pollutants. Energy conservation measures sometimes limit the amount of outside air that enters.
Mixing chamber	Mixes predetermined percentages of outdoor and indoor air	Dampers may not allow the entry of adequate amounts of fresh air.
Air filters	Remove particles from air as it leaves the mixing chamber. Some also remove gases.	If not cleaned regularly, filters can reduce ventilation rates and raise indoor contaminant levels.
Heating and cooling coils	Warms or cools filtered air as it is blown across the coils	Excess moisture provides breeding grounds for biological pathogens. Leaks from combustion sources may release particulates into the air.
Humidity controls	Add or remove water vapor from heated or cooled air	If not properly controlled and maintained, humidity levels may be incorrect. Devices can be sources of biological contaminants.
Supply fans and ducts	Push air throughout building	Ducts can become sources of dust, mold, bacteria, and other pollutants.
Return air systems and exhaust fans	Collect indoor air and push it from the building	If these are inadequate, too much stale air is left in the building.

Adapted from: Tate, N. (1994). *The sick building syndrome.* Far Hills, NJ: New Horizon Press.

HEATING, VENTILATION, AND AIR-CONDITIONING SYSTEMS (HVAC)

In the words of one author, HVAC systems are the mechanical lungs of a building (Tate, 1994). They vary in size, depending on the building they service, but generally consist of the same basic components: heating, cooling, and ventilating units; ductwork; filters; exhaust fans; and fresh-air intake units. (See Figure 5.7.) Although an HVAC system is a common way to maintain appropriate temperature and humidity levels, it can also be the source of indoor air problems. In fact, according to investigators of

the National Institute for Occupational Safety and Health, improperly functioning HVAC systems, along with inadequate ventilation, accounted for more indoor air quality problems than all other factors combined (Tate, 1994). Table 5.5 presents a list of HVAC components in which air quality problems can develop.

MITIGATING INDOOR AIR PROBLEMS

Health problems among building occupants may or may not be related to indoor air quality. It is one of the most common causes, so it should be one of the prime suspects when illnesses appear to be associated with a person's presence in a building. As with many other health problems, prevention is always the best method. This requires anticipating and taking measures to avoid potential problems. At the same time, there are effective ways to deal with existing situations. Whether preventing problems or solving existing ones, the following six steps are recommended:

1. Source management
2. Ventilation
3. Filtration
4. Maintenance program
5. Exposure control
6. Education

Source Management

Source management means minimizing or eliminating pollutants, always the best and most effective first step. Sources can be managed in several ways. The first is by substituting safer products and methods, when possible, such as less toxic cleaning products (see Chapter 9 for suggestions) or using solid wood products instead of those made of formalde-

hyde-containing particleboard (see Chapter 4 for information about the health effects of formaldehyde). Designers should specify building materials and furnishings with the lowest possible emission potentials. In cases where substitution is not possible, consider ways to enclose the source of pollution. For example, copy machines and printers can be placed in a dedicated room without desks or workstations. These rooms should be vented directly to the outside, possibly with extra exhaust fans. Finally, encapsulation of potential contaminants is suggested for areas that can be sealed off. For example, well-sealed drywall can separate plastic pipes, wire-covers, and other materials that typically emit VOCs into the living area of a house (Bower, 2001).

Ventilation

Ventilation means circulating fresh air into a structure, usually by means of replacing indoor air with outside air (Figure 5.8). Because indoor pollution sources, not those from outside air, are the primary cause of indoor air problems (U.S. Environmental Protection Agency, 1995, "The Inside Story"), moving outside air to the inside is usually the most effective way

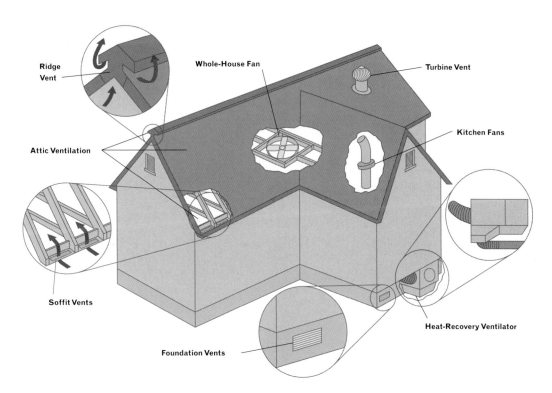

FIGURE 5.8 Examples of natural and mechanical methods for ventilating a structure.

to prevent the accumulation of unhealthy levels of air pollutants. Not only does fresh air dilute indoor pollutants, it replenishes the oxygen used up by the building inhabitants. And it simultaneously carries off the carbon dioxide (CO_2) produced by the occupants. Carbon dioxide levels should not exceed 1,000 parts per million (ppm) (Shaw, 1997). One way to ensure that CO_2 does not reach unacceptable levels is to install a CO_2 ventilation demand detector that automatically adjusts the total outdoor supply rate as needed (Shaw, 1997). Other important reasons for supplying fresh air are to lower the temperature of indoor air that has been raised by human bodies and to clear out unpleasant odors.

Outside air can enter a structure in the following three ways:

1. **Infiltration:** air enters through cracks, holes, and various unplanned openings in walls, floors, and around windows and doors (also called "random ventilation").
2. **Natural ventilation:** air moves through opened windows, doors, roof ventilators, etc.
3. **Mechanical ventilation:** purposeful movement of air from the outside through exhaust fans and central air-handling systems.

The rate at which outdoor air replaces indoor air is called the **air exchange rate.** The

amount of air can be expressed in cubic feet per minute (cfm) or liters per second (L/s). The rate at which air should be exchanged, whether naturally or mechanically, depends on factors such as the number of occupants in a building, the amount of outgassing from the building, including its equipment and materials, and the type of activities that take place inside. For example, the greater the number of occupants, the higher the levels of carbon dioxide reached in a given period of time. This is very relevant information because if a remodeling project is done to increase the capacity for occupants in a space, ventilation rates must also be increased to handle the increased concentrations of carbon dioxide and higher temperatures. Table 5.6 contains ASHRAE's minimum ventilation rates for various types of facilities during normal operations.

Mechanical ventilation, usually part of a central heating and air-conditioning system, involves five processes:

1. Supplying fresh air from the outside
2. Conditioning this air by heating, cooling, filtering, humidifying, or dehumidifying
3. Mixing the indoor and outdoor air
4. Moving the mixed air into the building
5. Removing stale air from the building

Mechanical ventilation systems have various operation modes to handle different conditions. The normal mode, used when buildings are occupied, is usually shut down when buildings are empty, such as during nighttime and on weekends. Without ventilation, indoor pollutant levels tend to rise. When this happens, the flushing cycle provides a faster air exchange rate. This cycle is used to clear the air before workers or the public arrive to use the building. Some ventilation systems also have an enhanced mode to provide even more clearing capacity during activities such as renovating, painting, and installing new carpeting.

Most home heating and cooling systems do not include mechanical ventilation. Fresh air must enter through infiltration or natural ventilation. Depending on how tightly a

TABLE 5.6 MINIMUM AIR EXCHANGE RATES

LOCATION	CUBIC FEET PER MINUTE PER PERSON
Auditoriums	15
Cafeterias	20
Conference rooms	20
Kitchens	15
Libraries	15
Office spaces	20
Smoking lounges	60
Spectator sport arenas	15

Source: O'Reilly, J.T., Hagan, P., Gots, R., & Hedge, A. (1998). *Keeping buildings healthy: How to monitor and prevent indoor environmental problems.* New York: Wiley-Interscience.

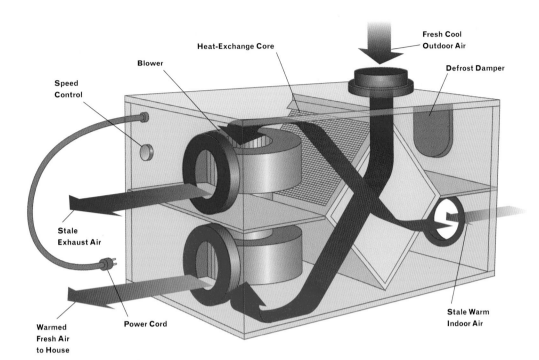

Speed Control

Blower

Heat-Exchange Core

Fresh Cool Outdoor Air

Defrost Damper

Stale Exhaust Air

Power Cord

Warmed Fresh Air to House

Stale Warm Indoor Air

FIGURE 5.9 Heat exchangers provide efficient means of heating and ventilating by taking advantage of indoor and outdoor ambient air temperatures.

house is built, the time that it takes for a full replacement of indoor air ranges from one-half to five hours (Morgan, 2003). In the case of new homes that are tightly built to conserve energy, mechanical ventilation systems are available. These are especially useful for clients who live in climates with very long winters in which months go by without the windows being opened. A product that designers might recommend is an energy-efficient heat recovery ventilator. Also called an energy recovery ventilator (ERV) or an air-to-air heat exchanger, these devices work with an electrically powered fan that forces indoor air past outdoor air through a heat exchanger. (See Figure 5.9.) In this way, fresh air is brought indoors and heated, at least partially, by the outgoing air.

All homes, whether or not equipped with a central ventilation system, should have exhaust fans in the kitchen and bathrooms and any other areas where pollutants and odors might be produced, such as workshops and art studios. Exhaust fans are essential on combustion appliances, such as gas stoves, to prevent buildups of carbon dioxide and airborne particulates. Another way to increase the rate of air entering a house is to run a window air

conditioner with the vent control open. Attic and basement fans are also good methods of clearing areas that tend to become polluted. Operable windows are desirable for letting in air, but features to protect small children from falling out should be considered. (See Chapter 9 for information about window safety.)

Office buildings, on the other hand, usually have less natural ventilation and, therefore, must depend on mechanical ventilation systems. This is especially true in newer buildings, which tend to have lower ceilings and large, nonoperable windows (Kroemer and Grandjean, 1997). In the 1970s, at the same time that tighter buildings were increasing the need for ventilation, air exchange requirements were lowered as part of energy conservation measures (O'Reilly, et al., 1998). These simultaneous circumstances may have led to the increase in indoor air quality problems, such as sick building syndrome, that we are seeing today. Buildings in which chemicals are used routinely, such as beauty salons and dry cleaners, particularly need good ventilation. Designers must address these important issues, which contribute to the well-being of both employees and customers.

Although ventilation is the best way, after source management, to ensure good indoor air quality, there are a number of problems designers should be aware of that can interfere with its effectiveness:

1. Overall systems are sometimes not built and installed according to the original blueprints (O'Reilly et al., 1998). This illustrates the importance of taking a systemic approach to the built environment. For example, if the placement of electrical outlets is changed by one contractor, the heating system contractors might have to add unplanned bends to the ductwork, a change that reduces airflow.
2. Indoor air returns are placed too high, so they pull air out only from the highest layers rather than from the breathing zone (Dul and Weerdmeester, 1993).
3. Intake vents are placed near parking or loading zones or trash Dumpsters so that fumes and smells are pulled into the building.
4. Air supply and return vents are located adjacent to each other in an occupied space so that the fresh air doesn't have a chance to circulate throughout the room.
5. Air vented from undesirable indoor areas, such as restrooms, is redirected into workspaces.
6. Elevator shafts, stairwells, spaces between walls, and ceiling plenums serve as pathways for pollutants and smells. Service elevator rooms are often a storage area for potential pollutants such as cleaning supplies and paints, which exacerbates the problem (O'Reilly et al., 1998).
7. Businesses, such as restaurants and print shops, are added to buildings whose ventilation systems were not designed to handle their needs.
8. Large spaces are partitioned to add offices and the new walls or dividers, including those that do not reach the ceiling, restrict the circulation of fresh air.
9. Furniture, boxes, and other items block air supply and return vents so that outdoor air cannot reach the breathing zones.

Even good ventilation cannot remove all traces of certain contaminants, such as tobacco smoke. This is why it is important for designers to practice source management and plan separate, enclosed areas for activities such as smoking, complete with their own exhaust systems to outside locations where pollutants cannot come back through intake vents. This can be illustrated by the experience of staying in a nonsmoking hotel room that nonetheless smells of tobacco. This happens when air is recirculated without adequate exchange rates to clear it of pollutants.

Some air pollutants are the result of temporary, purposeful activities such as painting, stripping floors, and using craft supplies. In these cases, care should be taken to ensure adequate ventilation, such as by opening windows and using exhaust fans. Workplace projects that emit pollutants into occupied spaces should be done when the fewest number of people are present. In addition, care should be taken to exhaust air to the outside; close or cover paint containers; seal air returns with plastic in areas that are under renovation; modify the HVAC system so that air from work areas is not circulated throughout the building; and use good housekeeping techniques to control dust (O'Reilly et al., 1998).

Filtration

Filtration refers to several methods for removing particles and gases from the air. At least some level of filtering is part of heating and air-conditioning systems in order to protect both the HVAC equipment and the general well-being of occupants. These filters are not designed to remove all pollutants from the air. This is the purpose of air cleaners, which come in various sizes. Large, central air cleaners can be installed to filter air throughout a house or building, but they require the constant running of a relatively noisy fan. At the same time, efficient portable room units are available and these might actually be better than central units at cleaning the air of the room they are located in (Binggeli, 2003). Thus, if clean air is especially important in certain rooms, such as the bedroom of someone with asthma, this type could be the best choice.

The effectiveness of an air cleaner depends on two factors: (1) how well it collects pollutants from the air (expressed as a percentage efficiency rate); and (2) the amount of air it pulls through the filtering unit (expressed in cubic feet per minute). Overall air-cleaning performance depends on both. For example, if a filter removes 99 percent of a pollutant, but the air-flow rate is only 10 cfm, it will take a long time to process the air in a typical 1,000 square foot room (U.S. Environmental Protection Agency, 1990, "Residential Air"). One method for expressing overall efficiency is the **clean air delivery rate (CADR),** which is the volume of filtered air delivered by an air cleaner each minute—efficiency of the system multiplied by the air flow of the system. For example, if an air cleaner has a CADR of 250 for smoke particles, this means it should reduce smoke particle levels to the same concentration as would be achieved by adding 250 cubic feet of clean air each minute (U.S. Environmental Protection Agency, 1990, "Residential Air").

If an air cleaner uses dense, highly efficient filters, the motors on the fans must be strong enough to overcome the filter's resistance. This is why small, tabletop models are relatively ineffective: their motors and fans are simply not large enough for the task. The fact is that even the most efficient small air cleaners cannot remove most allergens quickly enough to prevent adverse effects to those who are sensitive to them. For example, most animals shed dander more quickly than can be handled by smaller models, rendering them essentially useless for people with pet allergies. Therefore, air cleaners, even the larger models, generally are helpful only when used along with vigorous efforts to remove the source of allergens (U.S. Environmental Protection Agency, 1995, "The Inside Story").

If the decision is made to use an air cleaner, several general types are available: mechanical filters, ion generators, electronic air cleaners, and gas phase filters. Mechanical filters are installed in ductwork or in portable devices in which a fan forces air through the filter. They work much like a paper coffee filter. Some consist of flat panels made of loosely packed materials such as coarse glass fibers, animal hair, and vegetable fibers. These filters are most efficient at collecting large particles, but do not trap the smallest, most respirable-size particles (U.S. Environmental Protection Agency, 1990,

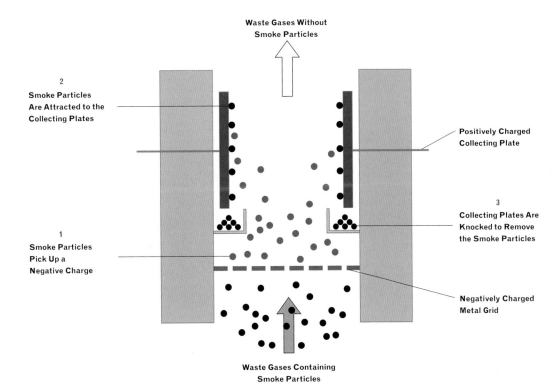

Waste Gases Without Smoke Particles

2
Smoke Particles Are Attracted to the Collecting Plates

Positively Charged Collecting Plate

3
Collecting Plates Are Knocked to Remove the Smoke Particles

1
Smoke Particles Pick Up a Negative Charge

Negatively Charged Metal Grid

Waste Gases Containing Smoke Particles

FIGURE 5.10 Electrostatic precipitators clean air by collecting and disposing of particulates inside the air filter itself. This is a cleaner method than having charged particles attach themselves to room surfaces.

"Residential Cleaning"). Pleated mechanical filters are usually better able to capture respirable particles because they use smaller, more densely packed fibers or paper and have more surface area. High-efficiency particulate air filters (HEPA) are the most effective at removing particles of all sizes. To qualify as a HEPA filter, it must be 99.97 percent efficient at removing respirable particles from the air. Because HEPA filters offer a lot of resistance, they require strong, relatively noisy fans. This is why their use is mainly restricted to facilities such as hospitals and laboratories. They can be used in residential air cleaners when people require extremely clean air.

Electronic air cleaners use the principle of static electricity. The simplest type of electronic air cleaner sends electrons into the air, which charge airborne particles. These particles then become attracted to noncharged surfaces, such as walls, floors, furnishings, and people. Because this can result in soiling as the particles accumulate on surfaces, **electrostatic precipitators** can be a better choice. These also work by charging airborne particles, but they use a fan to pull them back into the unit, where they are captured on a series of flat plates. (See Figure 5.10.)

The air cleaners discussed above remove particles—but not gases—from the air. Gas removal is based on adsorption, the accumulation of gases on a solid or liquid surface. Activated charcoal, which is used in gas masks, is commonly used in these filters. There is a lot of resistance with an adsorption filter, so they tend to have larger surface areas and require more powerful, expensive motors. For this reason, they are rarely used in homes.

Air cleaners that intentionally produce ozone, a gas, are not generally recommended. In spite of claims by some manufacturers to the contrary, ozone can react with the organic material that makes up the human body and cause harmful effects on health (U.S. Environmental Protection Agency, 2006, "Ozone Generators"). Although individuals' reactions to ozone vary, symptoms can include chest pain, coughing, shortness of breath, throat irritation, the worsening of asthma, and inter-

ference with the immune system (U.S. Environmental Protection Agency, 2006, "Ozone Generators").

Maintenance Program

All types of buildings, including homes, need a proactive rather than a reactive maintenance program (O'Reilly et al., 1998). As discussed previously, a common contributor to air quality problems is inadequate monitoring and maintenance of heating, air-conditioning, and ventilation equipment: air conditioners and humidifiers can provide breeding conditions for mold and bacteria; unchanged furnace and air cleaner filters can become clogged with dust and other particulates; and ductwork can harbor dust, mold, and other contaminants. Other indoor climate problems can be the result of leaky roofs, unattended mold, and radon entering a structure from the underground crawl space. Routine monitoring should focus on identifying areas that can contribute to indoor air problems and then promptly fixing any that need attention. Table 5.7 presents an example of a home maintenance schedule.

Exposure Control

Exposure control can be achieved by careful planning. For example, school remodeling projects that are likely to release contaminants into the air are best done when students are not on campus: during weekends, holidays, or between academic sessions. Likewise, major maintenance projects in office buildings, such as carpet cleaning, should be carried out when the fewest number of people are in the building. And as discussed previously in the chapter, areas in which potential contaminants and irritants are being used should be sealed off as much as possible.

Education

Education of home owners, parents of school-age children, occupants of buildings, and the public at large can contribute to safer air quality. Knowing which products and activities are potentially harmful can help prevent air quality problems from happening in the first place. As the case of carbon monoxide poisoning in

TABLE 5.7   MAINTAINING INDOOR AIR QUALITY IN THE HOME

FREQUENCY	ACTIONS
Monthly	• Test smoke and carbon monoxide alarms • Check memory on carbon monoxide alarms for peak levels
Two times/year	• Clean and inspect dehumidifier
Four times/year	• Clean exhaust fans and vents in kitchen and bathrooms • Change or clean air-handling filter • Clean and inspect ventilation system filters
One time/year	• Have heating, cooling, filtration, and ventilation systems professionally inspected • Have furnace and water heater serviced • Have fireplace and flues checked and serviced • Change batteries in fire alarms, smoke detectors, and carbon monoxide monitors • Properly dispose of old stored household chemicals • Inspect house, including windows, for signs of moisture intrusion • Clean or replace humidifier pad on central humidifiers • Inspect perimeter of home to ensure 5% slope and fill in if it has settled • Inspect outside exhaust hoods for debris and blockage

Adapted from American Lung Association Health House. Retrieved August 15, 2007, from www.healthhouse.org/maintenanceguide.asp.

the Pacific Northwest (see Box 5.6) shows, a lack of information can be harmful—even deadly.

SCHOOLS AND INDOOR AIR QUALITY

The indoor air quality of schools deserves special mention because school buildings are at particular risk for air quality problems. A number of government reports and thousands of anecdotal reports highlight the extent of these problems. For example, a nationwide survey conducted in 1995 by the U.S. Government Accounting Office reported that more than 50 percent of schools have problems that affect their indoor air quality (U.S. Environmental Protection Agency, 2006, "IAQ Tools"). In a radon investigation conducted in 29 schools across the country, the EPA discovered that most of them had inadequate ventilation and that nearly 20 percent had at least one room with radon levels above the level at which the EPA recommends remedial action (U.S. En-

vironmental Protection Agency, 2006, "IAQ Tools").

School buildings of all ages have a wide variety of air quality problems, including mold, especially in regions of the country such as the Southeast; VOCs from furnishings, carpeting, and building materials; chemicals from cleaning products; bacteria; and airborne pesticides. There are several factors that account for the high number of schools with indoor air quality (IAQ) problems:

- No federal laws and relatively few state and local laws regulate air quality in schools. For the most part, schools are locally controlled.
- Construction of new schools is sometimes poorly monitored. Examples include building sites located on or near previous toxic waste or garbage dumps and construction materials getting wet before they are installed, leading to the formation of mold.

BOX 5.6   A REAL-WORLD EXPERIENCE

In late 2006, the western portion of the state of Washington suffered what one physician called "a carbon-monoxide epidemic." As a result of a strong windstorm in December 2006, more than 1.5 million residents in the Pacific Northwest were without electric power at some point during the storm. Hundreds of thousands of people remained without power for several days during which temperatures dropped to the 20s. In an effort to stay warm, cook, and provide light, many people used portable generators and charcoal grills inside their homes. Both produce carbon monoxide in sufficient quantities that when not ventilated properly, as usually happens when these appliances are used indoors, carbon monoxide can build up to dangerous levels. In this case, at least 100 people became ill and two died as a result of carbon monoxide poisoning. Unfortunately, many people don't understand the sources or the dangers of carbon monoxide. Designers can help educate their clients, as well as the general public, about the danger of using nonvented combustion devices indoors.

Source: CBS News. Seattle, Dec. 18, 2006. Retrieved January 10, 2007, from http://www.cbsnews.com/stories/2006/12/18/national/printable2275545.shtml.

- Many school buildings are quite old, built before the use of potentially dangerous products such as asbestos insulation and lead was prohibited.
- School budgets are usually limited, both for initial building and follow-up maintenance. The least expensive rather than the most healthy methods and materials are often used.
- Schools are densely populated relative to other facilities, so levels of emitted body moisture and carbon dioxide, as well as body heat, are higher.
- Some school boards and administrators ignore suspected IAQ problems, which then magnify and become more difficult to remediate.
- Many schools use portable classrooms to handle expanding student populations. These buildings typically contain high levels of pressed-wood products, such as particleboard, that emit formaldehyde. To make matters worse, many portables have poor ventilation systems.

These problems can have serious consequences. The fact that children are developing physically places them at increased risk of possible harm, relative to adults, from all kinds of pollutants. (See Chapter 8 for more information about specific effects on children.) Also, asthma and allergies, discussed in Chapter 3, are increasing at an alarming rate, especially among children. It is believed that these increases are largely due to poor indoor air quality. Many of these children spend most of their waking hours in school buildings, so their exposure times can be quite long, even if pollutant levels are low.

Implications for Designers

Air quality in schools should be of concern to interior designers because as a society, we have a responsibility to protect the health of children.

A number of steps can be taken to help improve the air quality in schools. A first line of defense is to prevent dirt and pollutants from entering the building. For example, double-entry doors can prevent soil and other debris from being tracked into the building. Walk-off mats, extending inward between 9 and 15 feet, should be placed immediately inside the second doors to further clean and dry shoes and boots (Nally, 2002). Flooring inside the school should be sturdy enough to withstand vacuuming several times a day, if necessary. Carpeting is not recommended for classrooms, hallways, or other high-use areas because it harbors microorganisms, dust, and potentially harmful residues. Many carpets also emit VOCs from the carpeting material itself, the backing, and/or the adhesives. Healthy flooring alternatives include wood, ceramic tiles, cork, and linoleum (Nally, 2002). Regardless of the type, it is preferable that flooring be nailed down because most adhesives contain harmful solvents. In addition to flooring, all school surfaces, including furnishings and built-ins, should be easy-to-clean to prevent the need for using extremely strong cleaning products.

Other school building problems are more systemic. For example, moisture, which often leads to mold infestations, should be carefully monitored and reported immediately. Leaky roofs, relatively expensive to repair or replace, are a common problem. Extremely high humidity is another. Heating, ventilation, and air-conditioning systems can also present problems, spewing out contaminants and circulating them throughout the school. These systems should be inspected at least annually, more often if air problems are suspected. Even when ventilation systems are adequate, they can be sabotaged by a common practice at elementary and high schools: lining up idling school buses next to buildings where the exhaust can be sucked up into vents. Buses should park as far away from the building as is practical or at least a good distance from the vents.

Another significant problem in some schools is the use of pesticides. To avoid the associated health problems—such as asthma attacks—in both children and adults, many schools are adapting what is called Integrated Pest Management. This is a strategy for taking measures to prevent pest problems from happening in the first place. Pesticides are then used only as a last resort and the least-toxic chemicals are used. In cases where pesticides are used, the school should notify parents in writing before the applications so children with respiratory problems can be kept at home.

Good ventilation systems are extremely important in schools. Because of their high-density, vulnerable populations of children, air exchange rates in schools should be at least 15 cfm per student on a continuous basis. When the rate is lower, serious IAQ problems can result (Bayer et al., 2000). The varied activities that take place in schools can require even higher air exchange rates and dedicated exhaust fans in some areas. Examples include art and cooking classrooms, science labs, biology classrooms with live plants and animals, gyms, locker rooms, and indoor swimming pools.

A common problem today for many single-parent and working-couple families is the need to send children to school when they are ill due to a lack of day-care. Sneezing and coughing spew bacteria and viruses into the air through which they can easily travel long distances. Designers might consider suggesting that a special room, made comfortable for ill children and with its own exhaust system, be

incorporated into the school facility. To help those children who are old enough to stay home, but attend anyway so they won't fall behind, schools might consider using live cams and other technology to send class lectures and activities to sick children in their homes.

Many organizations, including the U.S. Environmental Protection Agency (see Box 5.7), have developed recommendations for creating

---

BOX 5.7 INDOOR AIR QUALITY TOOLS FOR SCHOOLS KIT

The Indoor Air Quality Tools for Schools (IAQ TfS) Kit, developed by the EPA, shows schools how to carry out a practical plan of action to improve indoor air problems at little or no cost using straightforward activities and in-house staff. The kit provides:

• Industry guidelines
• Best practices
• Sample policies
• Sample IAQ management plan

The kit is cosponsored by the National Parent Teacher Association, National Education Association, Association of School Business Officials, American Federation of Teachers, and the American Lung Association.

Available at: http://www.epa.gov/iaq/schools/toolkit.html#Problem%20Solving%20Wheel

---

BOX 5.8 THE SUSTAINABILITY CONNECTION

Attending to indoor air quality is not only important for maintaining human health, it can prevent wasting materials, as in the following examples:

• If solid wood rather than particleboard cabinets are chosen for a kitchen, they will not have to be replaced if future occupants of the home are sensitive to formaldehyde.
• When particulates, as from a fireplace, are properly exhausted to the outdoors, interiors are not dirtied so that they need frequent cleaning and eventual replacement.
• Devices such as heat-exchangers reduce the amount of energy needed to heat and ventilate buildings.
• Preventing moisture problems to prevent polluting mold also prevents the need for expensive repairs and reconstruction.

healthier schools. These groups are gathering and publicizing information about building materials and products that can be used to replace dangerous substances. An example of a substance of concern is PVC (polyvinyl chloride), commonly called vinyl, a widely used synthetic material that can contain dioxin, one of the most toxic substances ever tested (Nally, 2002). One study found that children exposed for extended periods to PVC flooring have an 89 percent higher risk of bronchial obstruction (Nally, 2002). Therefore, designers who are working with schools should research the materials being planned or already used in schools for their potential harmful effects. Although scientific research has not confirmed all the links between indoor air problems and negative health effects, applying the Precautionary Principle, described previously, certainly makes sense when dealing with the lives of children.

GLOSSARY TERMS

Air exchange rate

Building-related illnesses

Clean air delivery rate (CADR)

Dehumidifiers

Effective temperature

Electrostatic precipitator

Humidifier

Humidity

Infiltration

Insensible perspiration

Mechanical ventilation

Natural ventilation

Percentage efficiency rate

Precautionary Principle

Radiation

Reflex sweating

Relative humidity

Sick building syndrome

Source management

Thermal comfort

Thermal conduction

Thermal regulation

Thermoregulatory

Threshold limit value

Ventilation

LEARNING ACTIVITIES

1. Conduct a survey of the occupants of a room of your choosing to determine their perception of the temperature. (There should be at least ten people; the more sampled, the better.) How many are experiencing thermal comfort? How many perceive the temperature as too warm? As too cool? If the perceptions vary, how might that be explained? What suggestions could you make as an interior designer to provide comfort for more occupants?

2. Choose a room with a variety of surfaces. Check the temperature of each one by hand and list them in order from coolest to warmest. Conduct your investigation at different times of the day. How do these surfaces influence the effective temperature (the weighted average between air temperature and radiation temperature, more closely related to human perception) of the room? Are the effects negative? If so, what could you do as an interior designer to help mitigate these effects?

3. Create a checklist of indoor pollution sources and conduct an investigation of your living quarters. List the sources you identify and create an action plan to decrease their potential effects on the indoor air quality of your residence.

4. Suppose a client tells you that she has multiple-chemical sensitivity. What does this mean? Explain how it would affect your work with her as an interior designer.

5. Research and write a report summarizing the latest findings on possible harmful emissions from office equipment used in both the workplace and the home.

6. Visit a building in which you can locate some of the indoor and outdoor vents. Using the criteria listed in this chapter, are the vents properly placed? Are there obstructions that decrease their effectiveness? If there are problems, how might they be resolved?

SUGGESTED WEB SITES

1. American Lung Association Health House
www.healthhouse.org/index/asp
This program began in 1993 to provide the residential building community with information needed to build homes that provided ventilation, filtration, and moisture control. This Web site contains dozens of suggestions for both builders and home owners to achieve and maintain good indoor air quality.

2. U.S. Environmental Protection Agency
Indoor Environmental Division
www.epa.gov/iaq/index.html
This government site includes information on all aspects of indoor air quality. The following articles and fact sheets, found by clicking the "A to Z Subject Index," are only a few examples of the many that provide information of value to interior designers:
• Air Toxins
• Multiple-Chemical Sensitivity/Sick Building Syndrome
• Ozone Generators That Are Sold as Air Cleaners
• Design – IAQ Design Tools for Schools
• Humidifier Fever
• Portable Classrooms
• Radon-Resistant New Construction
• Ventilation and Air Quality in Offices

3. U.S. Environmental Protection Agency
"Indoor Air Pollution: An Introduction for Health Professionals"
www.epa.gov/iaq/pubs/hpguide.html
Despite its title, this booklet has valuable information for interior designers. The "Remedial Action" sections list environmental changes that designers might suggest to clients to help alleviate adverse health effects.

4. National Library of Medicine and National Institutes of Health
Medline Plus
www.epa.gov/iaq/index.html
This consumer-oriented Web site includes links to dozens of sources of information about indoor air quality, its effects on health, and how it can be improved.

5. Centers for Disease Control and Prevention and National Institute for Occupational Safety and Health
"Building Air Quality: A Guide for Building Owners and Facility Managers"
www.cdc.gov/niosh/baqtoc.html
This reader-friendly guide includes extensive information and tools for identifying and mitigating indoor air problems. It also has case studies with suggested solutions.

REFERENCES

Alabama Cooperative Extension System. News Line. (April 1, 2000). *Scented candles harbor soot, warns expert.* [Electronic version]. Retrieved January 1, 2007, from www.aces.edu/dept/extcomm/newspaper/soot_phenom.html

American Lung Association, Environmental Protection Agency, Consumer Product Safety Commission, and American Medical Association. (1994). *Indoor air pollution: An introduction for health professionals.* (EPA No. 402-R-94-007). Washington, D.C.: U.S. Government Printing Office. 2006.

Baechler, M. C., Hadley, D. L., Marseille, T. J., Stenner, R. D., Peterson, M. R., Naugle, D. F., et al. (1991). *Sick building syndrome: Sources, health effects, mitigation.* Park Ridge, NJ: Noyes Data Corporation.

Baron, R. A. (1976). The reduction of human aggression: A field study of the influence of incompatible responses. *Journal of Applied Social Psychology, 6,* 260–674.

Bayer, C. W., Crow, S. A., and Fischer, J. (2000). Causes of indoor air quality problems in schools: Summary of scientific research (revised edition). Oak Ridge, TN: Energy Division Oak Ridge National Laboratory.

Binggeli, C. (2003). *Building systems for interior designers.* Hoboken, NJ: John Wiley & Sons.

Bower, J. (2001). *The healthy house: How to buy one, how to build one, how to cure a sick one* (4th ed.). Bloomington, IN: The Healthy House Institute.

Canadian Centre for Occupational Health and Safety. (January 9, 2006). *OSH answers:*

Thermal comfort for office work. Retrieved January 7, 2007, from www.ccohs.ca/oshanswers/phys_agents/thermal_comfort.html.

Cotton, (1986). Violent crime incidents in Indianapolis increase with increasing temperature. *Journal of Applied Social Psychology, 16,* 786–801.

Dul, J., & Weerdmeester, B. (1993). *Ergonomics for beginners: A quick reference guide* (2nd ed.). New York: Taylor & Francis.

Fanger, P. O. (1972). *Thermal Comfort.* New York: McGraw-Hill.

Fountain, M., and Arens, E. A. (1993). Air movement and thermal comfort. *ASHRAE Journal, 35,* 27–30.

Holmes, J. R. (1994). *How much air do we breathe?* (Research Notes: Brief Reports to the Scientific and Technical Community. No. 94-11). Sacramento, CA: California Environmental Protection Agency, Air Resources Board.

Kroemer, K. H. E., & Grandjean, E. (1997). *Fitting the task to the human: A textbook of occupational ergonomics* (5th ed.). New York: Taylor & Francis.

Morgan, M. T. (2003). *Environmental health* (3rd ed.). Belmont, CA: Thomson Wadsworth.

Nally, S. (2002). *Creating safe learning zones: The ABCs of healthy schools.* Falls Church, VA: Center for Health, Environment and Justice.

National Institute for Occupational Safety and Health. (1997). *Indoor Environmental Quality.* Retrieved November 29, 2007, from www.cdc.gov/niosh/ieqfs.html

National Institutes of Health. (July 27, 2006.) Chemicals in many air fresheners may reduce lung function. *NIH News.* Retrieved August 7, 2006, from www.nidhs.nih.gov/oc/news/airfreshener.htm

Neighbors, M., and Tannehille-Jones, R. (1999). *Human diseases.* Clifton Park, NY: Thomson Delmar Learning.

O'Reilly, J., Hagan, P., Gots, R., and Hedge, A. (1998). *Keeping buildings healthy: How to monitor and prevent indoor environmental problems.* New York: Wiley-Interscience.

Schoer, L., and Shaffran, J. (1973). A combined evaluation of three separate research projects on the effects of thermal environment on learning and performance. *ASHRAE Transactions, 79,* 97–108.

Shaw, C. Y. (1997). *Maintaining acceptable air quality in office buildings through ventilation.* [Electronic version]. (Construction Technology Update No. 3). Ottawa, Canada: Institute for Research in Construction. Retrieved November 29, 2007, from http://irc.nrc-cnrc.gc.ca/pubs/ctus/3_e.html

Tate, N. (1994). *The sick building syndrome.* Far Hills, NJ: New Horizon Press.

Thompson, A. Breathing easier indoors. (November–December 2004). *Smart homeowner.* [Electronic version]. Retrieved February 22, 2007, from www.smart-homeowner.com/articles/8640

U.S. Environmental Protection Agency. (January 2007). *Health risks: Exposure to radon causes lung cancer in non-smokers and smokers alike.* Retrieved January 13, 2007, from www.epa.gov/radon/healthrisks.html

U.S. Environmental Protection Agency. (August 2006). *IAQ tools for schools: Frequently asked questions.* Retrieved January 17, 2007, from www.epa.gov/iaq/schools/scfaqs.html

U.S. Environmental Protection Agency. (August 2006). *Indoor air facts no. 8: Use and care of home humidifiers.* Retrieved January 15, 2007, from ww.epa.gov/iaq/pubs/humidif.html

U.S. Environmental Protection Agency. (August 2006). *Ozone generators that are sold as air cleaners.* Retrieved December 7, 2006, from epa.gov/iaq/pubs/ozonegen.html

U.S. Environmental Protection Agency, Office of Air and Radiation. (February 1990). (EPA Document No. 40/1-90-002.) Washington, DC: Author.

U.S. Environmental Protection Agency. (1995). *The inside story: A guide to indoor air quality.* (EPA Document No. 402-K-93-007). Washington, DC: Author.

Wyon, D. P. (1970). Studies of children under imposed noise and heat stress. *Ergonomics, 13,* (5): 598–612.

We all recognize that we are going through a time of tremendous change. And we all have to take part in solving this for our own common future.

—Dr. Susan Roaf

CHAPTER **6**

Energy Systems

LEARNING OBJECTIVES

1. **Explain how dependence on fossil fuels affects the environment and human health.**
2. **Describe the alternative forms of energy being developed and applied today.**
3. **Give examples of how designers can help clients make good decisions about techniques and products that conserve energy without harming human health.**

Energy plays a substantial role in modern life and has become a major consideration in the built environment. It adds comfort to our structures in the form of heat, light, and cooling, enabling us to live free of the restrictions of weather conditions and seasons. At the same time, our use of energy has come at a price to both ourselves and the earth. Examples include drilling for oil, digging through mountains to mine coal, and disrupting wilderness areas to obtain natural gas. Simultaneously, the conversion of these raw materials into usable energy through combustion is creating enormous amounts of pollution that have dirtied both the natural and built environments, particularly the air. This in turn leads to health concerns because when the particulates resulting from combustion are inhaled, they can cause chronic respiratory ailments such as

asthma. When designers create interiors that reduce the need for energy from combustible resources, those professionals contribute to the health of both the earth and the humans (and other life-forms) inhabiting it. For example, designers can recommend that windows be located on southern exposures of homes and buildings to take advantage of the sun's path throughout the year, thus obtaining a renewable and nonpolluting heat source. They can also design lighting systems that take advantage of natural daylight as much as possible, thus reducing the need for lighting, which consumes a significant amount of energy.

Global warming is a topic of increasing concern and discussion. This phenomenon is directly related to the way most of our energy is generated. Finding alternative and renewable sources of energy, while concurrently working to reduce our current consumption, are activities that must be given priority. Energy should be of particular concern to building professionals, including interior designers, because about 40 percent of generated energy is consumed by buildings, the same amount used by transportation (Kibert, 2005). The following statistics demonstrate the impact of these figures in terms of harmful emissions produced by buildings in 2002 in the United States:

- 47 percent of sulfur dioxide
- 35 percent of carbon dioxide
- 22 percent of nitrogen oxide

Thus, responsible designers should become involved in conservation efforts by learning about construction and energy-conserving and health-preserving strategies, as well as renewable forms of energy, to help their clients make more informed decisions.

SOURCES OF ENERGY

Fossil fuels supply almost 80 percent of the world's energy supply. Fossils are remnants of organisms that lived millions of years ago; these are exactly what these fuels are made of—microscopic plant and animal life that settled on the ocean floors eons ago. Over the millennia, they accumulated in vast numbers and were gradually buried by thick layers of sediments (materials that settle to the bottom of a liquid), such as sand and clay. As these layers became heavier, the resulting pressure and high temperatures converted them to **hydrocarbons** (chains of carbon and hydrogen atoms) that, in turn, became the crude oil, natural gas, and coal we now use to heat our buildings and run our cars.

Oil, gas, and coal have enabled humans to develop and enjoy comfortable modern lifestyles. This convenience has also created unintended consequences. For example, for hundreds of years, Londoners burned coal to combat England's damp, cool climate. Despite its warming properties, coal burning (both residential and industrial) is particularly dirty and London became known for smoke-filled air that irritated the lungs. This air pollution problem actually became fatal in December 1952, when as many as 12,000 people died as a result of a huge layer of fog and smoke that originated from industrial sources such as coal furnaces and blanketed London for five days (American Lung Association, 2004).

Fossil fuels present many problems, the majority of which are related to negative effects on human health and life quality. The first problem is that fossil fuel resources are finite, meaning that once we have depleted the supplies available under the earth's surface, they are gone. Using current exploration and extracting technology, optimistic estimates are that oil will be available for 100 more years. Natural gas and coal supplies are somewhat larger and might be expected to last 125 and 200 years, respectively. These numbers may not sound dire to those living today but, in fact, these are very short periods of time when considered in light of the thousands of years that humans have inhabited the earth. In addition to the environmental damage caused by extracting a finite resource, its eventual scarcity will lead to higher prices. The effect of supply and demand is demonstrated by the fluctuating of gasoline prices. The price of natural gas and oil for heating homes has started to outpace the budgets of many low-income families, especially seniors, who have difficulty paying for basic necessities.

The second problem with fossil fuels is that energy is secured from them by combustion (burning). The combustion of hydrocarbons produces carbon dioxide, a gas that constitutes 82 percent of human-made greenhouse gas emissions (National Energy Information Center, 2004). **Greenhouse gases** are chemical compounds that allow the sun's rays to enter the earth's atmosphere and then trap the heat of these rays as they reflect off the earth's surface. Many scientists believe that this process is gradually raising the overall temperature of the air close to the earth as well as the water in the oceans, resulting in the phenomenon known as **global warming.** The danger is that even very small increases in these air and water temperatures can cause changes in the earth's climate that affect everything from the growth of crops to the melting of glaciers and the polar ice caps. Greenhouse gases have increased by about 25 percent in the last 150 years. It is believed by many that this increase is due to the growth of industrialization and the demand for energy (National Energy Information Center, 2004). During the last 20 years, about 75 percent of human-caused carbon dioxide emissions have been the result of burning fossil fuels (National Energy Information Center, 2004).

There are several ways that designers can help reduce greenhouse gases. For example, they can encourage clients to buy lower-energy appliances such as those approved by the ENERGY STAR program (discussed in this chapter). They can also encourage the purchase of high-quality, long-lasting furnishings to save on the energy resources required in furniture production.

A third problem with fossil fuels also relates to their combustion: the release of gaseous chemicals, including sulfur dioxides and nitrogen oxides, into the air during the burning process. These gases interact in the atmosphere and form fine particulates that can travel long distances on the wind. When inhaled into the lungs, they can cause heart disorders and lung diseases such as asthma and bronchitis (U.S. Environmental Protection Agency, 2007, "Effects of"). When particulates reach high enough levels of concentration, they can cause fatal respiratory harm. Although engineers, not interior designers, plan the ventilation systems that influence the entry of outdoor pollutants into built structures, designers should know about the quality of the air in the vicinity of their clients (discussed in detail in Chapter 5). With this information, they can provide a higher level of service to stakeholders (including clients and/or occupants of the building). For example, a designer who works with a home owner in a highly polluted area needs to determine the ages of household members. If young children live in the home, the designer might consider including additional indoor play areas because the lungs of these children are still developing and, therefore, more vulnerable to the particulates present in polluted air.

In addition to chemical particulates, nitrogen oxides combine with volatile organic compounds, described in Chapter 4, to form ozone. Although ozone is beneficial when high in the earth's atmosphere, where it serves as a shield against the sun's harmful ultraviolet (UV) rays, it is harmful when it exists near the earth's surface. When inhaled, ozone poses a significant health risk, especially for children with asthma (U.S. Environmental Protection Agency, 2007, "Ozone"). Exposure to even small amounts of ozone can result in serious respiratory irritation—even death (see Chapter 4 for more information about ozone). In addition to directly harming human health, ozone can also kill vegetation and trees, thus indirectly affecting human well-being. Besides promoting the formation of ozone, the sulfuric, carbonic, and nitric acids generated by fossil fuel combustion fall back to the earth as **acid rain.** In large quantities, acid rain can make soils too acidic, kill plants, weaken trees, injure fish and other water species, and destroy objects made of certain stones, such as marble.

Finally, the dependence of the modern world on fossil fuels has contributed to conflicts, including wars, over access to oil resources, with injuries, deaths, and significant environmental destruction as a result. Thus, there are many ways that our heavy dependence on fossil fuels and our overuse of energy are negatively affecting the earth and all its life systems. The search to find alternative sources of energy has been under way for decades, but efforts to conserve energy must be increased and maintained if we are to preserve our planet as we know it.

Implications for Designers

As discussed in the previous section, the developed world's dependence on fossil fuels has led to a multitude of problems that threaten the health of all living beings, including plants. Interior designers, as well as other concerned members of society, have an obligation to learn about and take part in alleviating the problem. For designers, there are two specific implications. The first relates to reducing our dependence on fossil fuels. Designers can suggest alternative energy resources and recommend energy-saving products and techniques— perhaps including products and techniques they use themselves—described in this chapter, to their clients. Examples include updating traditional fireplaces to improve their heating capability, increasing the entry of natural light into rooms in order to decrease the need for artificial lighting, and creating window treatments that reduce the entry of summer heat and winter cold.

The second implication for designers is the use of heat-mitigating strategies for structures within environments where the extensive use of hardscape makes them particularly susceptible to increases in air temperature, ozone, and particulates. Although no city to date has implemented comprehensive plans for reducing heat, there are a variety of strategies that can help:

- Use highly reflective building materials on flat surfaces such as walkways, driveways, parking areas, and roofs. Light-colored roofs can reduce the amount of heat absorbed into the structure by as much as 80 percent (Lawrence Berkeley Laboratory, n.d.).
- Group buildings to allow room for trees and other solar-dissipating vegetation (Stone, 2005).
- Increase the amount of tree canopy cover. In addition to providing shade, experiments have shown plants to be helpful in removing greenhouse gases, such as carbon dioxide and nitrogen oxide, from the air (Fujii et al., 2005).
- Install roof and patio gardens to absorb carbon dioxide and provide a cooling effect as plants give off moisture.

EMBODIED ENERGY

Saving energy must become a priority for all built-environment professionals. There are many ways to achieve energy savings, thereby reducing the need for fossil fuels, in both new construction and existing structures. We often think of energy use simply in terms of what is needed to light, heat, and cool our buildings. There are many factors, including the materials and methods used to create the building in the first place, that significantly influence the overall use of energy. The term **embodied energy** refers to the amount of energy used

in the entire life cycle of a structure. The following are examples of the factors considered when calculating embodied energy, whether for an office desk or an entire building:

- Extracting raw materials, as through logging and mining, to use in manufacture or construction
- Transporting raw materials to the sites where they are processed, as in lumber mills and foundries
- Processing and/or manufacturing products from natural materials
- Packaging building materials and products
- Transporting products and materials to construction sites
- Transporting workers to construction sites
- Building the structure
- Remodeling, repairing, cleaning, and maintaining the structure once it is built
- Heating, cooling, and lighting the structure over its life span
- Demolishing and hauling away used materials when remodeling or taking down the structure
- Storing or destroying used materials

In addition to the energy needed to perform these functions, two other important factors are included when calculating embodied energy: the depletion of the natural resources used and the impact on the environment from the removal of these materials. For example, if wood is obtained through clear-cutting (logging practice in which all trees are felled and removed from a forest area), the supply of trees has been depleted until new ones can grow, the land may be susceptible to damage from erosion due to the lack of vegetation, wildlife have lost their habitat, and there are fewer trees to absorb the carbon dioxide exhaled by people and other living creatures. This example demonstrates that the total effect of man-made structures can be significant.

Implications for Designers

One of the most important factors in reducing the amount of embodied energy is building long-life, durable, and adaptable buildings

(Milne and Readon, 2004). Designers can make significant positive contributions to environmental, energy, and human-health conservation by taking a holistic approach and carefully considering all the materials and energy requirements involved in new construction and remodeling projects. Box 6.1 contains a list of suggestions for conserving embodied energy.

Designers should also consider the long-term consequences when deciding how to decrease embodied energy. For example, in a cold, windy climate, it might ultimately be cost-effective to spend more on the initial materials for walls and insulation, if their manufacture is relatively energy-efficient, in order to save on heating costs over the life of the building. Some decisions that appear to be cost-savers, such as installing cheap glue-down carpeting, may actually be more expensive in the long run in terms of replacement and disposal costs. (Another factor in the carpeting example is the possibility of VOC emissions and their impact on human health, as discussed in Chapter 4.)

Recycling building materials has been identified as an effective way to save embodied energy, believed to be as much as 95 per-

cent for products such as aluminum (Milne and Readon, 2004). An ecologically friendly phrase suggests that we "reduce, reuse, and recycle." On a large scale, there is increasing interest in the construction of buildings that can be deconstructed, rather than demolished,

---

FIGURE 6.1A AND B Antiques and items from architectural salvage companies can be incorporated into the built environment, adding beauty while saving resources.

(A)

(B)

and their materials salvaged. On a smaller scale, designers might suggest that clients consider purchasing high-quality used furnishings or antiques made of solid wood. Or that they recycle furnishings they already own through reupholstering, painting, or creatively modifying. Not only can these pieces add character and interest to interiors, their use eliminates the need to spend the energy and resources to convert trees into new furnishings. Used rugs, decorative objects, and even parts of buildings can be attractively incorporated into many decors. (See Figure 6.1a and b.)

CARBON FOOTPRINT

The term **carbon footprint** was developed to describe the impact of human activities in terms of the amount of greenhouse gases produced, measured in units of carbon dioxide. A carbon footprint consists of two parts:

1. The primary footprint is the measure of carbon dioxide emissions through the burning of fossil fuels. This includes domestic use, such as heating a house with an oil furnace, and transportation, such as driving a car that is fueled with gasoline.
2. The secondary footprint is a measure of the carbon dioxide emissions associated with the whole life cycle of products used; in other words, the embodied energy of the product, discussed in the previous section.

According to the estimates of the non-profit organization carbonfootprint.com, 36 percent of the typical person's footprint is related to the built environment:

- 15 percent for gas, oil, and coal
- 12 percent for electricity
- 9 percent for buildings and furnishings

Implications for Designers

Carbon footprints provide an easy way to visualize each person's contribution to the consumption of fossil fuels. Even more important, the concept emphasizes how each individual plays a role in contributing to the problems caused by the heavy use of fossil fuels. Designers might consider using this concept to discuss with clients how their choices influence their use of these fuels. For example, electricity generation is a major producer of carbon emissions and, as mentioned previously, constitutes 12 percent of the average American's carbon footprint. This information might be used to demonstrate to a client the advantage of incorporating natural lighting as well as changing light lamps to more efficient types, as discussed later in this chapter. Other simple actions that designers can recommend include insulating hot water tanks located in unheated garages and basements; installing systems to recycle gray water (wastewater from washing, cooking, and other non-toilet-generated activities); and creating systems to make recycling easy and convenient. A related issue is the disposal of items such as batteries and fluorescent lamps. Designers should know about local collection and disposal policies so they can make recommendations to their clients.

Size of Homes

In spite of growing interest in decreasing the size of our carbon footprints, there is a trend that contradicts the concept of sustainability and energy conservation: American houses are getting bigger. During the last 50 years, while the average family size has decreased, the square footage of the average home has increased by 18 percent. At the same time, the number of houses with garages has increased 80 percent (Winchip, 2007). The trend continues today, even as concern for global warming becomes a frequent topic of conversation all across the country. According to the U.S. Census, between 1900 and 2005, the number of homes with at least four bedrooms rose from one house in six to one house in five. In 2007, the fastest-growing type of house had five or more bedrooms (Ohlemacher and Foy, 2007). Even if some of these homes are built to be highly efficient in terms of heating, cooling, and lighting, recall from the discussion about embodied energy that the total process of building and maintaining structures must be included when considering our total consumption of fossil fuels. Larger-sized buildings obviously use more resources, such as building materials, furnishings, flooring, wall finishes, and maintenance products, than smaller ones. They also tend to emit more pollutants, thus having a larger negative impact on human health.

Designers can participate in reversing this trend by encouraging clients to reduce the size of buildings (Winchip, 2007). One strategy is to create what might be called "smart interiors" that maximize the efficiency of space. The first step in designing efficient interiors is to identify the needs and habits of clients to determine the amount and organization of interior space that will best address their needs (Winchip, 2007). The second step is to perform a spatial analysis to identify traditional rooms that can be eliminated and to determine ways to optimize the space in rooms that are actually needed (Winchip, 2007). For example, many families no longer require both a living room and family room. Combining the two into one well-planned area for entertainment such as watching television and visiting with friends can reduce square footage as well as the need for infrequently used furnishings.

The trend toward extremely large kitchens is problematic because of their popularity. This feature is emphasized in many new homes and many remodeling projects focus on enlarging and adding features to kitchens. For example, two kitchen sinks in a two-person household is not uncommon. At the same time, Americans are cooking less frequently and eating out more often. According to data collected by the Department of Energy in 2001, only 32 percent of households cooked at least twice daily; more than 27 percent cooked less than once a day (Raloff, 2002). Reversing the trend from overly large to smaller, well-designed, and energy-efficient kitchens would contribute to reducing wasted resources.

Wise Use of Space

"Flex rooms" refer to rooms that can be used for more than one purpose. For example, rather than having a dedicated guest room that is only used occasionally, the space can also serve as a hobby room or office. Furnish-

FIGURE 6.2 This clever piece of furniture expands the uses of a room by serving as a bookshelf, desk, and bed.

ings such as daybeds, pull-down beds, armoires that contain desks and foldout tables, and wall units make an easy transition from one use to another. (See Figure 6.2 for an example.) Laundry rooms, if located near an outside door, can double as mudrooms. The concept

FIGURE 6.3 A small home office can be tucked under stairs to take advantage of space that might otherwise be wasted or used as a collecting point for little-used items.

FIGURE 6.4 Vertical storage can greatly increase storage capacity as well as making items easy to see and access.

of flex rooms can also apply to office buildings. For example, conference rooms that are used infrequently can double as libraries and project areas when large table space is needed.

"Found space" is another technique to increase usable space. For example, closets and hidden spaces, such as under a stairway, can be outfitted in a number of useful ways:

- Storage areas
- Small work areas with a desk and file cabinet (see Figure 6.3)
- Cozy play areas for children
- Retreats for reading or napping

The average American family today has more belongings than ever before. As a result, a common design problem is finding sufficient storage that keeps order while at the same time not using large amounts of space. Even many families that purchase larger homes find themselves overwhelmed by the sheer quantity of possessions that comprise modern life. **Vertical storage** is a method that involves using wall space effectively. For example, covering a laundry room wall with painted pegboard with pegs, containers, and shelves of various configurations can be used to store items such as household and hobby supplies. Garages, frequently catch-alls for infrequently or never-used items, can incorporate vertical storage for

gardening supplies, tools, and sporting goods. (See Figure 6.4.) A popular method of maximizing garage space and storing seasonal items such as holiday decorations is a system of overhead shelves and baskets.

CARBON NEUTRAL

Carbon neutral means maintaining a balance between producing and using carbon, especially emissions of carbon dioxide. Its relation to the carbon footprint is that in achieving a carbon-neutral state, the size of one's footprint is reduced. Becoming carbon neutral is an active process that consists of three steps:

1. Measuring an organization's or individual's footprint by inventorying the greenhouse gas emissions generated. In the case of a person, the actual measurement could include a survey of energy requirements. This could include heating and cooling costs and electric bills for lighting.
2. Developing goals and strategies to reduce these emissions. Home owners who want to reduce their consumption of oil-generated heat, for example, might consider installing double-glazed windows.
3. Purchasing offsets, which means engaging in carbon-combating activities such as planting trees or investing in renewable-energy projects like wind turbines. For an individual, this might consist of planting additional shrubs in the garden or the community.

NET-ZERO ENERGY

Net-zero energy, as its name implies, refers to a building that has a net energy consumption of zero over a typical year. Energy consumption can be measured in at least three ways, each with its own methods of offsetting or "zeroing out":

1. The monetary cost of the energy. A common method for bringing the cost to zero is selling the extra energy produced by a building, such as through solar collection

panels, to an **electricity grid** (a large, complex system of equipment and wiring that produces and transmits electrical power to many customers).

2. The amount of energy used, as expressed in kilowatts for electricity or cubic feet for natural gas. This can be balanced out by producing equal amounts of energy onsite, as with a windmill.

3. The amount of carbon estimated to be emitted through the combustion of fossil fuels needed to supply the energy consumed. Again, this can be neutralized by planting trees that consume carbon dioxide and by reducing amounts of energy consumed.

At present, net-zero buildings are not common in the United States. Two U.S. Department of Energy programs are conducting research and creating partnerships with private builders to construct cost-effective, zero-energy homes. These programs, **Building America** and **Zero-Energy Homes,** have the following objectives:

- Produce homes on a community scale that use on average 30 percent to 90 percent less energy than traditionally built homes.
- Integrate onsite power systems leading to "zero-energy" homes (ZEH) that will ultimately produce as much energy as they use by 2020.
- Help builders reduce construction time and waste.
- Improve builder productivity.
- Provide new product opportunities for manufacturers and suppliers.
- Implement innovative energy- and material-saving technologies (U.S. Department of Energy, 2007, "Building"); U.S. Department of Energy, 2003, "Moving").

A number of major American builders have constructed net-zero-energy homes, including a 300-house subdivision in San Diego built by SheaHomes (U. S. Department of Energy, 203;

Moving Toward Zero Energy Homes). The major energy-saving features of these homes, some of which are discussed in this chapter, include the following:

- Photovoltaics (solar panels)
- NightBreeze (an integrated heating, ventilation cooling, air-conditioning, and fresh-air ventilation system developed by the California Institute for Energy Efficiency and the California Energy Commission)
- Insulation under the slab on which a house is built to reduce heat loss
- Cellulose insulation (made from recycled wood)
- Solar water heaters
- Masonry (concrete, brick, and stone) walls to store heat

Implications for Designers

The concepts of carbon neutral and net-zero energy, like the carbon footprint, can be useful tools for discussing energy needs and consumption with clients. Although generally applied to large organizations rather than to individuals, they provide a way to visualize complex issues. At the same time, increasing numbers of Americans are interested in building energy-efficient or even zero-energy homes. Many others want to incorporate more energy-efficiency strategies in their remodeling and home renovation projects. Designers should be aware of the various programs and methods so that they can make sound recommendations to clients and knowledgeably work with builders on the increasing number of projects that involve energy-efficient buildings. For example, clients may not associate their desire for large homes, discussed previously, with a large carbon footprint. If designers can help clients identify their reasons for wanting larger spaces, they might help them see that such spaces are not actually necessary to achieve their lifestyle goals.

Designers, as built-environment professionals, should be advocates of energy efficiency, thus representing the needs of both individual clients and the community as a whole. In fact, sustainability issues and practices, such as energy conservation, are now included in the standards for accredited interior design programs (Winchip, 2007).

RENEWABLE ENERGY SOURCES

As recently as 150 years ago, renewable resources supplied 90 percent of U.S. energy. Today they make up only 6 percent of U.S. energy consumption (Sexton, Marin, Zilberman, 2006). Research is moving forward to reverse this trend, and renewable and alternative energy sources are being developed to replace our dependence on fossil fuels. Natural forces, such as the sun and wind, have always been used as power and heat sources. After being largely replaced by the industrialized world with fossil fuel energy sources, they are now showing great promise to once again supply us with the vast amounts of energy we consume each day. The four major technologies that interior designers are most likely to encounter are solar, wind, biomass, and geothermal. Knowing about these forms of energy, including products that may not yet be widely used, will put designers in the forefront of a rapidly growing group of concerned people who are looking for safe and healthy alternatives to replace fossil fuel energy and heat sources.

SOLAR ENERGY

The sun has great potential as a heat and electrical source, providing energy that does not produce air pollution, greenhouse emissions, or wastes that must be buried. Solar energy has been used throughout history; for example, Greek and Roman architects designed buildings and oriented them to best take advantage of the sun's light and heat. The current disadvantages of solar energy relate to the initial costs of securing it—a major reason why solar energy is not widely used in the United States. In countries whose governments have subsidized the development of solar technology, annual increases in the quantity of energy produced by solar power have skyrocketed. Recent examples include 45 percent in Japan and 43 percent in Europe (Johnson and Washington, 2004). Some industry specialists predict that technological developments will make solar-produced energy affordable for homes in the near future (Johnson and Washington, 2004), so it is very likely that today's designers will work on buildings and homes that make extensive use of solar energy. They should therefore be familiar with this technology (including its effects on interiors).

Solar Heating Systems

There are two types of solar heating systems, passive and active. In passive solar, the sun provides energy and the building itself acts as the collection, storage, control, and distribution systems. Using passive solar is most successful when plans for its use are included in the original design of a building because many factors, starting with site selection and how the structure is placed on the site, must be considered. Related to the building site, the following elements affect the success of passive solar heating:

- Topography
- Location of trees
- Latitude (distance from the equator)
- Location of adjacent buildings (Winchip, 2007)

Factors related to the building itself include:

- Shape
- Fenestration (windows)
- Orientation (how it sits on the building site)
- Heat absorption of its materials
- Insulation
- Room configurations (Winchip, 2007)
- Thermal mass (materials that absorb heat, such as concrete, stone, and water)

Implications for Designers

A key factor in successful passive solar heating is the use of extensive glazing on the side of the building that receives maximum sun exposure year-round. In the northern hemisphere, this is the south side; in the southern hemisphere, it is the north side. It is important to keep the appropriate side clear from obstructions during the months when sunlight is scarcest. The most effective strategy is to plant deciduous trees, tall plants, or vines on the prevalent sun side: in summer, the leaves provide shade; in winter, the lack of leaves allows sunlight to enter the building. An additional benefit of using trees is their self-cooling mechanism that occurs when they take up water from the ground to evaporate through their leaves. This evaporative cooling lowers the temperature of the surrounding air (Binggeli, 2003). Other shading options, listed in order of effectiveness, include:

- Shrubs
- Trellises
- Overhangs
- Awnings
- Shade screens
- Window coatings
- Interior shades

During cold months, the issue is obviously retaining heat, rather than deflecting it. To accomplish this, floors and walls on sun-facing exposures should be made of heat-absorbing materials. Designers might consider brick, concrete, stone, and tile (Winchip, 2007). Window coverings and shades should be chosen to control night heat loss during cold months and to prevent excessive heat entry on warm summer days. (See Figure 6.5.) The most effective window coverings are light colored on the side facing the window and made of an insulating material (Binggeli, 2003). They should also fit tightly and cover the whole window to help prevent warm or cold air from entering the room. Painted surfaces, fabrics, and furnishings exposed to direct sunlight for several hours a day should be made from fade-resistant fabrics and colors.

The term "thermal mass" refers to floors and walls designed to absorb and store sunlight and then pass the heat to the interior.

When decorating rooms with such walls, it is important not to place furnishings or use wall hangings where they could block the flow of radiant heat entering the room.

Clients who are remodeling might be interested in solar hot water systems in which water runs through roof-mounted tubes where it is heated by the sun. Even if desired temperatures are not reached, the water is warmed enough to reduce the load on the conventional hot water heater. According to the U.S. Department of Energy,

FIGURE 6.5 Translucent shades are available to prevent the heat of unwanted sun while allowing light to enter.

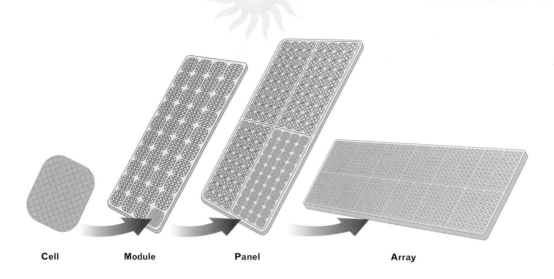

Cell   Module   Panel   Array

a solar water-heating system usually costs more initially to purchase and install, but is likely to save money—as well as nonrenewable resources—over the long run. The Department further reports that water-heating bills can drop 50 to 80 percent when solar power is used (U.S. Department of Energy, 2005, "Economics").

Active Solar Systems and Photovoltaics

Active solar-energy collection systems include special collecting panels along with pumps, fans, and other mechanical equipment to distribute heat energy throughout a building.

The basic component of solar collection systems is the **photovoltaic** (PV) cell, a device that converts sunlight into electricity. You might have used a solar-powered calculator, which operates using one solar cell. Grouped together by the thousands, these cells comprise PV modules. The modules are then combined into panels that are then joined to form arrays. (See Figure 6.6.) Arrays can convert large enough quantities of solar energy into electricity to supply the needs of entire buildings.

A technique known as **building-integrated photovoltaic (BIPV) technologies** is adding PV to building components including windows, skylights, siding shingles,

and metal shingles and tiles. As shown in Figure 6.7, these additions can be very attractive. Because PV systems are modular, they can be added, removed, and reused during their expected lifetime of 30 years. This flexibility increases their sustainability value.

PV glazing modules, also called photovoltaic windows, combine pleasing architectural accents, light entry, and sources of renewable energy. These modules can be incorporated into both new and existing buildings. They are fabricated by using two panes of glass with PV modules attached to the front of the inside pane. Because PV glazing is not completely transparent, it is best used for nonview windows, skylights, greenhouse windows, facades, and curtain walls (nonbearing layers hung on the outside of a building).

Currently, the costs of purchasing and installing PV modules are high compared to buying energy created by fossil fuels. This means that even though the long-term costs are extremely low, the initial costs are too high for many consumers. As technology advances and production increases, the costs are expected to decrease. This has already happened in Japan, where the price of PV modules has dropped two-thirds since 1994. In some cases, structures that produce more energy than needed can sell the extra energy to the local electrical grid.

FIGURE 6.7 Photovoltaics can be attractively integrated into a building's design. In the Solaire Building in New York, they are the shiny blue/purple surfaces that not only convert sunlight into electricity but add textural interest.

Implications for Designers

Designers might consider suggesting the use of photovoltaics to clients who have the means to purchase and install them. Over the long run, this technology can prove to be a healthy and cost-effective means of producing electricity. Photovoltaic windows, because of their translucency, can be good choices for rooms in which light is desirable and privacy is necessary. This might include bedrooms, bathrooms, and rooms that face busy streets.

As with other types of renewable-energy sources, a variety of programs are in place to assist with the cost of implementing photovoltaics. Designers should become informed about those that could benefit their clients.

WIND ENERGY

Wind power, like the power from the sun, has been used by humans for thousands of years. The ancient Egyptians may have sailed the Nile in wind-powered boats (Binggeli, 2003), and other early civilizations developed wind-powered water pumps and grain mills. Today, electrical energy that can be stored is produced as the blades of large turbines are turned by the wind. Wind-generated energy is the world's fastest-growing form of renewable-energy production, increasing an estimated 25 percent annually (Kibert, 2005), possibly because wind turbines and accessories pay for themselves in energy savings faster than most other types of energy production (Binggeli, 2003). It has also been encouraged by the Production Tax Credit of 1.9 cents per kilowatt hour of electricity produced for the first ten years of operation (Environmental and Energy Study Institute, 2006, "Wind").

Profitable generation of electricity now takes place on large-scale wind farms, such as those in southern California and west Texas. In fact, the cost per kilowatt hour has decreased dramatically in the last 20 years; this decline is expected to continue. Although wind energy is generally collected through large fields of wind turbines, single turbines are also available for powering individual buildings.

Wind turbines are clean, nonpolluting producers of electricity. In 2004, wind farms produced about 16 million kilowatts of electricity that, if produced by an average mix of fossils fuels, would have released the following into the atmosphere:

- 10.6 million tons of carbon dioxide
- 56,000 tons of sulfur dioxide
- 33,000 tons of nitrogen oxides (Environmental and Energy Study Institute, 2006, "Wind")

Implications for Designers

Wind turbines can be a good choice for people building in remote sites that don't have electrical service. Although this would seem rare today, there is growing interest in returning to more rural lifestyles. This trend could increase as the number of baby boomers retire and leave cities and suburbs in search of a quieter, more natural lifestyle.

BIOMASS

"Biomass" refers to fuels derived from plant materials such as trees, grains, wood wastes, aquatic plants, and animal and municipal solid waste. Thus, biomass can serve the double role of a clean energy source with reduced sulfur emissions and a method of removing waste that might otherwise be dumped into landfills. At the same time, it is important to note that biomass, if not used properly, can present health hazards. For example, millions of people in developing countries cook in unvented indoor spaces over fires fueled by charcoal, wood, dung, and crop scraps. The combustion of these materials is often incomplete and produces harmful inhalable particulates as well as carbon monoxide, nitrogen oxides, and other toxic compounds. This is of concern because as many as half of the world's population depends on biomass as a main source of fuel (Winchip, 2007). For this reason, advancements in developing clean methods of harnessing biomass energy have been necessary to make it a potentially viable energy source. Another concern about biomass is that allocating crops such as corn to biofuel production will raise the price of basic foods and cause millions to starve. But research is ongoing to make fields much more productive and the conversion of crops to fuel extremely efficient with almost no waste. Plants and trees are now being grown for the single purpose of becoming fuel. As they grow, these crops remove carbon dioxide from the air; when they are harvested, they supply a clean source of energy. Another important area of research is using all plant material, much of which used to be discarded as waste, for producing energy. In addition to more traditional forms of biomass, algae is being investigated as a potential major provider of biofuel.

At present, only a small percentage of U.S. energy needs are met with biomass, although the American Bioenergy Association believes that the United States has the capability of replacing all the country's gasoline usage and all its nuclear power if this form of energy were fully exploited (Kibert, 2005).

Implications for Designers

The majority of biomass research and development deals with fuel for cars and other means of transportation. At the same time, biomass is a fuel source that can be used directly by consumers in the home, under their control, as opposed to receiving it over electrical lines from a mass-production source. There are a number of biomass heating appliances that designers might suggest to ecologically concerned clients.

Pellet-Fueled Appliances

These appliances, similar in appearance to woodstoves and fireplaces, burn pellets that are produced from sawdust and wood shavings. The pellets provide a clean source of heat and, as a by-product of lumber and furniture production, they are environmentally friendly. Pellet appliances burn efficiently, create almost no smoke, and produce less odor than other wood-burning appliances. Their efficiency is based on the fact that compressed pellets contain less moisture than wood and, therefore, have a higher combustion efficiency (available energy that is converted to heat). Because they create so little smoke, they can be vented using a relatively small metal tube that passes through a wall or the roof to the outside, rather than requiring a full-sized chimney or stovepipe. Wood pellets also offer a net-zero effect: when trees used as stock are replanted, they absorb the carbon dioxide that results from burning the pellets (Pahl, 2003). Pellet appliances are a healthy choice because the sawdust is held together by natural wood resins and binders, so they usually contain no chemical additives that can negatively affect health when they burn.

Another advantage of pellet appliances, as opposed to traditional woodstoves, is that they are thermostatically controlled, with the pellets automatically feeding into the appliance. This means that constant tending is not necessary, an especially important feature for the growing number of families in which all adult members work away from the home. Because these appliances emit less smoke and particulates than woodstoves, they are approved in regions where wood-burning appliances are restricted or even banned (Pahl, 2003).

Pellet-appliance use is generally most economical in regions where there are large supplies of sawdust. The stoves come in several varieties to fit many decors and home styles, including the following three main types:

1. *Freestanding,* in which the appliance stands on legs or a pedestal. This type is the most flexible because it can be located almost anywhere in the living space.
2. *Fireplace inserts,* which can be installed in most existing masonry fireplaces.
3. *Built-in appliances,* which can be used to give the look of a traditional fireplace without the expense of constructing a mortar fireplace.

Clients who are considering the installation of a pellet appliance should first check the availability and current price of pellets in their area. If they decide to purchase a stove, they should carefully consider the following factors:

- Appropriate size for area to be heated
- Type and grade of pellets that can be burned in the stove

- Ease and expected frequency of routine maintenance
- Availability and cost of professional service
- Dealer's owner training program and materials
- Special features
  - Self-igniter system
  - Remote thermostat control
  - Glass air wash (cleans front glass so fire is visible)
  - Imitation logs for fire viewing
  - Large drawer for collecting ash residue
- Backup power if the stove is the main source of heat
- Warranties

Finally, costs should take into account the pellet appliance itself, the installation, and the price of pellets.

Woodstoves

Fireplaces were used for cooking and heating for centuries and continued to be used in the United States in the 1700s. Most were inefficient and dangerous, with heat going up the chimney, and smoke and sparks entering the living space. Benjamin Franklin developed a stove with a hoodlike enclosure in the front and airbox in the rear. This design created a much safer and more efficient heating unit and is the predecessor of the many configurations of woodstoves available today. Woodstoves may be appropriate choices for clients who want to heat limited areas without depending on fossil-fuel appliances. They also provide a coziness that some other heating devices lack. Because the radiant heat from woodstoves cannot be moved long distances or through walls, they are best used in larger, multipurpose rooms such as kitchen/family-room combinations. In the open-space or great-room designs that have become popular, a woodstove can be located where it delivers heat to the most areas possible. Woodstoves can be particularly economical sources of heat for people who have easy and inexpensive access to wood (otherwise, this can be expensive if the wood must

FIGURE 6.8 Cast-iron woodstoves come in many styles.

1. Steel: Cut into panels, steel stoves heat up quickly and tend to have a modern, boxy appearance.
2. Cast iron: Fluid and poured into a mold, cast iron can be formed into any shape. For this reason, it offers the widest variety of shapes, styles, and ornamentation. (See Figure 6.8.)
3. Soapstone: Stoves are constructed with a combination of soapstone and cast iron. When polished, soapstone has the elegant appearance of marble. At the same time, it absorbs heat, which it continues to radiate after the fire has died down.

The location, preparation of surrounding area with noncombustible materials, and proper installation are all essential for the safe operation of a woodstove. Proper maintenance and safety precautions are also necessary. For example, properly seasoning a new stove is critical so that the metal expands and contracts gradually. Improper use, even in the beginning, can ruin a new woodstove (Pahl, 2003).

Masonry Heaters

Masonry heaters are simple, efficient heating appliances that have been used in Northern Europe for hundreds of years. Although they can be purchased in the United States and are commonly seen at sustainable-living conferences and trade shows, masonry heaters are infrequently used in this country. It is expected that as information about them spreads, more people will be interested in using them because of their many advantages over other types of heating.

Masonry heaters operate on the principle of thermal mass: a quick, hot fire in a combustion chamber heats up the surrounding material, which then slowly radiates the heat into the surrounding area, where is it then absorbed by the walls, floor, ceiling, and furniture. Because the fire burns quickly, most of the energy potential is taken from the fuel and there are very low emissions. This makes masonry

be ordered and delivered, especially in non-forested areas).

Because of their potential to emit smoke particulates that can be harmful, the U.S. Environmental Protection Agency has developed standards for woodstoves to reduce the number of potentially harmful emissions. All stoves sold after July 1, 1992, must be certified and carry a permanent EPA label stating they have been tested. Clients considering the purchase of used woodstoves should be aware of this and those who are remodeling and already have older woodstoves might consider replacing them with certified models.

Woodstoves are available in three materials:

heaters among the most efficient users of cord-wood for heating purposes. It also makes it a viable option in regions where woodstoves are banned because of particulate pollution. The heaters are safe, especially for families with young children and pets, because the fire is not continually burning and because the outside surfaces are not hot to the touch.

The thermal mass itself can be created in many forms and incorporated into the design of any home. Custom designs can be adapted to any decor style and even stand as unique works of art. Because a masonry heater weighs several tons, a strong foundation is necessary.

Biomass Furnaces

Furnaces that burn wood, wood-waste pellets, corn, and other biomass are currently available for consumers who have access to sufficient quantities of these fuels. Like traditional oil and gas furnaces, they are large units capable of heating an entire house by passing warm air through ducts. Although wood-fired furnaces are becoming more popular in Europe, they are rarely used in the United States. They can be purchased and installed and could become more commonly used in the future as a substitute for fossil-fuel furnaces.

GEOTHERMAL

The term "geothermal" refers to the solar energy heat absorbed by the earth. In fact, up to 47 percent of the sun's energy that strikes its surface is absorbed by the ground (Pahl, 2003). This represents an enormous amount of energy that can be harnessed by heat pumps to heat and cool buildings and provide hot water. **Heat pumps** work by circulating a refrigerant that absorbs heat from the earth, air, or water and then is pressurized so that its temperature is raised to over 160°F. Now in a gaseous state, the refrigerant passes through a heat exchanger where the heat is transferred to water or air that is then circulated throughout the home or building via ductwork. Compared with traditional heating sources, the pumps are very efficient because they simply move heat rather

than creating it through combustion. This not only saves money for the consumer, it reduces greenhouse gas emissions. More and more people are recognizing the potential of heat pumps as a clean, efficient, and constantly renewable form of energy.

Two kinds of heat pumps are available: air-source and ground-source. As the name implies, an air-source pump draws heat from outdoor air through a system of pipes that contains a refrigerant. This type of heat pump works best in climates with moderate winters where temperatures are rarely below freezing (Pahl, 2003). Ground-source heat pumps, also called geoexchange systems, on the other hand, consist of loops of pipes buried in the ground or submerged in water sources, such as ponds. The earth is capable of storing heat year-round and at a depth of 6 feet, the temperature remains stable between 45 and 70°F (7 and 21°C) (Geothermal Heat Pump Consortium, 2003). This is why ground-source technology is more efficient in cold climates that have very cold winter air. Because ground-source systems require excavating and installing loop systems, they are more easily installed during new construction. With good planning, they can be added to established buildings and homes.

Heat pumps are also capable of replacing traditional air-conditioning units. This is accomplished by reversing the motion of the fan in the pump unit so that it pulls warm air out of a building and releases it into the air or the ground outside.

The operation of heat pumps requires a small amount of electricity, so they are not completely independent of other energy sources. ENERGY STAR-certified pumps are recommended because they use the least amount of electricity. (ENERGY STAR is discussed later in this chapter.)

Implications for Designers

Heat pumps, especially ground-source types, may be viable choices for clients who are seeking alternatives to fossil-fuel systems. Although the initial costs of these systems is higher than

BOX 6.2   VIEW TO THE FUTURE

Fuel Cells

Fuel cells are another exciting alternative energy possibility. The process for producing clean energy involves converting chemical energy into electricity.

In a fuel cell, hydrogen and oxygen molecules are brought together to create water and generate electricity. Among the various types of fuel cells, proton exchange membrane (PEM) fuel cells are of great interest because they operate at relatively low temperatures, have high power density, and can vary their output quickly as demand changes (Kibert, 2005).

Fuel cells can produce energy that is fed into electrical grids or they can generate heat and power on site for buildings, including single-family homes. The Long Island Power Authority in New York has started installing fuel cells in businesses and houses as part of its Clean Energy Initiative. One of the first installations was in a McDonald's restaurant in 2003 (Long Island Power Authority, 2003).

future is the development of solar-assisted heat pumps.

One of the major barriers to wider use of this technology is a lack of public awareness, according to some people. Designers not only have responsibilities to their clients but also to the world at large. Providing clients with information about the wide variety of alternative energy sources can help overcome the lack of awareness about this and other renewable energy sources. Becoming knowledgeable about renewable energy sources and promoting their use is part of being a responsible citizen. Designers are in a good position to become part of the solution to a serious problem rather than maintaining the status quo—a position that is ultimately unsustainable.

for fossil-fuel-based systems, those costs are decreasing as the number of installations are increasing. It is important to note that these initial expenses are offset, especially in colder climates, by a significant reduction in fuel costs.

Important factors when considering the feasibility and best type of a heat pump system include:

- Climate
- Availability and appropriateness of outdoor space for ground-source system
- Availability of a deep water well in a colder climate where this would be the preferred heat source
- Home or building structure
- Availability of qualified installation and maintenance professionals
- Possibility of combining with existing hot-air furnace
- Comparative costs of heat pump versus other systems
- Source of electricity needed to run the system. The overall positive contribution to both human health and the environment will be based to some degree on the source of the electricity. A solution that might become more affordable in the

IMPROVING ENERGY EFFICIENCY

Renewable energy sources are needed, and the United States has lagged in developing the technology necessary to produce those sources economically. At the same time, Americans can and should make serious efforts to conserve energy. Designers can have a significant role in these efforts. Whether a project involves new construction, remodeling, or just a simple update on a home or other type of building, addressing energy efficiency should be a top priority. Energy-efficient measures in buildings can help the environment, improve the health of its occupants, and add to its resale value (Alliance to Save Energy, 2005). For example, replacing an older heating and cooling system, which can account for as much as half of a home's energy costs, can improve ventilation and provide cleaner air, a proven health benefit. Replacing single-pane windows that are frequently covered with heavy drapes to prevent the loss of heat in winter and entry of hot sun in summer with high-efficiency double-pane windows will enable occupants to enjoy more light throughout the year.

Increasing a home's energy efficiency requires a systemic approach. A house is complex and contains many components, each of which can greatly affect the others. And it's inadvisable to simply substitute one problem for another. For example, if all the leaks in a home are sealed, but air contaminants are present, this can result in health problems for the occupants. But some measures that reduce energy loss help to prevent other problems. For example, sealing duct air leaks, through which a typical home loses up to 20 percent of its conditioned air (U.S. Environmental Protection Agency, n.d. "Duct"), can also help prevent high humidity levels in the home that lead to mold, mildew, and musty odors (U.S. Environmental Protection Agency, n.d. "Mold"). Double-pane windows, for example, have at least two benefits: providing more light and possibly preventing moisture problems.

A whole-house systems approach to energy efficiency considers the interaction of the occupants, the home's site, the local climate, and the following house components:

1. Appliances and electronics
2. Sealing
3. Insulation
4. Windows, doors, and skylights
5. Lighting and daylighting
6. Space heating and cooling
7. Water heating (U.S. Department of Energy, 2005, "Whole-house")

Owners of homes and commercial buildings can hire consultants to perform energy audits and evaluations. They can also use simple do-it-yourself procedures and computer programs to perform energy audits and identify the most effective energy-saving strategies. For example, the Home Energy Saver Web site at http://hes.lbl.gov is an easily accessible, Web-based program developed by Lawrence Berkeley Lab, a Department of Energy national laboratory. This interactive site enables the user to obtain a customized energy bill breakdown by entering a zip code and answering a set of basic questions, such as the square footage of the home and local fuel prices. The program can also create a customized set of suggestions for energy-saving improvements. The Web site

---

BOX 6.3 CONSIDERATIONS FOR PASSIVE DESIGN

- Local climate: sun angles and exposures, wind velocity and direction, air temperature, and humidity
- Site conditions: terrain, vegetation, soil conditions, water table, microclimate, relationship of other buildings
- Building aspect ratio: ratio of the building's length to its width
- Building orientation: room layout, glazing
- Building massing: energy storage potential of materials, color, and windows
- Building use: occupancy schedule and use profile
- Daylighting strategy: components (skylights, light shelves, louvers, etc.)
- Building envelope: geometry, insulation, windows, doors, air leakage, ventilation, shading, thermal mass, color
- Internal loads: lighting, equipment, appliances, people
- Ventilation strategy: cross-ventilation potential, paths for routine ventilation, chimney effect potential

Source: Kibert, C. (2005). *Sustainable construction: Green building design and delivery.* Hoboken, NJ: John Wiley and Sons.

---

also has a module titled "Making It Happen" that contains hundreds of links to products, service providers, utilities, and online reading materials, making it a valuable resource for both designers and their clients (Chen, 1999).

PASSIVE DESIGN

Passive design was defined by Randy Croxton, a pioneer of ecological design, as allowing a building to "default to nature" (Kibert, 2005). It requires a holistic, comprehensive approach that considers how a building might be constructed to take advantage of every available natural resource, such as sunlight, wind, vegetation, and land forms, to supply its heating, cooling, ventilating, and lighting needs. This is a departure from conventional planning and building that tends to emphasize complying with only those building codes in effect and minimizing construction costs as much as possible.

As is shown in Box 6.3, passive design involves many factors. It begins with a consideration of the natural features of a building site and follows through to the selection of individual building components. Sophisticated computer simulation tools are typically used to take into account the large number of variables involved with each individual building.

Although architects and engineers are the professionals most involved in the passive design of aspects of buildings, interior designers also make decisions that influence the effectiveness of passive design. For example, they can help plan room layouts, which affect ventilation; make decisions about glazing to control heat entry and loss; and determine the most effective use of natural light to decrease the need for artificial lighting.

TIGHT CONSTRUCTION

Tight construction is the practice of sealing as many leaks as possible in a structure for the purpose of making it more energy efficient. This is because air leaks cause warm air to be pulled into attics or to the outside, and cold air to be drawn into a building. Initiated in the 1970s as part of new construction in response to the energy crisis at that time, tight construction has become a controversial practice. Many people believe that it has reduced indoor air quality and increased the number of building-related health problems because of the decrease in ventilation and flow of fresh air (see Chapter 5), which can cause higher temperatures and humidity levels as well as increased odor retention (Morgan, 2003). At the same time, the potential annual energy savings from reducing drafts in a home range from 5 to 30 percent per year (U.S. Department of Energy, 2005, "Do-it-yourself"). When all the unintentional holes and cracks in a house are added together, the total, known as the effective leakage area, can be surprisingly large.

In light of the health-related problems created by the use of fossil fuels, creating healthy tight buildings is an important challenge. In addition to wasted energy, "loose" houses and buildings can have uncomfortable drafts, high humidity levels, and pollution if air is pulled in through soil or cracks in the foundation. In approaching this problem, it is important that professionals again view buildings as entire systems in which the various components work together to create a healthy, energy-efficient environment (Bower, 2001). It is important to understand that many indoor air problems are the result of unhealthy building materials rather than tightness. In these cases, even a great deal of infiltration (entry of outdoor air through leaks) may not be enough to disperse airborne contaminants. Thus, the selection of healthy products for building, furnishing, and maintaining a structure is related to the conservation of energy.

A second cause of indoor air problems in tight buildings is an inadequate ventilation system, which provides a good example of how the components of a building interact. When sealing the windows and other leaks, the need for increased ventilation must be considered. Without an adequate supply of outdoor air, unavoidable indoor pollutants, such as human body odors, can reach unacceptable levels. Buildings that have already been constructed tightly should be checked for adequate ventilation. For buildings being tightened for energy conservation, there is a good chance that additional ventilation will be needed. This is especially important in structures where a fuel is burned, because all combustion appliances must have an adequate air supply. A general rule is to provide 1 square inch of vent opening for each 1,000 Btu of appliance output heat (U.S. Department of Energy, 2005, "Do-it-yourself"). In some structures, such as older, multifamily housing, it may be necessary to add mechanical ventilation systems to maintain acceptable air quality (Envall et al., 2003). Although most single-family residences do not have mechanical ventilation systems, some healthy-home professionals believe they might be worth the investment, especially in very tightly built homes located in climates that don't allow windows to be open during most of the year. (See Chapter 5 for more information about ventilation.)

Another cause of poor indoor air quality, apart from tightness, is improper maintenance of the HVAC systems. This can lead to the circulation of dirty air, moisture that harbors mold and bacteria, and the necessity of using strong cleaning products that emit chemicals that simply add to the problem. (See Chapter 5 for more information on indoor air quality.) Incorporating the use of healthy building materials and reducing contaminants (see Chapter 4), as well as providing the components of good air quality should allow the use of tight building techniques to increase energy efficiency without compromising air quality.

Implications for Designers

Clients may want to conduct their own search for air leaks, in which case they should check for airflows through the following places:

- Electrical outlets
- Switch plates
- Window frames
- Baseboards
- Weather stripping around doors
- Fireplace dampers
- Attic hatches
- Wall- or window-mounted air conditioners
- Openings for pipes and wires
- Mail slots
- On the outside of the house, places where different building materials are joined are often the sites of leaks. These include all exterior corners; the places where siding and chimneys meet; and the areas where the foundation and bottom of exterior brick, stone, or siding meet (U.S. Department of Energy, 2005, "Do-it-yourself").

If it is difficult to find leaks, the following procedure to lower inside air pressure and make infiltrating air easier to detect can be done:

1. Close all exterior doors, windows, and fireplace flues.
2. Turn off all combustion appliances, such as gas-burning fireplaces and hot water heaters.
3. Turn on all exhaust fans, such as those located in the kitchen and bathrooms (U.S. Department of Energy, 2005, "Do-it-yourself").

4. Test the locations listed previously for leaks.

If tightening existing buildings is undertaken, the sealants and insulation products must be carefully considered because they could contain unhealthy components. Caulking products, for example, emit volatile organic compounds (VOCs), discussed in Chapter 4, that pollute the air and can be irritating for some people. The products have been improved in recent years, but to learn about the contents of specific weatherization caulking brands, designers can consult the National Library of Medicine's Household Product's Database at http://householdproducts.nlm.nih .gov/index.htm.

INSULATION

Humans have used insulation for centuries to protect themselves against the elements. Today it is used throughout buildings to prevent excessive heat entry during warm seasons and heat loss during cold seasons. It is installed inside walls and roof systems, under floors, around foundations, and around hot water heaters and ductwork, as shown in Figure 6.9. Different types of insulation are compared by their ability to prevent the flow of heat; in other words, their ability to resist. Thus, the rating system for insulation is based on their resistance-value or R-value; the higher the value, the greater the insulating ability. As an example, a brick has an R-value of 0.20 per square inch, while fiberglass batt insulation has an R-value of 3.17 per square inch (Bower, 2001). The appropriate R-value for a building is determined by local climate; this can be calculated by following the U.S. Department of Energy's instructions at www.ornl.gov/sci/roofs+walls/insulation/ ins_05.html. Having too little insulation can result in an uncomfortable building, and too much is a waste of resources.

In the past, natural materials such as cotton, straw, feathers, and moss were used as insulation. In the twentieth century, man-made insulation was deemed to be better and became popular. Problems have been associated with

FIGURE 6.9 Locations that should be insulated to prevent energy-losing air leaks.

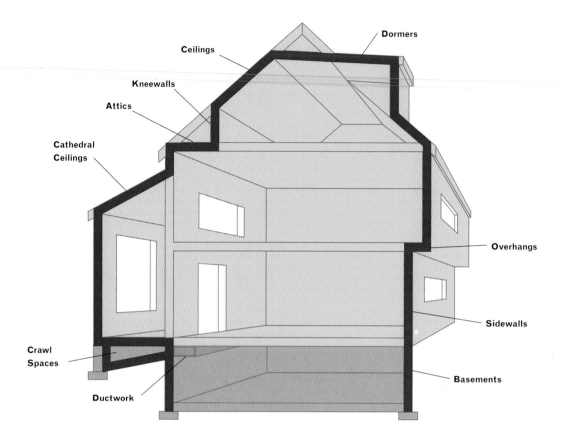

FIGURE 6.9 Locations that should be insulated to prevent energy-losing air leaks.

these products. For example, asbestos was used around heating systems for many years until its dangerous health effects were discovered. In the 1970s, widely used urea-formaldehyde foam insulation caused unacceptably high formaldehyde levels in many homes. Most insulation today is made of fiberglass, mineral wool, or cellulose (wood fiber) (Kibert, 2005). Both fiberglass and mineral wool release small inhalable fibers when they are disturbed. In fact, fiberglass is listed as a possible carcinogen. These products are safe if they are carefully installed and separated from the living space (Bower, 2001). Cellulose, on the other hand, is considered to be nontoxic (Kibert, 2005).

Another form of modern insulation being increasingly used is spray-on foam. Made of polyurethane that is pumped through pressurized spray nozzles, it is the same material used to insulate refrigerators, freezers, and booster rockets for space shuttles. The foam can be applied quickly and expands to provide excellent coverage of nooks and crannies. As states establish energy-savings programs, sprays have gained popularity. Some utility companies of-

fer rebates for customers who upgrade their insulation, which is important because this type of insulation, while generally more efficient, costs more than traditional materials. Part of the additional cost is for professional installation because foam, unlike sheets of fiberglass, for example, cannot be installed as a do-it-yourself project by the home owner. In the past, spray foams contained formaldehyde and other VOCs, in addition to containing aerosol propellants that contribute to greenhouse gases. Polyurethane foam does not contain formaldehyde.

A product that uses a different method of retaining heat is made of shiny foils that, when installed in sheets within walls, reflect radiant energy back to its source. The foils do need sufficient airspace to be effective. Foils reportedly rarely cause health problems (Bower, 2001).

In response to the demand for greener, more earth- and health-friendly products, some companies are developing innovative insulation products. These include a return to use of natural components, such as the manufacture of insulation from recycled cotton and denim scraps (Green Home Guide, 2007). In addition, many new spray foams are being produced from natural plant materials, such as soy, which do not emit VOCs. Designers should keep current on these new products as they come to market.

Implications for Designers

Although most people do not experience health problems with any of the types of insulation discussed in this section, before making decisions about insulation, designers should determine if clients are chemically sensitive or have allergies. Even "safe" components like cotton are treated with fire retardants that may cause more of a problem than a traditional product such as fiberglass, which is not treated with chemicals. Table 6.1 contains examples of insulation types and materials. When reviewing the potential health risks, it is important to remember the following:

1. Added chemicals are not inherently bad; in fact, their purpose may be to secure materials in place, prevent fires, control dust, and control pests that consider insulation a source of food.
2. Proper installation techniques will prevent most insulation problems. It is important to keep insulation materials separate from living areas, both during the initial installation and subsequently through good house tightening.
3. The majority of people are not bothered by the negligible amounts of insulation that manage to enter the living space. Chemically sensitive people should select nontoxic products without fibers.
4. Manufacturers are solving many insulation problems. For example, Air Krete has developed a nontoxic spray product that does not mold or shrink (Bower, 2001; Johnson and Lundberg, 2004).

It is important to know that even good insulation products can be dangerous if they are not installed properly. In fact poor construction practices have caused most of the health problems linked to insulation (Bower,

2001). Fiberglass fibers, for example, can produce symptoms if they are inhaled into the lungs. Some people have reported numerous debilitating health conditions, and a group called Victims of Fiberglass believes that fiberglass should be removed from all homes (Bower, 2001). It is widely believed that poor installation techniques were the cause of these problems because the fibers never should have been allowed to enter the homes' living spaces. This presents an additional argument for tight construction, discussed previously, because it reduces the chance for such fibers, as well as other chemicals used to manufacture insulation, to migrate from attics and crawl spaces. Preventing insulation from getting wet before, during, and after installation is important to prevent bacterial growth and odors.

Insulation can cause fire hazards if it touches metal or masonry openings around furnaces, hot water heaters, or chimneys, as they become very hot. Another precaution when adding insulation to older existing structures (or when installing a new furnace) is to check for the presence of asbestos. Although it is generally not dangerous if undisturbed, it can release inhalable fibers if it is moved. If it must be removed, certified professionals should handle the job. (See Chapter 4 for more information about asbestos.)

ROOFS

Roofs expose large expanses of space to the elements and, therefore, greatly influence a building's energy consumption. Very large roofs, such as those in shopping malls, can reach 150°F in warm summer climates. This amount of heat can raise the temperatures in the areas some distance from the mall (Kibert, 2005). Roofs with a high **albedo,** which is the measure of a property's reflectivity of solar radiation, can significantly decrease both indoor and surrounding heat. Light-colored roofs have high albedo. Researchers at Lawrence Berkeley Labs estimate that buildings with light roofs use 40 percent less energy than similar buildings with dark roofs (Kibert, 2005). The

TABLE 6.1 EXAMPLES OF TRADITIONAL INSULATION MATERIALS

TYPE	HOW IT IS MADE	POTENTIAL PROBLEMS
BATT		
Fiberglass	Melting sand and spinning it into glass fibers	Fibers may be held together with a formaldehyde-based resin
Rock wool	Heating rock and drawing it into fibers when it melts	Can contain contaminants; chemicals are used to bind it into batts
Cotton	Fibers are bound together in batt form	
LOOSE-FILL AND BLOW-IN		
Cellulose	Chopping up old newspapers	Treated with insecticides and fire retardants
Chopped fiberglass	Loose fiberglass, rather than bound into batts	Very small fibers that can be inhaled
Rock wool	Loose rock fibers	Fibers can be inhaled; product off-gases
Vermiculite	Mica-like mineral puffed up by heating	May contain small amounts of asbestos
Perlite	Silicate volcanic rock puffed up by heating	Very dusty and can be inhaled
Polystyrene beads	Expanded balls of synthetic foam	Contain fire retardants
SPRAY-IN-PLACE		
Polyurethane	Aerosol foam	Contains MDI, a chemical that off-gasses during application, but is quite stable after the foam cures
Magnesium oxide and sodium silicate	Spray	Nontoxic (components of Air Krete)
Fiberglass and cellulose	Mixed with very small amount of water or glue and sprayed	Mold can grow if improper (too much) amount of water is used during application

Adapted from: Bower, J. (2001). *The healthy house* (4th ed.). Bloomington, IN: The Healthy House Institute.

Solar Reflectance Index (SRI) is a rating system for roof reflectivity. Numbers indicate the percentage of solar energy that is reflected off the roof. For example, roofing with an SRI of 48 would reflect back 48 percent, thus considerably lowering the heat potential of a sunny day.

Implications for Designers

Remodeling and renovation projects can offer opportunities for clients to consider changing roofs if doing so can lead to energy savings, as well as improved safety. If it is not feasible to change a dark roof, then adding plants to the landscape and designing other cooling strategies for the interior can help dissipate the heat absorbed by the roof. These might include adding a window to increase cross-ventilation, installing attic fans to pull heat from the structure, or increasing the insulation in the ceiling to block the entry of heat.

WINDOWS

Window surfaces are a major source of heat loss and gain and thus an important factor when considering energy efficiency. Window performance is measured in several ways. The first is solar heat gain, expressed as the **solar heat gain coefficient,** or **SHGC,** and represents the fraction of solar energy that enters the window and becomes heat. SHGC is expressed as a value between 0 and 1; the lower the value, the less heat produced. The location of windows is the main consideration when choosing the optimal SHGC. For example, windows with a southern exposure whose purpose is solar heating should have a high SHGC. Windows with a western exposure that receive the hot afternoon sun might require a lower SHGC. The arrangement of rooms within a structure will therefore also influence the choice, for example, a bedroom that receives late afternoon sun and becomes uncomfortably warm for sleeping.

The second performance-measuring factor is the **visible transmittance,** or VT. This value is also expressed between 0 and 1 and refers to the visible spectrum that is allowed through the glazing. The higher the number, the more daylight is allowed to enter. Thus, rooms in which bright light is desired would have high-value VTs; areas subject to glare, such as workplace offices, might do better with a lower VT value (Kibert, 2005). SHGC and VT work together to determine heat and brightness. A ratio called the light-to-solar-gain, LSG, provides a guide: the higher the LSG, the brighter the room without adding excessive heat (Kibert, 2005).

A third value measures the efficiency of glazing (window plus frame) to retain heat within a building. It is expressed as a U-value in terms of the conductance of the materi-

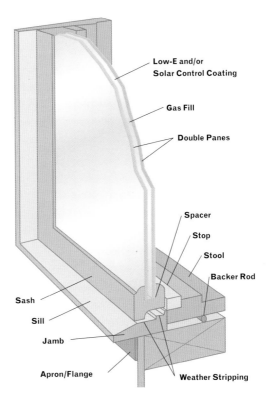

Low-E and/or Solar Control Coating

Gas Fill

Double Panes

Spacer

Stop

Stool

Backer Rod

Sash

Sill

Jamb

Apron/Flange

Weather Stripping

FIGURE 6.10 Energy-efficient windows incorporate many features to reduce the passage of heat and cold.

als: the higher the number, the more heat is conducted, and therefore lost. Some states are adopting minimum U-values for newly built homes.

A final important factor used to determine window performance is the infiltration of the assembly or how much air leaks in and out of the frames or between the glass and the frame. These areas can be sources of drafts and, therefore, heat loss from interiors.

Implications for Designers

Designers are in a position to inform their clients about various options available for improving the performance of their windows. To achieve maximum energy efficiency, old windows can be replaced with new, energy-efficient windows, such as ENERGY STAR-approved models. (See Figure 6.10.) These windows can be made to include the best performance values, discussed previously, for each area of the home or building.

Glass panes are now being manufactured with a coating that increases their efficiency. These work well for most people, but chemically sensitive individuals may be bothered by the off-gassing of the chemicals used in the coating. It is recommended that these sensitive individuals test coated glass before it is installed, or choose another type of glazing. In addition to coated glass, a new energy-efficient glass, known as low-E glass, has been developed. This glass works like a mirror, using a layer of metal a few molecules thick to reflect energy that would be otherwise passed through the window back into the interior. If overheating is the problem, glazing with low-E coatings can be applied to the outside of windows to reflect heat away from the structure. In addition to controlling heat loss and entry, these coatings block much of the incoming ultraviolet light that fades curtains, carpets, and other colored surfaces (Bower, 2001). Low-E coatings are the equivalent of adding a second pane of glass to a window and are rated in terms of emissivity value, which is the amount of heat transmitted through the glazing (Kibert, 2005). Because of the expense of installing new windows, consumers should explore the various rebates and tax credits for which they might qualify. Designers can help clients by staying up-to-date with local information.

A less expensive alternative to new windows is the addition of a second layer to existing single-pane windows, also known as storm windows. These second layers can be added directly to the original panes in the form of sheets of glass, plastic panels, or plastic film. While relatively economical, the plastics can turn yellow and degrade over time (U.S. Department of Energy, 2005, "Storm").

A relatively new product is high-tech window film composed of a laminate of polyester and metallized coatings. Applied to the insides of windows, the film reduces the amount of heat that passes through the glass and almost completely eliminates ultraviolet radiation. Low-emissivity films are now available, working in much the same way as low-E glass. Contrary to films produced in the past, the newer types are clear and free of distortion. If a client is interested in a solar control film, it is important that professionals who are properly trained perform the installation.

A more effective type of storm window consists of two or more panes of glass placed 1/4 to 3/4 inches apart. It is the existence of the air space, rather than its width, that determines the energy efficiency. Thus, adding more air spaces increases the efficiency. This can even be done by suspending plastic film between two panes of glass (Bower, 2001). Another way to decrease heat transfer is the introduction of a gas, such as argon, krypton, or carbon dioxide, between the layers, but this is a more complicated procedure.

A cutting-edge window technology that promises to reduce energy use while increasing human comfort is called the "smart" window. With the touch of a control device, a smart window changes its properties from clear to darkened. The following examples, explained here and illustrated in Figure 6.11, apply three types of technology:

1. Suspended particle devices (SPD): Particles that arrange themselves randomly are suspended between two pieces of glass that have been coated with a transparent conductive material. When electricity is applied, the particles line up and allow light to pass through. SPD windows offer transitional lighting between clear and translucent.

2. Liquid crystals: The same polymer dispersed liquid crystals (PDLS) that give us the numerals on clocks and calculators behave much like SPDs: when electricity is applied, they line up and light passes through. PDLS windows are either clear or dark with no intermediate.

3. Electrochromic: These windows darken when electricity is added. The technology is based on materials that change color when energized by an electrical current. The windows are either clear or dark.

If traditional windows cannot be replaced or altered, the careful selection of window coverings can help control the amount of light and heat that enter a room. Consider using coverings with the following characteristics:

• Nonwoven with high yarn counts to reduce glare

SPD SMART WINDOWS

PDLC SMART WINDOWS

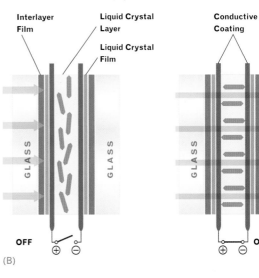

ELECTROCHROMIC SMART WINDOWS

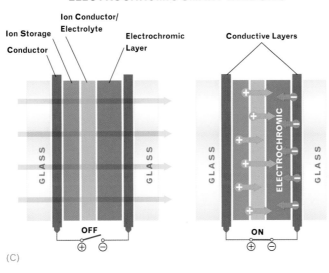

FIGURE 6.11A, B, AND C (a) When electricity causes the particles to line up, light passes through the glass. (b) When electricity causes the liquid crystals to line up, light passes through the glass. (c) When electricity is added, the glazing material darkens.

- Directional properties to redirect solar energy
- Directional shading to control light transmittance
- Shades with variable tilt angle so they can be adjusted as needed
- Pleat structure and orientation that maximizes the redirection of light (Grasso et al., 1997)

LIGHTING

Lighting consumes huge amounts of electrical energy because nearly every U.S. building and home depends on electric lighting. In fact, about 22 percent of the electricity consumed in the United States is for lighting (Banwell

et al., 2004). In commercial buildings, lighting is estimated to account for 40 percent of the electricity used (Winchip, 2007). The method for supplying much of this light, up to 90 percent in homes, is the extremely inefficient incandescent lamp (Banwell et al., 2004). This inefficiency is because the lamps produce light by pushing electrons through a small wire, an effort that expends 85 to 90 percent of its energy for producing heat rather than light.

An answer to this problem is to increase the use of fluorescent lighting, which has been used in commercial buildings and schools for many years. Fluorescent lamps work by passing an electric current through a tube containing a gas or vapor. They use up to 80 percent less energy than incandescent lamps, last up to eighteen times longer, and generate very little heat (Winchip, 2007). Until recently fluorescent lamps were rarely used in the home. This is beginning to change with the development of the compact fluorescent lamp (CFL) in which the traditional long tubes are bent into short tube forms that are more the size of an incandescent lamp. The EPA reports that CFLs use at least two-thirds less energy than standard incandescent lighting, generate 70 percent less heat, and last up to ten times longer (U.S. Environmental Protection Agency, n.d., "Light"). Stated another way, replacing a 60-watt incandescent lamp with a 13-watt CFL can save the consumer at least $30 in energy costs over the life of the lamp (U.S. Environmental Protection Agency, n.d., "Information").

Government-sponsored programs are encouraging consumers to replace as many incandescent lamps as possible with compact fluorescent types, especially in areas of high use, such as kitchens and living rooms. It is estimated that if every household replaced five incandescent lamps with compact fluorescents, American consumers as a group would save about $6.5 billion in annual energy costs and prevent greenhouse gases equivalent to the emissions of more than 8 million cars (U.S. Environmental Protection Agency, n.d., "Light").

But note that fluorescent lamps do contain mercury. The EPA reports that it is a very small amount enclosed inside the tubing and, therefore, is not a potential health hazard. The EPA does recommend that care be taken if a lamp should break. The area involved should be wiped with a wet paper towel and the broken lamp and pieces wrapped or placed inside a bag before being discarded. The agency also advises consumers to check with their local disposal companies to find out if lamps can be placed in with other household trash.

Implications for Designers

It is highly recommended that designers select lighting fixtures and lamps that will function with compact fluorescents. It is expected that with current campaigns encouraging the use of CFLs, many more fixtures will be designed to accommodate them. Fluorescent lamps now

come in a variety of shapes and include features such as dimming, so they can be used for ambient and indirect lighting in homes. Long fluorescent tubes can be used in homes by incorporating features that will hide them, such as coves and valances (Banwell et al., 2004). Because of the long life of these lamps and the infrequent need for changing, they can be a good choice for the elderly (Banwell et al., 2004), as well as reducing the risk of falls from ladders for the population in general.

In buildings that use fluorescent tube lights, it is important that electronic ballasts, matched to the light tubes, are used. This results in both energy savings and user satisfaction because the quality of light is better. Dimmers, whether they are automatic or user-controlled, have also been shown to save energy.

To achieve the utmost efficiency, all components of the lighting system must be energy-efficient and coordinate with one another. These components include:

- Lamp: electrical light source unit, commonly called a bulb
- Luminaire: unit containing the light source unit, housing, control device, and switch. Commonly called a light fixture.
- Ballast: control device that starts a lamp and controls the electrical current during operation (Winchip, 2007; Winchip, 2005)

Automatic timers are another energy-saving strategy. Building occupants generally tend to leave lights on once they are turned on. Timers can be used to dim lights during lunch hours or in unoccupied rooms, such as conference rooms or bathrooms.

DAYLIGHTING

Daylighting refers to the use of natural light as the primary source of interior illumination (DiLouie, 2006). This is light that comes through windows and other translucent media, skylights, and other openings. When discussing natural light, it is important to distinguish between sunlight and daylight. Daylight refers to desirable natural light as opposed to direct sunlight, which is usually too bright and warm for interiors (Winchip, 2005). The challenge is to capture daylight while avoiding the harshness of sunlight (Winchip, 2005).

Natural light has several advantages over artificial light. First is the fact that it relies on a free source of energy and therefore can save very large amounts of electricity. Some sources estimate that with daylighting, energy consumption for lighting can be reduced by 30 to 70 percent (Tetri, 2002).

In addition to saving energy, daylight as a source of illumination has been shown to be more satisfying and healthy for building occupants. As discussed in Chapters 7 and 10, views through windows are deemed desirable by building occupants, especially in the workplace and in health-care facilities. It is believed that increasing the use of daylighting may even decrease worker absenteeism (Kibert, 2005). (Because payroll is the highest cost of many businesses, this fact represents added savings beyond energy costs.) The use of natural daylight has been shown to increase children's learning when used in schools and worker productivity in the workplace (Kibert, 2005), which may be due in part to the fact that natural light increases visual acuity (Winchip, 2005). Kibert suggests that if this increased productivity were factored into the embodied-energy costs of a building, daylighting would likely become the lighting method of choice among businesses (Kibert, 2005).

The systems that make daylighting work must be well planned, designed, and coordinated. Planning begins by considering the following factors:

- Climate: typical number of sunny days
- Orientation of the building: direction of sunlight entering throughout the year
- Building's surroundings: adjacent buildings and structures, trees, hills, and other obstacles to light
- Location and number of windows
- Floor plan
- Type and location of activities performed by occupants and amount of light required for each (Winchip, 2005; Leslie et al., 2004)

Successful daylighting also requires the integration of natural and artificial light. This is because a balance must be maintained when the building is in use: when daylight is insufficient, artificial light must be provided for occupants; when daylight is adequate, artificial lights must be decreased to support the goal of saving energy. This balance is accomplished through a system of photosensors (light sensors) and controls that work together to maintain predetermined levels of light. These levels are calculated by identifying appropriate light for each interior zone based on the kind of activity performed in each, usage schedules, and so on. For example, lights in corridors might be lower than those in work areas, and all lights might automatically dim during the lunch hour.

Photosensors are typically located near windows where they can read incoming light levels. As daylight decreases to certain levels, controls are alerted to increase the amount of artificial light provided; the opposite occurs as daylight illumination increases. This process is called **daylight harvesting.** In some systems, the electric lighting is switched on and off based on signals received. A more expensive, but more satisfying system for building occupants uses dimmers that increase and decrease light levels gradually as the amount of daylight varies. This requires less visual adjustment on the part of those inside the building. An intermediate method is called "stepped controls" in which lights are progressively turned on and off.

In addition to sensors and controls, there are a variety of features and products that enhance daylighting:

- Window louvers, which control the amount of light entering the building
- Tilted ceilings, which reflect light into the interior
- Low-emissivity glass, which controls heat from the sun's rays
- **Light shelves,** which increase the amount of light entering a window. (See Figure 6.12.) Shelves with reflective surfaces are installed either inside or outside

FIGURE 6.12 Light shelves work by reflecting light off the ceiling deep into a room.

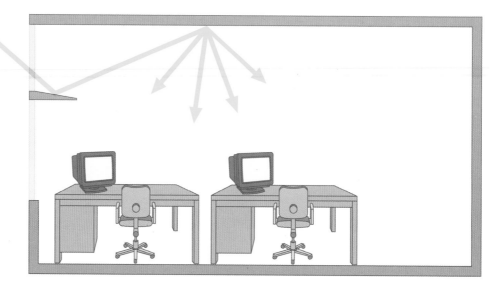

windows. They reflect light off their top surface onto the ceiling. From here, the light is dispersed into the room, thus greatly increasing the depth of the light's coverage from that of an ordinary window. Exterior light shelves can also double as sun shades.

- **Light tubes** (also called light pipes), which transport light from the outside to the inside of a building. The tube's opening is located on a roof or light-receiving exterior wall and contains a light-collecting device that directs light into the tube. Tubes are lined with highly reflective materials that enable them to transmit the light along their length. With a wide diameter, a tube can move light down to the first floor of a multistory building. Mirrors that track the sun are sometimes used at a tube's opening to maximize the amount of light collected.

Studies have found that combining various well-coordinated daylighting features results in more energy savings than individual components used separately. For example, when automatic window blinds are installed along with photosensors, the daylighting system is more effective (Leslie et al., 2004). On the other hand, there are factors that *decrease* the effectiveness of the system. In research conducted to identify the causes of daylighting system

failure, one example was due to interior colors and furnishings that were too dark; these decreased the brightness of the workspaces. Even though the sensors and other components of the daylighting system worked well, it was eventually abandoned because of worker complaints (DiLouie, 2006).

Implications for Designers

Successful daylighting relies on the coordination of many elements, so it is important that building professionals, including interior designers, work together when planning lighting. As mentioned in the previous section, interior design elements such as color can influence the effectiveness of daylighting. Another example involves perceived contrasts in value (light-dark). If a window admits very bright light, the interior walls near the window can seem dark. This can cause room occupants to turn on electric lights unnecessarily, thus defeating the energy-saving purpose of the system. Even worse, if the walls around windows are quite dark, it can be difficult or impossible for occupants to see objects. This condition, known as disability glare, is especially serious with older adults whose eyes take longer to adjust to various levels of light. Solutions to these problems include using light-colored walls between and near windows that admit substantial quantities of light, along with providing shading during periods of very bright sunlight.

Color also affects the efficiency of daylighting. For example, ceilings that reflect light from high windows or from light shelves should be painted in light colors using a matte finish to reduce glare. This is also true for walls located opposite windows and the openings around deep-set windows. Even the colors outside a building influence the amount of light reflected through the windows. For example, lightly colored ground and adjacent structures are more reflective and thus enable more light to enter.

The location and size of windows are important factors in daylighting. Adding windows to increase the entry of light, especially those with a southern (northern in the southern hemisphere) exposure, might be suggested as part of remodeling projects. A rule of thumb is that the surface area of windows should be at least one-fourth the area of the floor (Winchip, 2005).

The placement of windows is also important. Generally, the higher a window is located on a wall, the better it serves for natural lighting. This is because light entering these windows tends to bounce off the ceiling and thus enter the room more deeply than the light entering the window itself. Skylights are another addition that clients who have appropriate roofs and floor plans might consider. Because light enters from the top down, occupants benefit from more hours of sunlight and illuminated large areas. These advantages are increased when the skylight is set in a deep well with splayed sides (Winchip, 2005). Skylights are also good choices for interior spaces that lack sufficient natural light or for rooms in which privacy is important, such as bathrooms.

The direction from which natural light originates is also an important consideration. For example, light coming from the south (north in southern hemisphere locations) tends to vary in color and intensity. Rooms in which activities that require fine color discrimination are performed are therefore best located on the north (south) side of a building. This is why artists tend to prefer studios located with northern light exposures.

Interior obstacles that interrupt the entry of natural light should be avoided when possible. For example, daylight can be blocked by office partitions that are too high or poorly placed. Tall plants in windows, sometimes placed for decorative purposes, can block light. Some barriers that are part of the building's structure can be improved. For example, walls between rooms can be partially glazed to allow light to enter an interior space, such as a hallway. Transoms above doors can also be an effective way to allow light to enter rooms that lack or have limited daylight.

ENERGY STAR

ENERGY STAR is a joint program of the U.S. Environmental Protection Agency and the U.S. Department of Energy. Begun in 1992 to promote energy-efficient computers, it has grown to include energy-efficiency rating systems for thirty-five product categories and efficiency platforms for newly constructed homes. Table 6.2 contains examples of products currently included in the program. In addition, ENERGY STAR partnerships develop energy management strategies to help businesses save money while also helping the environment. The ENERGY STAR rating program has been used in at least 26,000 buildings across the country, with those that perform at top levels earning the designation of ENERGY STAR (ENERGY STAR, n.d., "About"). It is estimated that in 2006, using ENERGY STAR products helped Americans save $14 billion on their utility bills while preventing greenhouse gas emissions equivalent to those from 25 million cars (ENERGY STAR, n.d., "About").

ENERGY STAR offers many opportunities for savings in the residential sector, which, with more than 100 million households, contributes about 17 percent of the nation's greenhouse gas emissions (U.S. Environmental Protection Agency, ENERGY STAR, "The Power"). The EPA estimates that a home can

TABLE 6.2 EXAMPLES OF ENERGY STAR PRODUCTS AND ENERGY SAVINGS

PRODUCT	SAVINGS ABOVE STANDARD NEW PRODUCTS
Office Equipment	
• Home computer/monitor	27%
• Work computer/monitor	52%
• Copier	42%
• Fax	40%
Home Electronics	
• Televisions	24%
• VCRs	29%
• TV/VCRs	30%
• Audio	69%
Heating/Cooling	
• Central air conditioners	24%
• Gas furnaces	15%
• Programmable thermostats	20%
Appliances	
• Clothes washers	38%
• Dishwashers	25%
• Refrigerators	10%
• Room air conditioners	10%
Lighting	
• Fixtures	66%
• Bulbs	66%
• Exit signs	75%

Adapted from: Environmental Protection Agency. (July 2003). *ENERGY STAR — The power to protect the environment through energy efficiency.* (EPA Publication 430-R-03-008). Washington, DC: Author

realize energy savings of 25 to 30 percent by replacing older appliances and lights with EN-ERGY STAR products (U.S. Environmental Protection Agency, ENERGY STAR, "The Power"). It is important to understand that while the initial cost of some ENERGY STAR household appliances, such as refrigerators and washing machines, may be significantly higher than less-efficient models, the long-term savings will make up for this cost. The ENERGY STAR Web site, at http://energystar.gov/, provides information about specific products that qualify for its rating.

Implications for Designers

Designers can add value to their services by becoming familiar with ENERGY STAR products for businesses and homes, the cost-benefits of these products for their clients, and the business energy management systems. In some cases, designers might recommend replacing household appliances, such as during a kitchen remodeling project. In others, it might mean suggesting the replacement of structural elements, such as windows.

Designers should also learn about local rebates and tax credits available to customers who purchase ENERGY STAR products so that true costs can be factored in to home improvement projects.

MAKING EFFICIENT ENERGY AFFORDABLE

Programs at all levels of government are available to inform the public about renewable energy sources and ways to increase energy efficiency. In addition, some consumers are eligible for utility rebates and/or federal and state tax credits when they purchase certain energy-efficient products (see discussion of ENERGY STAR in previous section). Information about these programs is available at www.energy.gov/taxbreaks. Designers should explore the coverage details and dates for these programs to provide the best information to clients. The following categories of products, if they meet specific standards, may be eligible for tax credits:

- Windows
- Skylights
- Exterior doors
- Metal roofs
- Insulation
- Heat pumps
- Air conditioners

In addition, energy-efficient commercial buildings and homes that meet certain energy-reduction percentages entitle contractors to tax credits that they can pass on to home buyers (U.S. Department of Energy, n.d., "The Energy Policy").

GLOSSARY TERMS

Acid rain

Albedo

Biomass

Building America

Building-integrated photovoltaic technologies (BIPV)

Carbon footprint

Carbon neutral

Daylight harvesting

Daylighting

Electricity grid

Embodied energy

ENERGY STAR

Fossil fuels

Global warming

Greenhouse gases

Heat pump

Hydrocarbons

Light shelf

Light tube

Net Zero

Net-zero energy

Photovoltaics

Solar reflectance index

Solar heat gain coefficient

Vertical storage

Visible transmittance

Zero-energy homes

BOX 6.4 VIEW TO THE FUTURE

The EPA's ENERGY STAR program offers partnerships to all types of organizations in which senior executives make a commitment to superior energy management in their facilities. Future partnerships are being sought with organizations for which the EPA can develop new standardized measurement tools to improve energy usage.

The EPA is also exploring ways to adapt the rating system to the industrial sector, a large consumer of energy.

BOX 6.5 THE SUSTAINABILITY CONNECTION

Saving energy and reducing the use of fossil fuels is at the heart of sustainable design and construction. By definition, fossil fuels are unsustainable because they are finite: once depleted, they are gone and cannot be re-created. The truly sustainable forms of energy include wind, sun, and geothermal. Largely sustainable, if we tend the land well and continue to replant and reharvest, is biomass.

Although it may take years to fully develop renewable forms of energy and make them cost-effective for everyone, designers should strive continually to find new ways to create healthy interiors while at the same time helping their clients reduce the amount of energy they consume.

LEARNING ACTIVITIES

1. Investigate the current and predicted availability of renewable energy sources in your community. Write a report in which you discuss their initial cost, long-term operating costs, and potential influence on human health and the environment.

2. Design a flex room for a home or office building that is suitable for at least two uses. Draw a floor plan and include suggestions for appropriate furnishings.

3. Develop a resource file of vendors that provide products and services to improve energy efficiency. Examples: ENERGY STAR appliances, insulation, energy consultants, energy-efficient windows, light shelves, and pellet stoves.

4. Conduct an energy audit for your home or apartment (or that of someone you know) using the Web-based audit tool developed by Lawrence Berkeley Laboratory at http://hes.lbl.gov/. Based on what you learn, develop a written plan for ways to decrease energy consumption.

5. Design a room in a home that employs daylighting as the primary daytime light source. Assume the room has a southern (northern in the southern hemisphere) exposure. Include window locations, features such as light shelves and skylights, paint colors, outside plantings, and interior furnishings with the location.

SUGGESTED WEB SITES

1. Environmental Building News
www.buildinggreen.com
This Web site contains links to dozens of articles, a product directory, and a variety of case studies pertaining to all types of green building topics, including energy.

2. ENERGY STAR
www.energystar.gov
This is the official government site for ENERGY STAR products and information about the program.

3. U.S. Green Building Council
www.usgbc.org
The U.S. Green Building Council (USGBC) is a nonprofit organization composed of leaders from every sector of the building industry. Its purpose is to promote healthy, environmentally responsible buildings that contribute to improving human quality of life. The USGBC developed LEED, the Leadership in Energy and Environmental Design (LEED) Green Building Rating System, which is the nationally accepted benchmark for the design, construction, and operation of high-performance green buildings. This Web site contains information about all types of green topics, including energy efficiency.

4. Lawrence Berkeley Laboratory
http://lbl.gov/
This is a U.S. Department of Energy National Laboratories facility managed by the University of California. Scientists and engineers conduct both theoretical and applied research on a variety of topics. The lab publishes information consumers can use to learn about renewable energy sources, ways they can save energy in the home, and the results of ongoing energy research.

5. Energy Efficiency and Renewable Energy Consumer's Guide
www.eere.energy.gov/consumer
This U.S. Department of Energy agency Web site has links to all kinds of practical information for improving energy efficiency in the home, workplace, and community, including the Building America project.

6. Whole Building Design Guide (WBDG)
www.wbdg.org
The WBDG is a gateway to information on topics, including energy, from a "whole building" perspective. Its development and maintenance is a collaborative effort among federal agencies, private-sector companies, nonprofit organizations, and educational institutions. The dozens of articles and information pages

are segmented in three major categories: Design Guidance, Project Management, and Operations and Maintenance.

7. Alliance to Save Energy

www.ase.org

This organization provides information and news to update consumers and energy professionals with information on lowering energy bills, obtaining tax credits, refinancing and remodeling to improve energy efficiency, conducting energy audits, and buying energy-efficient products.

8. Hearth.com

http://hearth.com

This Web site brings together information about all types of biomass-burning appliances, such as pellet and woodstoves and fireplaces. It includes articles on general topics as well as descriptions of specific products.

9. Environmental and Energy Study Institute (EESI)

www.eesi.org

The EESI is a nonprofit organization dedicated to promoting environmentally sustainable societies. It provides information and public policy initiatives in the form of publications, briefings, workshops, and task forces. Included on its Web site are a series of fact sheets about a variety of renewable energy sources.

10. National Energy Information Administration

www.eia.doe.gov

This agency collects and compiles statistics about all types of energy. The Web site also contains consumer-directed articles about energy topics, including renewable energy sources.

11. Environmental Protection Agency—Personal Emissions Calculator

www.epa.gov/climatechange/emissions/ind_calculator.html

The EPA has developed an online calculator people can use to estimate their personal contribution to greenhouse gas emissions.

The Web site includes actions to take to lower those emissions. For each action chosen, the calculator displays the amount of emissions that would be prevented.

REFERENCES

Alliance to Save Energy. (2005). *Remodeling*. Retrieved June 22, 2007, from www.ase.org/section/_audience/consumers/refinanceremodel/remodeling

American Lung Association. (2004). *Health effects of ozone and particle pollution. Particle pollution: Deadly Then and Now.* Retrieved June 11, 2007, from http://lungaction.org/reports/sota04_heffects.html

Banwell, P., Brons, J., Freyssinier-Nova, J. P., Rizzo, P., & Figueiro, M. (2004). A demonstration of energy-efficient lighting in residential new construction. *Lighting Research Technology, 36*(2), 157–164.

Binggeli, C. (2003). *Building systems for interior designers.* Hoboken, NJ: John Wiley & Sons.

Bower, J. (2001). *The healthy house* (4th ed.). Bloomington, IN: The Healthy House Institute.

Chen, A. (March 18, 1999). Home Energy Saver Web site computes possible savings for homeowners. *Research News.* Retrieved June 6, 2007, from www.lbl.gov/Science-Articles/Archive/home-energy-saver-news.html

DiLouie, C. (May 1, 2006). Why do daylight harvesting projects succeed or fail? *EC&M.* [Electronic version]. Retrieved February 19, 2007, from http:/ecmweb.com/construction/electric/why_daylight_harvesting

ENERGY STAR. (n.d.). *About ENERGY STAR.* Retrieved November 30, 2007, http://energystar.gov/index.cfm?c=about.ab_index

Envall, K., Norrby, C., & Norback, D. (2003). Ocular, nasal, dermal and respiratory symptoms in relation to heating, ventilation, energy conservation, and reconstruction of older multi-family houses. *Indoor Air, 13*(3), 206–211.

Environmental and Energy Study Institute. (March 2006). *Wind energy resource base and incen-*

tives. [Online brochure]. Washington, D.C.: Author. Retrieved June 17, 2007, from www.eesi .org/publications/Fact%20Sheets/EC_Fact_ Sheets/Wind_ResourceBase&Incentives.pdf

Fujii, S., Cha, H., Kagi, N., Miyamura, H., & Kim, Y. (2005). Effects on air pollutant removal by plant absorption and adsorption. *Building and Environment, 40*(1), 105–112.

Geothermal Heat Pump Consortium, Inc. (2003). *How it works.* Retrieved June 21, 2007, from www.geoexchange.org/about/how.htm

Grasso, M. M.; Hunn, B. D.; & Rewerts, A. M. Effect of textile properties in evaluating a directional shading fabric. *Textile Research Journal, 67*(4), 233–247.

Green Home Guide. Product Directory. Retrieved February 24, 2007, from www .greenhomeguide.com/index.php/product_ detail/768/C237

Johnson, S., & Lundberg, T. (June 2004). High-end insulation. *Builder news,* 86–87.

Johnson, J., & Washingon, C. (June 21, 2004). Power from the sun. *Chemical & Engineering News.* [Electronic version]. Retrieved June 14, 2007, from http://pubs.acs.org/cen/ coverstory/8225/8225solarenergy.html

Kibert, C. J. (2005). *Sustainable construction: Green building design and delivery.* Hoboken, NJ: John Wiley & Sons.

Lawrence Berkeley Laboratory. (n.d.). *Cool roofs for hot climates.* Retrieved June 22, 2007, from http://hes.lbl.gov/hes/makingithappen/ no_regrets/coolroofs.html

Leslie, R. P., Raghaven, R., Howlett, O., & Eaton, C. The potential of simplified concepts for daylight harvesting. *Lighting Research and Technology, 37*(1), 21–40.

Long Island Power Authority. (February 26, 2003). *Plug Power fuel cell installed at McDonald's Restaurant, LIPA to install 45 more fuel cells across Long Island, including homes.* [Press release]. Retrieved June 21, 2007, from www .lipower.org/newscenter/pr/2003/feb26 .fuelcell.html

Milne, G., & Readon, C. (Last modified March 1, 2004). *Your home technical Manual: Embodied energy.* Retrieved February 23, 2007, from www.greenhouse.gov.au/yourhome/ technical/fs31.htm

Morgan, M. T. (2003). *Environmental health.* Belmont, CA: Thomson Wadsworth.

National Energy Information Center. (2004). *Greenhouse gases, climate change, and energy.* [Online brochure]. Retrieved February 19, 2007, from www.eia.doe.gov/oiaf/1605/ ggccebro/chapter1.html

Ohlemacher, S., & Foy, P. (May 23, 2007). More and more McMansions. *The Bulletin* (Bend, Oregon), pp. B1, B6.

Pahl, G. (2003). *Natural home heating: The complete guide to renewable energy options.* White River Junction, VT: Chelsea Green Publishing.

Raloff, J. (December 7, 2002). Home cooking on the wane. *Science News.* [Electronic version]. Retrieved June 13, 2007, from www. sciencenews.org/articles/20021207/food.asp

Sexton, S. E., Marin, L. A., & Zilberman, D. (Jan/Feb 2006). Biofuel and biotech: A sustainable energy solution. *Update: Agricultural and Resource Economics, 9* (3). University of California Giannini Foundation. Retrieved June 19, 2007, from www.agecon.ucdavis.edu/ outreach/update_articles/v9n3_1.pdf

Stone, B., Jr. (2005). Urban heat and air pollution. *Journal of the American Planning Association, 71*(1), 13–25.

Tetri, E. (2002). Daylight linked dimming: Effect on fluorescent lamp performance. *Lighting Research and Technology, 34*(1), 3–10.

U.S. Department of Energy. Energy Efficiency and Renewable Energy. (November 9, 2007). *Building America.* Retrieved November 30, 2007, from http://www.eere.energy.gov/ buildings/building_america/

U.S. Department of Energy. Energy Efficiency and Renewable Energy. (September 12, 2005). *Do-it-yourself home energy audits.* Retrieved June 17, 2007, from www.eere.energy. gov/consumer/your_home/energy_audits/ index.cfm/mytopic=11170

U.S. Department of Energy. (September 12, 2005). The economics of a solar water heater. Retrieved June 14, 2007, from www.eere .energy.gov/consumer/your_home/water_ heating/index.cfm/mytopic=12860

U.S. Department of Energy. (n.d.). *The Energy Policy Act of 2005: What the energy bill means to you.* Retrieved June 21, 2007, from www .energy.gov/taxbreaks.htm

U.S. Department of Energy. (December 2003). Energy Efficiency and Renewable Energy. *Moving toward zero energy homes.* [Online brochure]. Retrieved June 12, 2007, from www.eere.energy.gov/buildings/info/ documents/pdfs/35317.pdf

U.S. Department of Energy. Energy Efficiency and Renewable Energy. (September 12, 2005). *Storm windows.* Retrieved June 22, 2007, from www.eere.energy.gov/consumer/ your_home/windows_doors_skylights/Index. cfm/mytopic=13490

U.S. Department of Energy. Energy Efficiency and Renewable Energy. (September 12, 2005). *Whole-house systems approach.* Retrieved June 22, 2007, from www.eere .energy.gov/consumer/your_home/designing_ remodeling/index.cfm/mytopic=103

U.S. Environmental Protection Agency and U.S. Department of Energy. ENERGY STAR. (n.d.). *Duct sealing.* Retrieved June 22, 2007, from www.energystar.gov/ index.cfm?c=home_improvement.hm_ improvement_ducts

U.S. Environmental Protection Agency. (July 2003). ENERGY STAR—*The power to protect the environment through energy efficiency.*

(EPA Publication 430-R-03-008). Washington, DC: Author.

U.S. Environmental Protection Agency. (n.d.) *Information on proper disposal of compact fluorescent light lamps.* Retrieved February 25, 2007, from www.energystar.gov/ia/partners/ promotions/change_light/downloads/Fact_ Sheet_Mercury.pdf

U.S. Environmental Protection Agency. (n.d.) *Light lamps and fixtures.* Retrieved February 25, 2007, from www.energystar.gov/ index.cfm?c=lighting.pr_lighting

U.S. Environmental Protection Agency and U.S. Department of Energy. ENERGY STAR. (n.d.). *Mold, mildew or musty odors.* Retrieved June 22, 2007, from www.energystar.gov/index.cfm?c=home_solutions.hm_ improvement_moldmildew.

U.S. Environmental Protection Agency. (January 27, 2007). *Ozone.* Retrieved June 10, 2007, from www.epa.gov/epahome/ozone .htm

Winchip, S. M. (2005). *Designing a quality lighting environment.* New York: Fairchild Publications.

Winchip, S. M. (2007). *Sustainable design for interior environments.* New York: Fairchild Publications.

Creating Healthy Environments

Ergonomics provides the missing link in the modern health equation: control over the external environment where health problems originate.

—Gordon Inkeles and Iris Schencke

CHAPTER **7**

Ergonomics

LEARNING OBJECTIVES

1. **Define ergonomics and explain its purpose.**
2. **Explain the relationship between ergonomics and environmental health.**
3. **Describe how interior designers can apply ergonomic principles to the following elements of the built environment:**
   a. **Lighting**
   b. **Noise**
   c. **Space**
   d. **Furnishings**

Ergonomics, also called **human factors,** is the study of the fit between humans and their environment. It focuses on adapting the environment to humans, rather than vice versa, and provides interior designers with many principles and tools to create designs that best fulfill human needs. Many people associate ergonomics exclusively with the workplace, tackling such issues as computer keyboard design, but it has a much wider meaning and application. The British Ergonomics Society describes it as all-encompassing: "Ergonomics comes into everything which involves people. Work systems, sports and leisure, health and safety should all embody ergonomics principles if well designed" (The Ergonomics Society, n.d.).

Although humans can adapt to unsuitable conditions, such as chairs that don't fit them properly or counters that are too low, such adaptations often lead to physical problems, unacceptable psychological stress, inefficiency, and errors. Because ergonomics affects every aspect of our lives, including the home, the workplace, and buildings we access for leisure activities, a holistic approach to ergonomics is recommended, one that gives physical, physiological, and psychological effects equal weight (Bridger, 2003). This means that ergonomic principles should be applied throughout any design process, from the initial planning to the selection of furnishings. The ergonomic topics most relevant to interior designers, and therefore, covered in this chapter, are lighting, noise, space planning, and furnishings. Although interior designers are not ergonomists nor engineers, they should be able to identify and correct simple problems, such as furniture placement, and know when to refer more complex issues, such as faulty lighting systems, to the appropriate specialist.

HISTORY OF ERGONOMICS

Working conditions, the original impetus for the development of ergonomics, have been studied since the beginning of the Industrial Revolution, but ergonomics itself did not appear as a recognized field until World War II, when technology and the human sciences were systematically applied for the operation of complex military equipment. Following the war, ergonomic principles proved useful as industries developed in Europe and the United States (Dul and Weerdmeester, 2001). In a social justice context, ergonomics has come into its own as a more humane way of viewing human labor. People began to be seen as total individuals making a contribution to their work, rather than simply as workers (Dul and Weerdmeester, 2001). Modern ergonomics goes well beyond addressing workplace problems and today contributes to solving many social problems related to safety, health, comfort, and efficiency (Dul and Weerdmeester, 2001). The International Ergonomics Association (IEA) was founded in 1961 and today has forty-two federated societies located all over the world as interest in the subject continues to grow (International Ergonomics Association, n.d.).

THE NATURE OF ERGONOMICS

Human beings are complex organisms and buildings are complex structures, so it is not surprising that ergonomics, which explores their interrelationships, draws on a variety of human, natural, and social sciences. Table 7.1 lists the major contributing fields.

Although the goal of architects and interior designers is not to become ergonomic specialists, understanding the basic principles will enable them to create health-promoting environments for their clients. This is because **ergonomic design** provides for human comfort, safety, and satisfaction while creating conditions to promote and enable optimum human performance.

DETERMINING HUMAN NEEDS

Good ergonomic design begins with identifying the physical and psychological needs of the people who will be occupying the environment. "Participatory ergonomics" means consulting users of an environment early in

TABLE 7.1   FIELDS THAT CONTRIBUTE TO ERGONOMICS

Anatomy	Form and structure of living organisms
Anthropometrics	Measurement of the size, weight, and proportions of the human body
Biomechanics	Mechanics of a living body, especially of the forces exerted by muscles and gravity on the skeletal structure
Industrial design	Development of physical solutions to meet a particular need, including environments
Industrial management	Branch of engineering dealing with the creation and management of systems that integrate people, materials, and energy in productive ways
Information technology	All matters concerned with computer science and technology and with the design, development, installation, and implementation of information systems and applications
Mechanical engineering	Generation and application of heat and mechanical power and the design, production, and use of machines and tools
Physics	Matter and energy and their interactions
Physiology	Functions and processes of living organisms and their parts
Psychology	Science dealing with the mind, mental processes, and behavior
Toxicology	Nature, effects, and detection of poisons and the treatment of poisoning

the design process and involving them in the decisions that will affect them (Bridger, 2003). Mark Porter, a professor of design ergonomics at the University of Loughborough in the UK, suggests that "good design decisions can only be made if the right questions are asked at the right time" (Davis, 2007). Box 7.1 contains suggested techniques for assessing client needs. There are a number of advantages when users are involved in a design project: (1) initial design mistakes are more likely to be avoided; (2) acceptance by users is enlarged; (3) more ideas are generated; (4) bottlenecks are identified more quickly; and (5) human well-being is maximized (Dul and Weerdmeester, 1997). These kinds of assessments are particularly important when designing workplaces and other settings that will be used by a variety of individuals who have different needs.

Architects and interior designers sometimes work with ergonomists and engineers who conduct studies and provide technical recommendations. In other situations, it is up to the architects and interior designers to identify and apply ergonomic principles. Ergonomic considerations in home building or remodeling may seem like a novel idea, but individuals spend so much time there that it makes sense, from a health perspective, to apply ergonomics to make homes as safe and comfortable as possible. Consumers are becoming increasingly interested in finding ways to improve and maintain their health, and Web sites and books created for the public have increased general interest in ergonomic issues.

LIGHTING

Good lighting is of utmost importance in the built environment because sighted humans receive about 85 percent of their information through their sense of sight (Canadian Centre for Occupational Health and Safety, 2003). Lighting also affects our health in a number of ways, as discussed in the next section. In addition to human considerations, lighting systems must meet applicable codes, the client's budget, and fit into the overall architectural design. Further, lighting decisions are influenced by

---

BOX 7.1   TECHNIQUES FOR IDENTIFYING CLIENT NEEDS

1. Analyze documents and statistics (workplace).
2. Observe people in their current environment.
3. Interview users individually.
4. Conduct group discussions.
5. Distribute written questionnaires about preferences.

Adapted from: Dul, J., & and Weerdmeester, B. (2001). *Ergonomics for beginners,* (2nd ed.). New York: Taylor & Francis.

---

the federal government's energy conservation guidelines. (Recall from Chapter 6 that lights are a major energy consumer in the built environment.)

For these reasons, lighting should never be an afterthought. Rather, interior designers should strive to ensure that lighting plans are integrated into the total plan for the built environment and considered from the first step in the design process (Heinmiller, 2005).

In the workplace, increases in white-collar and computer occupations have made good lighting even more important now than in the past (Bridger, 2003). This is because doing paperwork and computer tasks can put severe demands on our visual systems. Lighting in offices is especially important because most people today receive the majority of their exposure to light in the workplace (Heil and Mathis, 2002). In spite of these facts, lighting is often taken for granted (Heinmiller, 2005). The Light Right Consortium, a membership organization of researchers and interested parties, suggests that "the real value of lighting is only now beginning to be understood and quantified" (Light Right Consortium, 2002).

Good lighting in the home, where we spend our time studying, reading, using computers, and pursuing hobbies, is also important. Whereas lighting decisions are often made based on what lamps and luminaires (lighting fixtures) look like, it is important that designers help clients choose lighting that is most suited for their needs. For example, while ceiling lights and decorative lamps are

FIGURE 7.1 A number of body processes function on 24-hour schedules known as circadian rhythms.

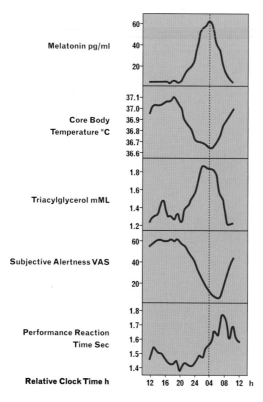

to adapt to different distances, and reduced visual acuity (Kroemer and Grandjean, 1997). In the workplace, these conditions can lead to loss of productivity, lower-quality work, more mistakes, increased accident rates, and more complaints from workers about vision problems. With increased levels of illumination, worker output increases and the level of rejected product decreases (Kroemer and Grandjean, 1997). An experiment conducted in schools showed that proper lighting decreased the pupil size of students and improved their reading accuracy and sensitivity to word contrast (Berman, et al., 1996).

Circadian Rhythms

Light is the major stimulus that regulates **circadian rhythms,** the human biological cycles that repeat approximately every 24 hours. Circadian rhythms involve a number of important body processes, including sleep-wake cycles, hunger, variances in body temperature throughout the day and night, arm and leg strength, flexibility, and the production and suppression of hormones that regulate certain body processes. (See Figure 7.1.) Disruption of these rhythms results in a variety of symptoms and conditions, including delayed sleep and seasonal affective disorder (SAD).

SAD is a form of depression that can include the following symptoms: decreased activity, sadness, irritability, changes in appetite, cravings for carbohydrates, changes in weight, changes in sleep habits, and menstrual difficulties (Miller, 2004). It is most often associated with the lack of daylight in extreme northern and southern latitudes from the late fall to the early spring. It can also affect night workers, who sleep during the day and miss being exposed to natural light. It is believed that SAD might be linked to levels of melatonin, a hormone that helps induce sleep. The production of melatonin peaks at night when it is dark; it could be that during long, dark winter days, the body interprets the lack of light as nighttime and produces too much melatonin. As a consequence, the body feels tired and ready to sleep during the day, when it should be alert.

typically installed to provide ambient lighting, appropriate task and reading lamps in the home are frequently lacking.

Effect of Light on Humans

The most obvious influence of light is on our vision, with 80 percent of the neural fibers from the eye transmitting signals to the visual cortex in the brain. But light actually affects two other human systems as well, the circadian and the perceptual. This is what happens with the remaining 20 percent of the nerves: they relay signals to nonvision parts of the brain and to other parts of the body, including those that control circadian rhythms and hormones (Miller, 2004).

Visual System

As discussed in Chapter 2, vision begins when light rays from an object enter the pupil and pass through the lens and interior of the eyeball to the retina. This is why the amount and quality of light play a critical role in the quality of sight. When there is insufficient light for the task at hand, visual fatigue can occur, causing a variety of symptoms: eye irritation and burning, double vision, headaches, reduced ability

Implications for Designers

Research about the effects of lighting on the circadian system offers designers opportunities to help their clients. For example, studies have shown that exposure to bright light, especially on awakening, helps relieve the depression experienced by people with SAD (Lewy et al., 1998; Terman et al., 2001). Thus, the availability of bright lights in areas frequented in the morning, as well as during the day, can be helpful to clients who live in locations with long, dark winter days and/or climates with heavy overcast for many months at a time. This "bright light area" might be the breakfast space in a home or residential facility. (See Figure 7.2.) In the case of dining rooms, a dimmer switch would be appropriate so that evening meals could be enjoyed in more subdued lighting. Bright light can also be provided by skylights, atriums, sunrooms, and courtyards, as well as by windows. (Note: Individuals who believe they have SAD should consult their physicians, because they could require treatment beyond exposure to the lighting available for general use.) On the other hand, dim light is recommended during the evening hours for those who have difficulty sleeping. Thus, designers should strive to provide light levels high enough for safety in bedrooms and sitting rooms, and yet low enough to help people prepare for restful sleep (Miller, 2004). With those who have trouble sleeping through the night, it may help to ensure total darkness during sleeping hours (Miller, 2004). This can be achieved through blackout curtains, shades, or blinds. In this situation, it is especially important that light switches are easily accessible from the bed to provide for safety when getting up during the night.

SAD-type symptoms can also affect night workers, who sleep during the day and miss the hours of natural daylight. Therefore, designing interiors for work environments such as hospitals, public safety buildings, and round-the-clock factories should include well-lit cafeterias and break rooms so that night personnel can get as much light exposure as possible. It is also recommended that bright light be available at the start of a work shift (Miller, 2004). The light levels should be higher at night than the levels provided for the same location during the daytime. Even for people who do not display SAD symptoms, it has been suggested that bright light exposure helps keep nightshift workers alert (Miller, 2004). People whose sleep-wake cycles have been interrupted report being alert for a longer time when they are exposed to high (3190 lx) or mid (230 lx) light levels than people who are exposed to low (23 lx) levels (Cajochen et al., 2000). Other populations who may benefit from bright architectural lighting include people who are institutionalized, imprisoned, retired, or homebound, and occupants of buildings that don't admit light effectively (Miller, 2004).

Researchers believe that the light levels needed for circadian functioning may be much higher than those needed for optimal vision and that longer exposure times may be

FIGURE 7.2 Brightly lit eating areas can provide the burst of morning light found to help decrease symptoms of seasonal affective disorder. It also assists the body in maintaining appropriate wake-sleep cycles.

necessary (Figueiro et al., 2002). It appears that to have a beneficial effect, light must be of the right spectrum, for a sufficient amount of time, and at specific times during the 24-hour cycle. Thus, our generalizations about what constitutes good lighting will likely change in the future as we learn more about its specific effects on the body (Rea, 2002). Because research continues in this area, it is recommended that interior designers periodically review the findings so they can provide the most up-to-date information and service to their clients.

Perceptual Systems

The term "perceptual effects" refers to how light is perceived and how it influences someone's mood. Studies suggest that light also affects mental performance and cognition (the mental process of knowing) (Knez, 2001), although the results have been mixed.

A number of lighting factors are believed to influence mood:

1. Size and source: large bright areas can stimulate a temporary surge of energy. Too much exposure can result in feelings of illness.
2. Direction: moderate to low levels of indirect lighting can promote relaxation and reduce eyestrain for general activities.
3. Color spectrum: warm white light and soft warm colors are uplifting, while intensely colored lights can cause eyestrain.

Cool white and cool colored lights can be calming, but may become cool and uninviting after long periods.
4. Color and texture of the items being lit (Nielson and Taylor, 2002).

Direct links to mood have been difficult to establish because so many variables contribute to mood (Boyce, et al., 2003). However, it makes sense to assume that poor general lighting that causes eyestrain and fatigue, especially in a work situation, will negatively affect a person's mood.

There is a general lighting category called "mood lighting," which usually refers to soft lighting that creates a sense of peace and coziness. A traditional example is the light emitted from a fireplace, representing warmth, comfort, and an emotional sense of home. In rooms in which a calming effect is desired, designers might choose recessed lights and dimmed table and floor lamps.

Some healthy-home experts believe that lights of different colors can improve both mental and physical health. Table 7.2 presents a list of colors and their suggested properties.

SOURCES OF INTERIOR LIGHT

Light can be provided by both artificial and natural sources, neither of which is inherently good or bad; both have advantages and disadvantages. Actually, how light is provided is

TABLE 7.2 THERAPEUTIC LIGHTING

COLOR	SUGGESTED EFFECTS AND USES
Blue	Calms the mind and promotes sleep. Do not use for reading.
Green	Best used with eyes closed to relax and speed the body's healing mechanism.
Orange	Combats depressions and lifts mood. Encourages friendliness and intimacy. Avoid in sleeping rooms if insomnia is a problem.
Pink	Provides a loving and nurturing environment.
Red	Arouses and encourages action. Also implies danger.
Violet	Aids in mediation and balancing the sides of the brain. Use only for short periods of time.

Adapted from: Chiazzari, S. (1998). *The healing home: Creating the perfect place to live with color, aroma, light and other natural elements.* North Pomfret, VT: Trafalgar Square Publishing.

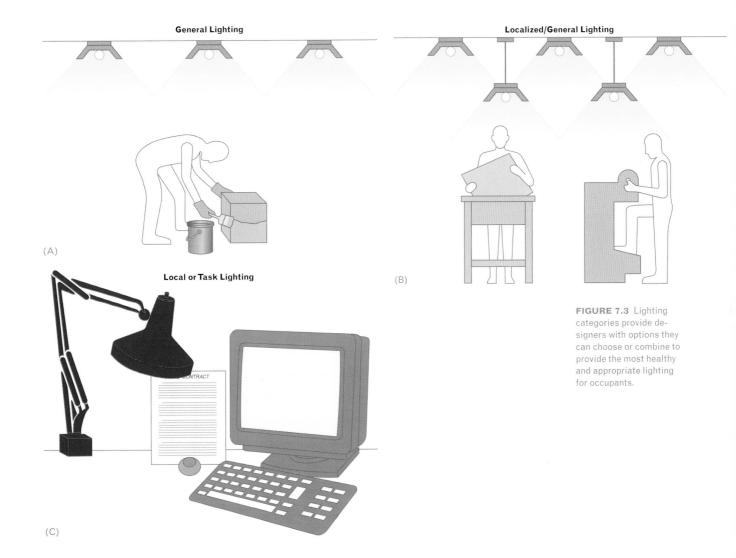

General Lighting

(A)

Local or Task Lighting

CONTRACT

(C)

Localized/General Lighting

(B)

FIGURE 7.3 Lighting categories provide designers with options they can choose or combine to provide the most healthy and appropriate lighting for occupants.

more important than the source of the light. For example, sunlight passing through a window and reflecting off a computer screen into the user's eyes is unsatisfactory, whereas well-directed light from an electrical source is helpful. Proper planning and installation are the determinants of success for selecting and combining light sources.

Regardless of the source, light can be provided in either a direct or indirect manner. Direct lighting, as its name implies, comes directly from its sources. Examples include sunlight entering a window and a task light focused on a desktop work area. Indirect lighting systems direct 90 percent of their light onto ceilings and walls, from which it is bounced back into the room. In most indoor settings, a combination of direct and indirect lighting is used (Kroemer and Grandjean, 1997).

Lighting can also be categorized as general, localized-general, and local (also called "task"), as illustrated in Figure 7.3. General lighting provides fairly uniform lighting. Localized-general uses a combination of ceiling and overhead fixtures to increase lighting levels in certain areas. Designers might choose this type of lighting for a dining room: ambient light for the whole room with a more directed light over the table. Local lighting increases the level of light directly over a specific area and its immediate surroundings. It is generally the best choice for tasks that involve close visual work such as reading, writing, and sewing. When choosing portable task lights, designers should be sure they include the following features: easy adjustment, cool lamp cover, no direct eye contact, and the ability to be positioned on either side of the user. If task lights are used for illuminating materials used when doing computer work, they should not reflect onto the screen. Reading lights in the home should also be adjustable and cool to the touch and have narrow beams that create a pool of light just wide enough to illuminate a large book (Inkeles and Schencke, 1994).

It is important that a task light is not the only light in a room. When there is high contrast that creates abrupt edges between the relatively small area illuminated by a task light and the surrounding space, eyestrain and fatigue can result (Nielson and Taylor, 2002). This is why ambient lighting, such as that provided by an overhead luminaire, should be included in rooms in which close-work activities, aided by task lights, will be performed. For example, the bedroom where a teenager does homework should have both ambient lighting and a good study (task) lamp. A common mistake in the home is lamps that have been chosen for their appearance rather than for suitability for their intended purpose. The results can be eyestrain and eye fatigue.

Artificial Light

Artificial light, supplied by electricity, can be described and measured in a variety of ways. Designers should have a very basic understanding of electrical light-source terminology to help them make good decisions about appropriate lighting systems for their clients. To start, it is important to know about how different aspects of electrically produced light are measured.

Lumen is the measurement for the light output from a source. **Illuminance** is the total amount of light falling on a surface and is measured in either **footcandles** (fc) or **lux** (lx), defined as follows:

- One footcandle is the amount of light that falls on a surface in a 1-foot radius of the source. This measurement is a lamp's lumen per square foot.
- One lux also measures light from a source and equals about 1/10 of a footcandle (therefore, 10 lux = 1 footcandle).

Illumination levels vary widely, from nighttime artificial light levels of 50 lx to full outdoor daylight levels of 100,000 lx (Kroemer and Grandjean, 1997). The minimum intensity for the human eye to visually detect obstacles is 10 lx (Dul and Weerdmeester, 2001). Because each environmental setting has a variety of illumination needs, determining the most appropriate lighting levels for each space requires observation and analysis of the activities performed in each space. See Table 7.3 for recommended ranges of light intensity for specific indoor areas.

Light intensity is measured in **candela** (cd). The following comparison gives a general idea of candela:

In an office with an illumination of 300 lx, a window surface would be 1,000–4,000 cd/m² (candela per meter squared), while a piece of white paper on a table would be 70–80 cd/m².

A **watt** is a measure of an electrical circuit to do work, such as producing heat and light. The efficiency of a lamp (bulb) is measured in lumens per watt (lpw); the higher the number, the more efficient the lamp. For example, an incandescent lamp rated at 40 lpw takes more energy to produce light than a fluorescent lamp at 105 lpw. The wattage of lamps (bulbs) should never be higher than indicated for a specific luminaire because this can present a fire hazard. Designers should always select lu-

TABLE 7.3 RECOMMENDED RANGES OF LIGHT INTENSITY

RANGE OF LUX	AREA
1–200	Orientation areas (corridors and storerooms)
200–800	Normal activities (reading normal print, operating machines)
800–3,000	Special applications (visual inspection tasks)

Adapted from: Dul, J., & Weerdmeester, B. (2001). *Ergonomics for beginners* (2nd ed.). New York: Taylor & Francis.

minaires that will provide sufficient light using the appropriate-size lamp.

Light can also be measured in terms of its ability to render colors accurately using a **coloring rendering index** (CRI). Using 100 CRI as the base, a full-spectrum fluorescent light is 91; standard cool white fluorescent is 68; and other fluorescents are 56 (Heinmiller, 2005). Color rendering is important in certain work situations as well as for areas used for activities such as art when choosing and accurately matching colors is important.

Incandescent Lamps

Incandescent, or filament, lamps produce light by passing an electric current through a tungsten filament. (See Figure 7.4a.) Once the filament heats to a high temperature, it glows and gives off light. These lamps are rich in red and yellow rays and create a pleasant, warm light. However, as discussed in Chapter 6, they are inefficient because more than half of their energy is converted into heat rather than light. Also, they burn out relatively quickly compared to other lamp types because fragments of tungsten deposit on the lamp's glass, causing

it to burn out. In spite of their inefficiency, they are still used for lighting in the majority of noncommercial settings.

Halogen Lamps

Halogen lamps are a type of incandescent lamp, but they differ in that the evaporated tungsten redeposits on the filament. This makes the lamp longer-lasting and more efficient. Halogen lamps become very hot and can pose a safety hazard, as discussed in Chapter 9. Designers should take care when recommending these lamps in settings where children or pets might knock them over. Also, they should never be placed where they might come into contact with flammable materials such as fabrics and paper.

Fluorescent Lamps

In fluorescent lamps, electricity is passed through mercury vapor. The tubes for fluorescent lamps are coated with a substance that converts ultraviolet rays into visible light. (See Figure 7.4b.) This is a much more efficient process than using a filament (fluorescent lights were first popularized as workplace

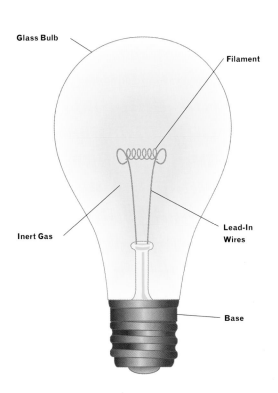

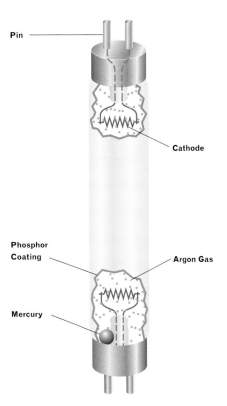

FIGURE 7.4A Incandescent lamps provide light by passing electrical current through a tungsten filament until it produces heat and glows.

FIGURE 7.4B Fluorescent lamps convert ultraviolet rays into visible light by passing electrical current through mercury gas. These lamps produce more light while producing less heat than incandescent lamps.

cost-savers). They also are capable of producing a high output of light; creating low luminance, if adequately shielded; and closely matching daylight (Kroemer and Grandjean, 1997).

Early fluorescent lights sometimes caused problems for users because they operated on alternating current, which can result in flicker. Studies have determined that although not everyone is affected negatively by light flicker, many people experience heightened arousal of the central nervous system (Küller and Laike, 1998). Some experts suggest that visible flicker has adverse effects on the eye because of the repetitive overexposure of the retina (Kromer and Grandjean, 1997). Other researchers have found that when flicker is eliminated by replacing magnetic ballasts with electronic ballasts, headaches are reduced and task performance increased (Wilkins et al., 1989; Veitch and Newsham, 1998a).

But newer fluorescent lighting has resolved these problems, and properly installed fluorescent lighting can be a good source of even, relatively shadowless, energy-saving light. Designers should be aware that if clients are having difficulty with older fluorescent lighting systems, the best recommendation may be to replace them with modern systems.

Full-Spectrum Artificial Light

The term "full-spectrum" was first used for describing certain electrical light sources by Dr. John Ott in the 1960s: "electric light sources that simulate the visible and ultraviolet spectrum of natural light" (Rensselaer Polytechnic Institute, 2005). There is no official, measurable definition; today it remains a marketing, not a technical term. The most common description used by producers of lighting products is that full-spectrum sources simulate sunlight or natural daylight. The problem with this definition is that daylight is never static, but varies by the position of the sun, amount of moisture in the air, and many other factors. No absolute point of daylight has been identified to which full-spectrum lamps can be compared.

Many health- and visual-improvement claims have been made for full-spectrum lamps. A report prepared by the Lighting Re-

search Center at Rensselaer Polytechnic Institute that examined the nature of and claims for full-spectrum lighting included the following conclusions:

- Contradictory claims are made by manufacturers about the nature of full-spectrum lamps (for example, some contain UV rays while others do not).
- Color rendering is excellent.
- Visual performance is no better than with other light sources under most circumstances (although individuals may perceive it as better and find it helpful for reading because the color is more saturated and white paper is brightened, causing dark letters to stand out).
- Health is not improved (in fact, short wavelength light is the most effective at regulating the circadian system).
- Psychological benefits may be achieved because of the appearance and perception of a natural environment, especially if this is a valued trait.
- The ultraviolet radiation in lamps is not enough to provide the production of needed amounts of vitamin D (Lighting Resource Center, 2005).

Daylight

Incorporating natural daylight into any built environment has many benefits, including increasing user satisfaction and decreasing energy costs. Surveys show that most people prefer daylight and views of the outside, but it is important to note that both artificial and natural light can result in eyestrain, sore eyes, blurred vision, and headaches (Boyce et al., 2003). In fact, daylight has not been found to be inherently superior to other light sources for performing visual tasks (Boyce et al., 2003). Researchers have found that when lighting distribution is adequate, there is little difference between natural and artificial light on the performance of everyday visual tasks (Santamaria and Bennett, 1981). In fact, if the level of natural light is inadequate for activities such as reading and writing and is not supplemented by artificial sources, the results can be eyestrain and fatigue. There is one area in which natural lighting is generally superior and that is in color rendering. Studies have found that when very fine color discrimination is needed, natural or "full-spectrum" artificial light is preferable (Boyce et al., 2003).

In spite of these findings regarding visual performance, individuals consistently indicate they prefer windows and daylight to interior offices. For example, a study on daylight and productivity found that people in windowed offices spent 15 percent more time on work-related tasks than people in interior offices (Figueiro et al., 2002). Others studies have shown that lack of access to windows correlates positively with job dissatisfaction, feelings of isolation, depression, and job stress (Leather et al., 1998). It is possible that people's attitudes about lighting affect their perceptions about its effectiveness. Studies conducted by Cuttle (2002) and Beckstead and Boyce (1992), for example, revealed a negative bias against electric lights, fluorescents in particular, as opposed to natural lighting. This may have been due to the poor quality of early fluorescent lights, which often flickered, a condition that has been linked to eyestrain and headaches.

The preference for daylight may also be influenced by the perceptual as much as by the visual. This is because windows, in addition to being a source of natural light, provide views of the outside world. Such views are restful on the eyes, allowing them to change focus as they look into the distance. They also provide a connection with nature and relieve feelings of being closed in. In fact, studies have shown that a view through a window to a natural setting is a reliable means of reducing stress (Boyce et al., 2003). (See Figure 7.5.) This may account for other findings that correlated views of nature to a decrease in calls to health-care providers from workers in various occupations (Boyce et al., 2003).

Implications for Designers

Desiring and benefiting from views of natural settings may be related to **biophilia,** a term coined to describe the proposition that humans have an innate need to connect with nature and other living things (Kellert and

FIGURE 7.5 Ideally, office windows should provide views of greenery and nature. When this is not possible, small gardens and plantings can be substituted.

Wilson, 1993). For example, green space has been positively correlated with feelings of good health. In studies of hospital patients, it has been shown that those who have views of nature from their hospital windows have faster recovery times and require fewer pain medications. Therefore, designers should endeavor to provide windows with natural views whenever possible. Such views are especially beneficial in facilities such as hospitals, nursing homes, and long-term care facilities. In urban settings, nature can be incorporated by providing gardens, plants on balconies and in window boxes, and plant-filled atriums and sunrooms.

Reflection

The reflective property of a surface depends largely on its color—the lighter the color, the higher the amount of reflection—as well as on its texture. Given two rooms of the same size and amount of lighting, one with white walls will feel very different than one with dark paneling, because much more light will be reflected off the white walls. Therefore, the room will seem much brighter and lighter.

Reflection is also related to safety. For example, light-colored walls and white concrete

TABLE 7.4   RECOMMENDED VALUES FOR SURFACE REFLECTIONS

SURFACE	REFLECTANCE
Ceiling	80 to 90%
Walls	40 to 60%
Machines and equipment	30 to 50%
Tabletops	25 to 45%
Floor	20 to 40%

Adapted from: Dul, J., & Weerdmeester, B. (2001). *Ergonomics for beginners* (2nd ed.). New York: Taylor & Francis.

Kroemer, K. H. E., & Grandjean, E. (1997). *Fitting the task to the human: A textbook of occupational ergonomics* (5th ed.). New York: Taylor & Francis.

flooring in a parking structure better reflect light than dark walls and asphalt flooring. The resulting higher luminance increases the ability of parking customers to see at night.

Implications for Designers

Reflection can be expressed as the percentage of light that is reflected back from a surface. Table 7.4 contains the recommended values for various surface reflections. In practical applications, lighting specialists recommend using light colors on the walls and partitions of offices and classrooms because light surfaces better distribute available light and fill in shadowed areas (Heinmiller, 2005). In addition to reflectance properties, dark walls are often perceived as gloomy, a characteristic that is psychologically undesirable (Shepherd et al., 1992). At the same time, excessive reflection in work areas can cause eyestrain and fatigue. It can also be inappropriate in areas intended for rest and relaxation.

Some reflections can be distracting, such as images reflected off television and computer screens that interfere with what a person is trying to see. Such items should be placed so that light from windows and artificial sources do not hit them directly.

Glare

Glare is defined as light that is brighter than the level of light to which the eyes are adapted. As light becomes brighter, the pupils decrease in size to restrict the amount of light entering the eye. When the light reaches a certain level of brightness, the pupils cannot become small enough for the retina to process the incoming light and the result is temporary blindness.

There are two kinds of glare: (1) direct, the result of looking into a light source; and (2) indirect, caused by light reflecting off a surface and into the eyes. Glare ranges from being simply annoying to causing physical discomfort. Over time, continual exposure to glare contributes to general bodily fatigue. When severe, it can result in loss of visual performance and impairment of vision, thus posing safety problems. These situations are why glare is one of the most important ergonomic considerations when designing offices (Kroemer and Grandjean, 1997).

As computers have become ubiquitous, studies of glare and how to avoid it tended to focus on computer screens. Other problems with glare have been identified, and interest in preventing these problems has increased (Heinmiller, 2005). In particular, overhead glare, caused by light fixtures, lamps, and sunlight from windows, seems to cause the most discomfort (Ngai, 1999).

Implications for Designers

As discussed previously, daylight and windows are perceived as desirable, but bright sunlight can be a source of glare and excessive contrast. It is important to remember that with lighting, more is not always better. Interior designers should review all windows and, when necessary, plan appropriate window coverings to prevent these problems. The kitchen is a room that's frequently overlooked in this regard. Windows here should allow light to enter but at the same time, have coverings such as adjustable blinds to prevent direct glare from sunlight and indirect glare from countertops and appliances. In offices, furnishings should be arranged so that desks and workspaces do not directly face windows. This is because when an individual faces a light source such as a window, the tendency is to bend the head forward to avoid the glare. Over time, this position leads to neck and back pain. Placing them at right angles to windows is one way to prevent glare while allowing occupants to enjoy window light and views.

The following suggestions can help prevent the glare generated by artificial lighting:

- Use shades or glare shields on all lights.
- Increase the angle of the line from the eyes to light sources to more than 30° from the horizon.
- Align fluorescent tubes at right angles to the line of sight (Kroemer and Grandjean, 1997).
- Use lamps (bulbs) with lower wattage or cool beams.
- Adjust the direction of the light source.
- Use baffles (louvers, grooves, grids, and lenses) to divert or diffuse glare (Nielson and Taylor, 2002).

Furnishings and equipment that reflect light also can be sources of glare, bouncing it into the room and into the eyes of its occupants. In the home, glare can be a problem in kitchens equipped with shiny-surfaced cabinets, metal appliances, and light-colored laminated tables and countertops. The placement of these surfaces should be carefully considered in relation to windows and other light sources to prevent annoying glare. In any well-lit room, it is best to select matte finishes for furniture and equipment.

FIGURE 7.6 Excessive contrast between the work area, in this case the computer screen and task light, and the surrounding area can cause eyestrain. More ambient lighting should be provided in this office.

When computer screens have glare from light sources, designers might suggest that antiglare screens be used. These are available in mesh, polarized, and optically coated, all in a variety of grades. The mesh causes the most distortion, but the monitor's screen type is most important when selecting an appropriate glare screen.

Contrast

Related to glare is contrast in brightness, an important consideration when designing a lighting system. High contrast among light sources in offices is consistently rated poorly by employees, with overall satisfaction increasing when there is high, evenly balanced brightness in the environment. (See Figure 7.6.) The problem is that when there are significant differences in levels of lighting, the eyes become fatigued by the need to constantly dilate and contract to adjust to various levels (Inkeles and Schencke, 1994). Some ergonomists suggest that the maximum luminous contrast in a room not exceed 40 to 1 (Kroener and Grandjean, 1997).

Implications for Designers

Designers should try to maintain a balanced level of brightness in a room in which all major objects and surfaces in the visual field appear about equally bright. When there is contrast, the following guidelines should be followed:

- Surfaces in the middle of the visual field should not have a luminance contrast of more than 3:1.
- The contrast between the middle field and the rim of the visual field should not exceed 10:1.
- The working field should be brightest in the middle and darker toward the edges
- Light sources should not contrast with their background by more than 20:1.

Style trends sometimes contradict these guidelines. For example, black furnishings might be placed against bright white walls, resulting in too much contrast. Black machines might be placed on white counters, or vice versa. At the same time, contrast can be used to convey information. For example, in dark or shadowy areas, or those frequented by older adults, designers can specify that light-colored paint be used on the edges of steps, curbing, or other areas where higher luminance will communicate important safety information.

LIGHTING AND PEOPLE

The goal of good lighting is to satisfy as many needs of its users as possible. Because people vary in their needs and preferences, generalizations about lighting cannot be universally applied. Even gender affects lighting needs and preferences, as seen in a study that found that regardless of the lighting conditions, women tended to evaluate room light as more cold and glaring than men (Knez, 2001). An additional finding was that in daylight white light, women performed better than men on long-term memory tasks.

Age is a factor that affects the sight of almost everyone. Starting at about forty, people need higher illumination levels, and the necessary levels increase with advancing age.

Therefore, higher levels of lighting should be provided for homes and facilities occupied by older adults. Adding task lighting in kitchens and bathrooms, for example, can help with reading medication and food labels and recipes. In kitchens, these lights might be installed under cabinets. Designers should ask clients about lifestyle habits that affect lighting needs. Examples of appropriate questions include:

- Where and when do you like to read?
- Do you have hobbies that involve doing close-up work?
- Is it important that you have good light for reading labels?

If a client enjoys reading the newspaper during breakfast, for example, a welcome addition to the eating area might be a good reading lamp to supplement overhead lighting.

Another important factor, as discussed in Chapters 8 and 9, is that the eyes of older people generally take longer to adjust to various levels of brightness. Designers, therefore, should ensure that transition zones are provided. For example, lighting in entryways used by older adults might have dimmer switches so the indoor entry can be brightly light during the day and more dimly lit at night so the transition from the outdoors is not too abrupt.

Of course, interior designers cannot be knowledgeable about all human variances, nor can everyone always be accommodated; however, learning as much as possible about the occupants of a specific environment, their characteristics, and the activities that will take place will result in more ergonomically sound lighting systems.

User Control

Studies have reported positive results when users have control over the light in their personal work areas. For example, when subjects were given personal control in a laboratory experience, they demonstrated more satisfaction with the lighting and comfort of the room and rated tasks as less difficult than those who did not have control (Boyce et al., 2000).

Another benefit was energy savings of 35 to 42 percent with the control group. A Canadian study found that workers who have control over lighting feel a general, positive sense of control in the workplace (Veitch and Newsham, 1998b). Individual lighting controls only work, however, if they are just that—individual. When control is shared by several occupants in one area, it can actually add to work stress and dissatisfaction if there is disagreement on desirable lighting levels (Moore et al., 2002).

One way to give office workers individual control is with furniture-mounted task lighting, such as under-cabinet fixtures or positionally adjustable lights (Heinmiller, 2005). It is important that any lights mounted at eye-level view, such as those installed under an overhead cabinet, should have an opaque front or the lens hidden from view to prevent shining directly into the eyes of the user.

Another system that provides user control is multilevel switching. This involves fixtures with three lamps, each controlled separately and, thus, allowing various levels of light. These systems have been found to save on energy because users tend to use only the amount of light necessary for their tasks (Heinmiller, 2005).

LIGHTING AND SAFETY

Adequate lighting is an important contributor to safety, both inside and outside the built environment. Lighting as a means of preventing falls, a major cause of injuries in the elderly, is discussed in Chapter 9.

Creative solutions are sometimes called for in addressing safety issues for specific populations. A study conducted in a nursing home will serve as an example (Taylor, 2006). Populated principally by older residents, nursing homes present special challenges during the night. This is because common problems among this group are sleep disruptions throughout the night and falls when getting into and out of bed. Sleep disturbances, which affect 40 to 70 percent of individuals over age 65, were made worse by mandatory bed checks on residents

performed at intervals during the night. On entering each room, the nurse would turn on an overhead light, frequently awakening the resident. In an attempt to solve both problems, amber-colored, low-level LED lighting systems were installed on the floors and around doorways. Connected to motion sensors, the lights turned on slowly when a nurse entered the room or when residents put their feet on the floor next to the bed. This innovative system drastically decreased the number of awakenings. Although it was not possible to determine how many falls were prevented, both nurses and residents reported that the lower levels of bathroom lighting were adequate.

While not all facilities can afford to install systems such as LED lights, such ideas can be considered for new facilities when planning the overall lighting systems. In addition, there are simple strategies that are often overlooked. For example, the location of light switches in relation to beds should be considered. These are often located out of reach of residents or in awkward locations. Designers can suggest repositioning switches in ways that do not incur great expense, but at the same time decrease the chances of falls.

Shadows can present problems when they darken areas that should be illuminated for security or safety reasons. Dark areas can interfere with vision and cause individuals to miss or misinterpret important visual information. For example, the edges of shadows may look

BOX 7.2 THE SUSTAINABILITY CONNECTION: LIGHTING

- Quality energy efficient lighting can reduce electrical consumption. New lighting systems that replace old technology may result in energy savings of 25 to 50 percent (Light Right Consortium, www.lightright.org).
- Studies are showing that daylight is a healthy and energy-saving source of light. Additional findings may cause more daylighting to be incorporated in the built environment.
- The best-known building accreditation program in the U.S. is the Leadership in Energy and Environmental Design (LEED), established in 1999 by the U.S. Green Buildings Council. Of the 57 credits in its rating system, one is for daylighting.
- Appropriate lighting helps sustain visual health.

BOX 7.3 VIEW TO THE FUTURE

Lighting

- Increased use of home offices and need to design and furnish using good ergonomics.
- Increased studies by groups such as The Light Consortium are encouraging wider attention to ergonomic lighting. The Consortium's purpose is to sponsor research to learn more about the effects of lighting on people, believing there is much that needs to be understood.
- In the future, we may be designing lighting not simply to retain and maintain human health and comfort, but to *improve* health and prevent and relieve disorders. Examples of current research topics include circadian functioning, Alzheimer's, and breast cancer.
- There may be more research about and testing of the biophilia hypothesis.

like edges that don't actually exist. Shadows can also increase feelings of insecurity because if people can't see what's ahead or to the side of them, they don't have enough reaction time if these are used as hiding places for criminals. To prevent such problems, designers should carefully consider the number and placement of luminaires. It is a good idea to check their effectiveness during nighttime hours before final installation is completed. Be sure that lights are not directed into the eyes and therefore blind users of the environment.

Because people feel safer as light levels increase, 3 footcandles of illumination throughout an area is recommended as optimal (Leslie and Rodgers, 1996). Not only can areas thus lighted be easily accessed and safely used, uniform illumination could also discourage crime. This is important in commercial establishments, such as restaurants and theaters, that want to attract customers in the evening.

TABLE 7.5 SPEED OF SOUND WAVES

MEDIUM	SPEED IN METERS/FEET PER SECOND
Air	340/1,115
Water	1,500/4,921
Steel	5,000/16,404

NOISE

Sound and hearing provide us with the means to communicate, share ideas, enjoy music, and help and support one another. We frequently seek out sound, as with phones and personal music players. At the same time, too much sound or sound that is meaningless—what we call noise—can range from being an annoyance to the cause of physical harm.

An estimated 14 million workers in the United States are exposed to hazardous noise. High-density workspaces and homes and schools located near highways and airports are often unacceptably noisy. Further, design trends today include many hard surfaces, including slate floors, granite countertops, and metal appliances. Because sounds reflect off these surfaces, noise can become excessive, especially when groups of people are present. These conditions present designers with challenges to create environments that balance our need for productive, pleasant sounds while reducing distracting, harmful levels of noise. Although some noise problems must be handled by acoustical experts, the majority of them can be solved by individuals such as interior designers, who do not have knowledge of architectural acoustics (Barkman, n.d.).

Production and Measurement of Sound

Sound is created when a mechanical movement creates waves of air pressure, much like when a tossed stone creates outwardly moving waves of water. The medium through which sound waves travel determines their speed—the denser the substance, the faster the speed. (See Table 7.5.) This is why trains can be heard through railroad tracks before the sound reaches our ears through the air. In the built environment, the transmission of sound through walls, floors, and ceilings varies with the density of the construction materials.

Recall from Chapter 2 that the ear hears by collecting and transmitting the vibrations produced by sound waves. What the ear perceives as loudness of sound is determined by the amount of energy (variation in pressure) carried by these sound waves. The unit of

TABLE 7.6 NORMAL SPEAKING VOICE AT A DISTANCE OF ONE METER

Quiet conversation	60–65 dB
Speaker at a conference	65–75 dB
Delivery of a lecture	70–80 dB
Loud shouting	80–85 dB

Adapted from: Source: Kroemer, K. H. E., & Grandjean, E. (1997). *Fitting the task to the human: A textbook of occupational ergonomics* (5th ed.). New York: Taylor & Francis.

measure for loudness is the **decibel (dB),** a logarithmic unit. This means that decibels, like the Richter scale used to measure earthquakes, represent a wide range of values in relation to one another. For example, with each increase of 3 dB, the power of the sound is doubled. One decibel is the smallest change the average human ear can detect and it takes 10 dB for the human ear to perceive a doubling in sound. Table 7.6 shows the decibel levels of human speech.

Sound waves do not need a clear path to travel. In addition to moving in a straight line, they can travel through objects, reflect off surfaces (reverberation), and move over and under obstacles (diffraction). When reverberated, sound waves bounce off a surface at the same angle they encountered it, much like cue balls on a billiard table. In the built environment, sound is reduced less quickly as it spreads around a room because of its ability to reflect off surfaces. This is important for designers to know because it could affect the design of rooms that might be affected by sound reverberation. For example, a room with high ceilings and walls consisting of windows may need acoustical panels or other soft materials on opposite walls or on the ceiling to help absorb sound waves to prevent echoing effects. Distance also affects sound, which loses energy, and therefore volume, as it travels through the air. Moving away from its source, its loudness is reduced by about 6 dB for each doubling of the distance from the source, as illustrated in Figure 7.7.

Frequency is the number of pressure fluctuations, or vibrations, made by a sound wave. Frequency determines the pitch of a sound

and is measured in **Hertz (Hz)** with 1 Hz equal to one vibration per second. The closer the peaks of a sound wave, the higher the frequency. Conversely, the farther apart the waves, the lower the frequency. High-frequency sounds are perceived as louder and more annoying—think screeching noise—than lower frequency sounds. On the other hand, lower frequencies travel farther and can be heard at longer distances from their source. A young person can hear sounds ranging from 16 to 20,000 Hz, with the greatest sensitivity lying between 2,000 and 5,000 Hz. Much of human speech is in the 2,000 to 5,000 Hz range. Figure 7.8 contains examples of the frequencies of various common sounds.

Noise load includes not only the loudness of sound but also how often and for how long it occurs. Two units of measurement for noise load are the **continuous sound level,** which expresses the average level of sound energy during a given period of time, and the

FIGURE 7.7 Sound waves lose energy, and thus loudness, as they travel away from their source.

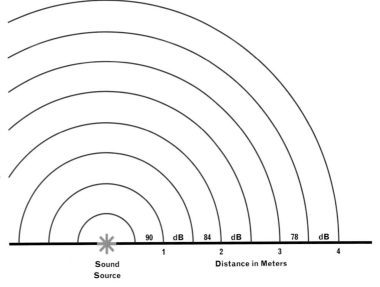

	90	dB	84	dB	78	dB
	1		2		3	4

Sound Source

Distance in Meters

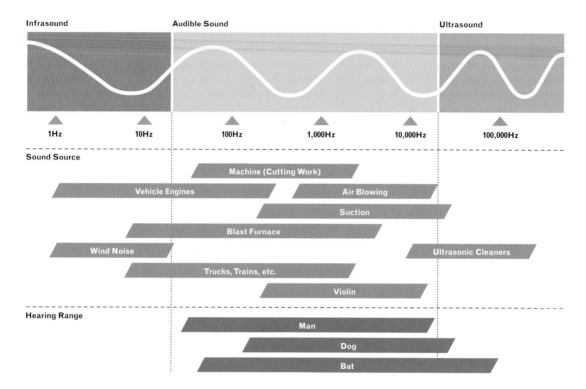

FIGURE 7.8 Examples of the frequencies of common sounds.

summated frequency level, which is the percentage of time that a designated decibel was reached or exceeded during a given period of time (Kroemer and Grandjean, 1997).

Effect of Sound on Humans

Our sense of hearing serves two major purposes: it enables communication and serves as a waking and alarm system. Much of the animal world relies on hearing for survival; humans

share this trait. For example, loud or continuous noise stimulates the autonomic nervous system, which controls body functions without our awareness. This stimulation then causes physiological effects that are symptomatic of stress, listed in Box 7.4. In other words, excessive noise can trigger the "fight or flight" response. In addition to causing fatigue, over time these reactions can place a burden on the heart and circulatory system (U.S. Department of Labor, n.d.). Even children's blood pressure has been found to slightly rise in the presence of excessive noise. This is a concern because we do not know the long-term effects of this change and whether these children will tend to have high blood pressure and other cardiovascular problems as adults (Evans and Lepore, 1993). It is also possible that excessive environmental noise and vibration negatively affect fetal and neonatal development because of the many developmental changes taking place then at the cellular level. (See Chapter 8 for more information about fetal and child physical development.)

Hearing Loss

Sound levels above 80 dB can impair hearing by damaging the sound-sensitive cells of the

---

BOX 7.4 PHYSIOLOGICAL REACTIONS TO NOISE

- Raised blood pressure
- Accelerated heart rate
- Contracted blood vessels
- Increased metabolism
- Slowed digestion
- Increased muscular tension
- Secretion of stress hormones: epinephrine, norepinephrine, and cortisol

Adapted from: Kroemer, K. H. E., & Grandjean, E. (1997). *Fitting the task to the human: A textbook of occupational ergonomics* (5th ed.) New York: Taylor & Francis.

Occupational Safety and Health Administration. *Noise control: A guide for workers and employers.* Retrieved February 2, 2006, from www.nonoise.org/hearing/noisecon/noisecon.htm.

Cornell News release. Retrieved February 27, 2006, from www.news.cornell.edu/releases/march98/noise.stress.ssl.html.

TABLE 7.7   EFFECTS OF VARIOUS SOUNDS

SOURCE	DECIBELS	EFFECTS
Jet engine	120–150	Permanent damage
Jackhammer	110–120	Severe noise fatigue and permanent damage
Loud orchestra	100–110	Extreme noise fatigue
Subway train	85–90	Noise fatigue; onset of pain; ear protection advised above this level
Car	65–75	Noise fatigue
Conversation	50–60	Noise fatigue if nearby
Whisper	30–40	No noise fatigue

inner ear. Hearing loss may be temporary at first, but continual exposure to loud sounds can result in noise-induced hearing loss. Cell damage usually takes place slowly, so that by the time the person notices the problem, irreparable hearing impairment has already occurred. Hearing loss can also happen as the result of a onetime exposure to a sudden, loud sound such as a gunshot, which can register as high as 180 dB. People suffering from noise-induced hearing loss may also experience tinnitus, a continual ringing in the ears, which has no cure (U.S. Department of Labor, n.d.). In most industrialized countries today, noise deafness is a common occupational hazard (Kroemer and Grandjean, 1997). Table 7.7 contains common sounds and their effects on hearing.

A current trend in residential construction, the home theater, brings a new challenge for preventing hearing loss. The use of multi-speaker systems at sound levels similar to those used in commercial theaters (most of which are too loud for health) could lead to an increasing number of hearing problems (Morgan, 2003). In these situations, designers can suggest that sound-absorbing walls and ceilings be installed to help control the noise generated.

Physiological Effects

Even when noise does not cause permanent hearing loss, exposure to continual noise can result in impaired mental alertness, annoyance,

irritability, and difficulty understanding speech (Kroemer and Grandjean, 1997). People doing tasks involving mental activity and concentration are especially sensitive to sporadic or high levels of noise. Because of the potential health hazards of excessive noise, the Occupational Safety and Health Administration (OSHA) has set standards that establish limits on workplace noise exposure for given time periods, shown in Table 7.8. In addition, the limit for average exposure during an 8-hour period is 90 dB and exposure to a onetime noise must not exceed 140 dB.

TABLE 7.8   OSHA LIMITS FOR SOUND LEVELS

HOURS OF EXPOSURE	SOUND LEVEL AVERAGE OVER THE TIME PERIOD
8	90
6	92
4	95
3	97
2	100
1 ½	102
1	105
½	115
¼ or less	115

Adapted from: U.S. Department of Labor, Occupational Safety and Health Administration, (n.d.) *Noise control: A guide for workers and employers*. On line publication, available at: www.nonoise.org/hearing/noisecon/noisecon.htm.

Noise as Distraction

Noise does not have to be especially loud to be disturbing to workers, as evidenced in surveys of office workers who report that the conversations of other people are what they find most disruptive. In a survey of 411 office workers conducted by Nemecek and Grandjean in 1971, 46 percent responded "talking" or "conversation" when asked what kinds of noise disturbed them (Kroemer and Grandjean, 1997). This problem has persisted, as evidenced by the results of a survey conducted more recently by Herman Miller, Inc. on privacy issues. Most respondents agreed with the statement "When I am working in my workspace, I'm distracted by conversations of my immediate neighbors" (Herman Miller, 2002). It is generally believed that it is not the loudness of the person talking that is distracting but the content, because it piques the curiosity of even the unintended listener. This presents a dilemma for the modern, open-office plan, which is intended to provide a more democratic, sharing, team-oriented workplace but has the downside of increased noise and decreased worker productivity. This is problematic because noise can interfere with complex mental activities, especially those that depend on the interpretation of information.

It can also make it difficult to learn certain kinds of dexterity skills (Kroemer and Grandjean, 1997).

Children's learning appears to be affected by noise levels in their schools. Noises typically generated in schools include chairs scraping, talking, shuffling feet, faulty fluorescent lights, equipment, and traffic. Schools located near airports and train tracks experience even higher levels. Young children are particularly affected when noise inhibits their ability to hear and understand their teachers. This is because they do not have the vocabulary and experience needed to fill in meanings when words are missed (Chobot, 1997). When hearing is a constant problem, language development skills and the ability to learn can be decreased. Researchers also believe that children chronically exposed to noise may suffer from attentional deficits (Evans and Lepore, 1993). As with adults, one of the most problematic distracters for children is meaningful speech.

This is why schools, as well as preschools and day-care facilities, should be checked for noise levels. When necessary, designers can suggest a number of remedies:

- Attach dampening material to the bottoms of chair feet.
- Use carpets, drapes, and/or curtains.
- Install bookshelves on hard-surfaced walls.
- Apply corkboard to walls.
- Install suspended acoustic tile on ceilings (see Figure 7.9).
- Install weather stripping on classroom doors.
- Damp and seal openings, such as those around pipes and ventilating ducts (Chabot, 1997).

Sources of noise depend on the type of environment. In addition to conversation, the following are common disruptors in the built environment: moving air and gases, flowing liquids, movement in ducts, machines that vibrate, people walking about, and automobile traffic. Box 7.5 contains a more comprehensive list of typical noise sources.

FIGURE 7.9 Acoustical ceiling tiles, which absorb sound waves and thus decrease the levels of sound in a room, come in a variety of styles.

Implications for Designers

Acoustics, the study of sound and sound waves, can be applied to significantly improve human comfort and health. Surveys have shown that attention to acoustics is often an afterthought in the design process. Worse, and more expensive to resolve, are problems that surface after a facility has been in use for some time. In new construction or in remodeling, there are at least four ways that noise can be reduced: absorption, blocking, masking, and proper space planning.

Absorption

Absorption involves using porous materials that are filled with air pockets in which sound waves bounce around and lose some of their energy due to friction. What happens is that rather than producing sound, they produce heat, which is then released into the environment. The rating for the absorbency of materials is expressed by an **absorption coefficient,** or the percent of sound absorbed. Ratings of 180 to 200 appear to be the industry standard (Steelcase, 2000). Depending on the specific environment, absorption can be achieved in many ways, as listed in Box 7.6 and illustrated in Figure 7.11.

Floors can be made more sound-absorbing by using vinyl or thick linoleum. Residential interior designers can also look for simple ways to reduce noise levels. For example, rubber mounts can be installed under appliances such as refrigerators, dishwashers, and clothes washers and dryers; rubber mats can be placed under small appliances, such as blenders and mixers. Plastic can be substituted for noisy metal items such as garbage cans with clanging lids.

But interior designers should also make sure the use of sound-absorbing materials does not introduce other health-related problems. For example, heavy draperies and the liberal use of upholstered furniture may reduce the noise that enters a bedroom that faces a busy street. At the same time, these fabrics would cause problems for clients with dust-mite allergies. In this case, other methods such as

blocking, discussed in the next section, might be more appropriate. Designers must consider all aspects of their clients' needs when making ergonomic decisions.

Blocking

Blocking involves the use of dense materials to cut off the direct path of sound. These materials contain little space between their molecules and, therefore, cut off the direct path of sound

---

BOX 7.5 TYPICAL NOISE SOURCES

Communication
• Conversation
• Telephones
• Paging and announcements
• Bells, buzzers, horns
Transportation
• Walking
• Elevators
• Escalators
• Motor vehicles
• Trains
• Aircraft
Productive Activities
• Keyboarding
• Office equipment
• Cleaning and service equipment
• Printing and duplicating
• Kitchen equipment
• Construction and repair
• Manufacturing equipment

Entertainment
• Radio and television
• Voices
• Musical instruments
• Movies
• Sports
• Shooting
HVAC Equipment
• Lighting ballasts
• Air diffusers
• Air conditioners
• Transformers
• Plumbing
• Toilets
• Pumps and fans
• Compressors

BOX 7.6 EXAMPLES OF METHODS FOR ABSORBING SOUND

• Acoustical ceiling tiles
• Acoustical wall coverings
• Upholstered furniture
• Carpeting
• Fabric window coverings
• Divider panels
• Absorption baffles hung from the ceiling
• Panels attached to studs
• Absorption chambers

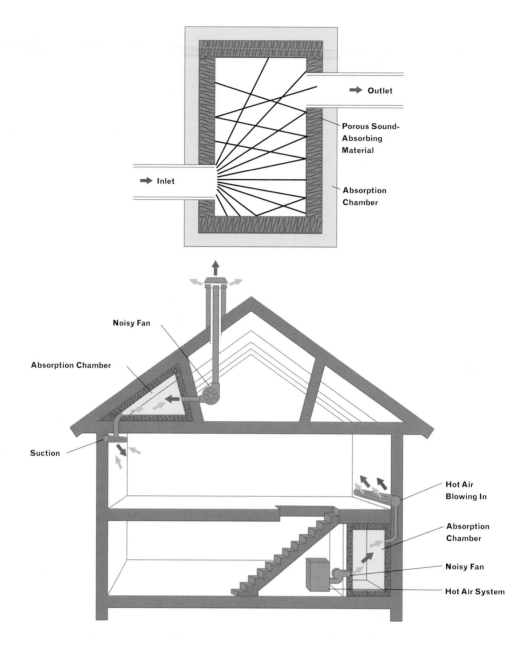

waves attempting to pass through them. Examples of such materials include solid masonite, metal, and hardboard. (Note that chemicals emitted from hardboard might influence the selection of blocking materials.) The ability of a material to block sound is indicated by its **sound transmission class (STC)** or its **noise reduction coefficient (NRC).**

Sound blocking becomes more necessary as more people are crowded into smaller work spaces and must work—and talk—within only a few feet from one another. Therefore, the rating systems just described are helpful when selecting panels to create cubicles in open-office spaces. An STC rating of 18 or greater or an NRC of at least 0.60 is recommended for panels (Steelcase, 2000). Interior designers should be aware that even panels with high ratings for blocking sound can be ineffective when combined with hard ceilings and walls (Herman Miller, Inc., 2002). This is because the sound from inside one cubicle simply bounces off the ceiling and enters into another. In addition, there is disagreement on the most effective height for panels that separate work areas. Research also found that "study participants with higher walls were not necessarily more satisfied with their acoustical privacy than those with lower walls" (Herman Miller, Inc., 2002). A height that at least blocks line-of-sight between space occupants, thus eliminating direct transmission of sound, seems logical. Therefore, it is generally recommended that partitions be at least at least 60 inches high to be an effective sound barrier.

Another problem that decreases the effectiveness of blocking is leaks, which can wreak havoc with a well-designed acoustical system. Leaks are, in fact, a major cause of uncontrolled noise. This is because a very small opening lets in a disproportionate amount of noise. For example, a 0.3 percent hole in relation to the total square footage of a barrier will reduce the wall's blocking efficiency by 75 percent (Barkman, n.d.). Actions such as drilling holes for electrical cords can be expensive mistakes in terms of acoustical effectiveness. Common spots where leaks are identified include seals between walls and between walls and windows and doors that do not fit tightly. Designers should check for these problems in existing structures as well as considering ways to prevent them in new and remodeled construction. Some remedies are fairly simple, such as installing thick, foam-backed weather stripping around doors, especially those leading to the outside of a building.

Sound blocking is also helpful in healthcare facilities, schools, and any other location in which some degree of quiet and/or privacy is necessary. In homes, designers can use sound-blocking materials to enclose laundry rooms that are adjacent to bedrooms; noisy appliances located near areas intended for relaxation; and home theaters and entertainment centers.

Interzonal Rating Systems These systems have been developed, in addition to the rating systems described previously, for measuring sound absorption and blocking. Many acoustical professionals now believe that noise reduction coefficients can be misleading because they measure absorbency without hang-on components, such as the shelves and other accessories found attached to most cubical walls. The ratings also do not specify how well speech frequencies will be absorbed. In other

FIGURE 7.11 In this office setting, acoustical panels have been supplemented by baffles hung on the walls.

words, the NRC and STC rating systems do not measure the real world (Herman Miller, Inc., 2002). Many experts therefore believe that interzonal rating systems are better predictors of speech privacy. These systems take into account a variety of factors. See Table 7.9 for descriptions of the three rating systems and their effectiveness in blocking human speech.

Sound Masking

Sound masking means using background noise to cover distracting sounds. It may seem contradictory to create more sound to correct a noise problem. Sound masking is based on the principle that it is not simply loudness but relative loudness that is distracting in the work environment. By introducing even, continuous sound that is just a little louder than the distracting sounds, they will be eliminated. Sound masking also solves the problem of being distracted by conversation content because it makes human speech difficult to understand and, as such, it becomes simply background noise (Gabriel, n.d.).

A sound-masking system employs electronic devices that generate a sound at around

TABLE 7.9 INTEGRATED ACOUSTICAL RATING SYSTEMS

MEASURING SYSTEM	RATING NUMBER	PERCENT OF SPEECH UNDERSTOOD
Noise Isolation Class (NIC)	16	54%
Measures speech privacy provided	18	34%
by panels in various configurations	21	8%
Articulation Class (AC)	<202	54%
Measures the sound reflective	220	34%
characteristics of an acoustical	256	8%
material when used in conjunction		
with partial-height space		
Articulation Index (AI)	1.00	90%
Measures combined speech pri-	0.23	54%
vacy performance of all elements,	0.16	34%
including ceiling, walls, panels, and	0.05	8%
sound-masking system		

Adapted from: Herman Miller, Inc. (2002). *It's a matter of balance.* Zeeland, MI: Author.

Retrieved February 16, 2007, from www.sonaretechnologies.com/whitepapers/wp_Matter_of_Balance.pdf.

48 dB, which is perceived as a hum. The sound signal is distributed to speakers, usually placed above the ceiling in the plenum. The hum created by a sound-masking system has been compared to the effect of an air conditioner hum or the sound of running water. The use of sound masking is not limited to large, open offices but can be used any place where auditory privacy and mental concentration are needed.

Space Planning

Interior designers should evaluate noise sources to determine optimal space planning. In offices, for example, they should identify equipment that creates noise and can distract workers. When possible, noisy equipment should be put in soundproof rooms or closets. When they cannot be isolated, they should not be located in corners where there are two walls that sounds can bounce off of. Desks should be positioned away from foot traffic and in ways that discourage occupants from calling across distances to one another.

In settings such as hotels, rooms should be insulated from elevators, entrances, and other noisy areas. Ice machines, for example, should be located where they do not disturb guests. Designers might create buffer areas between noisy and quiet areas. For example, storage and filing rooms might be placed between classrooms and the gym in a school. The important thing to realize is that every environment has its own issues and space-planning requirements for eliminating unacceptable and health-threatening levels of noise.

INTEGRATED APPROACH TO NOISE CONTROL

Design professionals generally agree that an integrated approach is best for controlling noise (Steelcase, 2000). For example, in a nonfactory work setting, there are a variety of elements that contribute to the control of noise, such as:

1. Ceiling systems: absorb
2. Furniture systems: absorb and block
3. Sound-masking systems: mask and cover
4. Carpeting: absorb and block
5. Space planning and furnishings: separate and absorb

Interior designers must first survey interiors carefully to identify sources of noise. This applies to all types of buildings, not just offices. In homes, they need to learn about the hearing ability and noise tolerance of all occupants, as well as activities that generate noise. They also need to consider various methods of reducing the noise and the trade-offs that must be balanced for maximum results. For example, highly absorbent surfaces can soak up the sounds produced by a sound-masking system and make it ineffective. Dense surfaces meant to block sound may reflect it back in annoying ways, such as echoes. Another problem is when good acoustical panels, used to enclose workspaces, are innocently sabotaged by large glass-covered pictures, shelving, bulletin boards, and other hard objects attached to the sound-absorbing material. This happens because smaller workspaces, built in the interest of saving costs, leave their occupants little room for placing needed items. Interior designers should look for storage and office organization methods that reduce the need for such attachments. These might include desks with drawers on either side of the knee space and efficient desk caddies. Adequate storage for infrequently used items should be provided outside the cubicle space to prevent the need to attach extensive shelving to acoustical panels. (This also eliminates clutter and the feelings of being closed in experienced by many office workers.)

Sometimes the attempt to solve one ergonomic problem results in another. For example, diffusers are frequently placed over light sources to prevent glare. Their large hard surfaces reflect sound waves back into the room or cubicle, not a desirable effect. This is why it is so important to develop an overall plan, considering all factors, at the beginning of a project.

Privacy Zones

Completely eliminating sound is neither reasonable nor desirable. In fact, having some noise is best in most settings because most people find total silence unnatural (Dul and Weerd-

---

BOX 7.7 VIEW TO THE FUTURE

Noise

- Problems in office settings are expected to grow due to the use of workteams.
- Continuing rise in real-estate values will force even more workers into a given space and, therefore, more noise problems.
- Increasing use of speaker phones, voice-activated computers, and video-conferencing provide new noise sources.

---

meester, 2001). At the same time, noise control systems can be designed to achieve various levels of privacy, depending on the needs of those in the environment. For planning purposes, three levels of speech privacy have been identified: interzonal (confidential), zonal, and regional. Table 7.10 contains a description for each level, along with the requirements for achieving each.

Exterior Noise

Noise from outside built environments is becoming increasingly loud and potentially harmful to health. One study determined that 70 percent of the residents living within a major airport flight pattern reported being bothered by aircraft noise. Further, these residents believed that it interfered with their daily activities, including sleep (Bronzaft et al., 1998). Individuals exposed to excessive exterior noise tend to suffer the negative health effects described previously in this chapter. In addition, there is evidence that high levels of noise negatively affect children and their learning. In a study conducted at a school located near elevated train tracks, it was found that children on the quieter side of the school tested one year higher in reading than those whose classrooms were adjacent to the tracks (Bronzaft and McCarthy, 1975). The same results were obtained in later studies by other researchers (Green et al., 1982; Evans and Maxwell, 1997).

The implications for architects and interior designers are in the planning and layout of buildings. Airports and other noise producers cannot be eliminated, but rooms

TABLE 7.10 PRIVACY ZONES

SPEECH PRIVACY GOAL	WHAT'S HEARD	WHAT'S NEEDED
Interzonal (confidential) Privacy	10% of what's said in next workstation	Perfect coordination of all architectural, furniture, and planning elements for best balance of panel height, sound absorption, sound blocking, and sound masking
Zonal Privacy	50% of what's said in next workstation, but less than 10% from two workstations away	Very sound-absorbent ceiling, good sound-masking system, and appropriate sound-blocking panels
Regional Privacy	Nothing too disturbing (20 to 30% of what's said two workstations away, and less than 10% from 40 to 50 feet away)	Adequate sound absorption in ceiling and sound blocking in panels, and some masking (either electronic or from heating and ventilation system)

Adapted from: Herman Miller, Inc. (2002). *It's a matter of balance.* Zeeland, MI: Author.

Retrieved February 16, 2007 from www.sonaretechnologies.com/whitepapers/wp_Matter_of_Balance.pdf.

can be arranged and soundproofing methods employed to make the noise as least disruptive as possible.

ERGONOMICS IN THE WORKPLACE

The design of the spaces in which we work has a significant effect on our quality of life. Our posture and movements, repeated day after day, influence how we feel and perform. Applying ergonomic principles to the design and selection of workspaces and furnishings increases our chances for wellness. This is because pain and health problems can result when individuals try to adapt themselves to the workplace in the name of efficiency. The truly healthy, efficient, productive, and sustainable activity is just the reverse—adapting the environment to the individual—and can be achieved through proper choices.

Movement and Body Posture

The shift from the factory to the office has brought a new set of challenges for maintaining safety in the workplace. In the past, most injuries were due to strenuous movements such as lifting and pushing; today, they are often due to not enough movement. This is because maintaining one position, known as **static effort,** results in a prolonged state of muscle contraction. During this time, the blood vessels are compressed and this restricts the blood from flowing through the muscles. When muscles are moving, they receive up to 20 times more blood than when they are resting (Kroemer and Grandjean, 1997). This is why excessive static load can cause general fatigue, along with inflammation of the joints and tissues. Older individuals are especially prone to these conditions (Kroemer and Grandjean, 1997).

TABLE 7.11 STATIC LOADS AND BODY PAIN

WORK POSTURE	POSSIBLE CONSEQUENCES AFFECTED
Standing in one place	Feet and legs; possibly varicose veins
Sitting erect without back support	Extensor muscles of the back
Seat too high	Knee; calf of leg; foot
Seat too low	Shoulders and neck
Trunk curved forward when sitting or standing	Lumbar region; deterioration of the intervertebral discs
Arm outstretched, sideways, forwards, or upwards	Shoulders and upper arm; possibly periarthritis
Head excessively inclined backwards or forwards	Neck; deterioration of the intervertebral discs
Unnatural grasp of hand grip or tools	Forearm; possibly inflammation of tendons

Source: Kroemer, K. H. E., & Grandjean, E. (1997). *Fitting the task to the human: A textbook of occupational ergonomics*, (5th ed.). New York: Taylor & Francis.

A problem associated with sitting for long periods of time is compression of the intervertebral discs in the spine, resulting in strain. It also restricts the movement of fluid-bearing nutrients to the discs. These conditions are the cause of many back problems. Table 7.11 contains a list of health conditions associated with excessive static load.

A workplace health problem of growing concern is cumulative trauma disorders, described in Chapter 3. These are caused by movements repeated continually over a period of time. Ensuring that the joints are properly positioned (in addition to taking breaks from the repetitive actions) can help prevent these disorders.

Implications for Designers

While movement is healthy for the body, incorrect movements can be damaging to the musculoskeletal system. When planning work configurations in any setting, including schools and homes, designers should provide people with the means to easily do the following:

- Maintain the joints in a neutral position
- Keep work close to the body
- Avoid bending forward for extended periods of time
- Avoid repeatedly twisting the trunk
- Avoid sudden movements
- Alternate postures fairly often (Dul and Weerdmeester, 2001)

A joint is in a neutral position when it is not bent. For example, the wrist is in a neutral position when it is aligned with the forearm and the hand. The neck is in a neutral position when it is in alignment with the spine, rather than being bent forward, backward, or from side to side. Maintaining neutrality prevents muscle strain and injury to the nerves that travel through the joints. This is why it is important to set up computer workstations so that the wrists do not bend when the worker is keyboarding. The hands should be at elbow height, with the elbows bent at a 45° angle. If the user has to bend in any direction the wrists while using the keyboard, either the keyboard or the chair—or both—should be adjusted so that the forearms are kept parallel to the keyboard. If a mouse is used, there should be space to place it on the same level as the keyboard. Placing it too low or high or too far away can result in shoulder, wrist, elbow, and forearm discomfort. The chance of incurring repetitive motion injuries, discussed in Chapter 3, can be reduced when proper ergonomics are applied to workstation setups.

Counters and work tables should be high enough to prevent the need to bend the neck forward or to bend the body at the waist. The average-sized head weighs between 10 and 11 pounds, which explains why bending and holding it forward for long periods is a common cause of neck strain. It is recommended that when working, the angle of the head not be bent more than 30° (Chaffin, 1973). At the same time, working surfaces that are too high can also cause discomfort in the neck and shoulders (Kroemer and Grandjean, 1997). If people of various heights will be sharing a work area, designers might consider adjustable tables or providing surfaces of different heights. A good feature on an adjustable table is a display that shows the height; this makes it easy for users to find their preferred settings each time they use the surface (see Figures 7.12 and 7.13). If heights cannot be individualized for workers or occupants using home kitchens, for example, it is recommended that as many workspace components as possible be made

adjustable. And when adjustable heights are not possible, it is best to accommodate the tallest people and provide platforms or footrests for shorter people. When low work surfaces are unavoidable, designers can provide chairs or stools so that tall individuals can perform tasks while sitting.

Office Furniture

The Centers for Disease Control and Prevention (2000) suggests that standard office furniture is generally unsuitable because it cannot accommodate everyone's needs. New employees are typically assigned the desk and chair used by the previous occupant with little or no consideration of the individual's size or physical characteristics. The same is true for schools and other public facilities. Classroom desks with attached chairs come in a one-size-fits-all style, when in reality, children vary greatly in size and shape.

Implications for Designers

In offices, chairs are the most critical piece of furniture for workers who sit all or most of

FIGURE 7.12 Adjustable desks that raise and lower easily are good choices when people of different sizes will be using them.

the day. In the past, chairs were a sign of status: wooden chairs for typists; thinly upholstered for the senior clerk; thickly upholstered for the office manager; and swivel, leather-upholstered for the director (Kromer and Grandjean, 1997). We now know that chairs are more than status symbols; the correct chair promotes wellness and productivity, while the wrong chair invites aches and pains. For example, backache, a common reason for absenteeism from work, is often the result of improper seating. In spite of this knowledge, a Washington State ergonomist recently reported that one of the two most common problems he sees in offices is chairs that do not fit the people using them (Fetters, 2005).

A good chair is sized to the individual, meaning it is not so high from the floor that the user's feet dangle from the edge, nor so deep that the user must scoot forward in order to bend the knees. The most important feature is sufficient back support to support a significant amount of the weight of the upper body in order to reduce strain on the discs in the spine. This support should incorporate the natural inward curve of the low back. If the chair back does not protrude sufficiently to fit this curve, a lumbar roll or cushion should be provided. It is suggested that the back of the chair be adjusted so that the trunk and legs form an angle between 90 and 115° (Centers for Disease Control and Prevention, 2000). In fact, it is easier on the back to *not* sit up straight all the time because this position stacks the vertebrae directly on top of each other, thus increasing the pressure on the discs. Reclining slightly shifts this body weight onto the chair and off the vertebrae and discs. Designers should be aware that people often select chairs for initial comfort, rather than for features that will ensure long-term healthy seating. For this reason, understanding the criteria for good chair selection is important—and this information can be shared with clients. The ergonomic considerations for selecting a chair are listed in Box 7.8 and examples of ergonomic chairs are shown in Figure 7.14.

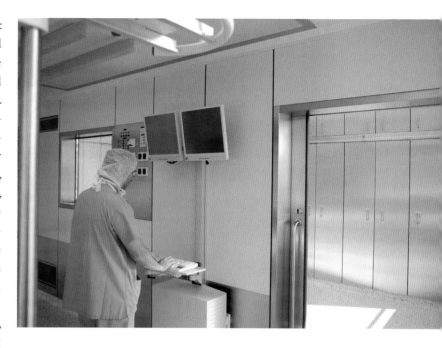

FIGURE 7.13 This adjustable stand, used by medical personnel, can accommodate the needs of shift workers who are likely to be of different heights.

Desks and workspaces should be high enough so that a fist fits between the seated user's knees and the bottom of the surface. Another test of proper distance is whether users can cross their legs under their desks. There should also be sufficient room to stretch and move the legs. This is important because without movement, gravity pools blood in the legs and feet, creating a sluggish return to the heart. These recommendations apply to all types of arrangements in which people sit for long periods of time, such as at school desks and reception counters.

The surface area of a desk should be adequate to accommodate everything needed to accomplish one's tasks. A common error is not considering the footprint, or total space needed, for supplies and equipment. As desks become filled with computers, telephones, printers, fax machines, and other labor-saving devices, along with document holders, papers, and other work supplies, the space diminishes until it is difficult to work without reaching, continually moving items, and forcing the body to accommodate to the clutter. Space should be provided for computer monitors to be placed directly in front of the user at an even line of sight from the eyes to prevent bending at the

BOX 7.8 ERGONOMIC CHECKLIST FOR WORK CHAIRS

☐ Lumbar back support at the appropriate height for the user
☐ Waterfall front edge that slopes downward
☐ Adequate padding
☐ Five spokes that run smoothly
☐ Padded adjustable armrests that do not force user to raise shoulders or move arms away from the body
☐ Easy-to-use adjustments for seat height, back angle, seat tilt, and armchair height
☐ Seat depth appropriate for user; legs should not press against edge of seat
☐ Swivel feature to prevent need to twist body

neck. If monitor height cannot be adjusted, a platform should be provided to elevate it as necessary. There should also be enough room to move the monitor forward or backward to assume a comfortable distance from the eyes. A common problem is sitting too close to the monitor. Designers should suggest that workers arrange surfaces so that material being read while working on the computer is about the same distance from the eyes as is the computer screen. This prevents the eyes from having to refocus when shifting back and forth.

A convenient accessory in situations where different people use the same monitor, as at a reception or an order desk, is a monitor arm that allows forward, backward, and up and down movement.

Keyboard trays can be helpful. They allow the monitor to be placed closer to the edge of the desk and thus easier for many people to see, especially those who are nearsighted. Also, most people prefer to write at a height slightly higher than the one for keyboarding. Keyboard trays should be stable and contain space for a mouse, if needed. This prevents the user from reaching to a different height every time the mouse if used.

Frequently used supplies can be attached to walls or panels with shelving and/or tool racks to free up the horizontal surface area. (Recall the need for *integrated ergonomic planning*. Consider that objects placed on sound-absorbing walls can reduce their

FIGURE 7.14 Properly fitting chairs are one of the most important ergonomic considerations for people who sit for extended periods of time. Ergonomic chairs are available in a variety of styles and colors.

BOX 7.9 EXPERT SPOTLIGHT: Stress at Work

Janetta Mitchell McCoy, Ph.D.
Associate Professor
Interdisciplinary Design
Institute
Washington State University
Spokane, Washington

Stress occurs when environmental demands tax or exceed the adaptive or coping abilities of an individual. People who are stressed at work may not only experience difficulty in concentrated thinking and doing their work but are more likely to become physically ill (McCoy & Evans, 2004). While a brief or momentary stressful event may be easily addressed and cause only temporary interruption, prolonged or more severe stress can adversely impact the worker's health and performance. Given the ubiquitous, permanent nature (and cost) of any organization's facility, it is important to know if the physical work environment is a source of prolonged stress. Typical symptoms of stress include fatigue, tension, and anxiety, each with the ability to compromise the high-level cognitive function so typically important in today's sophisticated office work environment.

Theoretical dimensions of stress include job satisfaction, affective appraisal, and motivation. Outcome measures include individual task performance as well as the social interaction related to team performance. By identifying environments that support or compromise each of the theoretical dimensions, we may link relevant physical components that ameliorate or exacerbate stress at work.

The physical office environment influences the experience of stress in multiple ways. Risk factors in the physical office environment include spatial organization, architectonic details, ambient conditions, and resources, as well as the view or visual access from the workspace. The degree to which these factors support task performance and social interaction link them to stress.

Spatial organization determines the level of enclosure, adjacencies, density, and territoriality of an office and may ameliorate stress by providing functional opportunities to do the work effectively and efficiently without undue distraction or threat. The opportunity to think and concentrate on work, along with controlling the number and level of distractions, may minimize job stress. Architectonic details, the overall aesthetic of the environment, including ornament and materiality, should reflect the individual, team, and organizational identity, as well as the values and norms of the organization. Meaningful, appropriate markers of status and territory may encourage job satisfaction, motivation, and social interaction. Ambient conditions include illumination, heating, ventilation, and sound; these are the most researched physical stressors. Thermal discomfort, noise, and poor air quality, as well as the inability to control these conditions, have been linked to performance and social interaction. Resources should allow the work to be done efficiently and effectively. Resources that are in poor repair, inaccessible, unavailable, or inappropriate to the task at hand have been linked to job satisfaction and motivation. Likewise, ergonomic features or the lack of ergonomic planning have been linked to worker health and motivation. Views into adjacent workspaces or from windows have not been directly related to stress; however, there is limited evidence that views of nature may reflect higher job satisfaction and have some restorative value, counteracting stressful work.

The apparent role of the physical characteristics of the environment on work may be subtle, but this does not imply a minor role. The cost of ignoring the relationship of the physical environment and workplace stress may be devastating; the benefit of addressing these issues through design may be healthier workers, stronger organizations, and, by association, a stronger society.

dampening effect.) Shared storage areas, outside the immediate workspace, are recommended for infrequently used items and files to prevent crowded work areas, dust, and trip hazards.

Some people have found the sloping desk top to be comfortable and convenient. It can be built into the desk top or provided separately. Used for reading and writing tasks, it prevents the need to bend the head forward.

Raised sections of desk tops that enable both sitting and standing while working are growing in popularity. In addition to reducing excessive static load, some individuals claim it enhances their creativity and work performance (personal communication with Dave Ellis, June 1999).

Interior designers must always consider individual characteristics. Even people of the same height can differ in their needs, such as an appropriate work-surface height. This is because bodies vary, as in waist-length compared to total body height, arm length, and vision. When selecting for ergonomic fit, one size certainly does not fit all.

ERGONOMICS IN THE HOME

Ergonomics in the home can play a significant role in the health, comfort, and even the interpersonal relationships of family members. For example, living and family rooms can be arranged either to promote conversation and interaction or to encourage television-watching.

The kitchen is a major work area in the home, so ergonomic principles should take precedence over style (Inkeles and Schencke, 1994). Kitchens are often designed with an emphasis on size and decor without regard to comfort and practicality (Goldbeck, 1994). Or they are set up to accommodate appliances instead of humans. In fact, kitchen size matters much less than the layout of the three essential work centers: cooktop/oven, sink, and food storage areas (which includes the refrigerator). U-shaped kitchens are recommended as ergonomically best because they eliminate much walking, provide ready access to items needed for preparing food, and provide sufficient areas for counter space. When space does not allow the U shape, then work centers should be designed so that movement around the kitchen takes place within a triangle. Examples of common design errors in the kitchen that reduce efficiency and convenience include refrigerator doors that do not open in the correct direction; doors and drawers that, when opened,

collide with one another; pullouts, such as cutting boards, that prevent access to other areas; and heavy traffic paths that cut through the work areas. Box 7.10 contains examples of questions to ask when designing an easy-to-use kitchen.

Home Appliances and Electronics

Appliances, lighting, and electronic equipment should be selected for how they best serve human needs. Ergonomic factors to consider include the following:

- Noise generated: select quiet models
- User interface: look for models that are easy to operate
- Easy, safe access: install refrigerators with freezers that do not require bending to remove items and ovens at chest level to prevent bending over to lift hot foods while getting a blast of hot air in the face
- Prioritized: place the television and other entertainment equipment where they do not dominate life. For example, do not arrange all chairs to face the television set, making human interaction and conversation secondary.

Box 7.11 contains examples of specific questions to ask when purchasing a refrigerator. Designers can use this as a guide to develop similar questions for use when selecting or recommending other home appliances for clients.

Home Furnishings

Ergonomically sound home furnishings can be both attractive and healthy. Designers should choose sturdy, well-constructed chairs with padded seats and lumbar support. Each family member should have a personal, ergonomic chair that swivels and includes a separate padded footstool (Inkeles and Schencke, 1994). Footstools are recommended instead of (or in addition to) reclining chairs with an attached footrest if smaller family members will be using the chair. This will ensure that their feet do not dangle when the chair is in the upright position. Seating that is too soft and does not provide support for the back may seem comfortable at first, but can cause musculo-skeletal discomfort after extended periods of sitting. Some chairs in the house should either swivel or be movable so they can be arranged to comfortably carry on a conversation.

Bedrooms and their furnishings should be planned to promote sleep. Sleep deprivation is becoming a serious health problem: this could be due in part to bedrooms where decoration dominates function. Beds and mattresses should be chosen to provide support, as well as being easy to clean.

Home Offices

According to a survey by the American Furniture Manufacturers Association, almost one-third of Americans have a home office (Michael, 2001) and this number is almost certainly increasing. Although most people do not use this office for doing "paid work," ergonomic principles should be followed. The same survey reported that 55 percent of respondents spend more than five hours a week in their home office. Appropriate workspace, seating, and lighting are worth providing.

But for a growing number of Americans, the home has become the principal workplace. This presents ergonomic challenges because home-based workers, whether telecommuters or self-employed, tend to adapt to the space and furniture they already have. This is partly due to the expense of buying the proper furnishings (Croasmun, 2004); it is also related to the fact that "work furniture" may clash with the overall decor. In fact, stylish, health-promoting furniture that complements home decor is now available (Michael, 2001). Designers should use the same guidelines for selecting home-office furnishings as those given for offices away from the home.

Adequate space is another home office problem. Using the kitchen table or a corner of the family room generally does not provide enough, nor does it provide the quiet and privacy needed to concentrate. It is best if the

---

BOX 7.10 HOW COOK-FRIENDLY IS THE KITCHEN?

Will the cook have:
- to walk far from the sink to the stove with a pot of water?
- enough space to perform activities such as slicing, chopping, and mixing?
- room to store items near where they are used, such as olive oil near the stove?
- space to work with others in the kitchen?
- the ability to easily wash dishes and access the dishwasher?

Does the cook prefer:
- one or two sinks?
- a range or separate cook top and oven?
- an eating area in the kitchen?

---

work area can be closed off from the general noise and distraction of the average household. Lighting, discussed earlier in the chapter, is another often-overlooked element in the home office.

Ergonomics for Children

Many children today have their own computers. Unfortunately, these are often not set up to accommodate children's smaller sizes and so the youngsters end up working with elbows and wrists forced into awkward angles (Canadian Safety Council, 2006). Although there is little research about the physical effects of computer use on children, it seems safe to assume that harmful effects may be occurring, given what we know about the seriousness of computer-related injuries in adults. Some children spend many hours on the computer,

---

BOX 7.11 QUESTIONS TO CONSIDER WHEN CHOOSING A REFRIGERATOR

- How much bending will be required? Bottom-mounted freezers might be best for shorter individuals, but can pose back problems for taller people.
- How much noise does the motor make? Are there noisy defrost or ice-making cycles?
- Are items easy to access? Does it have slide-out shelves?
- Can items be viewed? Are the compartments transparent?
- Can frequently used items be conveniently located?
- Is there sufficient space to fully and conveniently open the door?

BOX 7.12 A REAL-WORLD EXPERIENCE

I recently visited a community college in the northeastern part of the United States. After sitting at a table in one of the classrooms, I lifted my arms and noticed linear indentations. Upon examining the table more closely, I realized it had rather sharp edges where the plaster edging met the laminated top. Too sharp for comfort! This is a typical mistake which neither manufacturers nor purchasers of tables notice.

In the student center of the same college, banks of window and large skylights were used to bring in loads of daylight, surely a welcome feature during the winter. However, the tops of the tables chosen for this area were of shiny, light-colored materials that created quite a glare during bright days, such as those in July when I was visiting.

---

comparable to that spent by adults on the job. Therefore, the same principles described in the section on workplace furnishings apply to home computers. For example, the height of the keyboard and monitor should enable children to maintain neutral positioning of the wrists and neck. If all family members share a computer, designers should recommend an adjustable desk, keyboard tray, and chair. If necessary, children should be supplied with a pillow to support the back and a footrest to prevent the feet from dangling.

JUSTIFYING ERGONOMIC COSTS

At a time when health-care costs are skyrocketing and growing numbers of employers are finding themselves unable to provide full health insurance benefits to workers, meth-

---

BOX 7.13 VIEW TO THE FUTURE

General Ergonomics

- Increased emphasis on inclusive design, an ergonomics approach to design that seeks to meet the needs of all users, including those with physical, sensory, or cognitive impairments due to illness, injury, aging, or circumstances.
- Better ergonomic tools will become available for use by nonergonomists, such as computer-based, 3-D anthropometric models.
- More consideration of ergonomic needs for our growing aging population.
- Growing interest in ergonomically designed "smart" homes.

---

ods for reducing injuries and illnesses should be championed. The related costs are usually the highest expense of any business, so that applying ergonomics to increase worker wellness and decrease absenteeism and turnover is likely to pay for itself in the long run. At the same time, improved ergonomics can increase productivity and reduce product rejects. In built environments outside the workplace, good ergonomics can contribute to improving the health and comfort of those who use and occupy the environments.

From a purely business and financial point of view, some improvements related to ergonomics can produce direct economic benefits. For example, a study by the Building Owners and Management Association (BOMA) found that pleasing interior environments rent more quickly and for higher rates than those of lesser quality (Baier, 1999). Some ergonomic features, such as good lighting, have been shown to increase customer satisfaction. And although walls with windows cost more to construct, it is believed that the presence of windows has a positive effect on rental values (Boyce et al., 2003). Building accreditations for office buildings often give extra points for widespread daylighting, so that feature has the potential to increase the value of property (Boyce et al., 2003). There is also evidence that daylight in retail space increases the time customers spend in the space and, therefore, can increase sales (Boyce et al., 2003).

Increasing productivity will be more and more important in the face of global competition. Attending to lighting and noise issues and designing and furnishing ergonomically sound workstations, all proven to affect productivity, are cost-effective in the long run.

GLOSSARY TERMS

Absorption coefficient

Acoustics

Anthropometrics

Articulation class

Articulation index

Biophilia

Candela

Circadian rhythms

Color rendering index

Continuous sound level

Decibel (dB)

Ergonomic design

Ergonomics

Footcandle

Frequency

Glare

Hertz (Hz)

Human factors

Illuminance

Lumen

Lux

Noise-induced hearing loss (NIHL)

Noise isolation class

Noise load

Noise reduction coefficient (NRC)

Sound masking

Sound transmission class (STC)

Static effort

Summated frequency level

Watt

LEARNING ACTIVITIES

1. Choose a facility, such as a public library or health-care center, to visit and evaluate for sound ergonomics in three areas: lighting, noise, and furnishings. Examples of questions to ask yourself: Is the lighting adequate for the activities to be performed? Are the noise levels acceptable? Are there furnishings to accommodate people of different shapes and sizes? Write a description of your findings and include suggestions for how the environment might be improved. Include drawings and illustrations.

2. Visit a lighting store, either in person or online, to find task lights and reading lamps for various rooms in the house. Create a resource file with examples of various styles for each room.

3. Conduct research and prepare a report on various types of acoustical materials, such as panels, tiles, and double-glazing. In which type of environments is each recommended? How do they compare in cost? Which are more suitable for use in workplaces? Which are best for homes?

4. Visit a home furnishings store to review sofas and chairs. Do they tend to be stylish rather than ergonomically sound? Is there a large selection of sizes and shapes to accommodate different body types? How might manufacturers better meet the needs of the public?

5. Do an ergonomic analysis of a classroom in your own school or another. Which factors could be improved to enhance student health and learning? How might these improvements be made?

6. Choose a room in the home to design in which you apply ergonomic principles. Include a description of your work: how you chose the lighting, furnishings, room layout, and so on. Explain why each component of the room is ergonomically sound.

SUGGESTED WEB SITES

1. Design Council (UK)

http://designcouncil.org.uk

This site contains a section on ergonomics for designers.

2. Design Lights Consortium

www.designlights.org

This site contains case studies of actual designs, including descriptions and photos.

3. The Ergonomics Society (UK)

www.ergonomics.org.uk

The Ergonomics Society gives explanations of ergonomics, how to apply ergonomics, and examples of ergonomic design.

4. ErgoWeb

www.ergowerb.com

This site contains a great deal of practical information, such as short case studies, designing the home office, and an extensive buyer's guide for ergonomic products.

5. Illuminating Engineering Society of North America

www.iesna.org

The IESNA is the recognized technical authority on illumination. The society has written over 100 technical publications to address the needs of all lighting professionals.

6. International Ergonomics Association
www.iea.cc
This is a good Web site for students who want to learn more about the study of ergonomics. It includes explanations of the domains and specialties and access to articles on a variety of topics.

7. Lighting Research Center, Rensselaer Polytechnic Institute
www.lrc.rpi.edu
This research center is one of the most prominent in the field of lighting. The Web site contains information about research projects and links to abstracts and articles on various lighting topics. Included is a section on light and health.

8. U.S. Occupational Health and Safety Administration
http://osha.gov/SLTC/noisehearingconservation/index.html
This government Web site contains links to information about noise measurement and control in the workplace.

REFERENCES

Baier, R. D. (September 1999). Customer Service Made Easy: Deliver What Office Tenants Want. *Heating Plumbing Air Conditioning (HPAC) Magazine.* 41–45.

Barkman, A. (n.d.) Solving acoustical problems—sound difficult? It's not. *Office Journal.* [Electronic version]. Retrieved February 17, 2007, from www.ccrllc.com/images/Haworth%20Acoustics.pdf

Beckstead, J. W., & Boyce, P. R. (1992). Structural equation modeling in lighting research: An application to residential acceptance of new fluorescent lighting. *Lighting Research and Technology,* 24, 4, 189–201.

Berman, S., Fein, G., Jewett, D., Benson, B., Law, T., & Myers, A. (1996). Luminance-Controlled Pupil Size Affects Word-Reading Accuracy. *Journal of the Illuminating Engineering Society,* 25, 1, 51–59.

Boyce, P., Hunter, C., & Howlett, O. (2003). *The Benefits of Daylight through Windows.* Troy, NY: Rensselaer Polytechnic Institute.

Boyce, P. R., Eklund, N. H., & Simpson, S. N. (2000). Individual Lighting Control: Task Performance, Mood and Illuminance. *Journal of the Illuminating Engineering Society,* 29, 131–142.

Bridger, R. S. (2003). *Introduction to Ergonomics, 2e, Instructor's Manual.* New York: Taylor and Francis.

Bronzaft, A., & McCarthy, D. P. (1975). The Effect of Elevated Train Noise on Reading Ability. *Environment and Behavior* 7, 4, 517–528.

Bronzaft, A., Ahern, K. D., McGinn, R., O'Connor, J., & Savino, B. (1998). Aircraft Noise: A Potential Health Hazard. *Environment and Behavior,* 30, 101–113.

Cajochen, C., Zeitzer, J. M., Czeisler, C. A., & Dijk, D. (2000). Dose-Response Relationship for Light Intensity and Ocular and Electroencephalographic Correlates of Human Alertness. *Behavioural Brain Research,* 115, 1, 75–83.

Canadian Centre for Occupational Health and Safety. (Updated January 27, 2003). *Why is Lighting Important?* Retrieved February 12, 2007, from www.ccohs.ca/oshanswers/ergonomics/lighting_general.html

Canadian Safety Council. (January 11, 2006). *One size still doesn't fit all: Kids and computer use.* Retrieved January 23, 2006, from www.ergoweb.com/news/detail.cfm?id=1248

Centers for Disease Control and Prevention. (2000). *Computer Workstation Ergonomics.* Retrieved February 26, 2006, from www.cdc.gov/od/ohs/Ergonomics/compergo.htm

Chaffin, D. B. (1973). Localized Muscle Fatigue—Definition and Measurement. *Journal of Occupational Medicine,* 15, 4, 346–354.

Chobot, J. L. (1996–1997). Providing an optimal acoustic environment for young children in classrooms. *EITA Newsletter.* Early Intervention Training Institute.

Croasmun, J. (2004). If Telecommuting Is a Pain, Ergonomics Can Be the Solution.

Ergonomics Today, Online newsletter available at www.ergoweb.com/news/detail .cfm?id=997

Cuttle, C. (2002). Identifying the human values associated with windows. *International Daylighting,* 5, 3–6.

Davis, G. (Updated August 22, 2007). Ergonomics. Retrieved December 1, 2007, from http://www.designcouncil.org.uk/ en/About-Design/Design-Techniques/ Ergonomics-by-Gary-Davis/

Dul, J., & Weerdmeester, B. (2001). *Ergonomics for Beginners* (2nd ed.). New York: Taylor & Francis.

The Ergonomics Society. (n.d.) *About ergonomics.* Retrieved January 23, 2006, from www.ergonomics.org.uk/ergonomics.htm.

Evans, G.W., and Lepore, S. J. (1993). Non-auditory effects of noise on children: A critical review. *Children's Environments,* 10(1):42–72.

Evans, G.W., & Maxwell, L. (1997). Chronic noise exposure and reading deficits: Effects on language acquisition. *Environment and Behavior,* 29, 5, 638–656.

Fetters, E. (January 17, 2006). Properly positioned for pain prevention. *The Herald —Everett, WA.* Retrieved February 17, 2007, from www.heraldnet.com/stories/05/01/17/ 100bus_pain001.cfm

Figueiro, M. G., Rea, M. S., Stevens, R. G., & Rea, A. C. (2002). *Daylight and productivity— A possible link to circadian regulation.* Paper presented at the 5th International Lighting Research Symposium: Palo Alto, CA. Retrieved February 17, 2007, from www.lrc.rpi.edu/ programs/lightHealth/pdf/daylightProductivity .pdf

Gabriel, O. (n.d.) *A whoosh of air masks unwanted sounds.* Retrieved February 16, 2007, from www.ccrllc.com/images/A%20Whoosh %20of%20Air%20Masks%20Unwanted%20 Sounds.pdf

Goldbeck D. (1994). *The smart kitchen: How to design a comfortable, safe, energy-efficient, and environment-friendly workspace.* Woodstock, NY: Ceres Press.

Green, K. B., Pastenack, B. S., & Shore, R.E. (1982). Effects of aircraft noise on reading ability of school age children. *Archives of Environmental Health,* 37(1), 24–31.

Heil, D. P., & Mathis, S. R. (2002). Characterizing free-living light exposure using a wrist-worn light monitor. *Applied Ergonomics,* 33, 4, 357–363.

Heinmiller, G. (March 2005). Lighting: What makes a well-lighted space? *Building Operating Management.* [Online publication]. Retrieved February 8, 2006, from www.facilitiesnet.com/bom/article. asp?id=2640

Herman Miller, Inc. (2002). *It's a matter of balance.* Zeeland, MI: Author. Retrieved February 16, 2007, from www.sonaretechnologies.com/whitepapers/wpMatter_of_ Balance.pdf

Inkeles, G., & Schencke, I. (1994). *Ergonomic living: How to create a user-friendly home & office.* New York: Fireside Books.

International Ergonomics Association (n.d.). *The Discipline of Ergonomics.* Retrieved January 22, 2006, from www.iea.cc/ergonomics.

Kellert, S., & Wilson, E.O. (1993). *The Biophilia Hypothesis.* Washington, D.C.: Island Press/Shearwater Books.

Knez, I. (2001). The Effects of Colour of Light on Nonvisual Psychological Processes. *Journal of Environmental Psychology,* 21, 2, 201– 208.

Kroemer, K. H. E., & Grandjean, E. (1997). *Fitting the Task to the Human: A Textbook of Occupational Ergonomics* (5th ed.). New York: Taylor & Francis.

Küller, R., & Laike, T. (1998). The impact of flicker from fluorescent lighting on well-being, performance, and physiological arousal. *Ergonomics,* 41, 4, 433–447.

Leather, P., Pyrgas, M., Beale, D.; & Lawrence, C. (1998). Windows in the workplace: Sunlight, view, and occupational stress. *Environment and Behavior,* 30, 6, 739–762.

Leslie, R. P., & Rodgers, P. A. (1996). *The outdoor lighting pattern book.* New York: Mc-Graw-Hill.

Lewy, A. J., Bauer, V. K., Cutler, N. L., Sack, R. L., Ahmed, S., Thomas, K. H., Blood, M. L., & Latham Jackson, J. M. (1998).

Morning versus evening light treatment of patients with winter depression. *Archives of General Psychiatry,* 55: 890–896.

Light Right Consortium. (2002). *Lighting values.* Retrieved November 30, 2007, from http://www.lightright.org/pdfs/Lighting Values_2002.pdf

Michael, R. (2001). The Office Workstation at Home. *Ergonomics Today,* Online newsletter available at www.ergoweb.com/news/detail .cfm?id=332

Miller, N. (January 2004). *Light and health: The new drugs.* Presentation at the 2004 annual conference of the International Association of Lighting Designers: Vancouver, Canada. Retrieved February 17, 2007, from www.iald .org/pdfs/Light_and_Dark_The_New_ Drugs.pdf

Moore, T., Carter, D.J., & Slater, A.I. (2002). User attitudes toward occupant controlled office lighting. *Lighting Research and Technology,* 34, 3, 207–219.

Morgan, M.T. (2003). *Environmental Health* (3rd ed.). Belmont, CA: Thomson/Wadsworth Learning.

Ngai, P., & Boyce, P. (1999). *The effect of overhead glare on visual discomfort.* Paper presented at 1999 conference of the Illuminating Engineering Society of North America. Retrieved February 17, 2007, from www.lrc.rpi .edu/resources/pdf/22-1999.pdf

Nielson, K. J., & Taylor, D. A. (2002). *Interiors: An introduction* (3rd ed.). New York: McGraw-Hill.

Rea, M. S. (2002). *Light—Much more than vision.* Keynote presentation at the 5th International Lighting Research Symposium: Palo Alto, CA. Retrieved February 17, 2007, from www.lrc.rpi.edu/programs/lightHealth/pdf/ moreThanVision.pdf

Rensselaer Polytechnic Institute: Lighting Resource Center. (Revised March 2005). *Full-spectrum light sources.* Retrieved November 30, 2007, from http://www.lrc.rpi.edu/programs/ nlpip/lightingAnswers/fullSpectrum/abstract .asp

Santamaria, J. G., & Bennett, C. A. (1981). Performance effects of daylight. *Lighting Design and Application,* 11, 31–34.

Shepherd, A. J., Julian, W. G., & Purcell, A. T. (1992). Measuring appearance: Parameters indicated from gloom studies. *Lighting Research and Technology,* 24, 4, 203–214.

Steelcase. (2000). *Workplace acoustics: Sound, noise, and effective work.* Grand Rapids, MI: Author.

Taylor, J. (2006). Advanced lighting technologies enhance residence care. *Nursing Homes.* [Electronic version]. Retrieved February 9, 2006, from www.nursinghomemagazine .com/Past_Issues.htm?ID=4552

Terman, J. S., Terman, M., Lo, E., & Cooper, T. B. (2001). Circadian time of morning light administration and therapeutic response in winter depression. *Archives of General Psychiatry,* 58: 69–75.

U.S. Department of Labor, Occupational Safety and Health Administration. (n.d.) *Noise control A guide for workers and employers.* Online publication, available at www.nonoise.org/ hearing/noisecon/noisecon.htm

Veitch, J., and Newsham, G. (1998a). Lighting quality and energy-efficient effects on task performance, mood, health, satisfaction and comfort. *Journal of the Illuminating Engineering Society of NA.* National Research Council of Canada, Institute for Research in Construction. Ottawa, ON, Canada.

Veitch, G., & Newsham, G. (1998b). *Consequences of the perception and exercise of control over lighting.* Presented at the 106th Annual Convention of the American Psychological Association: San Francisco, CA.

Wilkins, A. J., Nimmo-Smith, L., Slater, A., and Bedocs, L. (1989). Fluorescent Light, Headaches, and Eyestrain. *Lighting Research and Technology,* 21, 1, 11–18.

If we're not designing for human beings, what
are we designing for?
—Ronald L. Mace, architect

CHAPTER **8**

Creating Healthy Environments for Specific Populations

LEARNING OBJECTIVES

1. **Describe potential effects of the built environment on the physical development of infants and children.**
2. **Give examples of how designers can both protect and enhance the physical development of children.**
3. **Describe the scope of disabilities that affect working-age Americans.**
4. **Explain age-related changes and how designers can help mitigate their effects on older adults.**
5. **Explain the function of the Americans with Disabilities Act of 1990 and how it impacts the work of the designer.**
6. **Provide examples of technical standards created to meet the Americans with Disabilities Act of 1990.**

Americans have an increasing awareness of and concern for the welfare of everyone in our country, regardless of age or ability level. We share the belief that all members of our society should be provided with what they need to maintain their health and well-being.

Fortunately, most young and midlife adults can generally take care of themselves. There are, however, many individuals who because of their age or special conditions are more vulnerable and need extra assistance. In this chapter we will discuss three groups of such individuals: children, persons with disabilities, and older adults.

Children, even before they are born, are entitled to a safe and nurturing environment that promotes healthy growth and development. At the other end of the life span, many older adults are undergoing changes that negatively affect their well-being. These individuals, like children, deserve to enjoy the highest possible level of life quality. Helping older adults to achieve this quality begins with accepting the consequences of aging as part of the natural life cycle, rather than as circumstances to be dreaded and ignored. Second, designers must learn to make the environmental alterations necessary to fully attend to the needs of the elderly, currently the fastest-growing segment of our population. Finally, in addition to recognizing the needs of children and older adults, we are becoming increasingly aware of the special requirements of individuals with varying physical, mental, and emotional abilities and working to find better ways to include them in mainstream society.

The built environment has a particularly strong influence on children, persons with disabilities, and older adults. As such, designers have exciting opportunities to make this influence a very positive one, taking actions that range from eliminating pollutants that harm the development of young children to making buildings safe and accessible for persons with limited mobility.

CHILDREN

Human children, unlike most other living creatures, are born completely helpless and go through a relatively long period of physical and mental development before attaining self-sufficiency. While four-legged creatures can stand, walk, and begin to suckle within minutes of birth, children take years to become independent and self-sufficient. Providing a safe and nurturing environment in which children can develop into healthy adults is one of our society's most important responsibilities. Designers, along with parents, teachers, and others, have many opportunities to protect and enhance children's health. However, this requires a basic understanding of how children respond to the built environment and, in turn, how the built environment affects them.

As we saw in Chapter 2 in the discussion on birth defects, a child's potential for harm as a result of the environment begins before birth. For example, exposure to tobacco smoke or alcohol can lower birth weight, a factor that is linked with infant mortality and the future health of infants who survive.

Once children are born, they may look a great deal like their parents. However, it is a mistake to think of children as simply "little adults," especially as we create built environments to meet their needs. This is because children have unique physical and biological characteristics that make them especially vulnerable to environmental hazards. There are a number of reasons for this increased vulnerability and these are discussed in the following sections.

Metabolism, Absorption, and Distribution

The smaller body size of children results in a higher metabolic rate, which means that they consume more oxygen relative to their body weight. Therefore, given the same con-

centration of an airborne pollutant, a child will inhale a disproportionately high amount of the pollutant when compared to an adult. For example, if a normal six-month-old child and a full-grown adult breathe air with the same level of radon, the child's body will receive twice the exposure as the adult during the same time period (Bearer, 1995). The same higher exposure rate applies to food and liquids because children consume more calories per pound of body weight than do adults. Thus, a child's exposure when ingesting given amounts of a substance is much higher. This is illustrated in the case of an infant who is nourished with formula prepared with water: the amount of liquid consumed by the infant each day is equivalent to an adult drinking liquid equal to thirty-five cans of soft drinks (Bearer, 1995). This explains why consumption of lead-contaminated drinking water results in higher blood levels of lead in infants than in adults who drink from the same water source.

Lead that is ingested not only introduces a harmful substance into the body, it displaces minerals that a child's body needs. For example, if a child were to chew on wood covered with lead-containing paint, the amount of lead absorbed into the body would be five times that of an adult who ingested the same amount of paint. Therefore, the child suffers a double harm: large amounts of lead in the body and a lowered capacity to absorb necessary calcium (Bearer, 1995). This is why the same lead exposure levels may not affect an adult at all while having catastrophic results on a child, such as a decreased IQ and a weakened skeletal system.

Another route of absorption is through the skin. Because fetuses and newborns have not developed the epidermis (layer of dead skin cells), one of the body's first lines of defense, their skin surface is particularly absorptive and places them at risk for illness. Therefore, avoiding contact with potentially irritating substances and keeping everything that comes into contact with the baby's skin extremely clean during the first weeks of life is very important.

The distribution of chemicals, both helpful and harmful, once they enter the body and the manner in which they are distributed often depend on the stage of physical development of the individual. For example, many drugs become more diluted in newborns than in adults. This means that they spread out to relatively larger areas of the baby's body. Once distributed, certain substances such as lead tend to be retained in children's bodies in higher amounts and for longer time periods than in the bodies of adults. A related problem is the inability of immature organs, such as the livers and kidneys of infants, to efficiently flush harmful substances from the body (Craven, 2003).

Implications for Designers

The differences between children's and adult's bodies clearly demonstrate why children are especially vulnerable to pollutants. Designers who are working on any built environment that is used by pregnant women and children must take special care when selecting building materials, flooring, paints, furnishings, and other potentially harmful substances and materials. (Chapter 4 contains information about specific contaminants.)

Because cleanliness is important for babies of all ages, furnishings such as changing tables and infant seats should be easy to clean and disinfect without leaving a potentially irritating residue.

Physical Development

As children mature physically, they pass through various developmental stages in terms of growth rate, hormonal levels, and biochemical makeup. Their body organs and systems are growing and maturing, which is why normal development can be disrupted by exposure to harmful elements in the environment, such as pesticides, mold, and metals. Table 8.1 contains a summary of environmental risks to child development.

Development of the Cells

Recall from Chapter 2 that cells, the body's basic building blocks, reproduce by dividing in an orderly way called mitosis. Because this process is essential for normal development, its disruption, such as from certain chemicals,

can lead to serious physical and mental problems. In addition to cell division, an important part of organ growth is carried out by a process called **differentiation,** in which cells are taking on specific tasks within the body. A common trigger for differentiation is signals from hormones. Problems can occur in the presence of certain chemicals, such as chlorinated insecticides, that mimic hormones and interfere with normal maturation (Bearer, 1995). Another important process in physical development is **cellular migration,** in which cells move to specific destinations in the body where they will subsequently function. Neurons, for example, originate near the center of the brain and then migrate out to predestined areas throughout the layers of the brain (Bearer, 1995). Normal migration of cells in fetuses can be disrupted by chemicals, such as the ethanol in alcoholic beverages, resulting in what is commonly called **fetal alcohol syndrome.** Because these types of cell activities are critical for the normal development of children, they provide us with another argument for the importance of taking care when designing environments for children.

Development of the Lungs

The body's organs continually develop in size and function throughout childhood. Among the most vulnerable are the lungs, bones, and brain. The lungs, for example, continue to form new air sacs. Recall from Chapter 2 that it is in these sacs that oxygen and carbon dioxide are exchanged. While this growth in the number of air sacs increases the child's risk of absorbing airborne chemicals into the bloodstream, it is also important that it not be interrupted because increasing the total absorptive area in the lungs enables the body to take in necessary amounts of oxygen as the child grows and reaches adult size.

Implications for Designers   Clean air is critical for proper lung development. Thus, ensuring minimal levels of VOCs, proper ventilation, and access to fresh outdoor air are especially critical actions when designing environments for children. (Chapter 5 contains information

TABLE 8.1 ENVIRONMENTAL RISK FACTORS FOR CHILDREN AT DIFFERENT STAGES OF DEVELOPMENT

DEVELOPMENTAL STAGE	BIOLOGICAL VULNERABILITIES	EXPOSURE PATHWAYS
Newborn zero to two months	Brain: cell migration, neuron myelination, creation of neuron synapses Lungs: developing air sacs Bones: rapid growth and hardening	Food Water Indoor air Mold Chemicals
Infant/Toddler two months to two years	Brain: creation of synapses Lungs: developing air sacs	Food Water Indoor air Floors Chemicals Stimulation from television
Preschool child two to six years	Brain: dendritic trimming Lungs: developing air sacs, increasing lung volume	Food Water Indoor air
School-aged child six to twelve years	Brain: specific synapse formation, dendritic trimming Lungs: volume expansion	Food Water Indoor air Toxins in arts and crafts supplies
Adolescent twelve to eighteen years	Brain: continue synapse formation Lungs: volume expansion Reproductive system: maturation of ovaries, testes, ova, and sperm; development of female breasts	Food Water Air Occupational hazards

Adapted from: Bearer, C. (Summer/Fall 1995). Environmental health hazards: How children are different from adults. *Future of Children*, 5, 2, 11–26.

about maintaining a healthy indoor climate.) This is true in homes, day-care centers, and schools. Unfortunately, environments occupied by children are not always optimal. For example, day-care centers are frequently housed in private homes and buildings not specifically designed for children. They may be housed in a church basement, for example, which lacks the necessary ventilation for the paints and craft materials that often comprise the activity agenda. Designers must consider appropriate alterations to safeguard children's health in cases like this when they are placed in multipurpose facilities.

Asthma and respiratory-related allergies in young children, discussed in Chapter 3, can result in poor lung function and respiratory diseases later in life (Lowe et al., 2004). It is important, therefore, that designers identify ways to protect all children from common respiratory irritants such as mold, formaldehyde, and secondhand cigarette smoke and make a concerted effort to learn about any allergies or asthma that children affected by their projects already have or that they may be genetically predisposed to. Homes and other environments inhabited mainly by children should be free of items that tend to collect dust, pollens, and pet hair, such as heavy bedding and carpeting (Craven, 2003). In addition, moisture should be carefully monitored to prevent the formation of mold, a known cause of asthma in some individuals.

Development of the Brain

The brain and nervous system develop in a two-step process. First, neurons are produced during **gestation** (period between conception and birth) at the astounding rate of over one half million per minute. The second part of the process involves what we might call the wiring of the brain: the growth of dendrites and the creation of billions of synapses, which, as you recall from Chapter 2, are the points between the neurons at which the transmission of nerve impulses takes place. The production of synapses, called **synaptogenesis,** is most active all through gestation and well into the second year of life (Eliot, 1999). The importance of this process is illustrated by the fact that intelligence depends in part on the extent of the brain's network of synapses. Therefore, anything that interferes with synaptogenesis can cause lowered intelligence or even mental retardation. In fact, effective synaptogenesis is critical to the entire future functioning of the child's brain, including perception, thinking, vision, and language (Eliot, 1999).

During this period of intense synapse production, the brain actually creates many more connections than are needed for even high-level functioning. Therefore, another process begins after age two, that of **dendritic trimming,** in which the brain actively removes some synapses so that those that remain will perform more specific functions (Bearer, 1995). In a sense, it is a case of, "use it or lose it," which is why environmental influences that stimulate brain functions are so important during this period.

A third critical aspect of brain development that occurs concurrently with synaptogenesis and dendritic trimming is **myelination.** Myelin is a fatty substance that coats the axons of most neurons, creating what is called the **myelin sheath.** To understand the importance of myelin, it is necessary to know two facts about neurons: (1) the impulses that transmit messages through the nervous system are electrical in nature and (2) many thousands of neurons are bundled together to form nerve fibers. A major function of myelin is to prevent electrical interference between the neurons, much like the plastic coating on electrical wires that keeps the metal from coming into direct contact and shorting out. Another very important function of myelin is increasing the speed of the transmission of electrical signals (Eliot, 1999). Multiple sclerosis (MS), a degenerative autoimmune disease in which the body destroys its own myelin sheaths, provides us with an example of what can happen when these sheaths are damaged or missing and nerve transmissions cannot be conducted properly. Myelination in children can be disrupted by conditions such as poor nutrition (Eliot, 1999). Research is ongoing and it is possible that other substances in the environment can interrupt the process.

Implications for Designers Of significance to designers is the fact that the number and formation of specific synapses are influenced by an infant's environment, specifically by the stimuli, opportunities to learn, and activities that engage the brain in problem-solving and other mental challenges. Research by neurobiologists has confirmed that animals raised in enriched environments, which consist of a variety of sensory stimuli and activities, have larger brains than those raised in impoverished environments. Thus, designers should incorporate a variety of sights, sounds, smells, shapes, and textures into nurseries for infants and young children (Wade, 1998). Studies have also shown that a critical part of an environment that stimulates a child's future ability to deal with words in a conceptual manner is hearing adult speech (Wade, 1998; Eliot, 1999). This is why places for adult-child interaction should be provided. These might include a rocking chair in the nursery for holding and talking to infants and reading to older children; and safe areas where babies can be placed in rooms where parents and caregivers are likely to be working, such as the kitchen and home office. It should be noted that although stimulating surroundings are important, it is possible to overstimulate infants, in which case their brains tend to stop taking in sensations (Wade, 1998), so care should be taken not to have too much noise or too many visuals going on at the same time.

The following loss of synapses, or dendritic trimming, occurs at the incredible rate of up to 20 billion per day between early childhood and adolescence (Eliot, 1999). These extremely complex brain processes are accomplished through chemical and electrical cues, and if they are disrupted by environmental hazards such as lead, the result can be brain impairments. This was demonstrated in a study that used magnetic resonance imaging (MRI) to explore brain function. The researchers found that childhood lead exposure has a significant and persistent impact on developmental brain reorganization that is responsible for language function (Weihong, et al., 2006). It is worth repeating here that the environments of young children directly and permanently influence the structure and function of their brains (Eliot, 1999) and, as such, designers must pay particular attention when creating them.

Development of the Bones

Bones, which form the framework for a child's body, grow throughout childhood and into adolescence. Bone is living tissue that is continually renewing itself as bits of old bone are removed and replaced with new tissue. Throughout childhood and adolescence, bones grow in size and mass (density), which typically reaches 90 percent of its adult total by age 18 in girls and 20 in boys (National Institute of Arthritis and Musculoskeletal and Skin Diseases, 2005). The bone mass attained in childhood and adolescence is an important determinant of lifelong skeletal health. It can

even be said that osteoporosis, discussed in Chapter 3, is "a children's disease with consequences in older adulthood" (National Institute of Arthritis and Musculoskeletal and Skin Diseases, 2005).

Aside from determinants outside our control, such as gender and race, proper nutrition and physical exercise are the two most important factors that influence the formation of strong bones. The two most important bone-related elements of nutrition are calcium and vitamin D. Adequate supplies of calcium, a mineral present in a variety of fresh foods, are an important component of the hard parts of bones. Thus, an adequate supply of calcium is essential during childhood when the bones are growing. It is vitamin D that enables calcium to leave the intestine and enter the bloodstream, thus becoming available to the bones. It is important to know that in addition to food sources, vitamin D is manufactured in the skin following direct exposure to sunlight.

Implications for Designers

Strong, healthy bones require physical exercise and calcium. Therefore, creating inviting outdoor areas that provide access to sunshine and movement is an important design consideration for children of all ages.

Activities that require movement, such as sports, contribute to healthy bones because, like muscles, bones grow stronger with use. Because the most beneficial activities are those that require the skeleton to bear weight, such as the examples in Box 8.1, creating areas that accommodate such activities should be a priority when designing children's environments.

Many homes, in-home day-care centers, and preschools do not allocate sufficient space for activities that help build bones and develop the large muscles. Even infants need exercise and this requires safe environments in which they can roll over, crawl, and begin learning to walk. Toddlers need "corralled open spaces" in which to practice walking and to improve their coordination and balancing skills (Weinstein and David, 1987). If existing space is limited, consider the use of movable, stackable furniture that can be easily pushed to one side, thus providing a play area during designated times. Suggestions for creating permanent play spaces that promote the development of coordination and balance include wavy floors and ramps, and temporary spaces with pellets and foam, mats, and net climbers (Weinstein and David, 1987).

When planning both indoor and outdoor spaces for children, pathways must be considered because even good play areas will not be used if there are not clear paths to get to them (Weinstein and David, 1987). For example, if a hedge divides grassy play areas in a park, a clear pathway should be created connecting one to the other.

A variety of interesting elements, such as bright colors and rough textures, should be incorporated into the play areas of infants and young children. This is important for several reasons. First, variety in the environment promotes general infant development (Weinstein and David, 1987). Second, infants use these elements as environmental clues to find their way around when crawling and learning to walk (Weinstein and David, 1987). Third, young children are very much in the present and extremely observant of their surroundings, so offering variety within their space will stimulate them to further explore their environment and thus move about (Weinstein and David, 1987). Finally, touch is a critical sense for children under age three, so providing varieties of texture can arouse the senses and encourage exploratory movements (Weinstein and David). Figure 8.1 contains an example of a well-designed play area.

The Effects of Television on Child Development

In addition to obvious hazards such as pesticides, lead, and radiation, an item that has become an integral part of our culture may also interfere with the healthy development of children: the television set. Research with animals has shown that stimulation such as the type provided by television viewing may interfere with synaptogenesis. Studies have also shown a positive correlation between the numbers of hours of television viewed daily by infants

---

BOX 8.1   BONE-BUILDING ACTIVITIES

Aerobics
Basketball
Dancing
Gymnastics
Hiking
Ice/field hockey
Inline skating
Jumping rope
Lifting weights
Running
Skateboarding
Skiing
Soccer
Tennis
Volleyball
Walking

Adapted from: National Institute of Arthritis and Musculoskeletal and Skin Diseases. *Kids and their bones: A guide for parents.* Retrieved November 17, 2006, from www.niams.nih.gov/hi/topics/osteoporosis/kidbones.htm.

---

and preschoolers and the incidence of short attention spans, attention deficit hyperactivity, and impulsivity by age seven (Elias, 2004). For these reasons, the American Academy of Pediatrics recommends that children under the age of two do not watch any screen entertainment (television, videos, DVDs, or video games) and

FIGURE 8.1 An example of a well-designed play area.

fact, an increasing number of children today are showing early signs of these diseases, such as increased cholesterol levels in the blood.

Television watching may also inhibit the development of gross motor skills, which takes place at a dramatic rate between the ages of two and six. This is because the hours spent in front of the set tend to displace the physical activities needed to transform clumsy two-year-olds, who frequently fall and bump into things, into youngsters who can ride tricycles and climb ladders (Berger, 1980).

Implications for Designers

In view of the potential negative impact of television on young children and teens, health-promoting bedrooms and play areas for these age groups would not include a television set. This recommendation presents quite a design challenge for many families because, according to a Kaiser Family Foundation survey, the following percentages of young children have a set in their rooms: 19 percent under age one, 29 percent ages two to three, and 43 percent ages four to six (Kaiser Family Foundation, 2006). The designer might suggest the substitution of activity areas for playing with toys, playing games, and pursuing hobbies. For example, items to encourage reading include a bookshelf within the child's reach, a comfortable child-sized chair, and good lighting (see Figure 8.2). If a child's room does not have a television set, it is especially important to create a climate that is pleasing to the child, which means that his or her preferences about color and furnishings should be solicited when designing the room.

Parents' habits play a major role in the television viewing habits of young children. The Kaiser survey mentioned previously included focus groups with parents, many of whom reported that they placed a television in their child's room to free up other televisions to watch their own shows. Other reasons given for allowing children to watch television were to keep the child occupied so parents could do things around the house, to help the child fall asleep, and as a reward for good behavior. There are, in fact, ways that homes can be

FIGURE 8.2 Children's rooms should be inviting and encourage healthy play.

that preschoolers over age two be limited to two hours a day. It should be noted that there is not total agreement on the effect of television on attention deficit disorder. The Attention Deficit Disorder Association, for example, does not believe that television is a causal factor (Jaksa, 1998).

In addition to its potentially negative influence on the brain, excessive television viewing has been linked to the growing problem of childhood obesity and low fitness levels (Robinson, 2001). Obese children are more likely to be obese as adults, thus increasing their lifetime risk for heart disease, cancer, and diabetes. In

arranged to reduce television viewing. As suggested in Chapter 7, television sets do not have to be the center of attention in living areas. The designer could, for example, organize the seating to emphasize people-to-people interactions rather than television viewing. Another idea is to provide tables for games and music equipment in central locations to encourage alternative, more socially engaging entertainment. In this way, parents who normally watch television themselves, while sending children off to seek their own entertainment, might be prompted to engage the family in "togetherness" activities.

A specific area of the home in which the presence of a television should be discouraged is in the one allocated for eating. This is because family meals help children learn to socialize and communicate. Studies have shown that teens who frequently participate in family meals have lower odds of tobacco, alcohol, and marijuana use; better grade point averages; higher self-esteem; and fewer incidences of depression and suicidal thoughts (Eisenberg, et al., 2004). Instead of placing the television in or near the dining area, an attractive art piece or collection of family mementos, such as items collected on a recent vacation, can be substituted in its place. A display of the children's work, such as pictures or craft pieces, can also be displayed for the dual benefits of enhancing their self-esteem and providing a subject of conversation.

A design consideration for the parents who reportedly use television as a form of babysitting their young children is to include spaces in rooms in which mothers and other caregivers perform household tasks where children can safely play. Two popular floor-plan trends, the adjoining family room and kitchen and the more recent great-room style, might accomplish this, but for the fact that these rooms typically feature a television set, often a very large one. The Child Development Institute goes so far as to suggest that parents discourage viewing and snacking by locating the set away from the main living area and out of range of the refrigerator (Child Development Institute, n.d.). A more practical solution for many families may be to place the set in a cabinet, as in the popular armoires, so that it can be hidden behind a door when not in use.

Microenvironments

A microenvironment is a small unit within an environment. For example, the air in an enclosed room consists of horizontal layers. If radon is present in a room, there will be horizontal levels of air, also called breathing zones, with each level containing a different level of radon concentration. The heaviest concentrations will be near the floor where infants crawl and the next heaviest will be at around two feet, the level of a toddler's mouth and nose. At six feet above the floor, where a tall adult male breathes, the radon levels will be lower. The fact that children often inhabit more contaminated microenvironments, combined with their smaller body size, is another reason why they are at higher risk for airborne contaminants. Floors provide us with an example of how a specific microenvironment is used differently by children and adults: in this case, crawling and playing versus standing and walking. Obviously, spending time close to floors places infants and small children at greater risk for inhaling pollutants such as volatile organic compounds (VOCs) emitted by synthetic carpets and residue from flea bombs. (Chapter 4 contains more information about VOCs and other contaminants.) The fact that young children often inhabit floor-level microenvironments may explain, in part, the rising incidence of childhood asthma that was discussed in Chapter 3.

A prominent exploratory behavior of children from about age six months to two years is placing most objects within their grasp into their mouths, an action that certainly increases their risk of transferring bacteria, toxic chemicals, and other hazards present on floors from their hands to their mouths. From these examples, we can see that it is not uncommon for children and adults to live in different microenvironments when they are in the same structure or even in the same room. Designers must be able to identify microenvironments and their unique characteristics so

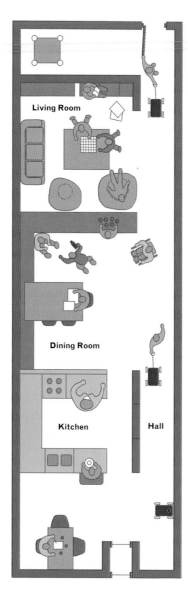

tive play is especially important in very cold or hot climates where young children cannot always play outside. Noncluttered hallways, with tough cleanable wall covering, can be used for riding indoor wheeled toys. Family rooms, or a section of a great room, can be child-proofed so that children can move about without bumping into things.

Ideally, a large dedicated playroom or area in a finished basement can be provided for the active play that encourages the development of large muscle groups. At the same time, many children enjoy doing quieter activities, such as painting, crafts, and model building. Whenever substances such as paints and glues are used, adequate ventilation is extremely important to remove any toxic fumes. This is also a consideration in the case of homeschooling because in addition to craft supplies, items such as whiteboard markers release toxic fumes. These examples illustrate how it is critical for designers to learn about all members of a household, as well as the types of activities that will take place in the home.

Nurseries and Bedrooms

Nurseries should be planned with the physical needs of infants in mind. It is important to remember, for example, that newborns cannot regulate their body temperature by moving about, or adding or removing clothing and covers (Phillips, 2002). The overheating of babies while they sleep has been identified as a possible risk for sudden infant death syndrome (SIDS), the leading cause of death in infants aged one month to one year (Nemours Foundation, 2005, "Sudden Infant"). Thus, it is necessary to have uniform heating and cooling in their sleeping area, maintaining the temperature between 67 and 69°F. Another important fact to know is that babies are highly sensitive to light.

Recommendations for the nursery include using window coverings that block bright light and using dimmer switches with light fixtures and lamps. To avoid overwhelming the senses of infants, choose soft or neutral colors for walls and furnishings (Phillips, 2002). These also work well to soothe active toddlers

they can protect and promote the health of all individuals who will occupy a given built environment.

Designing Environments for Children

The entire home, not just bedrooms and playrooms, should be considered in terms of meeting children's needs. (See Figure 8.3.) As discussed previously, children require a variety of components to develop fully and healthily, including freedom from contaminants, space in which to move about safely, and sensory stimulation. Meeting their needs requires knowing the children and their individual interests, as well as creating child-friendly spaces throughout the home. Providing adequate covered or indoor space where children can engage in ac-

when it is time for bed (Phillips, 2002). These colors are good sustainable choices because they allow for more flexibility as children's tastes change; rather than repainting a room, for example, furniture and accessories can be changed. On the other hand, play areas are best done in bright, primary colors, although it is recommended that the child's response, even a nonverbal one, be solicited when selecting colors.

An important design consideration is the location of sleeping areas for children. Keeping the cribs and bassinets of very young infants in the room where the parents sleep has been associated with a lower risk of SIDS. Even after they are sleeping in their own bedrooms, many young children feel more secure if their room is located near their parents' room. They also tend to prefer sharing a room with a sibling. In shared rooms, privacy can be provided with a room divider such as double-sided shelving, curtains, or half-walls. Another consideration when siblings of different ages share a room is the safety of the younger one. Any items that might pose a risk to a young child should be stored in a high place or cabinet that prevents easy entry.

Bedrooms for children of all ages should be as sleep-promoting as possible because physical, emotional, and intellectual well-being depend on getting sufficient sleep. Ensuring quiet for those who live near highways, train tracks, or other noise-producers during the night may require the use of double-paned windows and sound-dampening materials. Temperatures should not be too warm, and rooms should be designed to reduce potential allergens, such as dust, that can cause sleep-disrupting coughing and other respiratory symptoms.

While it is known that infants and very young children require many hours of sleep, a less-known fact is that adolescents need more than preteens or adults: up to 9.2 hours (Carpenter, 2001). A second important fact about teen sleep needs is that changes in sleep patterns, sleep/wake systems, and circadian timing systems have been associated with puberty (Carskadon, 1999). Recall from Chapter 7 that

circadian rhythms control various body functions, including the sleep cycle. During adolescence, it appears that the natural cycle shifts to both later sleep times (often after 11 P.M.) and corresponding later awake times.

Adolescent sleep difficulties have been associated with behavior problems; poor grades; depression; negative moods such as anger, sadness, and fear; and accidents on the job involving hazardous equipment (National Sleep Foundation, 2000). The most tragic result of teen sleep deprivation is the 50,000 fatigue-caused car crashes that occur each year involving young drivers (Carpenter, 2001). Although designers cannot control such factors as school starting times, deemed by many experts to be too early to accommodate the typical adolescent sleep cycle, they can help create environments that are conducive to sleep. For example, locate bedrooms for teens as far away as possible from the noisiest areas of the house. Provide soothing places to relax before bedtime, such bathtubs and comfortable chairs for reading or listening to quiet music. Because lighting is an important factor in controlling the circadian system (see Chapter 7) and teens seem to be especially sensitive to the awakening effects of bright light before going to bed, installing a dimmer switch on their bedroom lights and lamps is recommended. (On the other hand, exposure to bright light upon arising in the morning signals the body it is time to wake up.) Ensuring that the mattress and pillows are suited to the teen's preferences can also help make falling asleep easier. Although the majority of teens have televisions in their bedrooms, this may not be a good idea. An eighteen-year longitudinal study revealed that nighttime viewing by teens contributes to sleep problems, including difficulty falling and staying asleep, difficulty falling back asleep, nightmares, and irritability upon waking (Johnson et al., 2004). Another problem related to television in the bedroom is the tendency of viewers to fall asleep while the set is on, in which case the flickering light can inhibit restful sleep (National Sleep Foundation, 2000).

Computers and Children's Health

Computers in the home, providing enhanced opportunities for both learning and entertainment, are increasing in popularity. In many homes, computer ownership is an assumed part of modern life and more than one computer is not uncommon. A major concern with children's computer use in the home, as well as in school, is ergonomics. Recall from Chapter 7 that the purpose of ergonomics is to ensure a good fit between people, the things they do, and the objects they use. Unfortunately, most computer systems are designed for the body of a twenty-five-year-old man (Nemours Foundation, 2005, "Computer-Related"). The resulting poor positioning and lack of proper body support for children, combined with the hours some of them spend at a computer, can cause repetitive stress injuries (Nemours Foundation, 2005, "Computer-Related"). Thus, the arrangement and furnishings for computer use, as well as electronic game playing, should be appropriate for children in size and form. A specific example of poor ergonomics for children is the use of the typical office chair. Designed for an adult, it is too large and, as a result, children's legs hit the edge at an inappropriate point and the feet dangle rather than being placed on the floor. Pressing the legs against the edge of a chair can interfere with proper blood circulation. Another problem is that adult-sized chairs are too deep, requiring children to lean forward, thus depriving themselves of proper back support. This causes stress on the neck, back, and spine. In the absence of appropriate child-sized chairs, some children choose small wooden chairs that are too hard for extended periods of sitting. There are several ways that designers can reorganize computer stations to better meet the needs of children:

1. Choose a chair that fits the child. If individuals of various ages must use the same chair, select one that is fully adjustable, along with an appropriate pillow that provides back support for the child.

2. Arrange the desk or table so that the monitor is close enough for the child to see without leaning toward the screen or jutting the chin forward, actions that put stress on the neck.

3. Place the keyboard and mouse within easy reach. Again, if people of various sizes will be using the system, strive for maximum adjustability in the setup: a workstation with adjustable heights and a keyboard and mouse area that can be raised and lowered.

4. Install wrist pads on keyboards and consider using a curved or split-design keyboard to promote a more natural position for hands and wrists.

Video Games and Children's Health

Video games comprise a rapidly growing segment of the entertainment industry, generating almost $10 billion in sales in the United States in 2004 (Walsh et al., 2005). According to one study, more than half of children age four to six have played video games, with at least 25 percent playing several times a week (Kaiser Family Foundation, 2006). Another study reported that children today ages two to seventeen average seven hours a week watching video games (Gentile & Walsh, 2002). Playing video games for extended periods of time presents problems similar to those of viewing television in that it detracts from participating in physical activity and experiencing the real world.

In addition to the time spent, the content of the games worries many adults. This is because the most common scenes in many popular games include killings, thefts, and other acts of violence. In fact, some content analyses show that as many as 89 percent contain some violence (Children Now, 2001), with many also containing explicit sexual or pornographic content. It is believed that many parents are unaware of the violent or sexual content of the games their children are playing. This is a worrisome finding in view of the fact that a growing number of studies are linking violent games and aggressive behavior in youth (Anderson and Dill, 2000). Furthermore, it is believed that violent games have even more influence on behavior than movies or television because the games are interactive, violent behavior is rewarded, and participants repeat the moves and behaviors over and over. Reported aggression in youth that may be linked to game playing includes physical fights, getting into arguments with teachers, and displaying a generally hostile attitude (Gentile et al, 2004). At the same time, violent content can give children the impression that the world is a violent and mean place in which others cannot be trusted (American Academy of Pediatrics, 2000).

Implications for Designers

Parental or other adult monitoring of game content and amount of playing time appears to be a protective factor in the development of aggressive behaviors (Gentile et al., 2004). Because most eight- to seventeen-year-olds play video games at home, the implication for designers is to locate computers and television monitors so that game playing can be monitored. If computers are located in teens' bedrooms to accommodate their study needs, consider placing them so that the screen can be seen from the hallway. In public places, games should be located where adults can easily see the screens. For example, a video arcade might include a coffee shop where adults can congregate and discreetly supervise their children. In any environment, including schools, computers can be placed with their backs toward a wall to enable supervision of content.

Enhancing Child Development with Music

Music has been an integral part of the human experience from the beginning of history, serving as an important part of life's milestones, ceremonies, and religious services. Music is of such significance that it has played a part in the creation myths of some cultures. Although music has long been acknowledged as a means to inspire, calm, and provide enjoyment, it is now believed that it may have additional positive benefits. Research begun during the 1980s and 1990s revealed that

---

BOX 8.2 THE SUSTAINABILITY CONNECTION

Children's Furniture

Children grow so quickly that many furnishings are used for relatively short periods of time. When purchasing these items, think in terms of future use, as in these examples:

- A sturdy, attractive toy chest can be used later for storing any number of items. If it is constructed of cedar, it will serve well for linens and clothing, as cedar is a natural moth repellent.
- Adjustable wooden chairs in which the seat and footrest move up and down can provide comfortable seating from infancy to adulthood.
- Furniture that converts, such as a wooden crib that dismantles to create items such as chairs and climbing frames, or into larger beds as the child grows, allows the family to attractively recycle furniture already owned (See Figure 8.4).

---

highly structured classical music, particularly that composed by Mozart, may influence the physical development of growing children, particularly the development of the brain. Recall that at birth an infant's brain has billions of neurons that have not yet been connected. It appears that the patterned nature of music may promote the creation of connections in the brain that form the patterns for speech and language. These patterns, in turn, influence behavioral and communication skills (Campbell, 2002). This has become known as the "Mozart effect." Music is also believed to play a role in helping infants interpret the huge amounts of sensory data they receive because the auditory nerve is the first sensory nerve to become functional (Campbell, 2002).

Proponents of the Mozart effect believe that "by connecting sound, movement, speech, and interaction with a musical component, it is possible to activate and integrate more of the brain than with any other education tool" (Campbell, 2002, p. 195). This view is supported by a study reported in 2006 by Canadian researchers who demonstrated that young children who take music lessons have different brain development and larger memory capacity than those who do not (Hawryluk, 2006; Fujioka, et al., 2006). It has also been demonstrated in a number of studies that children who receive regular music training, such as

FIGURE 8.4 Furnishings that can serve more than one purpose add to the sustainability of the built environment.

piano lessons, have increased spatial reasoning abilities, the building blocks for learning math and science.

In addition to enhancing brain development, music can influence good motor development through its rhythmic qualities. We've all seen young children bouncing, clapping, and dancing along to music. The ages from six to 18 months are marked by very rapid physical growth and maturation. During this period, children who have opportunities to move to music develop a basic sense of timing along with increased coordination, balance, body awareness, strength, and physical grace (Campbell, 2002).

Implications for Designers

Designers can suggest that access to music be provided, as well as room for free movement, in the environments commonly used by children: homes, day-care centers, preschools, and schools. Flooring should be such that children will neither slip easily, such as highly polished surfaces, nor catch their feet, such as on carpeting. With young children, proper storage of music-making devices is important so that small hands don't pull on tapes and remove CDs from their players, or worse, pull equipment onto themselves. Speakers should be placed high enough to prevent damage by young children who are curious to find out what is inside making the sound. Cupboards or cabinets for storing musical instruments should be provided in day-care centers and schools. In

the home, space for a musical instrument such as a piano might be planned.

INDIVIDUALS WITH DISABILITIES

A **disability** is generally defined as a condition that makes it difficult to carry on the normal **activities of daily living (ADLs),** such as getting dressed, shopping for groceries, preparing food, and remembering information. It may seem surprising to include "remembering information" as a disability, but if this condition interferes with daily living and limits an individual's function, it is a disability. Other examples that vary from more traditional definitions include learning disabilities and alcohol and substance abuse. Because of the wide range of disabling conditions, they have been categorized in a number of ways. For example, the 2005 Disability Status Reports prepared by Cornell University are divided into six broad classifications. Table 8.2 contains these categories along with data regarding their prevalence among disabled working-age people, defined as individuals ages 21 to 64 (Rehabilitation Research and Training Center on Disability Demographics and Statistics, 2005). The reported 12.6 percent of working-age people, given in the table, who have at least one disability translates into a very large number of individuals: 21,455,000. This means that in addition to the human cost of disabilities, the economic costs

TABLE 8.2   PREVALENCE OF DISABILITIES AMONG WORKING-AGE ADULTS

TYPE OF DISABILITY	PERCENT OF TOTAL WORKING POPULATION	NUMBER OF INDIVIDUALS
All types	12.6%	21,455,000
Physical	7.8%	13,313,000
Employment (unable to work)	7.3%	12,386,000
Mental	4.4%	7,526,000
Go-Outside-Home (unable to do so or very limited)	3.2%	5,336,000
Sensory	3%	5,074,000
Self-Care (unable to do so or very limited)	2.2%	3,712,000

Note that the percentages of the various disabilities total more than 12.6 percent due to the overlapping of some disabilities.

Source of data: Rehabilitation Research and Training Center on Disability Demographics and Statistics. (2005). *2005 Disability Status Reports*. Ithaca, NY: Cornell University. Retrieved November 27, 2006, from www.ilr.cornell.edu/ped/disabilitystatistics/.

are also high. A major reason is that many disabled persons are unable to work, either due to their conditions or to limited access to the workplace, and therefore cannot contribute to national productivity. The actual employment rate of working-age adults ranges from a low of 25.5 percent in West Virginia to a high of 53.3 percent in South Dakota (Rehabilitation Research and Training Center on Disability Demographics and Statistics, 2005). The inability to work leads to personal financial difficulties, with 24.6 percent of disabled persons living at or below the poverty rate as compared to 9.3 percent of persons without disabilities (Rehabilitation Research and Training Center on Disability Demographics and Statistics, 2005). Looked at another way, the median household income in 2005 for a person with at least one disability was $35,000 as opposed to $61,500 for the nondisabled.

The figures in Table 8.2 give us the numbers of working-age disabled adults, so they only reveal part of the picture. When we include children with disabilities and adults age 65 and older, we find that the total number of disabled Americans is actually around 50 million. The magnitude of this number is better appreciated when you know that this represents almost 20 percent of the total population who are more than five years of age, not institutionalized, as in a prison, or living in a nursing home (Kopec, 2006). This large percentage is due, in part, to the increasing number of older adults who are living into their eighties and nineties; many of them have conditions that limit their ability to function and are thus considered to be disabled.

OLDER ADULTS

Older adults represent the fastest-growing segment of the American population, a phenomenon that has been called "the greatest demographic change in human history" (Kotlifoff and Burns, 2005). The following numbers certainly back up this statement: in 2000, the population age 65 and older was 12.4 percent of the total; it is conservatively expected to be 19.4 percent in 2030. Thus, designers can expect to be working with an increasing number of older clients whose needs they must be able to address.

BOX 8.3 EXAMPLES OF DISABLING CONGENITAL DISORDERS

- Cerebral palsy: bilateral paralysis due to inadequate oxygen supply to the brain during fetal development, birthing, or infancy
- Cystic fibrosis: glands secrete abnormally thick fluids, which cause the most serious problems in the lungs, blocking bronchi and trapping bacteria
- Down syndrome: mild to severe mental retardation; child may also have a heart defect and other congenital abnormalities
- Muscular dystrophy: group of diseases characterized by degeneration or weakening of the muscles

Age-Related Changes and Disabilities

The disabling conditions experienced by children and younger adults tend to be caused by **congenital** conditions, such as those listed in Box 8.3, or by accidents that cause traumatic injuries, such as those involving the brain and spinal cord. On the other hand, many disabilities in older adults are due to the aging process, part of the natural life cycle, and/or the presence of chronic conditions such as arthritis, heart disease, and Alzheimer's disease, discussed in Chapter 3. In fact, the American Academy of Family Physicians reports that most people age seventy and older have two or three chronic conditions that interfere to some extent with their activities of daily living (Kopec, 2006). Table 8.3 contains a list of the types of everyday activities that many individuals over age sixty find difficult to perform.

As we discuss the changes due to aging, it is important to understand that aging in itself is not a disease; rather, many of the changes that occur are due to progressively diminished physical reserves that do not guarantee illness, but simply place older Americans at a higher risk for chronic conditions such as heart disease, cancer, and stroke. In our youth-driven culture, growing older is generally viewed as undesirable. As one author puts it, we grow old "against a background of avoidance and negativity" (Dychtwald and Flower, 1989, p. viii). Evidence of this avoidance is the fact that Americans spend billions of dollars each year in an effort to look and feel as young as possible.

TABLE 8.3 PERCENTAGE OF ADULTS AGE SIXTY AND OVER WHO HAVE ANY DIFFICULTY PERFORMING SELECTED FUNCTIONAL ACTIVITIES

ACTIVITY	PERCENT WHO HAVE DIFFICULTY
Stooping, crouching, or kneeling	51%
Standing on one's feet for about two hours	42%
Walking for a quarter of a mile	30%
Lifting or carrying something as heavy as 10 pounds	29%
Doing chores around the house	28%
Walking up 10 steps without resting	26%
Standing up from an armless chair	26%
Going out to do things like shopping, movies, or sporting events	22%
Sitting for about 2 hours	21%
Reaching up over one's head	18%
Participating in social activities	18%
Getting in or out of bed	17%
Using one's fingers to grasp or hold small objects	17%

Adapted from: Centers for Disease Control and Prevention. National Center for Health Statistics. (August 23, 2006). *Advance data from vital and health statistics.* No. 375.

The emphasis on youth in our society is also reflected in the fact that the American built environment tends to be designed for young people. Consider, for example, the design of many modern restaurants that feature multiple hard surfaces that raise the noise level and make it very difficult to hear, along with the use of low lighting, which makes reading menus all but impossible for many older adults.

Our desire to remain youthful may be the reason that many older adults are in denial about their disabling conditions. For example, they may decide it is better to forgo being able to hear than to suffer the perceived stigma of using a hearing aid; or to sit at home rather than use a mobility aid. This attitude is unfortunate because ultimately it lowers **life quality** for individuals at a time when they should be afforded respect and encouraged to live as comfortably and productively as possible. Designers have an opportunity to help remedy this situation in terms of the built environment by becoming aware of **age-related changes** and how these can best be accommodated. Common age-related changes are described in the following sections, along with applicable design considerations.

Designing for Changes in Vision

The changes that occur in the eyes are among the most significant of all bodily changes related to aging and for some people, the most debilitating. Vision changes typically begin at about age forty when many of us start needing "extra long arms" to read small print. This is due to a condition called presbyopia, discussed in Chapter 3, in which the eye lens hardens and cannot sufficiently change shape to accommodate close-up vision. Designers can ensure that lighting in places where reading or other close work is expected or necessary is bright and arranged to fall directly onto reading matter, such as books, sheets of paper, and forms in public agencies and menus in restaurants. Full-spectrum lamps can be helpful because they brighten the white background of papers so that the darker print stands out. In the home, good reading lamps should be placed wherever necessary, including the dining room table if this is where the morning newspaper is read. This is an example of why it is important to discuss lifestyle habits with clients, such as where they most enjoy reading or doing work such as sewing or other crafts. Reading labels correctly, such as on medications and household cleaning products, can affect health and safety, so consider installing adequate task lighting in bathrooms, bedrooms, kitchens, and storage areas. This additional lighting may require installing additional electrical outlets in these areas.

Some older adults experience decreased vision due to cataracts, glaucoma, and macular degeneration. (See Chapter 3 for more information about these conditions.) While cataracts can be removed surgically, the damage done by untreated glaucoma and the natural course of most cases of macular degeneration cannot be reversed. Good overall lighting is a key issue for the visually impaired. To help clients compensate for vision loss, general lighting should be increased by 20 percent in homes and facilities used by older people (Kopec, 2006). At the same time, extreme changes in light levels should be avoided because the muscles that control the pupils, which control the amount of light that enters the eye, respond more slowly in the older eye. Therefore, transitional lighting should be incorporated between the indoors and outdoors to give the eyes an opportunity to adjust.

At all ages it is more difficult to distinguish blues and greens than reds and yellows. In older people, this problem becomes even more pronounced because of the yellowing of the lens that comes with age (Medline Plus, 2004). For this reason, it is best to choose warm colors for home interiors and furnishings because this makes it easier to distinguish between items. At the same time, there should be some variety in colors and values so that furnishings do not seemingly blend together with each other and other surfaces into large indistinguishable masses. The selection of appropriate, easy-to-see colors also applies to items that affect personal safety, such as markings on the edges of stairs and curbs and signs that contain safety warnings.

Another common condition of the aging eye is sensitivity to glare, which makes it important to avoid using shiny, light-reflecting surfaces and furnishings and glossy paints in the environments of older adults. Many public buildings, including even medical facilities, have very shiny floors, perhaps in an effort to look clean and professional. However, these are more difficult for older adults to negotiate, so businesses and services that cater to this population should consider installing other types of flooring. At the same time, natural light, while an excellent source of light, may need to be reduced by tinting windows or using transparent coverings. Also, furniture should be arranged so that seated persons are not directly facing a window.

Decreased night vision is another change experienced by many older individuals because the pupil gets smaller, thus decreasing the quantity of light entering the eye. Designers can help compensate by placing bedside lamps so they can be turned on without leaving the bed; providing light switches in all entryways to rooms and halls that prevent the need to walk through darkened areas; placing night-lights in halls and bathrooms; and selecting outdoor lights that are on timers or sensitive to motion.

In addition to lighting, issues of contrast must be considered because they can be problematic for older people. One study found that the average seventy-five-year-old needs twice as much contrast to distinguish objects as well as a younger person; at age ninety, the need for contrast increases to six times as much (Brabyn, et al., 2000). Easy-to-implement suggestions for the home include painting the insides of cupboards white to provide maximum brightness and ease in finding objects, installing cabinet door handles and drawer pulls that contrast with the door fronts, and painting the edges of shelves to make them easier to distinguish. Clothes closet interiors are often too dark for distinguishing colors, matching shoes, and so on, thus robbing the visually impaired person the independence and confidence of dressing oneself properly. This can be remedied by adding or increasing lighting in both the closet and dressing areas.

The loss of peripheral (side) vision that often accompanies aging makes clear pathways especially important to prevent older persons from colliding with objects and falling. The installation of strip or runway-type lighting on baseboards in halls and other pathways is one way to provide clues to better the pathways and reduce the likelihood of falling (Slay, 2002).

In public places, issues of signage and directions can be problematic for low-vision and contrast-impaired persons. Ideas to help overcome this problem include using large, clearly defined letters and high contrast between the lettering and the background. These considerations are especially important in environments, such as assisted-living facilities, that cater for the most part to older adults.

A nonvision but uncomfortable eye condition is caused by the decrease in tear production, a natural change. Designers can help by ensuring adequate humidity, perhaps through the use of a humidifier, in drier climates or closed-in facilities that rely on drying, artificial heat. (However, as discussed in Chapter 5, humidifiers can cause bacteria and mold problems.)

Designing for Changes in Hearing

As with the eyes, the ears undergo changes as we age. The delicate structures that enable us to hear gradually deteriorate. This process includes thickening of the eardrum, decreasing its ability to vibrate, as well as changes in the tiny bones of the inner ear (Medline Plus, 2004). The associated progressive age-related hearing loss, called presbycusis, usually begins with difficulty hearing high-frequency sounds such as speech. Changes in the auditory nerve and the auditory processing center of the brain also negatively affect the sharpness of hearing. All these conditions are common among older individuals, with about 25 percent of people age 65 to 75 and 70 percent to 80 percent of those over age 75 having some degree of hearing loss (Medline Plus, 2006). Another condition that tends to affect older adults is tinnitus, or abnormal ear noise, which can interfere with normal hearing.

When planning the environment for hearing-impaired individuals, consider eliminating or at least decreasing the amount of background noise. One way is to select items that don't make a lot of noise, such as quieter appliances and air-conditioning systems. In public places that cater to the elderly, consider eliminating mood music and extraneous sounds. (This also helps the blind, who depend on the sound of their footsteps and cane taps for orientation and navigation.) A second method is to use sound-absorbing materials within the walls and between work spaces, acoustical tiles, soft surfaces such as carpeting and upholstery, and double-glazed windows to reduce street noise. (See Chapter 7 for more information about noise control.)

At the same time, there are some sounds everyone must hear for safety and convenience. For this reason, check the availability of low-pitched auditory warning devices on appliances, which typically are high-pitched and therefore inaudible with advanced presbycusis.

Conversation is an important means of communicating and staying connected with others. Designers can plan seating to help hearing-impaired persons more easily engage in conversation by arranging face-to-face rather than side-by-side seating. This might mean switching the traditional sofa in which people sit in a row with smaller chairs angled toward one another or clustered around a small table (see Figure 8.5). In addition to conversation, another enjoyable activity that becomes difficult when hearing is diminished is listening to music, radio, and television. This is especially true when there are other household members with normal hearing who find the volume needed by the hearing impaired to be intrusive or even painful to the ears. In these cases, there are devices that provide amplification as needed through earphones. Other possibilities include a private television located away from the center of the home that the older household members can watch at their preferred sound level.

Designing for Changes in the Musculoskeletal System

Aging bones become thinner as calcium, which is responsible for their hardness, is reabsorbed into the body. This process is especially pronounced in women during the first years following menopause, although it commonly occurs in both older men and women. Thinner bones break more easily and put older adults at increased risk for serious injuries from falls, as discussed in Chapter 9. The situation is further exacerbated by vision and hearing losses and problems maintaining balance, all factors that increase the chance of falling. This is why design considerations for the elderly should be comprehensive and coordinated so that the entire environment addresses all age-related changes, both present and possible in the future.

Another skeletal change is the compression of the intervertebral disks, which results in a

FIGURE 8.5 This seating arrangement has been designed to facilitate hearing and encourage conversation.

loss of height. This loss can be as much as five percent for men and six percent for women (Tiley, 2002). Designers can address this change by creating lower storage areas throughout the house and workplace. In addition, furniture may need to be scaled down to better fit the changing body.

The joints are common sites of discomfort for aging individuals because over the years, the cartilage on the ends of bones wears thin or even disappears.

This is accompanied by a decrease in the fluids that lubricate the joints. Together, these changes cause decreased flexibility, agility, and mobility, which inhibit everyday actions most of us take for granted in our younger years. A common example is getting out of a chair. One study showed that in a group of adults with a mean age of 82, nearly two-thirds couldn't rise out of a chair without using their hands (Alexander et al, 2001). Chairs, then, should be chosen that fit the individual and have arms sturdy enough to provide support for rising. All the dining room chairs in assisted-living facilities, for example, should have padded arms. Another consideration is to avoid front rungs in chairs because older people tend to move their legs back under the chair to assist them in rising. For individuals who are unable to rise from upholstered furniture, such as recliners, the type that mechanically rise and lift the person up to his or her feet may be a good choice. Another important thing to realize is that many elderly persons have shorter strides and don't lift their feet as high when walking as younger people, thus increasing their chances of tripping on stairs and small obstacles (McFadyen and Price, 2002). Safety-enhancing features include lower stair risers and door thresholds.

Reaching overhead can become a problem when **range of motion** and balance are compromised, so designers should look for alterations to reduce the amount of reaching required in the home. For example, clothing rods in closets should be between 20 and 44 inches above the floor, but in fact, many closets have them higher than this (AARP, n.d., "Safety"). In the kitchen, consider a side-by-side refrigerator-freezer to prevent the need to reach up and into a shelf full of frozen goods. Cabinets are often placed too high or too low and thus become difficult to access. This can be prevented by lowering upper cabinets to a maximum of not more than 48 inches from the floor. To prevent excessive bending and stooping, lower cabinets should be raised at least six inches above the floor (AARP, n.d., "Kitchen").

The laundry area often poses problems for the elderly and is, in fact, often one of the least accessible work areas in the home. If it consists of a washer and dryer sitting in a basement or garage, try relocating these appliances to a more convenient location. Regarding appliances, elevated, front-loading washing machines tend to be easier to use than top-loading models. Another helpful feature is nearby counter or table space for sorting and folding laundry. For individuals who have trouble standing at a counter, install one that is lower and has space underneath so they can sit to do their work.

When conditions such as arthritis affect the finger joints, as happens with more than 50 percent of people over age 60, the fingers become increasingly stiff and lose some dexterity (Dychtwald, 1989). This makes many daily actions quite painful, especially those that require twisting, pulling, and pushing with the hands. There are many changes designers can incorporate into the built environment to help alleviate these problems, including door openers that can be opened with a fist, such as long (at least five inches) levers; detachable handles added to controls, such as those on a stove; and single faucets that are controlled with a levered handle rather than a knob.

Along with changes in the bones and joints, the muscles tend to decrease in mass, tone, and strength, and muscle cells may actually decrease in total number (Neighbors and Tannehill-Jones, 1999). The results of these changes are illustrated in the following figures: hand strength is reduced by about 16 to 40 percent and arm and leg strength by about 50 percent (Tiley, 2002). Designers should look for ways to reduce the number of tasks requiring strength, such as in the following examples:

- Large, easy-to-open drawers that provide storage for pots and pans
- Heat-proof areas next to stovetops to enable the transfer of heavy pots full of food. (See Figure 8.6.)
- Extra-long spray hose at the sink to allow filling pots with water while they are on the stove
- Storage space for heavy items at chest level or slightly below to prevent having to reach over the head or bend down to retrieve
- Rolling cart for transporting items, such as groceries from an outside parking area, into the house
- Rolling carts or baskets for sorting clothes to eliminate the necessity of leaning over and carrying baskets that normally sit on the floor
- "Parking spots," such as under a counter, for carts so they don't obstruct pathways

Designing for Changes in the Skin

The skin of older adults becomes thinner, sometimes almost transparent, and retains less water, making it dryer and more prone to irritation and injury. It also loses its elasticity and subcutaneous fat, which results in the wrinkling associated with aging. This fat provides insulation and its loss means that the older person requires more protection from the cold. At the same time, the sweat and oil glands may function less efficiently, contributing to overheating and dry skin (Neighbors and Tannehille-Jones, 1999). Design considerations include the installation of climate-appropriate heating and air-conditioning systems and humidifiers. (Recall the caution regarding humidifiers.) The controls for these systems should be simple and easy to read, such as the large-print models that many companies are now making. The controls also need to be placed on walls at a height that can be seen by even the shortest older adult.

FIGURE 8.6 This kitchen is well designed for individuals who lack arm and shoulder strength. Note how the counters on either side of the range make it easy to slide heavy pots onto and off the stove.

Changes in the skin also decrease the sense of touch, an important sense that enables us to discern temperatures and feel pain. This is why many older adults are burned each year from water that's too hot. Although water at 130°F will give a bad burn, most water heaters are set at 140°F. It is recommended that heaters be turned down to a maximum of 120°F or that antiscald devices, which mix in larger amounts of cold water, be installed at sinks. Stove safety can be increased if the appliance has lights that indicate when burners are on. Mirrors secured to the wall behind a range can help in determining if burners are turned on and if steam is coming out of boiling pots.

Designing for Changes in the Cardiorespiratory System

The lungs of older adults become less efficient because of decreased elasticity. This can lower air intake by as much as 35 percent (Tiley, 2002), which reduces the lungs' ability to meet the body's demand for oxygen. This change is a major reason why older adults tire easily. At the same time, the heart and circulatory system are undergoing changes, including loss of elasticity in the blood vessels, loss of cardiac muscle contractibility, and loss of heart valve function. Combined, these changes contribute to decreased circulatory efficiency, which causes tiring with minimal exercise, cold extremities, slow healing, and increased risk for heart disease (Neighbors and Tannehille-Jones, 1999). Appropriate design measures to help the older person cope with these conditions include the elimination of stairs; the provision of easy-to-clean surfaces and furnishings; the installation of automatic features, such as garage-door openers; and the provision of low-maintenance landscaping.

AGING IN PLACE

Many older adults prefer to stay in their own homes as they age. Our homes are imbued with meanings such as those associated with creating a family, establishing holiday traditions, planting gardens, and expressing creativity. Thus, homes can be intertwined with our self-identities. It is even believed by many that remaining in one's home promotes better health, and efforts are being made to help older adults stay in their homes. A relatively new term, **aging in place** refers to planning and altering residences to make them more compatible to the needs of older people. (See

Box 8.4 for examples of stated needs of older adults.) The *Journal for Housing for the Elderly* defines aging in place as "not having to move from one's present residence in order to secure necessary support services in response to changing need" (Senior Source, n.d.).

A proactive approach to aging in place is to incorporate changes when remodeling or interior updating takes place. This may occur well before clients are in need of these modifications. However, doing so early has several advantages:

- It is easier to incorporate modifications when other changes are being made.
- Making changes may be more cost-effective during remodeling.
- Clients who are still working are more able to handle the expense of house modifications than when they are older and living on a fixed income.
- Modifications help accommodate visiting older relatives and family members who become temporarily disabled, as through an accident or illness.

Examples of proactive changes during a bathroom remodel might include adding such features as an elevated toilet; extra reinforcement in the walls for later installation of grab bars; space to allow walker or wheelchair entry; and a large shower stall with a low threshold, built-in shower seat, and height-adjustable showerheads. All these features can be incorporated without giving an "institutional" look, while at the same time preparing the room for possible future needs of aging occupants.

Many of the home modifications recommended by the National Aging in Place Council and other groups are similar to those already mentioned in this chapter or in other chapters. Additional suggestions that designers might suggest to clients of any age who are engaged in remodeling include the following:

- Bathrooms
  - Lowering one of the bathroom sinks and providing knee clearance under-

neath (this can double as a children's sink with a step stool stored beneath)

- Locating bathtubs so a person backing away from a sink is not likely to collide with and fall into the tub

- Avoiding sliding glass doors, which can move when grabbed or used to support the body

- Replacing porcelain bathroom fixtures with those made of polymer, which is easier on the body in case of falls

- Bedrooms
  - Creating closets with hanging rods and shelves at various heights (helpful for people of various heights at any age)
  - Installing sufficient lighting inside closets

- General
  - Installing rocker light switches located 36 to 40 inches above the floor (easier to use when hands are full, as when holding an infant in one arm and a bag of groceries)
  - Installing luminous light switches, especially in bedrooms, bathrooms, and hallways
  - Creating entryways with no steps and very little slope or with a ramp (also helpful with strollers and tricycles or a family member on crutches as a result of a skiing accident)
  - Widening doorways to at least 36 inches wide and putting off-set hinges on doors
  - Installing easy-to-open and -lock patio doors and screens
  - Replacing doorknobs with levered door handles (easier to open when hands are full)
  - Replacing regular thermostats with programmable models
  - Replacing faucets that turn using knobs with levered faucets
  - Using nonglare glass on artwork (makes viewing easier for everyone)
  - Raising electrical outlets higher from the floor

- Kitchen
  - Installing secondary catches in drawers to prevent accidental removal and falls resulting while trying to avoid being hit by a falling drawer and its contents
  - Selecting ranges with controls in the front
  - Installing at least one counter that is about four feet long to allow the person to lean on the counter and still have work space
  - Installing at least one counter about 10 inches below elbow height for tasks such as mixing and kneading dough
  - Creating removable cabinets that can double as serving carts

(Sources: www.seniorsource.com/ageinpl. htm; National Aging in Place Council; Ahmadi & Cotton, 1998; Ahmadi & Earhart, 1997)

Some home modifications would most likely be deferred until the occupants reach older adulthood and/or determine the need for them. These might include creating a bedroom on the main floor where one didn't previously exist; rearranging furniture to accommodate a wheelchair or prevent a person with poor eyesight from bumping into items; adding handrails in hallways; replacing chairs that have individual legs with those that are connected at the floor with bars or have loop-type supports to decrease the danger of tipping a chair and falling onto the upturned legs; replacing gas cooktops with electric to decrease the chance of igniting clothing; adding grab rails to the edges of kitchen counters; and converting a bedroom for live-in help.

As with any design project, the needs of the individuals involved must be considered. Not every adult will experience all the typical changes of aging; and some will have multiple changes that require careful planning and coordination to address all their needs. Designers working with older clients may want to consult an occupational therapist or gerontologist for assistance in creating the most supportive environment possible.

BOX 8.4   EXPRESSED NEEDS OF OLDER ADULTS

Answers from a Gallop poll of people over age 55 about what they might need help doing to stay self-sufficient and comfortable in their environments:

1. Opening medicine packages
2. Reading product labels
3. Reaching high things
4. Vacuuming and dusting
5. Going up and down stairs
6. Cleaning bathtubs and sinks
7. Washing and waxing floors
8. Using a shower or bathtub
9. Moving around the house without slipping or falling

Adapted from: Dychtwalk, Ken, and Joe Flower. (1989). *Age wave.* Los Angeles: Jeremy P. Tarcher, Inc.

Most older adults do very little to change their homes to make them safer and more convenient. Interviews with groups of the elderly have revealed the following reasons for the failure to implement home modifications:

• They have adapted to inconveniences, such as by using a step stool to reach cabinets, and thus do not perceive them as problems. (However, many falls occur from household step stools.)
• They do not know where to look for assistance or how to locate a competent and trustworthy contractor.
• They are concerned about the appearance of modifications and the resale value of their homes.

BOX 8.5   THE SUSTAINABILITY CONNECTION: UNIVERSAL DESIGN

The concept of universal design is at the heart of sustainability because it is proactive in addressing the needs of as many individuals as possible. When incorporated into the initial design and building of a structure, it reduces the need for future modifications that involve removing and replacing parts of the structure. It is also sustainable in terms of human health and well-being by providing features that make the environment user-friendly and supportive.

• They believe the costs would be prohibitive (Ahmadi, et al., 1999).

By being aware of these concerns, designers can better assist their older clients. For example, they can show them how changes can be attractively incorporated into their existing decor. They may know dependable contractors and suppliers and can benefit their clients by helping them avoid repair and home-improvement scams that often target the elderly. Designers should learn about funding resources such as reverse mortgages. Contrary to a traditional mortgage, the home owner receives money rather than paying it out each month. It is still a loan because the amount received is paid back when the house is sold, either before or after the death of the owner. Various financial assistance programs are also available, such as property tax deferrals and the Weather Assistance Program of the U.S. Department of Energy, which pays for the weatherization of homes of low-income persons. Many communities have locally based programs that assist the elderly with home modifications.

Notice how many of the recommendations listed in this section are suitable for people of all ages and abilities. This brings us to the concept of **universal design,** which means creating interiors that are suitable for people of all ages, sizes, and abilities. This would seem to be a sensible overall approach to design because it incorporates building features and elements and products to create interiors that work for everyone. As an example, in a home with occupants ranging from young children to mid-adulthood and visitors including grandparents, the needs of everyone would be better met if sinks and countertops of various heights were available.

Universal design is not the same as "barrier free" design, or meeting the ADA requirements discussed in this chapter. The concept is actually much broader in scope and addresses more than designing for the specific, identified needs of the elderly and disabled. More than removing barriers, its goal is to make interiors more useful and convenient for everyone, including the able-bodied.

OTHER HOME-BASED LIVING ARRANGEMENTS

Some older adults choose to move to smaller houses or condominiums that are more accessible; require less upkeep, especially the outside areas; and are less expensive to maintain (Hansen and Gottschalk, 2006). In this case, they may need assistance from designers to create a comfortable and truly accessible environment in their new surroundings.

When living in one's own home is no longer desirable, practical, or safe, an alternative chosen by some is to move in with others, such as younger family members. Designers can contribute to the success of such moves by creating spaces to comfortably accommodate the older household member(s). In addition to safety, it is suggested that the environment allow as much independence as is desired and possible for the older person (Lee and Callender, 1998). For example, it is best if the person has his or her own bedroom. Ideally, it should have windows to provide natural light, be large enough to have a sitting area and space for visitors, have its own thermostat for temperature control, and have a bathroom either attached or close by. It may also have to be modified somewhat better to meet the needs of its older occupant. (See Figure 8.7.) Changes to the overall home may include adding ramps, handrails on stairs and in hallways, and grab bars in bathrooms. It is important that these additions and changes are as aesthetically pleasing as possible and fit in with the decor of the house. In this way, the older person won't feel as if he or she has institutionalized the home and younger family members won't find the changes unappealing and disruptive.

SPECIALIZED LIVING FACILITIES

Designers may work on facilities built specifically for elderly and disabled persons, such as the following:

- **Adult day-care center:** provides activities, meals, and supervision during the day for adults who need assistance, including older and/or disabled persons
- **Assisted-living residence:** provides housing, meals, and personal care to individuals who need help with daily living activities but do not need daily nursing care
- **Continuing-care community:** provides a variety of living arrangements that support lifestyles as they change from independent living to the need for regular medical and nursing care
- **Long-term care facility** (nursing home): provides nursing and rehabilitative services on a 24-hour basis (Mitchell and Haroun, 2007)

Design Implications for Adult Day-Care Centers

A major problem with these centers is that many of them are housed in facilities originally designed for another purpose. One researcher refers to the prevailing character of most services as that of "the Church Basement," meaning a large, nondescript area in which many activities take place (Moore, n.d.). Because the number of adult day-care centers is likely to

FIGURE 8.7 This room is attractive and provides a healthy environment for young adults. However, it has several features that could present hazards or discomfort to older persons: the rugs present trip hazards, the lamps are placed too far from the bed, the bed is too high off the floor, and the wooden floor is highly reflective.

increase, designers may find themselves in a position to help create environments that are more suitable. This includes differentiating areas so that the visual distractions and feelings of being on display that occur in a large space are reduced; providing a sufficient number of accessible bathrooms; and creating a more personal character for visiting and dining, as by clustering tables in small groups. It is also recommended that transition zones be provided, especially if the center has clients with dementia. These include entryways and exits that are separate from the main activity and dining areas. Above all, designers must consider the characteristics of the population served and the activities planned in order to create center interiors that support each (Moore, n.d.).

Design Implications for Long-Term Facilities

The fear of being "put away" in an institution when they are older is dreaded by many Americans (Friedan, 1993). Studies have shown that many people have very negative perceptions of assisted-living and long-term care facilities. In fact, consumers in general don't perceive assisted-living buildings as being supportive and friendly places (Marsden, 2005). Although efforts have been made to provide needed services, little attempt has been made to learn about the preferences of residents regarding the physical environment (Marsden, 2005). Interviews with older adults and their families have revealed their desire to replicate, as much as possible, feelings of "home." Although a facility that serves a disparate group of residents and is also the workplace for staff cannot truly be "home" for residents, one study identified a number of elements that can be incorporated into the group-living environment to make it more homelike. When photographs of building exteriors and interiors were shown to the study participants, they identified the following preferences:

- Familiar housing cues: elements that reference the single-family house, such as porches, sloped roofs, gables, window shutters, a variety of window shapes and sizes, fireplaces, formal dining rooms, and informal living rooms. Exceptions were features such as covered walkways, not typically found in homes, but which increase usability and comfort of a facility.

- Protective enclosures: layers of enclosure from the site edge to the building interior, including sheltered walkways. Inside, residents prefer areas for eating and relaxing that are not part of the main circulation routes so they don't feel like they are "on display."

- Caring cues: attention to detail in design, such as quoins, lintels, molding, and other ornamentation. Window treatments, outdoor seating, bright cheerful colors, areas that encourage social exchange. Signs of good maintenance, both inside and outside.

- Human scale: variety of features that minimize the scale of the exterior, such as one-story buildings. Inside, examples include small groupings of tables and chairs, small bookcases, and ceilings of standard or only slightly higher height.

- Usability: exterior entries on grade, windows that allow seated persons to see outside, matte finishes to reduce glare, furnishings with padded but firm seating, adequate space to move about, and uniform natural light.

- Naturalness: lush landscaping, interior plants and flowers (not artificial), window views, natural materials such as wood and stone (Marsden, 2005).

Giving residents of group-living facilities as much independence and control over their lives as possible is a key positive influence on their physical health and life quality. Examples of ways designers can promote this include creating a floor plan that encourages residents to move about freely and easily and installing cameras and observation windows, when these are necessary for the safety of residents who might wander off or fall down out of the view of others, in ways that don't give residents a feeling of being watched (Martin, 2002). Also, individual resident rooms should be designed to be as adaptable as possible to the tastes of each new resident so they can, if they desire, bring their own furniture and decorative items (Dobbs, 2004). It has also been suggested that including residents' personal items in common areas creates a homier environment (Martin, 2002).

In addition to autonomy, social interaction and maintaining a personal support system have been identified as major determinants of health and quality of life (Mitchell and Kemp, 2000). As such, designers should create areas that encourage socialization: small groupings of tables and chairs in quiet areas; circulation routes throughout the building that encourage interactions among the residents; and inviting and cozy common rooms where residents can gather and engage in shared activities, such as group discussions, listening to music, making crafts, and playing games.

The final point to be made here about residential facilities is their frequent failure to provide easy access to the outdoors. We know that fresh air and sunshine have health benefits and studies have shown that older adults enjoy spending time outdoors (Rodiek and Fried, 2005). At the same time, outdoor areas in many facilities are either unappealing or inaccessible to residents (Rodiek and Fried, 2005). Features to increase time spent outdoors include easy ingress and egress; paved walkways; covered areas to provide protection from the weather; benches to rest on; fences that don't give the impression of being "locked in"; lots of grass, shrubs, and plants; and views that extend beyond the facility walls to give residents a sense of connection to the world beyond (Rodiek and Fried, 2005). See Figure 8.8 for an example of a well-designed residential facility.

OLDER WORKERS ON THE JOB

An increasing number of older adults are staying on the job beyond the traditional age 65 or are returning to the workplace. In fact, over half of all employed Americans report wanting to work past age 65 (Vital Aging Network, 2006). Reasons behind this trend include better health of older adults, the prospect of

FIGURE 8.8 This residential facility incorporates a homelike look and feel that are reportedly preferred by older adults.

a very long retirement as we live longer, and financial necessity. Also, many older people enjoy their work and are not enthusiastic about giving it up to pursue activities they view as less purposeful. As such, designers must rethink how workplaces accommodate older workers. Many of the changes that increase the safety and efficiency of older workers are in line with good ergonomics, as discussed in Chapter 7, and are relatively easy to put into place:

- Increase illumination and color contrast
- Use larger characters on signs and instructions and larger video displays
- Select appropriate furnishings, such as chairs with arms, in break rooms, cafeterias, and conference rooms
- Design adjustable workstations to fit the stature of various-sized individuals
- Provide seating, as possible, for tasks that normally require lengthy periods of standing
- Store supplies in ways to make heavy lifting unnecessary
- Reduce noise levels
- Lower sound-system pitches, such as on alarms
- Create storage to eliminate the clutter that increases chances for falls
- Install skid-resistant material for flooring and stair treads

BOX 8.6 VIEW TO THE FUTURE

Future Challenges for Universal Design and Accessibility

In the effort to increase accessibility, some ADA requirements have resulted in conflicts. An example is drinking fountains that extend out from walls to enable use by individuals in wheelchairs. A problem quickly developed for blind persons who were unable to detect these protruding fountains with their canes. As a result, accessible drinking fountains are now recessed into walls. Ironically, not all ADA specifications best fulfill the needs of the intended users. Changes based on the desires and multiple needs of the users may be contemplated in the future. Another possibility is that more flexibility will be incorporated into codes to allow for user input.

The ADA is designed principally to increase access to public buildings for persons in wheelchairs. However, these individuals make up a small fraction of the elderly and disabled who can benefit from design focused on increasing their ability to function as independently as possible in all types of built environments, including the home. More research and creative approaches are needed—and expected—in this area.

Many employers are not currently considering how an aging workforce will affect their long-range plans (Head, 2006). As such, designers have an opportunity to bring attention to the need to be proactive, as it is expected that by 2010, almost 17 percent of the American workforce will be 55 or older; by 2014, this group is expected to make up 21 percent of all labor force participants (Rix, 2006). The functional limitations presented by older workers need to be addressed for employers to take advantage of willing, experienced workers, as well as to be in compliance with the Americans with Disabilities Act, discussed later in this chapter.

DESIGNING FOR DISABILITIES

Individuals with disabilities include those who have disabilities throughout their lives and older adults who, because of age-related changes, have lost function. These groups represent a very large number of people who can benefit from the creation of cost-effective built environments adapted to their needs. Because disabling conditions are not always obvious, designers need to observe their clients and tactfully discuss with them any special needs that can be addressed by good design. The need to carefully listen and observe cannot be overemphasized because many people who experience gradual changes over time, such as hearing loss, may not notice the loss of function. It is also not uncommon for them to be in denial about it, such as when they insist that the television, painfully loud for everyone else in the room, is set at a normal volume. In these cases, designers must use tact and present suggestions for accommodations in the context of good design rather than as remediation.

Designers must also keep in mind that each disability situation is unique and that while guidelines exist for dealing with various classes of disabilities, design considerations must be tailored to the individual. This is especially true with clients who have more than one disability or in environments used by people who have a variety of disabling conditions. Also be aware that some accommodations that assist one person make life more difficult for another. For example, when curb cuts for wheelchairs were first installed, it was discovered that some visually impaired individuals, who depended on the curb as their cue to wait and listen for traffic, were stepping into the roadway without stopping. (This has since been remedied by the addition of a textured surface or railings to indicate a pathway into a street.) In another example, some facilities have lowered the placement of switches and controls so that persons in wheelchairs can reach them. Again, this is disorienting to the visually impaired person who expects to find them at the standard height.

The fact is that the number of clients with disabilities is going to increase in number. This is due, in part, to successful advancements in medicine that have enabled more people to survive events such as premature birth, car accidents, and strokes, but leave them with a disabling condition. This means that what was once a specialized area of design is now, and will become even more so, an area that all good designers must be able to address competently.

BOX 8.7 EXPERT SPOTLIGHT: Unique Needs of People Who Are Disabled

". . . A split level, which is a common way of building in this town, it seems. It creates all kinds of headaches; there are either four or five steps up and four or five steps down to get to the lower level from the entrance. It is nearly impossible for me to get in with my wheelchair, even for visiting . . . unless they literally carry me in."

(from Keith, a person with a disability, describing the houses on his street.)

Shauna Corry, PhD
Assistant Professor
IDEC, EDRA
University of Idaho
College of Art and Architecture
Department of Architecture and
Interior Design

How would you feel if you could not attend the funeral of a close friend because the restroom in the mortuary was not accessible? How would it affect you if you could not go to dinner at a friend or relative's house because the entrance had steps? These are situations that people with mobility disabilities face on a daily basis. The ability to interact with friends, spend the day shopping, or attend important life events is often denied by the design of the built environment. These situations vividly point out that issues of accessibility and visitability and the potential of not being able to function in an environment have a profoundly negative impact on quality of life for people with disabilities. Ultimately, the inability to participate equally in daily life activities can contribute to social isolation and a reduction in an individual's sense of self-identity and self-worth.

Practical Solution

Although there are numerous regulations that address accessibility in public places, people with disabilities still are excluded from major life activities because of physical barriers. Historically, solutions for this problem have been addressed by visionary organizations such as Adaptive Environments, the Center for Universal Design, and Concrete Change. However, the ultimate goal of creating an inclusive built environment will not be achieved easily.

A step toward meeting this goal is to increase understanding among professional designers, building owners, and society in general about the unique needs of people with disabilities. Such increased understanding would enhance the chances for systemic change and heighten awareness of discrimination in the built environment among these groups. If designers truly comprehend that they are responsible for another person's inability to participate fully in life, they should strive to solve the problem.

Empathetic exercises are often successful in communicating the challenges a person with a disability confronts daily. I have had jaded college students and naive fifth graders return from a sensitivity training exercise outraged that they could not shut the stall door in an "accessible" bathroom. That revelation is truly an "aha" moment and results in a much greater understanding of diverse user needs. Spending time with a person with a disability is also helpful in illuminating their unique needs. Experiencing daily struggles along with them even briefly underscores the challenges they face every minute of every day in negotiating the built environment.

Although the solution seems simple, learning about the unique needs of others and applying that knowledge requires a concentrated and sustained effort by all of us. Knowing that it will result in inclusive and democratic environments that treat all users equally should keep us on task and moving toward the future. A future where Keith will have the ability to visit his neighbors, and all people will have the opportunity to participate fully in life events.

AMERICANS WITH DISABILITIES ACT OF 1990

CAVEAT: The following is not to be regarded in any manner as legal advice. The laws referenced are simply some of the statutes affecting design mandates and are hereunder used to alert the reader to the existence of certain legal requirements in design.

Americans have become increasingly sensitive to the needs of individuals with disabilities over the last 80 years, initiated to a great degree by the return of large numbers of soldiers who suffered disabling injuries in World War I. Starting in the 1920s, public awareness, supported by legislative requirements, has steadily recognized the rights of people who have a wide range of disabilities, including physical, cognitive, emotional, and behavioral. This awareness has been translated into a variety of legislation, which culminated with the **Americans with Disabilities Act of 1990 (ADA),** a sweeping set of regulations whose goal is to ensure access for all Americans to all built environments and public services (Kopec, 2005). This means that designing with the needs of disabled and aging individuals in mind is not only the right thing to do, it is, in the case of public facilities and accommodations, the legal thing to do.

The ADA is the most recent in a number of government actions to more fully include disabled members of society who were previously kept hidden from public view. Today, on the contrary, disabled persons are encouraged to be as active and productive as their conditions permit, but they can only do so if public facilities are accessible to them. Under the ADA, this access is now a civil right. Because of the wide scope of the ADA and its influence on the built environment, it is essential that designers have a basic understanding of this act and what it encompasses. Lack of awareness has resulted in many construction and alteration projects, including those built by local governments, being inaccessible. As a consequence, some projects have been halted in midconstruction and others have had to be torn out and redone, both of which increase expense, inconvenience, and, in some cases, public ill will. Noncompliance can also result in being sued by the federal Department of Justice, the enforcement agency of the ADA.

The ADA is organized into five titles, listed in Table 8.4, each dealing with a specific area. Of these, Titles I, II, and III have the most impact on the built environment. Title I, whose principal purpose is to prevent employment

TABLE 8.4 THE FIVE ADA TITLES

Title I	Employment	Prohibits discrimination against applicants and employees because of a disability. Requires employers to make **reasonable accommodations** for disabled employees.
Title II	Public Services	Requires that public transportation and state and local government buildings and services be accessible.
Title III	Private Entities	Prohibits discrimination by places of public accommodation and services and commercial facilities.
Title IV	Telecommunications	Requires that relay services be provided for hearing- and speech-impaired people.
Title V	Miscellaneous Provisions	General and administrative provisions.

Adapted from: Harmon, S. K. (2005). *ADA guidelines: Past, present, and future.* Washington, DC: National Council for Interior Design Qualification.

TABLE 8.5 PLACES OF PUBLIC ACCOMMODATION

CATEGORY	EXAMPLES
Place of Lodging	Hotel, motel
Food or Drink Establishment	Restaurant, bar
Exhibition or Entertainment Facility	Movie theater, concert hall
Place of Public Gathering	Convention center, auditorium
Sales or Rental Establishment	Department store, supermarket
Service Establishment	Health clinic, beauty salon
Public Transportation Station	Train station, airport
Place of Public Display or Collection	Museum, library
Place of Recreation	Park, zoo
Place of Education	School, university
Social Service Center Establishment	Homeless shelter, children's day-care center
Place of Exercise or Recreation	Health club, golf course

Adapted from: Harmon, S. K. (2005). *ADA guidelines: Past, present, and future.* Washington, DC: National Council for Interior Design Qualification.

discrimination based on disability, may require an employer to make certain modifications to enable access for employees who are otherwise qualified to do their jobs. Examples include building a ramp, providing a workstation that can be used by a person in a wheelchair, enlarging the restrooms, and adding Braille to signage.

Title III, which addresses private entities and public accommodations, is very broad in scope, essentially including most nonresidential facilities that are open to the public. Categories and examples of public accommodations are listed in Table 8.5. There are some exceptions, which is why consulting the regulations is very important when planning any new construction or alterations. For example, places of lodging are exempt from the legislation if there are five or fewer guest rooms for rent and the proprietor lives in the building. Therefore, the exemption might apply to a small bed-and-breakfast facility. (At the same time, there may be applicable local codes regarding accessibility.) Also, a structure may be exempt from certain requirements if the site is such that features, such as an on-grade entrance, cannot be safely built. However, assumptions should

never be made about possible exemptions: always consult the proper regulatory authority.

The ADA requirements that ensure the highest level of accessibility are required for all new construction. **New construction** is defined as a new building, work done to fill in a gutted building, or the addition of tenant space in an existing building (Harmon, 2005). When accessibility features are included in the original designs, the cost is almost always less than making the needed changes for compliance later. Alterations to existing buildings must be accessible to the "maximum extent feasible" (Harmon, 2005, p. 47). **Alterations** are defined as changes that affect the usability of a facility. For example, if an entryway is moved or remodeled, it must be made fully accessible, regardless of the age of the building. And if the new entryway makes any previously accessible areas inaccessible, this must be corrected.

Existing buildings that house **places of accommodation** are not expected to meet all the technical standards set by the ADA, but nevertheless must engage in **barrier removal** to enable disabled individuals to use the facility (see Figure 8.9). Barrier removal is required if it is "readily achievable," which means it can

FIGURE 8.9A AND B
Examples of accessible features in the built environment.

be accomplished without much difficulty and/ or expense. This, of course, leaves much open to interpretation because the regulations do not define how much effort and expense must be expended to fulfill the requirements of the law. Title III does, however, include a list of priorities to consider when planning barrier-removal projects:

- Priority 1: Accessible approach and entrance
- Priority 2: Access to goods and services
- Priority 3: Access to restrooms
- Priority 4: Any other measures necessary (Adaptive Environments, 1995)

Americans with Disabilities Act Accessibility Guidelines (ADAAG)

The Americans with Disabilities Act itself is quite broad and contains vague language, a characteristic that is typical of this type of federal legislation that is trying to address a wide range of conditions. This does present a problem, however, because the act lends itself to various interpretations, which results in building owners, architects, and designers often being confused and at odds about how to correctly implement the regulations. To provide more specific minimum standards, the Access Board, which is the administrative body of the ADA, developed the **Americans with Disabilities Act Accessibilities Guidelines (ADAAG).** Although helpful, the ADAAG standards sometimes conflict because of the different needs for various disabilities, as dis-

cussed previously. Even so, it is recommended that designers become familiar with the overall content of ADAAG so they can refer to it as needed.

Designers should be aware that new standards, known as the ADA-ABA Accessibility Guidelines, are currently being reviewed for approval by federal agencies. Until they are approved, however, ADAAG remains in force. It is recommended that the new guidelines be reviewed. With standards that are completely new, such as those addressing the needs of disabled children, it is good policy to incorporate them into designs in anticipation of their final approval (Harmon, 2005).

Examples of barrier-removal projects, including technical specifications from ADAAG, are listed in Table 8.6. These are not intended to provide the final word on specific requirements, but are included here to show the scope and type of requirements and standards contained in the ADA and ADAAG. Before proceeding on any project, it is essential that the designer review all the potentially applicable codes and regulations.

Areas of Confusion

In addition to exceptions to the regulations and the broad nature of the ADA and some of the ADAAG language, there are other factors that make implementation of the ADA challenging, such as the complexity of some regulations. For example, some parts of buildings must be accessible while other parts do not have this requirement. For example, this might

TABLE 8.6   EXAMPLES OF BARRIER REMOVAL USING ADAAG SPECIFICATIONS

ELEMENT/ BARRIER	REQUIREMENTS	SUGGESTIONS AND TECHNICAL SPECIFICATIONS
Entrance must be accessible to people with a variety of disabilities, such as impaired mobility and blindness	• Route that does not involve stairs or steps • Walkways that don't have obstacles • Cane-detectable warning devices • Door that is wide enough for wheelchair entry • Space for persons using wheelchairs, walkers, or crutches to open the door • Door can be opened by persons with limited hand use	• Curb cuts or small ramps with textured surface to indicate where they begin and end • Ramp with a slope no greater than 1:12 • Railings between 34 and 38 inches high on ramps longer than 6 feet • Route at least 36 inches wide • Protruding objects on walkways at least 27 inches off the ground • Objects hanging overhead at least 80 inches off the ground • Entry door at least 32 inches clear • Entry door with at least 18 inches of space on the handle side
Parking	• Adequate parking spaces for those with disabilities • Accessible parking located near accessible entry, including pathway	• Space requirements: Total spaces: Access spaces 1 to 25　　　　1 26 to 50　　　2 51 to 75　　　3 76 to 100　　 4 • 1 of every 8 accessible spaces must be van accessible
Signs for goods and services	• Appropriate signs for people who are blind or have limited vision	• Raised characters between 5/8 and 2 inches high with high contrast • Text of sign information, including that on pictograms, in Braille
Restrooms	• Accessible to persons using wheelchairs • Usable by persons with muscular weakness or problems with balance • Identifiable by visually impaired persons	• Doorways at least 32 inches clear • One stall at least 5 feet square • Grab bars behind and on the side wall nearest the toilet • Toilet seat 17 to 19 inches high • Soap and towel dispensers within reach and operable with one fist • Clear text rather than ambiguous symbols to identify restrooms • Tactile signage identifying restrooms in addition to text

Adapted from: Adaptive Environments Center, Inc. and Barrier Free Environments, Inc. (1995). Checklist for Existing Facilities. Retrieved November 30, 2006, from www.usdoj.gov/crt/ada/racheck.pdf.

apply to a cookie manufacturing facility that is not considered to be a place of public accommodation but which offers public tours. In this case, the areas entered by the public must be barrier free or, in the case of a newly built factory, fully accessible. Another problem is the existence of state and local codes that sometimes conflict with ADA requirements. The general rule in these cases is that the most stringent standard must be used. Finally, there are often disagreements about who is responsible for identifying the applicable requirements: the property owner, renter or lessee, architect, or designer. It is essential that someone assume the responsibility because with ADA regulations being enforced by the federal Department of Justice, disregarding them can be costly.

It is not expected that designers will know all the guidelines for all types of buildings; rather, the examples in this chapter are presented to emphasize the need to be aware of the various guidelines and standards in existence, as well as the need to research prevailing accessibility requirements of any projects undertaken.

GLOSSARY TERMS

Absorption
Accessibility
Activities of daily living
Adult day-care center
Age-related changes
Alteration (Americans with Disabilities Act of 1990)
Americans with Disabilities Act Accessibility Guidelines
Americans with Disabilities Act of 1990
Assisted-living residence
Barrier removal
Cellular migration
Continuing-care community
Dendritic trimming
Differentiation
Disability
Fetal alcohol syndrome
Gestation
Life quality
Long-term care facility
Metabolism
Myelin sheath
Myelination
New construction (Americans with Disabilities Act of 1990)
Places of public accommodation
Range of motion
Reasonable accommodation
Synaptogenesis
Universal design

LEARNING ACTIVITIES

1. Design a bedroom that can be adapted to the needs of a child from birth to age sixteen in a sustainable way. Draw a floor plan and provide suggested colors, decor, and furnishings for the child at the following ages: infant, three, six, twelve, and sixteen. (Your designs should be for either a girl or boy.)

2. Visit a child day-care center, preschool, or school to investigate its appropriateness for the physical development of children. Write a summary of your findings, including suggestions for improvements. Include rationale for your suggestions.

3. Collect information and create a resource file of local contractors, services, suppliers, and products for making homes accessible.

4. Choose a private home to study in terms of its potential for aging in place. For each room, garage, and exterior, create a list of suggestions that would make the home safer and more convenient for aging adults. Then indicate which recommendations are more in line with universal design and could be implemented in advance; and which would be better implemented once specific changes occur and needs have been identified.

5. Investigate government programs and local funding resources available for helping the elderly and the disabled make needed modifications to their homes.

6. Visit a public building and imagine yourself to be negotiating your visit in a wheelchair. Write a description of its accessibility, including positive points and any areas you find in need of improvement.

SUGGESTED WEB SITES

1. U.S. Environmental Protection Agency America's Children and the Environment www.epa.gov/envirohealth/children
This government site contains links to dozens of pages covering trends in contamination, measurements of contaminants in the bodies of mothers and children, and environmentally influenced diseases in children.

2. AARP
www.aarp.org
Click on the "Family, Home, & Legal" tab, then on "Home Design" for information on universal design, specific home safety issues, and recommendations for various rooms in the home.

3. Senior Resources
http://seniorresource.com

Find information on aging in place, housing alternatives, physical changes that accompany aging, suggestions for home remodeling.

4. ADA Technical Assistance Centers
ADA Document Portal
www.ADAportal.org.
This portal contains links to more than 7,400 documents related to the ADA. It can be searched by keyword or by using the categories created to organize the materials.

5. U.S. Department of Justice
www.usdoj.gov/crt/ada/stdspdf.htm
From this site, you can view and/or download the ADA Code of Federal Regulations.

REFERENCES

AARP. (n. d.) *Kitchen checklist.* Retrieved November 26, 2006, from ww.aarp.org/families/home_design/kitchen/a2004-03-02-k-checklist.html

AARP, (n.d.). *Safety, lighting, and storage: closets.* Retrieved November 26, 2006 from www.aarp.org/families/home_design/safety_lighting/a2004-03-02-s-closet.html

Adaptive Environments (August 1995). *The Americans with Disabilities Act: Checklist for readily achievable barrier removal.* [Pamphlet] Washington, D.C.: National Institute on Disability and Rehabilitation Research.

Ahmadi, R., Stafford, P. B., & Earhart, C. (1999). *Home modifications: A market-based approach.* Retrieved August 22, 2007, from www.bsu.edu/classes/ahmadi/article1.html

Ahmadi, R., & Cotton, S. (1998). Lowering injury rates of LTC residents. First appeared in *Canadian Health Care Management,* April 1998, pages 44-45. Retrieved August 22, 2007, from www.bsu.edu/classes/ahmadi/article3.html

Ahmadi, R., & Earhart, C. (1997). Kitchen design improves quality of life, offers independence. First appeared in *Long Term Care Monitor,* April 1997, pages 26-28. Retrieved August 22, 2007, from www.bsu.edu/classes/ahmadi/article4.html

Alexander, N. B., Gross, M. M., Medell, J. M., & Hofmeyer, M. R. (2001). Effects of functional ability and training on chair-rise biomechanics in older adults. *Journal of Gerontology: Medical Sciences,* 56A, 9, M538-M547.

American Academy of Pediatrics, (July 26, 2000). *Joint statement on the impact of entertainment violence on children: Congressional public health statement.* Retrieved September 15, 2006 from www.aap.org/advocacy/realeases/jstmtevc.htm

Anderson, C. A. and Dill, K. E. (2000). Video games and aggressive thoughts, feelings, and behavior in the laboratory and in life. *Journal of Personality and Social Psychology,* 78, 4, 772-790.

Attention Deficit Disorder Association. (1998). *Fact sheet on attention deficit hyperactivity disorder.* Retrieved September 2006, from www.add.org/articles/factsheet.html

Bearer, C. (1995). Environmental health hazards: How children are different from adults. *Future of Children,* 5, 2, 11-26.

Berger, K. S. (1980.) *The developing person.* New York: Worth Publishers.

Brabyn, J. A., Haegerström-Portnoy, G., Schneck, M. E., & Lott, L. A. (2000). Visual impairments in elderly people under everyday viewing conditions. *Journal of Visual Impairment and Blindness,* 94, 12, 741-755.

Campbell, D. (2002). *Mozart effect for children: Awakening your child's mind, health, and creativity with music.* New York, NY: Quill (Imprint of HarperCollins Publishers).

Carpenter, S. (2001). Sleep deprivation may be undermining teen health. *Monitor on Psychology, 32,* No. 9. Retrieved September 22, 2006, from www.apa.org/monitor/oct01/sleepteen.html

Carskadon, M. (1999). When worlds collide: Adolescent need for sleep versus societal demands. *Phi Delta Kappan,* 80, 5, 348-353.

Child Development Institute, (n.d.). *Television and children.* Retrieved September 14, 2006 from www.childdevelopmentinfo.com/health_safety/television.shtml

Children Now. (2001). *Fair play? Violence, gender and race in video games.* Los Angeles, CA: Children Now.

Craven, J. (2003). *The healthy home: Beautiful interiors that enhance the environment and your well-being.* Gloucester, MA: Rockport Publishers, Inc.

Dobbs, D. (2004). The adjustment to a new home. *Journal of Housing for the Elderly.* 18, 1, 51-71.

Dychtwald, K., & Flower, J. (1989). *Age wave.* Los Angeles: Jeremy P. Tarcher, Inc.

Eisenberg, M. E., Olson, R. F., Neumark-Sztainer, D., Story, M., & Bearinger, L. H. (2004). The correlations between family meals and psychosocial well-being of adolescents. *Archives of Pediatrics and Adolescent Medicine,* 158, 8, 792-796.

Elias, M. (April 2004). *Frequent TV watching shortens kids' attention spans.* USA Today. Retrieved September 15, 2006 from www.usatoday.com/news/health/2004-04-05-tv-kids-attention-usat_x.htm

Eliot, L. (1999). *What's going on in there? How the brain and mind develop in the first five years of life.* New York, NY: Bantam Books.

Friedan, B. (1993). *The fountain of age.* New York, NY: Simon and Schuster.

Fujioka, T., Ross, B., Kakigi, R., Pantev, C., & Trainor, L. J. (2006). One year of musical training affects development of auditory cortical-evoked fields in young children. *Brain: A Journal of Neurology,* 129, 10, 2593-2608.

Gentile, D. A., Lynch, P. J., Linder, J. R., & Walsh, D. A. (2004). The effects of violent video game habits on adolescent hostility, aggressive behaviors, and school performance. *Journal of Adolescence,* 27, 1, 5-22.

Gentile, D. A. & Walsh, D.A. (2002). A normative study of family media habits. *Journal of Applied Developmental Psychology,* 23, 2, 157-178.

Hansen, E.B., & Gottschalk, G., (2006). What makes older people consider moving house and what makes them move? *Housing, Theory and Society.* 21, 1, 34-54.

Harmon, S.K. (2005). *ADA guidelines: Past, present, and future.* Washington, D.C.: National Council for Interior Design Qualification.

Hawryluk, M. (2006, September 28). Studies show learning music might boost IQ. *The Bulletin,* p. E1. (Bend, Oregon newspaper).

Head, L. (2006). *Workplace Accommodations for older workers: An examination of employer practice.* Presentation at Conference 2006. California State University at Northridge. (call for conference title). Retrieved December 3, 2006, from www.csun.edu/cod/conf/2006/proceedings/2776.htm

Jaksa, P. (1998). *Fact sheet on attention deficit hyperactivity disorder (ADHD/ADD).* [Fact Sheet]. Pottstown, PA: Attention Deficit Disorder Association.

Johnson, J. G., Cohen, P., Kasen, S., First, M. B., & Brook, J. S. (2004). Association between television viewing and sleep problems during adolescence and early adulthood. *Archives of Pediatrics and Adolescent Medicine,* 158, 6, 562-568.

Kaiser Family Foundation, (May 24, 2006). *New study shows how kids' media use helps parents cope,* [news release]. Retrieved September 22, 2006 from www.kff.org/entmedia/entmedia052406nr.cfm

Kopec, DAK. (2006). *Designing for the elderly population: The Americans with Disabilities Act and its implications for an aging america.* Washington, D.C.: American Society of Interior Designers.

Kotlikoff, L. J. & Burns, S. (2005). *The coming generational storm.* Cambridge, MA: The MIT Press.

Lee, A. J., & Callender, M. (1998). *The complete guide to eldercare.* Hauppauge, NY: Barrons Educational Series, Inc.

Lowe, L A., Woodcock, A., Murray, C. S., Morris, J., Simpson, A. & Custovic, A. (2004). Lung function at age 3 years: Effect of pet ownership and exposure to indoor allergens. *Archives of Pediatric and Adolescent Medicine.* 158, 10, 996-1001.

Marsden, J. P. (2005). *Humanistic design of assisted living.* Baltimore, MD: The Johns Hopkins University Press.

Martin, P.Y. (2002). Sensations, bodies, and the 'spirit of a place': Aesthetics in residential organizations for the elderly. *Human Relations,* 55, 7, 861-885.

McFadyen, B. J. & Price, F. (2002). Avoidance and accommodation of surface height changes by healthy, community-dwelling, young, and elderly men. *Journal of Gerontology: Biological Sciences.* 57A, 4, B166-B174.

Medline Plus. (Last updated November 6, 2006). *Age-related hearing loss.* Retrieved July 31, 2006 from www.nlm.nih.gov/medlineplus/ency/article/001045.htm

Medline Plus, (Last updated July 3, 2004). *Aging changes in the senses.* Retrieved October 14, 2006 from nlm.nih.gov/medlineplus/ency/article/004013.htm

Michell, J. & Haroun, L. (2007). *Introduction to health care.* Clifton Park, NY: Thomson Delmar Learning.

Mitchell, J. M., & Kemp, B. J. (2000). Quality of life in assisted living homes: A multidimensional analysis. *Journal of Gerontology: Psychological Sciences.* 55B, 2, P117-P127.

Moore, K. D. (n.d.) *Design guidelines for adult day services.* Retrieved August 21, 2007, from www.aia.org/SiteObjects/files/Diaz_Moore_color.pdf

National Aging in Place Council. (n.d.) *Making your home senior friendly.* Retrieved December 1, 2007, from www.naipc.org/AGuidetoAginginPlace/MakingYourHome-SeniorFriendly/tabid/76/Default.aspx

National Institute of Arthritis and Musculoskeletal and Skin Diseases. (Revised December 2005). *Kids and their bones: A guide for parents.* Accessed December 1, 2007, from http://www.niams.nih.gov/Health_Info/Bone/Bone_Health/Juvenile/default.asp

National Sleep Foundation, (2000). *Adolescent sleep needs and patterns:* Research report and resource guide. Washington, D.C.: National Sleep Foundation.

Neighbors, M. & Tannehille-Jones, R. (1999). *Human diseases.* Clifton Park, NY: Thomson Delmar Learning.

Nemours Foundation, (Updated last September 2005). *Sudden Infant Death Syndrome.* Retrieved October 5, 2006 from www.kidshealth.org/parent/general/sleep/sids.html.

Phillips, D. (2002). *Designs for a healthy home: An eco-friendly approach.* San Francisco, CA: SOMA Books.

Rehabilitation Research and Training Center on Disability Demographics and Statistics, (2005). *2005 disability status reports.* Ithaca, NY: Cornell University.

Rix, (April 2006). Update on the aged 55+ worker: 2005. *Data Digest* [Newsletter] Washington, D.C.: AARP Public Policy Institute.

Robinson, T. N. (August 2001). Television viewing and child obesity. *Pediatric Clinics of North America,* 48, 4, 1017-25.

Rodiek, S. D., & Fried, J. T. (2005). Access to the outdoors: Using photographic comparison to assess preferences of assisted living residents. *Landscape and Urban Planning.* 73, 2-3, 184-199.

Senior Source. (n.d.) *Aging in place.* Retrieved December 1, 2007, from www.seniorsource.com/ageinpl.htm

Slay, D. H. (2002). Home-based environmental lighting assessments for people who are visually impaired: Developing techniques and tools. *Journal of Visual Impairment and Blindness,* 96, 2, 109-115.

Tilley, A. R., & Henry Dreyfuss Associates, (2002). *The measure of man and woman: Human factors in design.* New York: John Wiley & Sons.

Vital Aging Network. *Fact sheet about older workers.* (2006). University of Minnesota. Retrieved December 3, 2006, from www.van.umn.edu/options/2b5_factsheet.asp

Wade, N, (Ed.), (1998). *The Science Times book of the brain.* New York, NY: The Lyons Press.

Walsh, D., Gentile, D., Walsh, E., Bennett, N., Robideau, B., Walsh, M., Strickland, S., & McFadden, D., (November 29, 2005). *Tenth annual MediaWise: Video game report.* Retrieved September 24, 2006 from www.mediafamily.org/research/report_vgrc_2005.shtml

Weihong, Y., Holland, S. K., Cecil, K. M., Dietrich, K. N., Wessel, S. D., Altaye, M., Hornung, R. W., Ris, D., Egelhoff, J. C., and Lanphear, B. P. (September 2006). The impact of early childhood lead exposure on brain organization: A functional magnetic resonance imaging study of language function. *Pediatrics,* 118, 3, 971-977.

Weinstein, C.S., and David, T.G., (Eds) (1987). *Spaces for children: The built environment and child development.* New York, NY: Plenum Press.

CHAPTER **9**

Safety Considerations

LEARNING OBJECTIVES

1. **Explain how the potential for various types of accidents changes over the life span.**
2. **Describe the various types of hazards that designers should consider when planning the built environment.**
3. **Provide examples of how good design can help prevent injuries and deaths in the built environment.**

Accidents have claimed human lives since the dawn of time. In the beginning of human history, hunters were often injured while trying to capture their prey or when they became the prey of another dangerous animal. Other injuries were caused by fallen trees or branches, rocks, and wet areas, often resulting in abrasions, punctures, or lacerations, which, if they became infected, could mean the death of the individual. Through much of history, unanticipated events were viewed as God's will and, as such, humans were powerless to avoid them. Over time, much of civilization as we know it has assumed personal control over life and worked to discover ways to prevent both accidents and illness.

At the same time, the development of the built environment, in spite of the protection and comfort it can afford, has created many additional sources of injury and has done little to eliminate the more mundane causes of injury. In fact, five of the six current leading causes of unintentional injuries and death in the United States are falls, poisoning, choking, drowning, and fire (National Safety Council, 2006, "Injury Facts"), many of which occur within the home. Although our homes have become safe havens from nature's elements, we are still at risk of injury and death from daily activities. In some cases, the built environment has actually increased the potential for injury. As mentioned previously, homes are the scene of many injuries: 13,592,000 injuries in 1997, or approximately 42 percent of all injuries requiring medical attention (National Safety Council, 2006, "Injury Facts"). In addition, approximately 18,000 people were killed by injury in the seven-year period between 1992 and 1999 (Allen, 2005). Workplaces are also the site of millions of accidents and several thousand deaths each year.

Designers can make a positive contribution to the promotion of safety in homes, workplaces, and public buildings by taking into account safety concerns and risk factors during the developmental design process. Notwithstanding, when making suggestions regarding safety and injury prevention, designers must be sensitive to the needs, preferences, and life circumstances of their clients because these factors strongly affect how people will react to prevention efforts (National Center for Injury Prevention and Control, 2006). It is therefore important for designers to get to know their clients and understand the individual and age-related concerns of those who will occupy the home or use a facility. In addition, they will want to know how long the occupants are likely to reside in a home, specific issues and concerns that an invited visitor might have (disabled person or small child, for example), and what kinds of activities will be pursued in the environment. Although some safety features are more germane to certain ages and individuals, good design should be universal and address the needs of people throughout their lives.

SAFETY OVER THE LIFE SPAN

We are all at risk for accidents related to the built environment as we carry out our daily activities of moving about, working, cooking, cleaning, and playing. Children and older adults are especially vulnerable. Within these two groups, the individuals most prone to having and dying from household accidents are under five years of age or older than 74. This is due, in large part, to their physical and developmental stages. It is also related to the quantity of time people of these ages spend in the home as compared to school-age children and the young and mid-adult population.

Children

Infants, of course, are totally dependent on others to provide for their safety, so their environment must be carefully planned to prevent accidents during those times when they are left alone, such as during the night in their crib. Starting at about ten months, children develop the ability to creep and crawl and, in some cases, even to walk. Thus, they are typically able to move about long before they acquire the **cognitive** abilities to judge the safety of situations. In other words, they are often able to leap before they know to look. Neither are

toddlers and young children completely physically developed, so they are prone to coordination problems that cause them to fall and bump into things (National Center for Injury Prevention and Control, 2006). A related problem is their lack of experience in knowing what is safe and what is dangerous: the surface of a hot stove, for example, doesn't look any more dangerous to them than the cool surface of a refrigerator door. Due to their intense curiosity and desire to explore their world, they are inclined to investigate both the surfaces. Likewise, when practicing their **motor skills,** bookshelves and tables are just as attractive for climbing as playground equipment designed for that purpose. In the toddler's mind, the table and bookshelf appear perfectly stable and unlikely to fall over.

Young children tend to be in a hurry and enjoy running, an activity that increases their risk for falls and collisions. This is particularly problematic when designing smaller homes and areas that are crowded with furnishings. In these situations, designers can help their clients determine what is really necessary and eliminate (or at least store until children are older) unnecessary pieces of furniture and other items that take up space. Baby- and toddler-proofing all areas of the home, discussed in more detail in the following sections on specific types of injuries, is an important way that designers can contribute to the health and well-being of children as they grow and mature.

Older children and teens are also susceptible to injuries. Major risk factors for these age groups are, as in younger children, incomplete cognitive development and inexperience. These deficits can present dangers for teens in particular because their physical size and strength are close to adult levels. As such, they are apt to be driving motor vehicles, using machinery, and engaging in unsupervised sports and activities. Also, their impulsiveness, inability to judge the safety of a situation, and willingness to engage in risk-taking behaviors can result in tragedy. Two examples illustrate these behaviors: half of all drownings of young males are alcohol-related and only 35 percent of high school students report that they

TABLE 9.1 CAUSES OF ACCIDENTAL INJURY DEATHS
THE NUMBERS RANK THE INCIDENCE OF THE INJURIES WITHIN EACH AGE GROUP.

AGE GROUP	DROWNING	FALLS	FIREARMS	FIRES, FLAMES	CHOKING ON FOOD OR OBJECT	MECHANICAL SUFFOCATION	MOTOR VEHICLE	NATURAL HEAT OR COLD	POISONING
Under 1 year	3			5	4	1	2		
1–4	2			3	4	5	1		
5–14	2		5	3		4	1		
15–24	3	5	4				1		2
25–34	3	4		5			1		2
35–44	4	3		5			1		2
45–54	4	3		5			1		2
55–64		2		4	5		1		3
65–74		2		4	3		1		5
75 and older		1		4	3		2	5	

Source of data: National Safety Council. (2002). *Injury Facts®, 2002 Edition.* Itasca, IL: Author.

always wear their seat belt (National Center for Injury Prevention and Control, 2006). Thus, home safety considerations, such as securing firearms in gun safes—discussed later in this chapter—continue to be important for children of all ages.

Older Adults

The physical changes that accompany aging, discussed in Chapter 8, are major factors in making older adults more vulnerable to injuries. A number of specific changes are responsible for increasing the risk of accidents, including a decrease in muscle mass that results in weakness, a condition often exacerbated by lack of physical exercise (National Institute of Arthritis and Musculoskeletal and Skin Diseases, 2005; National Center for Injury Prevention and Control, 2005). Osteoarthritis and other degenerative diseases of the joints also inhibit mobility. Poor balance increases the risk of accidents, especially falls.

All these risk factors can be mitigated by physical exercise, which increases muscle and nerve communication, thus improving both coordination and balance (Dahm & Smith,

2005). Further, muscles and tendons have sensory receptors called **proprioceptors** that play a key role in maintaining balance by sensing changes in tension and pressure and then relaying this information to the central nervous system. The practice of a special form of physical exercise, called proprioceptor training, can improve balance (Dahm & Smith, 2005). Another type of exercise shown to be very effective in increasing strength and improving balance is tai chi (Wolf, 1996; Li, 2005). Practiced throughout China, tai chi is an ancient form of martial arts that involves gentle circular movements combined with deep breathing. As designers, we are thus provided with additional reasons for providing appropriate spaces in homes and other environments used by seniors. In addition to conditions that inhibit free movement, diminished eyesight contributes to the incidence of accidents among the elderly. Good lighting, discussed in Chapter 7 and later in this chapter, can play a major role in preventing accidents in this population.

Table 9.1 shows the top five causes of accidental death for various age groups in 1999. Box 9.1 lists, ranked in order of occurrence, the top eight injuries treated in hospital emergency rooms in 2000 for all ages combined. Accidents related to the built environment, along with design strategies to aid in their prevention, are discussed in the following sections of this chapter.

FALLS

Our environment, both natural and built, contains a wide variety of surfaces and grades, so nearly everyone is at risk for a fall. In fact, when all age groups were combined in 1999, falls were the leading cause of unintentional injury hospitalizations and deaths after motor vehicle crashes (National Safety Council, 2002, "Injury Facts"). More specifically, falls are a significant cause of injury among children; the rate declines during adulthood until about age 70, when it rises dramatically and becomes the leading cause of accidental death (National Safety Council, 2002, "Injury Facts").

Children are frequently the victims of falls, many of which involve tumbling from one height to another, such as falling down stairs, off of furniture, or out a window. For infants, the greatest risks for falls occur on stairs, furniture, and baby walkers (Holtzman, 2005). Falls from windows present the greatest risk for toddlers (Holtzman, 2005). Children younger than five are especially prone to these accidents during the summer months (Morgan, 2003). Similarly, balconies present another high risk for falls. Finally, furniture presents a less obvious but common fall hazard for children. This is because once they can climb, anything that presents an opportunity to do so is fair game for young children.

Implications for Designers

It is important to consider all aspects of indoor environments that may present fall hazards for children. For example, to ensure the safety of infants and very young children, select furnishings that meet Juvenile Products Manufacturer's Association (JPMA) safety standards and have straps to secure the child. (See Box 9.2.) Because infants spend so much unsupervised time in cribs, it is essential that these items

---

BOX 9.1 CAUSES OF INJURIES RESULTING IN HOSPITAL EMERGENCY ROOM VISITS

1. Falls
2. Motor vehicle accidents
3. Striking against or struck by objects or persons
4. Cuts and impalings by objects
4. Natural and environmental factors
5. Overexertion
6. Poisoning
7. Pedacycles
8. Fire, flames, hot or corrosive materials, steam

Source of data: National Safety Council. (2002). *Injury Facts®, 2002 Edition.* Itasca, IL: Author.

---

be selected carefully. Many cribs built before 1991 have an unsafe design and therefore are not recommended (Holtzman, 2005). Whether a crib is used or purchased new, it should be sturdy, with no loose or missing parts. The distance from the top of the mattress to the top of the side rail should be at least 26 inches to prevent the older baby from climbing over the top (Lansky, 2002). To further protect the child from falling out of bed, the crib sides must latch securely and be difficult for children to operate so they cannot let them down.

When a child is 35 inches tall or able to climb out of the crib, it is time to move to a "big bed" (Holtz, 2005). A good strategy when a child starts sleeping in a regular bed is

---

BOX 9.2 PRODUCT SAFETY FOR CHILDREN

The Consumer Product Safety Commission is a federal regulatory body charged with protecting the public from "unreasonable risk of injury" from products. Children's products are often recalled when information is gathered after the fact about their safety. Recall information is available at 1-800-638-2772 or www.cpsc.gov. Another source of recall lists is the Web site of the National Safe Kids Campaign: www.safekids.org.

The Juvenile Products Manufacturer's Association (JPMA) is a trade association of American and Canadian companies that manufacture and/or distribute products for infants. Their mission is to help consumers keep babies safe through a safety certification program in collaboration with the American Society for Testing and Materials (ASTM). Products with the JPMA safety seal have met the high standards established by ASTM.

FIGURE 9.1 Cabinets without open shelves at low levels are safe choices when there are children in the household.

to place the mattress on or close to the floor. It is also a good idea to install soft flooring, such as a thick pad or gym mat, around the bed as a cushion against potential falls (Holtzman, 2005). Bunk beds, or elevated beds, are not recommended for young children, as they account for approximately 22,000 fall-related injuries each year (Morgan, 2003). If either type of raised bed is used because of space limitations, a rail should be installed to prevent accidental falls.

When choosing general furniture for the home, including the child's room, avoid pieces with wide footholds and shelves. Bookshelves, for example, might have a row of latched cabinets across the bottom. (See Figure 9.1 for an example.) (Be careful to select latches that allow children to get out of cabinets if they use it as a hiding place and lock themselves inside.) As another safety precaution, all heavy furnishings and appliances should be secured to the walls with angle braces or anchors to prevent them from tipping if a child does manage to climb onto them.

Collisions with objects that occur when children fall while running or climbing are common and the injuries suffered are often the result of colliding with sharp edges and corners. As such, the corners where two walls meet should be bull-nosed and certain items, such as glass coffee tables, should be avoided, along with furnishings that have sharp points.

Windows and Balconies

Because they pose a very serious threat, safe window design is essential. Windows that open for ventilation should be located at heights young children cannot reach, or the windows should open only from the top down. Because heat rises, this is also a more energy-efficient way to cool a room. If windows that open are already installed at lower levels, one option is to install window guards. Caution should be exercised to comply with local fire codes and ensure that the guards have quick-release mechanisms to facilitate escape in an emergency (National Safety Council, 2005, "Window Safety").

A less expensive solution than window guards is to use window-stopping devices that attach to the inside of the window frame to prevent it from opening more than four inches. An important thing to know is that insect screens are not designed to prevent falls, as they are not strong enough to withstand the pushes of even a small child. When selecting new windows, look for models that already have the stops installed. To prevent children from climbing and accessing windows, tables and other furnishings should not be placed near them. This is especially important in nurseries and bedrooms where children are left unattended in cribs and beds.

To help prevent falls from balconies, the spaces between the railings should be no wider than three inches so that small children cannot squeeze through the openings. In the case of wider spaces, screens or guards made of Plexiglass, plastic, or mesh should be installed. These guards should extend from floor to ceiling or at least to a height of six feet. As with windows, tables and other furnishings can present a climbing hazard and should not be placed against balcony enclosures. In addition, because children can be tempted to use railings as balance beams, ground-level patios should have shrubs and soft ground materials, such as wood chips, to reduce the degree of injuries from falls that occur in spite of preventive measures (National Safety Council, 2005, "Window Safety").

Playgrounds

Playgrounds are an important part of the built environment, providing children with opportunities for fun and exercise. Unfortunately, they are also the site of many falls. In fact, U.S. emergency rooms treat more than 200,000 children for playground-related injuries annually (Tinsworth, 2001), with falls accounting for about 80 percent of these injuries (National SAFE KIDS Campaign, Playground Injury Fact Sheet, 2004). Many are quite severe and include bone fractures, internal and head injuries, and dislocations (Tinsworth, 2001).

Implications for Designers

Most playground falls occur onto the surfaces located under equipment, not onto the equipment itself. Therefore, the type of surface materials used under ground equipment is critical to the safety and welfare of children because it is directly related to the degree and severity of the injury sustained. Unfortunately, a 2002 national survey found that 75 percent of public playgrounds lack adequate protective surfaces (National SAFE KIDS Campaign, 2004).

Safe surfaces should not be hard, meaning that asphalt, concrete, and packed soil should be avoided. Instead, loose fill materials, such as dense, well-maintained shredded rubber, wood chips, wood fiber, and sand, should be chosen (see Figure 9.2). These should reach a depth of twelve inches and extend at least six feet in all directions around play equipment (National SAFE KIDS Campaign, 2004). It is also possible to use rubber mats, synthetic turf, and other artificial materials that are designed to soften the impact of a fall. Regardless of the materials used, they must be maintained, with loose materials being replenished as needed. This effort pays off, as demonstrated in a recent study that found a 22 percent decrease in injuries after a state law in North Carolina required child-care centers to install proper surfacing (National SAFE KIDS Campaign, 2004).

BOX 9.3   A REAL-WORLD EXPERIENCE

As a child I was involved in gymnastics, but I had a hard time getting enough height to do a "front flip." So I came up with the ingenious idea to practice in my bedroom, trying to do this "front flip" from the floor onto my bed. However, I couldn't get enough running speed because my bedroom was rectangular, with my bed situated along the wall of the narrow side. Being the resourceful child that I was, I moved the bed to position it along the wall at the far end and started to practice. My running, combined with jumping and landing on the bed, made loud noises and my father came to investigate. Needless to say, he was not happy with the situation and pointed out that my bed was now situated directly under a third-story window. My actions could have resulted in me flying out that window. I include this story because as designers, we must be able to think like the inhabitants of the environments we create so that we can take precautionary measures to prevent accidents. In this situation, a good designer would consider the fact that there is a young gymnast in the home, which means the youngster would likely use the bed as a trampoline, the sofa as a lift, and the ottoman or coffee table as a vaulting box. In my situation, the designer could have included protective bars on the window, fastened the bed to the floor, or had the bedposts weighted with lead. It's important to understand that children are resourceful and innovative, and if we are to protect them, then we have to think more like them. Many experts even recommend that adults crawl around the floor of a house or other buildings inhabited by babies and toddlers, to see what kinds of hazards exist at that level.

A commonly neglected environment for children is the backyard of residential homes. It is estimated that only 9 percent of residential backyards have impact-absorbing surfacing materials around children's play areas. This may account for the fact that 70 percent of deaths resulting from play-equipment falls since 1990 occurred on home playgrounds (National SAFE KIDS Campaign, 2004). Hence, residential and landscape designers need to be aware of a variety of safety methods and

BOX 9.4   CULTURAL INFLUENCES ON BEHAVIOR

In the late 1950s and early 1960s, the first *Superman* series was aired on television. In that show, Superman would jump from a window, ledge, or balcony and fly through the air. Unfortunately, during the first years of this show many children plunged to their deaths because they thought that they could fly like Superman. This situation highlights the importance of designers to be aware of the different situations young people are exposed to and may try to emulate.

BOX 9.5   A REAL-WORLD EXPERIENCE

A nine-month-old girl, left in the care of youngsters while her mother was at work, was left alone with the door to the outdoor balcony left ajar. The baby managed to get out and climb over or crawl through the outside railing of the third-floor condominium where she lived. When spotted by a passing woman and her teenage son, the little girl was dangling from the railing, high above the sidewalk. The woman sent her son up the stairs to get to the child, but before he could reach her, she let go. Fortunately, the woman was able to catch her, saving the child from what could have been catastrophic injuries or death.

materials so they can educate and advise their clients who have children or young guests, such as grandchildren. In new construction or when a house is remodeled, an effective method of mitigating harm to children is to orient the home so that the primary windows face the play area. This enables the person responsible for the children to easily observe them as they play outside.

FALLS AMONG OLDER ADULTS

While falls can lead to catastrophic injuries for children, they pose an even greater danger to older adults. Annually, more than a third of individuals age 65 and older suffer at least one

fall (Hausdorff, 2001). This represents a very large number of people, as can be seen from the following figures: in 2003, more than 1.8 million adults over the age of 65 were treated in emergency rooms and more than 431,000 were hospitalized (Centers for Disease Prevention and Control, 2006, "Preventing"; National Center for Injury Prevention and Control, 2007, "Costs of Falls") with moderate to severe injuries such as hip fractures and head traumas. (See Chapter 3 for information about these injuries.) For many people, these types of injuries reduce their mobility and independence, and increase their risk of premature death (Sterling, 2001). In fact, 13,700 people age 65 and older died from fall-related injuries in 2003 (Centers for Disease Control and Prevention, 2006, "Preventing"), accounting for one third of unintentional-injury deaths for adults age 75 and older (National Safety Council, Injury Facts, 2002). Not only do falls have human costs of pain and suffering among older adults, they have high economic costs: in 2000, for example, the direct medical costs were $179 million for fatal injuries and $19.3 billion for nonfatal injuries related to falls (Stevens, 2005). It is estimated that direct medical costs for falls among older adults will reach

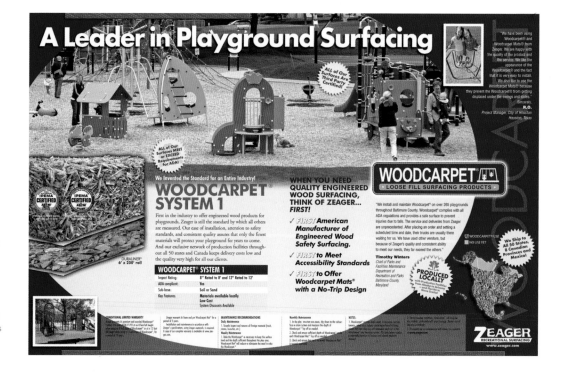

FIGURE 9.2 WOOD-CARPET by Woodcarpet Recreational Surfacing uses high-quality wood fibers to create a safe playground surface. The air between the wood fibers provides a cushion for the inevitable tumbles from playground equipment.

$43.8 billion by 2020 (Centers for Disease Prevention and Control, 2006, "Preventing").

In addition to the physical changes mentioned earlier in the chapter, reflexes slow down with age. This, in turn, slows down protective responses, such as grabbing onto something to slow or impede a fall (National Institute of Arthritis and Musculoskeletal and Skin Diseases, 2005). Besides reflexes, some of the measures taken to correct age-related visual impairments can actually increase the potential for falls. This happens because many prescriptions for eyeglasses call for bi- and trifocal lenses in which the bottom section is designed for close-up viewing such as reading. Looking through this portion of the lens, as is natural when looking down when walking, can distort vision and negatively affect depth perception. Another factor that contributes to accidents is the amount of medication taken by many older adults for chronic health conditions. This is because medications can interfere with balance and perception, thus increasing the risk for falls.

Implications for Designers

Obviously, designing environments that help prevent falls significantly contributes to the well-being of older adults. The importance of this effort will only increase in the coming years because the number of adults over the age of 65 is expected to more than double from 36.3 million in 2004 to 86.7 million by 2050, at which time they will comprise 21 percent of the total population (U.S. Census Bureau, 2006). Thus, there will be many opportunities to create designs to help prevent what could be a catastrophic number of injuries and deaths.

Flooring

As opposed to the majority of falls suffered by children and younger adults, who fall from one elevation to another, most falls among older people occur on the same level (not from one elevation to another) and from a standing height (Ellis, 2001). The two most common causes are tripping and slipping (National Institute of Arthritis and Musculoskeletal and Skin Diseases, 2005), which is why designers need to pay special attention to the flooring and flooring materials used when designing spaces for older adults. Walking surfaces should be smooth and even, but not slippery. All conditions should be considered, such as whether floors will become slippery when wet. Floors should also be easy to clean so that spills, such as grease in the kitchen, can be cleaned up easily.

Designers will also want to minimize changes in grade and not combine a variety of materials and different patterns along primary walking areas. Examples include avoiding the use of a patterned carpet surrounded by a solid border or carpeting that abuts linoleum or ceramic tile. Another trip hazard for older people is the use of thick carpets or thick underpads because the squishy nature can catch a person's foot, walker, or cane and lead to a fall. Also, once a surface material has been selected and installed, it should be kept clear and not covered with throw rugs or other flooring accessories. If there is a need for an entry rug or mat, such as in the cold or wet climates where snow, ice, or water could cause the floor to become slippery, be sure to secure the rug firmly to the floor with foam carpet backing, double-sided tape, or a rubber pad.

Even good flooring can be hazardous if there are trip hazards present. Obvious examples include unnecessary furnishings, clutter, and decorative objects along or within the primary walkway. Other trip hazards include electrical wires such as extension and telephone cords strewn across rooms. In today's electronic world, most computers, telephones, televisions, etc., require an attachment to an electrical outlet, a telephone jack, and/or a cable outlet. As such, potential trip hazards can be avoided simply by increasing the numbers of outlets per room. Because it is common for falls to occur when people are getting out of bed, a cordless telephone can be mounted on the wall (between 3 and 4 feet from the floor) and close to the bed.

FIGURE 9.3 There are a variety of grab bars available to make bathrooms safer without giving the room an institutional look.

power failure is a likely occurrence. In order to help prevent accidental falls in these situations, designers will want to include power-failure night-lights along primary walking areas such as hallways and in primary rooms such as bedrooms and bathrooms. (Note that night-lights should never be a substitute for good room lighting.)

Bathrooms

Bathrooms are one of the most dangerous areas of the home for older people, but there are a number of proactive measures that designers can implement to reduce the risks for falls. For example, when installing new showers and tubs, select models with nonslip surfaces. With existing fixtures, nonslip decals can be glued to the surface, and for individuals whose mobility or balance is impaired, grab bars can be installed next to toilets, in tubs, and in showers. (See Figure 9.3.) Be aware that a common error when installing a grab bar is the lack of adequate structural support. Improper installation is actually more dangerous than no bars at all because they give a false sense of security and when used, can pull away from the wall through the drywall and result in a bad fall. Most building codes now require that bars be capable of withstanding a 250-pound load. To support this weight, you must screw the grab bars into wall studs or into additional blocking because molly bolts, nails, or screws in Sheetrock are not adequate. Figure 9.4 shows an example of how a grab bar can be safely installed. Another problem is presented by single-unit fiberglass shower stalls because there is typically a one-inch gap between the shower wall and the wall of the building. The fiberglass shell does not have the strength to support a grab bar. There are wall-mount products that remedy this situation (National Safety Council, 2005, "Designs"). When installing grab bars for bathtubs, side-mounted units can be a good choice because they don't require breaking into a wall or tile.

Lighting

Good lighting is another important factor for preventing falls, especially for older adults. As discussed in Chapter 3, changes in light intensity present special challenges because of the decreasing ability of the eye muscles to quickly open and close in response to light. Therefore, contrast in flooring materials should be reduced as much as possible and transition zones should be incorporated in areas where people enter from bright outdoor light into dimmer interior lighting. Also, designers should plan the placement of light switches to be installed in convenient locations that prevent the need to walk through dark areas before finding a switch. As such, switches should be located at each end of a hallway, at the bottom and top of flights of stairs, and at each entryway to rooms that have more than one entrance. In many newer homes with rooms without overhead light fixtures, designers might consider installing overhead lights or including an outlet attached to a switch so that a lamp can be illuminated upon entry to the room. It is also recommended that guiding illumination be a minimum of 50 lux. (See Chapter 7 for more information about lighting.)

In climates known to have high winds, electrical storms, or even ice storms, consider that

Outdoor Areas

The last areas to be discussed in relation to fall prevention are those located outside a house or building. These include the walkways leading to the structure, entryways, decks, balconies, and porches. First, caution must be exercised to ensure that their construction will withstand prevalent natural forces and that surface areas will remain even. For example, in cold climates, frost heaves can cause concrete to buckle, and in desert areas the movement of the underlying sand can easily erode from underneath. To help prevent these actions from occurring, the designer will want to ensure that the contractor uses steel framing in the concrete pads and includes expansion joints between the concrete pads. Surfaces to avoid include wood-slatted decking and gravel paths, especially for people with limited mobility or vision, because of their uneven surfaces. Also, the spaces between wood slats present opportunities for catching heels and causing falls. Other often overlooked hazards include the use of potted plants in the walkway, overgrown bushes or plants along the paths (particularly those with thorns, such as rosebushes), and items suspended over walkways and around doorways, such as wind chimes and socks and hanging plants. It's a good design practice to ensure that all balconies, decks, and walkways remain unobstructed to ensure optimum visual access.

Aside from removing objects that impede walkways, visual access can be improved with good outdoor lighting. Such lighting might include sensor lights that automatically illuminate when the sun goes down or when there is movement. A common situation in which falls occur is when getting into and out of cars. This is frequently a result of inadequate lighting or insufficient amount of space to move freely. Lighting can be addressed simply by ensuring a bright overhead light in garages or including a light post along the driveway where the car is usually parked. On public property, local governments can be encouraged to place streetlights along areas where people park. Other safety precautions include designing adequate storage space to free garages of clutter and installing an automatic garage door opener. It's very important to ensure that only openers with an auto-reverse device are used so

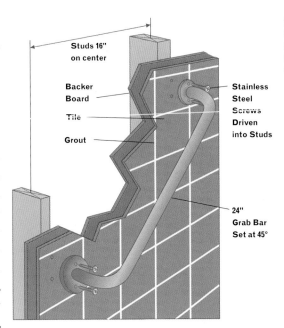

Studs 16" on center

Backer Board

Tile

Grout

Stainless Steel Screws Driven into Studs

24" Grab Bar Set at 45°

FIGURE 9.4 Grab bars must be attached to studs so they can withstand the pressure of weight without breaking.

that children and pets aren't accidentally hurt should they get in the way of a closing door. Likewise, these openers should incorporate a light that automatically illuminates when the door is about to open. This light should stay on until the person manually turns it off once they are safely in the house.

Stair Safety

All kinds of stair systems have been used in both indoor and outdoor construction since ancient times. In spite of their usefulness, they have always presented the danger of falling for people of all ages. Every year, thousands of people suffer injuries, with over 17 percent of home falls resulting in death occurring on stairs or steps (Runyan and Casteel, 2004).

Implications for Designers

There are many ways that designers can promote the building of safe steps and stairways, as indicated in the following suggestions:

1. Install handrails on both sides of all stairways, constructing them to extend at least one foot beyond the last step at both the top and bottom. Handrails should be easy to grasp and enable a firm grip. The ideal shape is round, about 1 1/4 to 2 inches in diameter. Check applicable codes for exact requirements. The rail should be smooth so the handgrip can be continuously maintained.

2. When new stairways are built, a good rule is to construct treads that are at least 11 inches wide and risers that are no more than 7 inches high. (It is important to note that each city, county, or state may have their own rules and regulations, so designers should always consult the local building codes.) Failure to have or to use handrails is a very common contributing factor for falls.

3. Avoid the use of thick carpets and underpads on treads because it's easy to catch the feet on them. Also, the squishy nature of thick carpeting can upset a person's balance.

4. Choose flooring for stairs and landing surfaces that doesn't require waxing because this can make them slippery. Also, matte finishes prevent glare that can interfere with vision.

5. Avoid visually distracting surfaces, such as patterns that make it difficult to distinguish one step from another.

6. With children or individuals with seriously impaired vision, install safety gates on both the top and bottom of stairs. Pressure gates, which attach to the side walls with pressure instead of screws, can be used at the bottom of stairs, but never at the top (Holtzman, 2005). Vertical rather than horizontal slats are safer and should be no more than 2 3/8 inches apart. Newer models made with Plexiglas or fine mesh are the best choices (Holtzman, 2005).

7. For child safety, stair railings should not be more than 3 inches apart to prevent small bodies or heads from sliding through.

8. On stairs used by the visually impaired, highlight the edges by painting them a contrasting color.

9. Paint the last basement step white so it is easy to distinguish from the landing.

10. When doors open directly into a stairwell, there should be a platform that extends beyond the swing of the door to prevent people from immediately stepping down.

CHOKING AND SUFFOCATION

Choking and suffocation, which cause injury or death by preventing the intake of oxygen needed to maintain life, are the fourth-leading causes of unintentional-home-injury death in the United States (Runyan & Casteel, 2004). As with falls, the risks for choking tend to be highest in young children and older adults (National Safety Council, 2002, "Injury Facts"). In fact, mechanical suffocation is the primary cause of unintentional-injury deaths of infants.

Babies are particularly at risk for suffocation because even when they can squirm and roll over, they may lack the motor skills and strength to lift their heads or move away from suffocating items. Young children are also at risk because they gain physical mobility much faster than they acquire cognitive and judgment skills, and hence they tend to place themselves in dangerous situations, such as playing with hanging ropes and in old refrigerators. Another characteristic of very young children that places them in danger of choking is their propensity to explore their world by putting all kinds of things into their mouths. Because the fingers and lips have the highest density of touch receptors, children learn about their environment by mouthing items.

Implications for Designers

Items that can present choking hazards should be avoided in environments where children reside or visit, such as in houses, day-care centers, and preschools. It is a good idea to ask clients about visits from young friends, grandchildren, nieces and nephews, and so on, so that proper planning can be done in advance. Hazards to watch for include furnishings and decorative objects that have removable small parts, such as buttons and trim.

Because people of various ages live together, designers should plan appropriate storage areas, out of a baby or toddler's reach, for the toys and hobby supplies belonging to other family members. It is a good idea to look carefully throughout the built environment, to the point of crawling on hands and knees, to find potentially dangerous objects. Even products whose principal purpose is to increase safety can be dangerous. For example, parents have been advised for years to cover electrical outlets, and a common product is a plastic single-outlet cover that is easily popped into the receptacle. This small item has been discovered to pose a choking hazard when removed, as when using the outlet for vacuuming, and not returned to the socket (Kansas Dept. of Health & Environment, 2000).

The list that follows contains design considerations to decrease the risk of suffocation and strangulation of infants and young children. Note that several suggestions relate to cribs. This is because they are the third-leading location of all accidental suffocation deaths in the home (Runyan & Casteel, 2004) and therefore, proper selection and maintenance are critical.

1. Choose cribs with slats that are no more than 2 3/8 inches apart to prevent the baby's head from getting caught. The same principle applies if rails are used on children's beds: the openings between the rails must be too narrow for a child to insert his or her head.
2. Select crib mattresses that fit snugly with no more than a two-adult-finger-wide space between the mattress and the perimeter. This prevents infants from getting their heads caught in this space and suffocating.
3. Cut the ends of any strings that tie onto the crib to 7 inches or less and do not hang mobiles within the baby's reach
4. Avoid the use of bumper pads in cribs. (If parents insist on using them, they should be made of a firm material or mesh.)
5. Locate cribs and the beds of young children away from curtains or any other hanging items the child might reach.
6. Use short cords on window coverings or consider using cordless window coverings. Also avoid chains, such as on hanging lamps; suspended decorations; and ring/beaded-type room dividers.
7. Select playground equipment with openings less than 3 1/2 or more than 9 inches,

such as between ladder rungs and guardrails, to prevent children from getting their heads trapped between them.
8. On playground equipment, avoid S-shaped hooks, which can catch clothing and cause strangulation, and hanging ropes with which children might play.
9. Ensure that appliances and other tightly enclosed items, like the examples shown in Figure 9.5, are discarded, have the doors removed, or are properly stored so that children cannot become trapped inside and suffocate. Although refrigerators have been required for the last 40 years to have latches on the inside that open, many appliance manufacturers are placing this

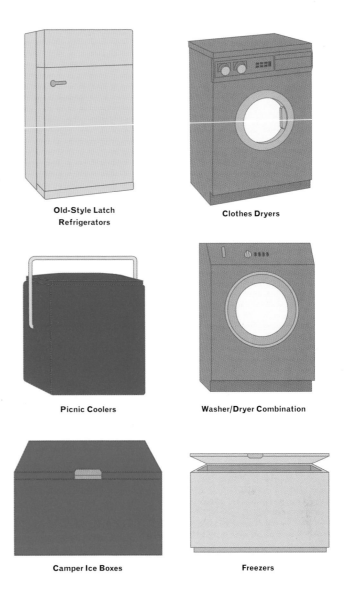

Old-Style Latch Refrigerators

Clothes Dryers

Picnic Coolers

Washer/Dryer Combination

Camper Ice Boxes

Freezers

FIGURE 9.5 Many common household items pose entrapment hazards for children who are curious by nature. Child-proof by removing the door, locking it securely, or wrapping it with a chain and padlock that cannot be removed.

BOX 9.6 SAFETY RULES FOR POOLS

- Enclose the pool with a fence at least 4 feet in height (higher if mandated by local codes), separating it from the yard and play areas.
- Avoid placing furnishings, potted plants, or other items onto which a child can climb next to the outside perimeter of the fence.
- Ensure that the pool is visible from inside the house.
- Use self-closing, self-locking gates with child-resistant latches that are at least 54 inches from the ground.
- Consider the installation of audible alarms on fence gates and house doors that open into the pool area.
- Install textured, slip-proof material on the pool deck.
- Separate the storage of ride-on wheel toys from the pool area.
- Provide out-of-child-reach and/or locking cabinets for storing pool and hot tub chemicals.

Adapted from: Lansky, V. (2002). *Baby proofing basics: How to keep your child safe.* Minnetonka, MN: Book Peddlers.

Holtzman, D. S. (2005). *The safe baby: A do-it-yourself guide to home safety.* Boulder, CO: Sentient Publications.

type of latch on other appliances as well (U.S. Consumer Product Safety Commission, n.d.). In homes with children, or potential young visitors, look for this feature when purchasing new appliances, such as freezers, clothes washers, and dryers.

DROWNING

Water, an essential component of human existence, has played an important part in our history. If you look at a map and note the location of major civilizations and cities, both past and present, you'll see that they are usually located near a convenient source of water. As such, water presents us with a paradox: while we cannot live without it, it can literally be the death of us, especially for children. Drowning is, in fact, the second-leading cause of death among children ages one to 14 and among the top five causes of death for teens and adults up to age 55 (National Safety Council, 2002, "Injury Facts"). Nearly one-fourth of all drownings occur in or around the home (Runyan & Casteel, 2004). Many of these deaths are children under the age of one who most frequently drown in bathtubs, buckets, and toilets that are full of water. This happens because

their heads are heavier in relation to their total body weight and strength and once they fall forward into a water-filled container, they have a hard time getting back up. On the other hand, the majority of drownings of older children take place in backyard swimming pools, hot tubs, and spas (Holtzman, 2005). (See Box 9.6 for pool safety considerations.)

Implications for Designers

Designers can incorporate a number of safety features into home design to prevent drownings:

1. Install lid guards on toilets to lock them down when not in use. Many children are fascinated by the swirling water and fall in as they lean over to investigate.
2. Place inflated covers over tub faucet handles to prevent children from turning on the water (Lansky, 2002).
3. Provide locking covers on hot tubs. (Note that children under age five should not use hot tubs at all because their smaller bodies and developing organs make them more sensitive to high water temperatures (Lansky, 2002).
4. Provide convenient storage for containers such as buckets to encourage their being emptied of water and put away.

POISONING

Modern science, especially chemistry, has provided us with many seemingly miraculous products that prevent and cure disease, help us live longer, and improve our lives in many other ways. At the same time, the accidental misuse of these products can result in tragedy. In fact, poisoning is the third-leading cause of unintentional-injury death for all age groups (National Safety Council, 2002, "Injury Facts") and the second-leading cause of unintentional-injury deaths that take place in the home (Runyan & Casteel, 2004), with 90 percent of all poison exposures taking place in the home (National Center for Injury Prevention and Control, 2006). Of these exposures, over 50 percent involve children under the age

BOX 9.7 EXPERT SPOTLIGHT: Swimming Pool Safety

Brett Kayzar, CCI
Principal
Quick and Reliable Home
Inspections, LLC

Home swimming pools can be an attractive feature for many people. But as a home inspector, it is my job to make sure we don't create extreme hazards along the way to creating the perfect backyard oasis. After all, swimming for humans is an acquired rather than a natural ability and creating an open, water-filled space in a backyard can pose many dangers.

To appreciate what pool and spa safety is all about, we must think in terms of the users. For example, blue is the favorite color of most children. So a blue-tiled pool filled with reflective blue shaded water tends to be a special attraction for kids at play. Even when not in use, pools are often protected with solar covers made of blue plastic. In addition to color, many backyard pools are designed with interesting shapes to appeal to both youngsters and adults.

The home inspector can help by studying ways to restrict direct access to pools. Many home owners build their pools strictly from an aesthetic point of view, without much thought to child or adult safety. However, it is essential that a pool or spa be protected from entry from all sides. This can be accomplished by a complete 4-foot fence enclosure encircling the pool, with openings no greater than 4 inches wide (see Figure 9.6). The fence should have latched gates that only swing outward when released and have self-closing devices or spring-loaded mechanisms that automatically latch closed when released. This type of enclosure may seem to counter an attractive design, but these safety requirements can be achieved through many methods. For example, the entire yard can be encircled by a fence, as long as the entry gates have proper latches. This arrangement keeps children from wandering uninvited onto the property. For children inside the home, alarm devices should be attached to every door that has access to the pool to sound a loud alarm anytime a door is opened. The goal here is to limit access, or at least "notify" everyone when access has been breeched.

Next on the list of safety features is lighting. In a situation with blue painted decks, blue trimmed pools, and blue solar covers, it can be difficult to see just where the concrete walkway ends and the water begins. A little lighting can aid a person in seeing changes in patterns, heights, and textures to avoid missteps. Perimeter lights can be both aesthetically pleasing and functional. Sensor lights can also act as an alarm, giving notice when someone has entered the pool area.

Another important consideration is the type of surfaces used around the pool. Although shale-slate, an oil-based stone, looks great, the polished slate can become a bit slick when wet. Nonslip decking will help prevent falls around and into the pool.

Finally there is the issue of solar covers. While they may look sturdy enough to walk on, it actually takes only a few pounds from a child or family pet to cause the cover to sink. And worse, the cover can wrap around its intruder like flypaper, trapping its victim in an airtight seal. Only rigid or solid construction covers are safe for walking, and these are only considered safe for use if they make a lock-tight or latched connection around the entire pool or spa.

of five (National Center for Injury Prevention and Control, 2006). This is because the same characteristics that put young children at high risk for choking—the tendency to place all kinds of things in their mouths and the inability to identify dangerous substances—also increase their chances of being poisoned. Curiosity leads them to sample whatever they can access, including medications, household cleaning products, or cosmetics.

Implications for Designers

For designers, the key word when dealing with poisons is "access." Finding ways to prevent young children from gaining access to harmful products can contribute to preventing thousands of hospitalizations and hundreds of deaths each year. This may seem a daunting task when we consider that consumers buy more than a quarter of a million different household products each year that are used in

FIGURE 9.6 Children of all ages are attracted to swimming pools. Fences and gates should be as impenetrable as possible. This example also blocks the view of the pool from the outside to further discourage youngsters.

home, using a drawing and/or checklist such as those illustrated in Figure 9.7 and Table 9.2 provide a good start.

There are basically two methods for reducing the hazards presented by these products: (1) substituting safer products and (2) designing proper storage. In addressing the first issue, that of product selection, we realize that it is outside the realm of the designer to give advice about personal products used in the home. Offering suggestions regarding cleaning and yard care products, in both homes and public buildings, is appropriate. This is especially true if these are given in relation to new furnishings and other items being purchased and installed as part of construction, remodeling, and decorating projects. The fact is that there are many substitutes for highly toxic products that are both safer and cheaper than many—or perhaps most—of those advertised to "work wonders." For example, nondetergent soaps, baking soda, vinegar, and lemon juice are highly effective for many cleaning needs. Even plain warm wa-

and around the home for medicating, cleaning, grooming, exterminating insects, and killing weeds (National Safety Council, 2004, "How to Prevent"). A methodical look at a typical

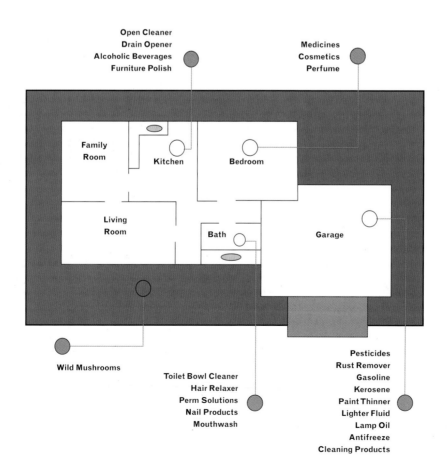

FIGURE 9.7 Common locations in the home for poisonous substances.

TABLE 9.2   HOME POISON CHECKLIST

KITCHEN
- ☐ medications
- ☐ drain cleaner-lye and bleaches
- ☐ furniture polish
- ☐ powdered and liquid detergents
- ☐ cleanser and scouring powders
- ☐ metal cleaners
- ☐ ammonia
- ☐ oven cleaner
- ☐ rust remover
- ☐ pills
- ☐ carpet and upholstery cleaners
- ☐ dishwater detergents
- ☐ alcoholic beverages
- ☐ moldy or rotten food

BEDROOM
- ☐ medications
- ☐ jewelry cleaner
- ☐ cosmetics
- ☐ perfume

LAUNDRY
- ☐ bleaches
- ☐ soaps and detergents
- ☐ disinfectant
- ☐ bluing, dyes
- ☐ spot removers or dry cleaners

CLOSETS, ATTIC, STORAGE PLACES
- ☐ rat and ant poisons
- ☐ mothballs
- ☐ sprays

BATHROOM
- ☐ medications
- ☐ drain cleaners-lye
- ☐ iron pills
- ☐ shampoo, lotions, and sprays
- ☐ creams
- ☐ nail polish and remover
- ☐ suntan products
- ☐ deodorants
- ☐ shaving lotions
- ☐ toilet bowl cleaners
- ☐ diaper pail deodorizers
- ☐ hair remover
- ☐ pine oil and bath oil
- ☐ rubbing alcohol
- ☐ boric acid
- ☐ room deodorizer
- ☐ camphor-containing products
- ☐ denture tablets

GARAGE, BASEMENT, WORKSHOP
- ☐ lye
- ☐ kerosene
- ☐ lime
- ☐ bug killers
- ☐ gasoline
- ☐ lighter fluids
- ☐ turpentine
- ☐ paint remover and thinner
- ☐ pesticides
- ☐ weed killers
- ☐ fertilizers
- ☐ antifreeze
- ☐ lamp oil

GENERAL
- ☐ flaking paint
- ☐ repainted toys
- ☐ broken plaster
- ☐ pet medications and products

Source: Washington Poison Center, www.wapc.org/safety.htm

ter is an excellent solvent for non-greasy dirt (Phillips, 2000). Table 9.3 contains ideas for many safe substitutes.

Pesticides

Pesticides, like other chemicals, have helped mitigate the harmful effects of insects, rodents, and fungi. Because they are designed to be toxic, many of them affect humans by causing cancer, as well as problems with the nervous, respiratory, reproductive, endocrine, and im-

mune systems. When ingested, they can result in death.

Avoiding the need to use toxic pesticides begins with prevention. Effective methods for making the environment unattractive to pests include eliminating the conditions they need for survival and preventing their entry into structures. Standing water, for example, supplies a ready drinking supply to various types of pests and should be avoided by regularly emptying collecting areas such as refrigerator

TABLE 9.3   EXAMPLES OF SAFE SUBSTITUTES FOR HIGHLY TOXIC PRODUCTS

TASK	SUGGESTED SUBSTANCE OR METHOD
Clear clogged drains	Mechanical means: plunger, gas or water-powered device, or auger (snake)
Deodorize	Baking soda (sodium bicarbonate)
Clean and polish metals	Baking soda (sodium bicarbonate)
Soften fabrics	Baking soda (sodium bicarbonate)
Inhibit growth of mildew and mold	Borax (naturally occurring, water-soluble mineral)
Clean and polish glass	Lemon juice and water; cornstarch and vinegar and water; or vinegar and water
Remove rust	Steel wool
Prepare walls for painting	TSP (trisodium phosphate)
Dissolve mineral deposits, remove stubborn stains, clean coffeepots	Vinegar
Cut stubborn grease	Washing soda (SAL Soda—sodium carbonate dechydrate, a mineral)
Freshen air	Open windows, use cut flowers, boil cinnamon and cloves, sprinkle borax in garbage and diaper pails
Clean oven	Baking soda and steel wool
Clean toilets	White vinegar, lemon juice, baking soda, borax, washing soda, or hydrogen peroxide

and air-conditioning drain trays. When designing kitchens, easy-to-clean surfaces, including floors, and proper storage areas encourage the removal of food sources for pests. Potential rodent foods, such as birdseed and bulk grains, should not be stored in garages; and attractive nesting materials, such as newspapers and cardboard boxes, should be disposed of. Potential entryways can be eliminated by installing screens on windows and doors; caulking all cracks, including those created by pipes and wiring; and using metal grates to cover attic vent openings. If pests are a problem in spite of these measures, the less-toxic methods listed in Table 9.4 may be used to fight them.

Safe Storage

Of course, even some of the safer alternatives are poisonous if ingested, especially by a child. It is also true that certain food products, such as vanilla extract, are poisonous if drunk in a large quantity. Therefore, designers should create secure and efficient storage for all types of foods, as well as potential harmful products, throughout the built environment. This will help eliminate problems such as those illustrated by one of the most common storage areas for many of the most toxic substances in the home: under sinks in kitchens and bathrooms. These locations contain some of the worst characteristics of good storage: they can be difficult for adults to reach, especially the elderly, while being at the perfect level for infants and toddlers. In addition, they are usually poorly lit and the space for placing items is deep so items tend to be stored in a jumble.

Conversely, safe storage must be inaccessible to children while at the same time be convenient for adults. To start, position cabinets out of a child's reach. This is not entirely

TABLE 9.4 ALTERNATIVES FOR TOXIC PESTICIDES

PEST	SUGGESTED SUBSTANCES AND METHODS
Ants	Red chili pepper, paprika, dried peppermint, or borax (depends on type of ants)
Fleas, ticks	Beneficial nematodes (specific types of microscopic round-worms that eat certain insects) in the yard, diatomaceous earth (crushed skeletons of prehistoric algae) Feed flea-susceptible pets brewer's yeast mixed with food or in tablets
Moths	Cedar blocks or chips, lavender sachets, pheromone scent traps
Roaches	Boric acid; equal parts sugar and baking soda
Rodents	Traps; mint-leaf sachets (deterrent); cat
Termites	Particular species of nematodes that eat them; professionally applied heat treatments; or sodium borate wood preservatives

Adapted from: Davis, G. A., & Turner, E. *Safe substitutes at home: Non-toxic household products.* Working paper. Retrieved February 16, 2007, from http://es.epa.gov/techinfo/facts/safe-fs.html.

Phillips, D. (2000). *Designs for a healthy home: An eco-friendly approach.* San Francisco: SOMA.

Holtzman, D. S. (2005). *The safe baby: A do-it-yourself guide to home safety.* Boulder, CO: Sentient Publications.

sufficient because most children are inquisitive and many are able to climb surprisingly well. Therefore, cabinets that hold medications and toxic products should have locks. These locks should be convenient for adults to use so they won't be tempted to leave items in more "convenient" places, such as on a lower, child-reachable counter. Shelving should be constructed to hold containers in an organized fashion to prevent adults from grabbing the wrong product.

Another reason for good organization in storage is to make the monitoring of household products easier. This is especially important with gases, aerosols, paint thinners, degreasers, and similar items because growing numbers of preteens and adolescents are using them as inhalants to get high. In fact, national surveys have revealed that more than 22.9 million Americans have abused inhalants at least once; 17.3 percent of eighth-graders have abused inhalants (National Institute on Drug Abuse, 2005). In one incident, twin sisters hospitalized for inhaling mothball fumes showed signs of serious addiction (Herrera, 2006). The consequences of this activity can be catastrophic, because long-term use of inhalants can break down myelin, the protective covering of nerve cells that helps transmit messages. Even worse, inhalants can result in death from heart failure or suffocation.

Product Safety

Another poison danger is the unintentional misuse of products by not following the label directions, a factor (along with alcohol and illegal drug overdoses) that contributes to poisonings of adults between the ages of 25 and 44. One reason this happens is that products are often purchased in the economy size and then transferred to other containers that don't have labels. Tragically, cases are reported of poisonous liquids being stored in food containers, such as soda pop bottles, which other adults then drink by mistake. Designers can help prevent these accidents by providing shelves that accommodate large containers, thus discouraging their transfer into inappropriate ones. They can also make sure that adequate lighting is available. Many garages, for example, house pesticides and other toxins, but tend to have poor lighting. A counter with a task light where one can read and carry out instructions for safe mixing and handling of products would be a safety-conscious addition to the garage, basement, and other storage areas.

Medications

Ironically, lifesaving and health-improving medications pose a major risk for poisoning among all age groups. Elderly adults are at an especially high risk because of the number of medications they take. For adults over age 55, misuse of medication accounts for many of the nearly 100,000 annual poison exposures (Cincinnati Children's Hospital, n.d.). Previously, we discussed locking cabinets as a way to protect children. There are some additional things designers can do to help older adults remain safe. Safety measures that designers can take to safeguard medications include the following:

1. Provide separate storage cabinets for medications: they should never be kept in the same area as foods or poisonous household products. This eliminates the risk of confusing products.
2. Install medication cabinets at eye level so items can be seen and reached easily. (In this case, it is critical that locks be installed if children live in or visit the household.)
3. Ensure that there is adequate lighting in the area where medications are kept. Many older adults, who typically take more medications than younger people, have vision impairments and require good lighting to read labels and instructions. Also, they may be taking a large number of drugs that can be similar in size, shape, and color, making sufficient light essential for distinguishing between medications. For clients who have health conditions that require them to take medications during the night, bedside lamps with easy-to-locate switches should be placed within arm's reach to discourage taking drugs in the dark and risking an error.
4. Include a conveniently located counter at an appropriate height for organizing and taking medications. Some people organize

a week's worth of pills at a time. If this is the case for a client, include legroom under the counter and a chair or stool so they can work in comfort.

ACCIDENTS WITH FIREARMS

Gun ownership, controls, and regulations continue to be debated in the United States. Gun rights groups argue that restrictions to ownership would infringe on our constitutional rights and leave law-abiding citizens unable to defend themselves against criminals. Many Americans also enjoy the recreational aspects of gun ownership, including hunting and trap-shooting (shooting at clay pigeons). On the other side are gun-control advocates who believe that limiting the types of guns owned, along with the enactment of mandatory safety laws such as trigger locks, would reduce the number of deaths and injuries inflicted by guns. Regardless of which side of the argument a person is on, the fact remains that firearms account for many deaths and injuries each year, as demonstrated by the following statistics:

- 1999: There were 28,874 combined intentional and unintentional firearm-related deaths (National Safety Council, 2002, "Injury Facts").
- 1999: Firearms were the fifth-leading cause of death for 5- to 14-year-olds and the fourth-leading cause for 15- to 24-year-olds (National Safety Council, 2002, "Injury Facts").
- 2000: An estimated 23,237 nonfatal unintentional firearm-related injuries occurred (National Safety Council, 2002, "Injury Facts").
- 2000: An estimated 49,432 assault and legal intervention firearm injuries took place (National Safety Council, 2002, "Injury Facts").
- 2000: 3,016 intentionally self-inflicted nonfatal injuries using firearms were reported.
- 2002: 1,830 children and teenagers were murdered with guns (WISQARS, Injury Mortality Report).

- 2003: 16,907 individuals died from firearm-inflicted suicides (Centers for Disease Control and Prevention, n.d., "WISQARS").

Implications for Designers

A surprising number of households with children, between 31 and 43 percent, report having at least one firearm (Rand, 2001). Of these households, only 46 percent report keeping their firearms in a lockbox or locked cabinet (Runyan & Casteel, 2004). The significance of these facts for designers is that almost all unintentional shooting deaths of children occur in or around the home, and research has shown that proper storage of guns and ammunition reduces the number of deaths and injuries. One study, for example, revealed that in states with laws regarding proper gun storage, unintentional shooting deaths of children younger than age 15 were reduced by 23 percent during the years covered by these laws (Cummings, et al., 1997). Another study concluded that storing firearms and ammunition separately in locked spaces appears to decrease the risk of unintentional gun injuries and gun suicide attempts among children and teens (Grossman, et al., 2005).

Many people believe that keeping a gun handy, such as under beds or mattresses or in unlocked bedroom drawers, is necessary for self-protection. Such guns are actually more likely to harm someone in the household than to help, supported by the fact that for every legally justifiable shooting (self-defense), there are 22 criminal, unintentional, and suicide-related shootings (Kellerman, et al., 1998).

In view of this statistic, it would seem that designers have an opportunity to help prevent both intentional and unintentional firearm incidences by using the following guidelines to help clients who own firearms safely secure them:

1. Select appropriate storage boxes or safes.
2. Locate the storage away from the reach of children. Although no system is foolproof, as seen with teens who use crowbars to break into **gun safes,** storing firearms in a less-accessible area will discourage their use.
3. Provide separate, locked storage for ammunition, preferably in a different area of the house.
4. Store firearms and ammunition separately from valuables, such as jewelry or electronic equipment, to keep them out of the hands of potential thieves.
5. Make sure that keys and combinations are not accessible to children.

FIRES AND SHOCK HAZARDS

For thousands of years, fires provided humans with light, warmth, and a means of cooking. Early fires also formed a nucleus for human grouping and eventually became tribal or communal fires (Semmelroth, n.d.). Their significance was such that in many early cultures fire was viewed as magical. Stories of its acquisition or discovery abound, one of the most famous being that of Prometheus stealing fire from the Greek gods. Today, in most parts of the United States, fires serve less utilitarian needs, but instead are more likely to provide us with enjoyment, feelings of coziness, and a sense of family. This is especially true in cold-weather climates and during holidays, such as Christmas. Consider the sentiments of that classic Christmas song (*Chestnuts roasting on an open fire . . .*), or the emotional impact of the words "home and hearth."

At the same time, fires present a serious danger in the United States, which has one of the highest fire-fatality rates in the industrialized world (Morgan, 2003). Fire is, in fact, one of the five-leading causes of accidental injury and the fourth-most-common cause of death in children (University of Virginia Health System, 2006). The human and financial costs of residence fires are high, as shown in the following statistics for 2004:

- 410,000 residential fires
- 3,225 civilians (nonfirefighters) killed
- 14,175 civilian fire injuries

- $6 billion in property damage (Karter, 2005)

Sadly, it is in the home where we like to feel safe that 90 percent of deaths due to burns or inhalation of smoke or fumes take place (Runyan & Casteel, 2004). Sometimes the very items that add to our holiday enjoyment, such as jack-o'-lanterns, candles, and Christmas tree lights, also add to the risks. At the same time, the incidence of nonfatal fire injuries in homes is lower than for deaths attributed to fire (Runyan & Casteel, 2004). As with other types of accidents we have discussed in this chapter, it is the very young and very old who suffer a disproportionate number of injuries and deaths from fire. The same issues that contribute to injuries and deaths from other causes apply here: these age groups tend to spend more time in the home; young children lack the experience and judgment to identify danger and escape from it; and many older adults have limited mobility and impaired senses.

Implications for Designers

Designers should incorporate fire safety into overall home planning. For example, if residents have impaired mobility, bedrooms should be located on the ground floor with or very near exits to the outdoors. Bedrooms should have telephones for calling the fire department (or for other emergencies). If a resident uses a wheelchair or walker, consider placing a ramp to the outside near the bedroom. Another fairly inexpensive safety measure, for all types of clients, is to replace any mattress made before the 1973 Federal Mattress Flammability Standard (U.S. Fire Administration, 2006, "Bedroom Fire").

Smoke Detectors

Most fatal residential fires take place between 11 P.M. and 6 A.M. when occupants are asleep and do not awaken in time to escape. This is why smoke inhalation, rather than burns, accounts for the largest share of injuries and deaths. Thus, a major fire-prevention implication for designers is that the homes of all clients should have **smoke detectors** installed to provide them with an important first line of defense against fire, especially in the night. Having a working smoke detector more than doubles the chances of house occupants to survive a fire (U.S. Fire Administration, 2007, "What You Need"). In addition to the information contained in Figure 9.8, the

FIGURE 9.8A AND B
Recommended placement of smoke detectors in the home.

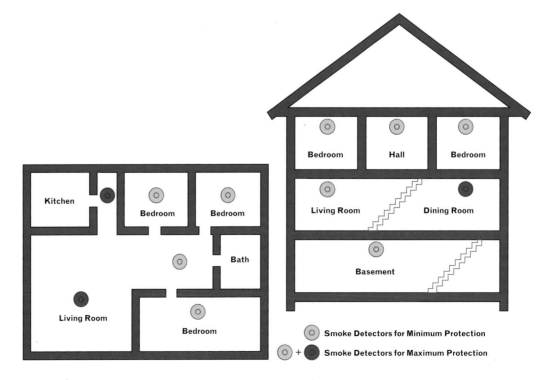

following list contains important considerations for the location and installation of smoke detectors:

- Carefully follow the manufacturer's instructions.
- Install them on every level of the building, including the basement.
- Place one in each sleeping area (required in new construction).
- Place one in the hall outside of sleeping areas (especially important if occupants sleep with the bedroom door closed).
- Locate on the ceiling, at least 6 inches from any wall; or on side walls, at least 6 to 8 inches below the ceiling.
- Avoid placing on uninsulated exterior walls because cold and heat extremes can adversely affect the batteries.
- Avoid placing near corners, in locations where drafts can impair the detector operation, or near fireplaces and woodstoves that can trigger false alarms.
- Place at each end of hallways longer than 30 feet and at the top of every stairwell (U.S. Fire Administration, 2007, "What You Need").

Although most smoke detectors are battery-operated, they can also be hard-wired into the home's electrical system with batteries as a backup in case of a power outage. If this arrangement is chosen, the installation should be done by a qualified electrician who places the detectors on their own circuit. Hard-wiring should be considered for houses with high ceilings that make it difficult to check and change batteries. It is also a good idea for older people and the disabled who are unable to maintain battery-operated models. Detectors can be made even more effective by connecting them to a lamp near the bed, a safety feature for the hearing impaired. Other special models include alarms that vibrate; these can be placed under the pillow of hearing and/or visually impaired individuals. The designer should check local smoke detector codes and services. In many communities, the local fire department will come to homes to give ad-

vice on proper placement and installation; some governmental agencies even provide free smoke detectors. See Box 9.8 to learn about the two types of smoke detectors.

Sprinkler Systems

Fire sprinkler systems, widely used in schools, offices, and other public buildings, are now more commonly installed in residences. While smoke detectors can alert residents to fire dangers, only sprinkler systems can actually extinguish fires. In addition, residential sprinklers are extremely sensitive and respond more quickly to fires than standard commercial and industrial systems. This is an especially significant advantage for those individuals, such as the elderly and disabled, who are unable to quickly leave the scene of a fire. Their benefit has been proven in studies conducted by the U.S. Fire Administration, which indicate that residential fire sprinklers have the potential to save thousands of lives, prevent many injuries, and save millions of dollars in property loss (U.S. Fire Administration, 2007, "Residential Sprinkler"). Along with the U.S. Fire Administration, the **National Safety Council** and other safety organizations recommend the use of home sprinkler systems (Runyan & Casteel, 2004).

Some communities, such as San Clemente, California, have enacted home sprinkler ordinances. If a sprinkler system is used, it should be listed by **Underwriters Laboratories** to ensure good quality and reliability (U.S. Fire Administration. "Residential Sprinklers"). Sprinklers are most easily installed during new

---

BOX 9.8   FACTS ABOUT SMOKE DETECTORS

There are two types of smoke detectors:

1. Ionization: radioactive material creates an electrical path that smoke molecules disrupt, thus triggering the alarm.
2. Photoelectric: contain a light source and photocell that is activated by light. Light from the bulb reflects off the smoke particles and is directed toward the photocell, which triggers the alarm.

Whichever kind is selected, it should have a testing laboratory label to ensure that the model has been tested under operating conditions.

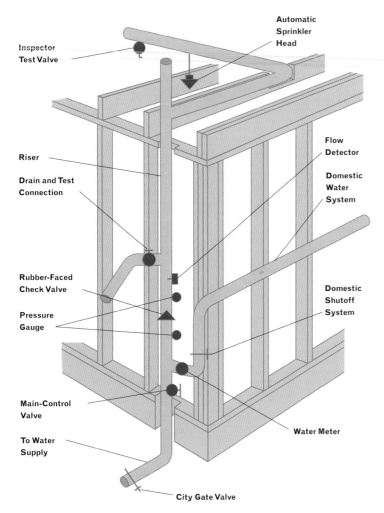

Inspector
Test Valve

Automatic
Sprinkler
Head

Riser

Drain and Test
Connection

Flow
Detector

Domestic
Water
System

Rubber-Faced
Check Valve

Pressure
Gauge

Domestic
Shutoff
System

Main-Control
Valve

To Water
Supply

Water Meter

City Gate Valve

FIGURE 9.9 Components of a residential sprinkler system.

construction or major remodeling projects, but can also be retrofitted to existing structures and aesthetically coordinated with any decor style (U.S. Fire Administration. "Residential Sprinklers"). The systems are not overly complex or prohibitively expensive to install. The use of plastic pipes, for example, has brought down the cost, and some insurance companies now offer discounts for homes with sprinklers. Figure 9.9 contains a diagram of the pipe arrangement used in a residential system.

Kitchen and Cooking Fires

While fire deaths tend to occur during sleep, the majority of home fires begin in the kitchen, and injuries incurred as a result of cooking fires are the leading cause of fire-related nonfatal injuries (Runyan & Casteel, 2004). Keeping kitchens and cooking areas safe should be part of every kitchen design. Because unattended items

on the stove are the most common cause of these fires, methods to deter leaving the kitchen can play an important part in fire prevention. Examples of design ideas include placing a telephone in the kitchen; including a small desk so that other tasks, such as paying bills, can be done without leaving the area; providing space for a radio and small television set so the individual doing the cooking is less tempted to leave the room; and combining the kitchen with other rooms, as is done in many newer open-style or great-room houses, to enable visiting in the kitchen area. To handle stove fires that do occur, it is recommended that storage next to the stove be included for large pan lids, used for smothering stovetop fires, and a multipurpose fire extinguisher. At the same time, storage space over stoves designed for storing food or frequently used items should be avoided to prevent the need to reach over hot burners and risk being burned.

An essential part of kitchen safety is the proper selection and use of kitchen appliances. Because two out of three reported home fires start with the range or stove, it is important to choose only those models that have been tested and approved by a recognized product testing facility (National Fire Protection Agency, n.d., "Cooking Safety"). It's also important that stoves and ovens are easy to clean so that food and grease don't accumulate, posing a fire hazard. Self-cleaning ovens, therefore, are a good choice. (Instructions for use must be followed very carefully because ovens reach very high temperatures during the cleaning cycle.)

Another design consideration is providing adequate counter and storage space around stoves and ovens so that nothing is placed too close to the cooking surface. Cloth items that might ignite, such as towels, oven mitts, and pot holders, should not be hung on oven doors or close to burners.

Although they don't cause as many fires as stoves, microwave ovens heat foods, liquids, and containers to very high temperatures and are the cause of more emergency room visits than any other cooking device, with scalds comprising almost half of the injuries suffered from their use (National Fire Protection Association, n.d., "Cooking Safety: Microwave"). A common problem with microwave ovens is placement. Frequently, they are too high and require reaching up, an action that increases the risk of spilling the contents. They also need to be placed near a counter "landing area" to prevent the necessity of carrying a hot cup or plate to the other side of the kitchen.

Appliances and Lighting

Clothes washers and dryers are taken for granted in most households, providing us with an easy means to take care of our laundry. They can present fire hazards, causing an average of 13,300 home structure fires a year. The leading cause of these fires is the failure to clean out flammable lint and dust. Designers can help prevent such fires by ensuring that these appliances are located in a way that allows easy maintenance. For example, dryer ducts should be accessible from both inside and outside the structure so they can be regularly cleared of lint, fibers, and dust. Proper storage should be provided in areas around laundry machines so that extra clothing, boxes, and other flammable items are not piled up on or around them. Also, new dryers should always be installed and serviced by a professional.

Lamps present a potential for fires, especially those containing halogen bulbs, which can heat to temperatures as high as 1,500°F. Although the Underwriters Laboratory standard for these lamps was revised in 1997 to require bulb shields (Office of Information and Public Affairs, 2004), older models are still being used. While the guards reduce the potential for fire, these lamps still must be treated with care. Important points to remember are to never place them near combustibles such as curtains, wall hangings, and bedding. It is also recommended that bulbs be a maximum of 300 watts (Office of Information and Public Affairs, 2004). In homes with children or pets, designers might consider other types of lighting, as halogen-lamp fires are often the result of a lamp being knocked over onto clothing or other combustible material (Ault, 1998).

When planning lighting for specific purposes, such as reading, provide lamps or fixtures that take bulbs of adequate wattage to supply the desired amount of light. For example, don't select lamps intended for ambience to use for reading, increasing the temptation to install a higher-wattage bulb than the light is designed to use and thus increasing the chance of overheating and fire.

Preventing Electrical Fires

Some electrical fires, which cause over 2,000 injuries each year, are caused by electrical system failures and appliance defects, but the majority are caused by misuse and poor maintenance of appliances, improper wiring, overloaded circuits, and improper use of extension cords. These are areas over which designers have some degree of control. In selecting appliances, for example, the U.S. Fire Administration recommends that only those that meet the Underwriters Laboratory (UL) standards for safety be purchased (U.S. Fire Administration, 2006, "On the Safety").

Designers can also ensure that structures have adequate circuits and enough outlets to handle the electrical needs of the residents. Today, when even our telephones need to be charged, it is a good idea to review the electrical needs of any home when remodeling or redecorating, with special attention given to older homes built before we had so many electricity-demanding devices. Outlets should be located where residents can reach to unplug small electrical items when not in use. This habit is recommended because electrical current continues to run through plugged-in appliances even when they are turned off. Certain appliances, especially those that create heat, such as space heaters, should always be plugged directly into an outlet; large appliances, such as stoves, must have their own circuit. All electrical cords, including extension cords, should be inspected periodically for fraying, cracks, and broken connections. If these are found, the cord must be replaced or the appliance replaced, as this presents a serious fire hazard.

BOX 9.9 EXTENSION CORD SAFETY

Use: Only cords marked "suitable for use with outdoor appliances" can be used outdoors. Never use an indoor extension cord outdoors because doing so can result in an electric shock or fire hazard.

Wattage: This is the amount of electrical current that can be carried by the cord. Appliances vary in the amount of wattage required for their operation and the cord must be capable of carrying that amount.

Size: Also called gauge, size is based on the American Wire Gauge (AWG) System, in which the larger the wire, the smaller the AWG number. For example, a 12-gauge wire is larger, and can power higher-wattage appliances, than a 14-gauge wire. Cord length is also an important consideration because the longer the cord, the lower the current-carrying capacity. For example, a 16-gauge extension cord less than 50 feet in length can power a 1,625-watt appliance, while a 16-gauge cord that is longer than 50 feet can only power an appliance up to 1,250 watts.

It is essential to read the instructions and wattage ratings for appliances and the extension cords that will be used with them. If an appliance indicates power usage in amps and volts, multiply these numbers to obtain the wattage. For example, the wattage needed for an appliance that uses 5 amps at 125 volts is 625 watts.

Adapted from: United Laboratories, Inc. (n.d.) *Products safety tips: Extension cords.* Retrieved October 18, 2006 from www.ul.com/consumers/cords.html.

Extension cords offer convenience and flexibility, but can be dangerous if they are allowed to fray, are too small for the power needed, or are run under rugs and carpets or buried under piles of books or clothing. In fact, electric cords of any kind should never be trapped against walls where heat can build up (U.S. Fire Administration, 2006, "Bedroom Fire"). It is important to remember that extension cords should never be used with stoves, microwaves, space heaters, and other heat-producing appliances. See Box 9.9 for additional information about the safe use of extension cords.

Fireplaces, Woodstoves, and Heaters

Fireplaces and woodstoves add pleasure to our lives, but must be properly used and maintained to avoid fires. Fireplaces should be guarded by heavy screens that are capable of stopping rolling logs and large enough to cover the entire opening of the fireplace so they catch flying sparks. Inside the chimney, out of our sight, is where creosote, a highly flammable by-product of combustion, builds up. To prevent creosote from accumulating to dangerous levels, chimneys should be inspected by professionals annually and cleaned, if necessary.

Woodstoves, increasingly popular as heating costs rise, cause more than 5,000 residential fires every year (U.S. Fire Administration, 1998, "Check"). Combustible items, including furnishings and decorative items, should be kept at least three feet away from the woodstove and its flue. Just as with fireplaces, creosote buildup should be monitored. If a client purchases a new woodstove, it should be solidly constructed out of materials like plate steel or cast iron metal.

Portable space heaters are useful for heating small areas or rooms that don't have central heating. They can be very dangerous, especially in rooms where there are many combustible items. Space heaters pose a special hazard in bedrooms, where they are commonly used, because of the presence of many combustibles such as clothing and bedding. As with woodstoves, combustibles should be kept at least

Another measure to prevent fires caused by circuit overloads is to install electrical circuit interrupters, in addition to the traditional circuit breakers that have been available for many years. **Arc-fault circuit interrupters (AFCIs)** continuously monitor for unintended arcs (discharge of electricity across a circuit), which they can distinguish from the normal arcing that occurs when a switch is operated. **Ground-fault circuit interrupters (GFCIs)** shut off a circuit when an unintentional electrical path is established between a source of current and a grounded surface. An example is when a person comes into contact with an energized part and his body becomes part of the circuitry. The National Electric Code requires AFCIs in bedrooms of new residential construction and GFCIs for receptacles in kitchens, bathrooms, outdoor areas, basements, and garages of new residential construction (National Fire Protection Association, 2002, "Electrical").

three feet from space heaters. Another danger in bedrooms is that they are frequently left on, unmonitored, while people are asleep. If space heaters are used, they should have a thermostat control mechanism and an automatic turn-off feature that activates if the appliance tips over.

Security Bars and Fire

Security bars, intended to keep criminals out and children in, present us with an excellent example of unintended consequences: in a number of incidents, they have trapped residents inside burning houses and apartments. After several tragic fires, involving windows with bars or nailed shut and doors blocked by heavy furniture, the Home Security and Fire Safety Task Force was founded to encourage the use of bars that can be opened from the inside by pulling a handle, pushing a button, stepping on a pedal, or kicking a lever. Designers working with clients who require such safety features should encourage them to choose devices that protect but do not trap, with opening methods appropriate for the ages and physical conditions of the residents.

OFFICE SAFETY

It is estimated that office workers sustain 76,000 fractures, dislocations, sprains, strains, and contusions each year (National Oceanic and Atmospheric Administration, n.d.). The leading types of accidents that result in these injuries are falls, strains and overexertion, being struck by or striking objects, and getting caught in or between objects (National Oceanic and Atmospheric Administration, n.d.). Other injuries include foreign substances in the eye, burns from hot liquids and fire, and electric shock.

Falls are frequently caused by poor planning or failing to pay attention. An example of the latter is tripping over open desk or file drawers. One design remedy is to locate furnishings with drawers out of walkways and away from doorways so that if they are accidentally left open, they present less of a hazard. Other common causes of office falls include

unsteady chairs, cords and wires strung in pathways, loose carpeting, boxes and equipment stored in halls and walkways, and inadequate lighting. Fortunately, these hazards are all preventable through the selection of proper furnishings, installation of adequate electrical outlets, repair or replacement of carpeting, creation of adequate storage, and provision of

FIGURE 9.10 Overloading outlets and circuits is common in offices that were not built when today's plethora of electronic and electrical devices were available. The example shown here presents a serious fire hazard.

BOX 9.10 THE SUSTAINABILITY CONNECTION

Safety and sustainability cross paths when creating healthy built environments, as seen in the following examples:

- Solar lights for driveways and entryways can absorb the sun's energy during the day and use it to provide safety lighting at night.
- Sturdy, well-built furniture is generally safer and likely to last longer as well.
- Natural alternatives to poisonous cleaning products and pesticides tend to be less harmful to the environment.
- Smoke detectors save lives, and they also frequently give warning so that structures can be saved, thus saving the need to use additional resources to rebuild.

Any measure taken to protect humans from harm can, by definition, be described as sustainable because its purpose is to sustain human health and well-being.

good lighting systems (lighting is discussed in Chapter 7).

Office areas can be crowded and as a business grows, conditions can worsen. The placement of furniture and equipment should allow individuals to work without having to stretch, reach, or strain. It should also prevent collisions of various kinds, both between people and objects and people and people. To avoid overcrowding, it is recommended that there be allotted at least 50 square feet per employee and at least three feet between desks. Pathways should be at least four feet wide. Also consider grouping employees who use the same office machines to cut down on the need to walk about, thus decreasing the chances of collisions.

BOX 9.11 VIEW TO THE FUTURE

As increasing numbers of Americans reach retirement age, designers will be called upon more frequently to create safe spaces for individuals with diminished hearing, eyesight, and mobility. The challenge will be to provide pleasant environments that will nurture the social and psychological well-being of older adults, while protecting their physical health and safety.

Many offices are filled with combustible materials, such as papers, fabric furnishings, and cleaners and chemicals. Designers can suggest that fire-resistant files or vaults be used for papers, books, and notebooks that are not used on a daily basis. Any fabrics used should be made from flame-retardant materials, and flammable products for cleaning or machine maintenance should be stored in fire-resistant cabinets.

Electrical current can pose a workplace hazard, especially in cases of older buildings whose circuits cannot safely accommodate the demands of modern equipment. (See Figure 9.10.) This problem is compounded when employees bring in additional "comfort appliances," such as coffeemakers and small space heaters. Good workplace design ensures that in addition to proper circuitry, heating is adequate and a break room is provided where coffee and other refreshments can be prepared and stored. Special attention should be directed to the placement of electrical cords to avoid pushing them against a wall behind bookshelves and file cabinets or running them over heating items such as radiators and steam pipes. If extension cords must be used where wiring is not possible, do not fasten them to walls or furnishings with staples or hang them from nails or wires.

Some large office machines have sharp corners and protrusions and should be situated away from the edges of desks and tables, which themselves should be located where they are highly visible, such as not immediately around a corner, and in areas that are not so crowded that bumping against them becomes inevitable. Small cutting and piercing machines, such as shredders, electric hole punchers, and electric staplers, should have adequate surface space allotted in a well-lighted area to ensure their safe use. This also applies to other sharp objects such as manual paper cutters. Another appliance with accident potential is the electric fan, which must have a substantial base to avoid tipping, as well as guarded blades.

GLOSSARY TERMS

Cognitive

Gun safe or cabinet

Motor skills

National Safety Council

Proprioceptors

Smoke detector

Underwriters Laboratories

LEARNING ACTIVITIES

1. Conduct a poison safety check of your residence using the checklist in Box 9.2 and the poison-locator in Figure 9.7. Are all products stored and labeled safely for the age of all residents and visitors? Write a report of your findings, including a description of any changes you make to help prevent accidental poisoning.

2. Design a safe bedroom for an infant. Include photos or drawings of furnishings and a floor plan with furniture placement. Write a brief description of how you have baby-proofed the room, such as how the crib meets safety requirements.

3. Create a home fire safety checklist. Organize your checklist by room or by type of hazard or safety feature, such as electrical appliances, heating appliances, and so on. Include smoke detectors and escape routes.

4. For one week, observe stairs in all the public and private places you visit. How do they rate for safety in terms of adequate lighting, flooring of stair surfaces and landings, size of landings, and handrails?

5. Collect a picture file of products available for reducing the risk of accidents in bathrooms. Use your findings to design a bathroom that incorporates safe flooring, grab bars, slip-proof tub and shower, and medicine storage. Look for ways to incorporate design elements to keep the room from looking "institutional."

SUGGESTED WEB SITES

1. National Safety Council
www.nsc.org
The NSC has up-to-date articles, fact sheets, and checklists for all aspects of safety, including fall prevention, safe windows, and poison prevention.

2. National Fire Protection Association
www.nfpa.org
This Web site contains fact sheets on all aspects of fire safety, including lists of prevention tips.

3. U.S. Fire Administration
www.usfa.dhs.gov
Explore the Citizen's section of this Web site for brochures on all aspects of fire safety. Of special interest to interior designers is the up-to-date list of fire-related product recalls.

4. National Center for Injury Prevention and Control
www.cdc.gov/ncipc
Find useful information on myriad safety topics. Booklets and information sheets prepared by the CDC in cooperation with other government agencies include checklists and prevention guides.

5. U.S. Consumer Product Safety Commission
www.cpsc.gov
This government agency creates standards for products, issues research reports, and maintains up-to-date lists of product recalls. This is a valuable resource for designers as they help clients choose furnishings and other products.

6. Safe Kids USA
www.usa.safekids.org
Safe Kids Worldwide is a global network of organizations whose mission is to prevent accidental childhood injury. It was founded in 1987 by the Children's National Medical Center with support from Johnson & Johnson. Their Web site contains injury-prevention tips and product-safety recalls specifically targeted to children.

7. U.S. Environmental Protection Agency
www.epa.gov
The EPA studies and reports on hundreds of safety topics related to the built environment, including pesticides and household cleaning products.

8. Occupational Safety and Health Administration
www.osha.gov
This division of the U.S. Department of Labor is charged with ensuring worker safety. Its Web site contains information on all aspects of injury and illness-prevention, including a new database developed with the EPA on chemicals commonly found in the workplace.

REFERENCES

Allen, I., (Ed), (February 2005). *Facts of life: Issue briefing for health reporters.* Health Behavior News Service, 10, 2, 1-2.

Ault, K. (April 9, 1998). *Data summary on halogen torchiere-style floor lamps.* Washington, D.C.: U.S. Consumer Product Safety Commission.

Centers for Disease Control and Prevention. (Updated August 26, 2006). *Preventing falls among older adults.* Retrieved December 2, 2007, from www.cdc.gov/ncipc/duip/preventadultfalls.htm

Centers for Disease Control and Prevention. (Last updated December 1, 2006). *WISQARS Injury Mortality Reports, 1999–2004.* Retrieved December 7, 2006 from webapp.cdc.gov/sasweb/ncipc/mortrate10_sy.html

Centers for Disease Control and Prevention. (n.d.) WISQARS 2003, United States: Suicide firearm deaths and rates per 100,000. Retrieved October 17, 2006, from http://webapp.cdc.gov/cgi-bin/broker.exe

Cincinnati Children's Hospital Medical Center. (n.d.). *Poison prevention: guidelines for older americans.* Retrieved September 26, 2006 from www.cincinnatichildrens.org/svc/alpha/d/dpic/prevent/older.htm

Cummings, P., Grossman, F. P., Rivara, F. P., & Koepsell. T. D. (1997). State gun safe storage laws and child mortality due to firearms. *The Journal of the American Medical Association,* 278, 13, 1084-1086.

Dahm, D., & Smith, J. (Eds.), (2005). *Mayo Clinic: Fitness for Everybody.* Rochester, MN: Mayo Clinic.

Ellis, A. A., & Trent, R. B. (2001). Do the risks and consequences of hospitalized fall injuries among older adults in California vary by type of fall? *Journal of Gerontology:Medical Sciences.* 2001:56A(11):M686-92.

Grossman, D. C., Mueller, B. A., Riedy, C., Dowd, M. D., Villveces, A., Prodzinski, J., Nakagawara, J., Howard, J., Thiersch, N., & Harruff, R. (2005). Gun storage practices and risk of youth suicide and unintentional firearm injuries. *Journal of the American Medical Association,* 293, 6, 707-714.

Hausdorff, J. M., Rios, D. A., & Edelber, H. K. (2001). Gait variability and fall risk in community-living older adults: A 1-year prospective study. *Archives of Physical Medicine and Rehabilitation.* 82, 8, 1050-6.

Herrera, C. A. (2006, September 14). Some kids find their high at home. *The Bulletin,* p. E,10. (Bend, OR).

Holtzman, D. S. (2005). *The safe baby: A do-it-yourself guide to home safety.* Boulder, CO: Sentient Publications.

Kansas Department of Health & Environment. (November 16, 2000). *Tis' the season for holiday safety.* [news release]. Retrieved February 6, 2007, from www.kdheks.gov/news/web_archives/2000/256.htm

Karter, M. J. (June 2005). *Fire loss in the United States during 2004.* [Abridged Report] Quincy, MA: National Fire Protection Association.

Kellermann, A. L., Somes, G., Rivara, F. P., Lee, R. K., Banton, J. G. (1998). Injuries and deaths due to firearms in the home. *Journal of Trauma-Injury Infection & Critical Care,* 45, 2, 263-267.

Lansky, V. (2002). *Baby proofing basics: How to keep your child safe.* Minnetonka, MN: Book Peddlers.

Li, F., Harmer, P., Fisher, K. J., McAuley, E., Chaumeton, N., Eckstrom, E., & Wilson,

N. L. (2005). Tai chi and fall reductions in older adults: A randomized controlled trial. *Journal of Gerontology: Medical Sciences,* 60A, 2, 187-194.

Morgan, M.T. (2003). *Environmental health.* (3rd Ed). Belmont, CA: Thomson Wadsworth.

National Center for Injury Prevention and Control. (November 2006). *The CDC injury fact book.* Atlanta, GA: Author.

National Center for Injury Prevention and Control. (Updated May 21, 2007). *Costs of falls among older adults.* Retrieved December 2, 2007, from www.cdc.gov/ncipc/factsheets/fallcost.htm

National Fire Protection Association, (n.d.). *Cooking safety.* Retrieved October 10, 2006, from www.nfpa.org/categoryList.asp?categoryID=282&URL=Research%20&%20Reports/Fact%20sheets/Home%20safety/Cooking%20safety

National Fire Protection Association, (n.d.). *Cooking safety: Microwave safety.* Retrieved October 10, 2006, from www.nfpa.org/itemDetail.asp?categoryID=282&itemID=27799&URL=Research%20&%20Reports/Fact%20sheets/Home%20safety/Cooking%20safety

National Fire Protection Association, (Last updated April 2002). *Electrical circuit-interrupters.* Retrieved October 10, 2006, from www.nfpa.org/itemDetail.asp?categoryID=285&itemID=19048&URL=Research%20&%20Reports/Fact%20sheets/Electrical%20safety/Electrical%20circuit-interrupters

National Institute of Arthritis and Musculoskeletal and Skin Diseases (2005). *Preventing falls and related fractures.* [Pamphlet] Bethesda, MD: National Institutes of Health Osteoporosis and Related Bone Diseases-National Resource Center.

National Institute on Drug Abuse. (Revised 2005). *Inhalant abuse.* Retrieved December 2, 2007, from www.nida.nih.gov/ResearchReports/Inhalants/Inhalants.html

National Oceanic and Atmospheric Administration. (n.d.) *Office safety training module.* Retrieved November 5, 2006, from www.labtrain.noaa.gov/osha600/mod27/2701----.htm

National SAFE KIDS Campaign (2004). *Playground injury fact sheet.* Washington, DC: Author.

National Safety Council. (Last updated February 14, 2005). *Designs on building safe homes for the elderly.* Retrieved September 10, 2006, from www.nsc.org/issues/ifalls/falfalls.htm

National Safety Council. (Last updated December 28, 2004). *How to prevent poisonings in your home.* Retrieved January 27, 2007, from www.nsc.org/library/facts/poisoning.htm

National Safety Council. (2002). *Injury facts: 2002 edition.* Itasca, IL: National Safety Council.

National Safety Council (2006). *Injury facts: 2005–2006 edition.* Itasca, IL: National Safety Council.

National Safety Council. (April 28, 2005). *Window safety checklist.* Retrieved September 19, 2006, from www.nsc.org/aware/window/checklst.htm

Office of Information and Public Affairs. (Updated April 8, 2004). *CPSC and industry announce corrective action to improve safety of halogen torchiere lamps.* Retrieved October 18, 2006, from www.cpsc.gov/cpscpub/prerel/prhtml97/97173.html

Phillips, D. (2000). *Designs for a healthy home: An eco-friendly approach.* San Francisco, CA: Conari Press.

Rand Health. (2001). *Research highlights: Guns in the family: Firearm storage patterns in U.S. homes with children.* Retrieved October 8, 2006, from www.rand.org/pubs/research_briefs/RB4535/index1.html

Runyan, C. W. & Casteel, C. (Eds.) (2004). *The state of home safety in America: Facts about unintentional injuries in the home,* (2nd ed.). Washington, D.C.: Home Safety Council, Library of Congress Control Number: 20041.

Semmelroth, E. (n.d.). *Before stoves there was fire: A brief history of fire and its uses.* Retrieved October 11, 2006, from www.antiquestoves.com/history1.htm

Sterling, D. A., O'Connor, J. A., & Bonadies, J. (2001). Geriatric falls: Injury severity is high and disproportionate to mechanism. *Jour-*

nal of Trauma-Injury Infection and Critical Care, 50, 1, 116-119.

Stevens, J. A., Corso, P. S., Finkelstein, E. A., & Miller, T. R. (2005). CDC economic analysis of fall-related injuries among older adults. *Injury Prevention,* 11, 5, 275.

Tinsworth, D., & McDonald, J. (2001). *Special study: Injuries and deaths associated with children's playground equipment.* Washington, DC: U.S. Consumer Product Safety Commission.

U.S. Census Bureau. (March 9, 2006). *Older Americans month: May 2006.* Washington, D.C.: U.S. Census Bureau News.

U.S. Consumer Product Safety Commission. (n.d.). *CPSC warns about child entrapment in household appliances and picnic coolers.* Washington, D.C.: The U.S. Consumer Product Safety Commission.

U.S. Fire Administration. (2006). *Bedroom fire safety helps you sleep sound at night.* [Brochure]. Emmitsburg, MD: Author.

U.S. Fire Administration. (1998) *Check your hot spots.* [Brochure]. Emmitsburg, MD: Author.

U.S. Fire Administration. (2006). *On the safety circuit.* [Brochure]. Emmitsburg, MD: Author.

U. S. Fire Administration. (Updated January 4, 2007). *Residential sprinkler systems.* Retrieved January 10, 2007, from www.usfa.dhs .gov/safety/sprinklers

U. S. Fire Administration. (Last updated January 4, 2007). *What you need to know: The impact of smoke alarms.* Retrieved January 10, 2007, from www.usfa.dhs.gov/safety/alarms

University of Virginia Health System. (Updated August 28, 2006). *Common childhood injuries and poisonings: Facts about burn injury.* Retrieved October 11, 2006, from www .healthsystem.virginia.edu/uvahealth/peds_ poison/burns.cfm

Wolf S. L., Barnhart, H. X., Kutner, N. G., McNeely, E., Coogler, C., & Xu. T. (1996). Reducing frailty and falls in older persons: An investigation of Tai Chi and computerized balance training. Atlanta FICSIT Group. Frailty and Injuries: Cooperative Studies of Intervention Techniques, *Journal of The American Geriatrics Society,* 44, 5, 489-497.

We shape our buildings, and afterwards,
our buildings shape us.
—*Winston Churchill*

CHAPTER **10**

Promoting Healthy Lifestyles

LEARNING OBJECTIVES

1. **Explain how excess body weight, lack of physical activity, and stress affect physical and mental health.**
2. **Give examples of how the built environment influences these three areas of health.**
3. **Describe interventions designers can take to help decrease the prevalence of overweight and obesity, increase rates of physical activity, and reduce incidences of stress.**

The United States spends more money on health care than any other country in the world, and the amount continues to increase. In 2004, approximately $2.0 trillion was spent on health care, or 16 percent of our annual gross domestic product (the market value of all final goods and services produced in a given period of time). Expressed another way, the $2.0 trillion represents $6,697 for each person in the United States (Office of the Actuary, n.d.). Table 10.1 shows the increases in various categories of health-care spending that were realized in 2005.

Much of this expense is to alleviate conditions, such as diabetes and heart disease, related to how we choose to live: our personal habits and the built environment. Many measures that would likely lower health-care expen-

ditures as well as raise our individual quality of life involve low- or even no-cost actions. For example, one study estimated that if each of the 88 million inactive Americans ages 15 and older were to participate in moderate physical activity, such as regularly taking a 30-minute walk, annual direct medical costs might be reduced by as much as $76.6 billion (Pratt, Macera, and Wang, 2000).

Ironically, many of the aspects of modern life that were originally conceived to improve the quality of life have had negative effects on health. Consider the development of suburban neighborhoods. The intention was to provide clean air, open space, and access to the outdoors, among other things. The consequences have been otherwise: green space has been destroyed, open spaces for children to play are gone, and people depend on cars for most of their transportation. The result has been a decrease in physical exercise and an increase in excess body weight.

Although the work of interior designers should focus primarily on the needs of their individual clients, there is a growing belief that all members of society should be proactive in encouraging wellness. This is especially true for problems like being overweight and lack of physical activity, which are creating a

TABLE 10.1 PERCENTAGE INCREASES IN HEALTH CARE SPENDING FROM 2004 TO 2005

CATEGORY	PERCENT INCREASE
Medicare	9.3%
Medicaid	7.2%
Prescription drugs	5.8%
Hospitals	7.9%
Physicians and clinical services	7.0%
Nursing homes	6.0%
Home health services	11.1%

Source: Office of the Actuary at the Centers for Medicare and Medicaid Services. Estimations of national spending on health care goods and services. Retrieved January 29, 2007, from www.cms.hhs.gov/NationalHealthExpendData/downloads/highlights.pdf

burden in both human suffering and financial responsibilities that will affect both current and future generations of Americans. The Surgeon General, in a 2001 report addressing America's growing obesity problem, invites input from all sectors of society: "The design of successful interventions and actions for prevention and management of overweight and obesity will require the careful attention of many individuals and organizations working together through multiple spheres of influence" (U.S. Department of Health and Human Services, 2001). This chapter explores current health issues and ways the interior designer can create environments that support healthy lifestyle choices.

OVERWEIGHT AND OBESITY

During the twentieth century, amazing advancements were made in medical science and public health. Results of this progress include lengthening the average American life span by about 30 years; conquering infectious diseases that were once leading causes of death; and vastly improving public health conditions, such as the availability of clean water and efficient sewage systems. Our perceived quality of life has improved. We have more comfortable living conditions and fewer heavy physical demands on our bodies; yet, in some ways,

these "improvements" have prompted negative consequences.

In a sense, life has become too good, and it may well be that our very prosperity has resulted in conditions that some health professionals are calling among the most important health challenges of the twenty-first century: overweight and obesity. Both have reached epidemic proportions among all age groups. In fact, more than half of the adults in the United States are affected. Results from the 2003–2004 National Health and Nutrition Examination Survey show that an estimated 66 percent of U.S. adults are too heavy: 34 percent are overweight and 32 percent are obese (National Center for Health Statistics, 2007). These statistics regarding overweight and obesity represent a trend of dramatic increases over the last 30 years, as shown in Table 10.2.

Weight-Related Health Problems

Overweight and obesity have become public health concerns because of their associated health risks. It is believed that the **morbidity** (ill health) resulting from these conditions may be as great as from poverty, smoking, or problem drinking (U.S. Department of Human Health and Human Services, 2001). Obesity (excessive body fat), in particular, can lead to conditions that cause disease as well as to a variety of diseases themselves. For example,

TABLE 10.2 PREVALENCE OF OVERWEIGHT AND OBESITY AMONG U.S. ADULTS

	1976–1980	1988–1994	1999–2000	2001–2002	2003–2004
Overweight or Obese	47.0%	55.9%	64.5%	65.7%	66.2%
Obese	15.0%	23.2%	30.9%	31.3%	32.9%

Results are from the National Health and Nutrition Examination Surveys (NHANES). Source of table: National Center for Health Statistics. (January, 2007). *Prevalence of overweight and obesity among adults: United States, 2003–2004.* Retrieved January 24, 2007, from www.cdc.gov/nchs/products/pubs/pubd/hestats/overweight/overwght_adult_03.htm

obesity can exacerbate high blood pressure, which is a significant risk factor for heart disease. (See Box 10.1 for examples.)

A serious disease related to overweight and obesity is **type 2 diabetes,** which appears to be reaching epidemic proportions for groups of all ages. Type 2 diabetes is a chronic condition that affects the way the body converts glucose (sugar) into fuel it can use. Instead of passing into the cells, the glucose remains in the blood, where it eventually reaches levels that can do serious damage to the nerves, small blood vessels, and kidney filters. In very serious cases, or if left untreated, type 2 diabetes can cause blindness and necessitate amputations, particularly of the feet and legs. Over time, diabetes can harm almost every major organ.

Economic Costs of Excess Weight

In addition to the health problems suffered by individuals, the economic burden of weight problems for individuals, society, and the country's health-care system is substantial. In 2002, direct costs of weight-related problems, meaning the costs of preventive, diagnostic, and treatment services, were estimated to be $61 billion. Indirect costs, referring to lost wages and future earnings lost by premature death, were $56 billion (U.S. Department of Health and Human Services, 2001). For type 2 diabetes alone, the estimated direct medical costs in 2002 were $91.8 billion, more than doubling in the five-year period beginning in 1997 (U.S. Department of Health and Human Services, 2003).

Another increase related to **morbid obesity** (extremely detrimental to health) is the hospital costs for bariatric surgery, in which the stomach is made smaller to decrease the amount of food a person can eat at one time. Between 1998 and 2002, the number of surgeries increased by 400 percent while the costs increased sixfold, to $928 million (Encinosa, et al., 2005). These costs are expected to rise dramatically in coming years, because these numbers still represent less than one percent of the more than 11.5 million adults who are clinically eligible for such surgery (Encinosa, et al., 2005). Table 10.3 contains examples of the costs of weight-related health conditions.

BOX 10.1 CONDITIONS AND DISEASES ASSOCIATED WITH OBESITY

Conditions
- Hypertension (high blood pressure)
- High blood cholesterol
- Increased surgical risk
- Psychological disorders such as depression
- Sleep apnea (interruption of breathing during sleep)
- Complications of pregnancy
- Breathing problems

Diseases
- Type 2 diabetes
- Heart disease
- Stroke
- Gallbladder disease
- Osteoarthritis
- Asthma
- Cancer: endometrial, colon, kidney, gallbladder, and postmenopausal breast

TABLE 10.3   COSTS OF WEIGHT-RELATED CONDITIONS AND DISEASES

CONDITION/DISEASE	DIRECT COST
Heart disease	$8.8 billion
Osteoarthritis	$5.3 billion
Hypertension	$4.1 billion
Gallbladder disease	$3.2 billion
Colon cancer	$1.3 billion
Breast cancer	$1.1 billion
Endometrial cancer	$310 million

Sources of information: Weight Control Information Network. National Institute of Diabetes and Digestive and Kidney Diseases. (August 3, 2006). *Statistics related to overweight and obesity.* Bethesda, MD: Author.

Overweight Among Children and Teenagers

Obesity is now considered by some to be the most common health problem facing children (Strauss and Knight, 1999) (See Figure 10.1.) Results from the 2003–2004 National Health and Nutrition Examination Survey (NHANES) reveal that 19 percent of children ages 6 to 11 and 17 percent of teens ages 12 to 19 are overweight. As Table 10.4 illustrates, the trends for weights of young people are similar to those for adults, and moving in the same unhealthy direction.

One study found that maternal obesity was the most significant predictor of child obesity (Strauss and Knight, 1999), linking the problem to the home and the family environment. As the authors of the study state, "To understand the obese child, one needs to remember that he accumulated his extra weight while living in a family that, wittingly or unwittingly, encouraged overeating and inactivity" (Strauss and Knight, 1999). This indicates the importance of the home environment, including the influences of the built environment, because we know that physical conditions always influence the quality of human activity (Cosco and Moore, 1999).

What makes excess weight among young people of particular concern is that their behavior lays the foundation for lifelong habits. Indeed, teenagers who are overweight are at high risk for being overweight or obese as adults (U.S. Department of Health and Human Services, 2001). Even more alarming is the fact that obesity-related health problems, such as type 2 diabetes, are now showing up during childhood and adolescence. Once considered a disease of older adults, type 2 diabetes among youth has become a major concern among health professionals. Although research on childhood diabetes is in its beginning stages (Rosenbloom et al., 2000), it is known that, as with adults, the risk factors for this disease are obesity and lack of physical activity, in that order.

FIGURE 10.1 The percentage of overweight and obese children and teens in the U.S. continues to grow. Public health officials are concerned about the future of these young people.

TABLE 10.4 PREVALENCE OF OVERWEIGHT AMONG CHILDREN AND TEENS

AGE	1971–1974	1976–1980	1988–1994	1999–2000	2001–2002	2003–2004
6–11	4.0%	6.5%	11.3%	15.1%	16.3%	18.8%
12–19	6.1%	5.0%	10.5%	14.8%	16.7%	17.4%

Source: Results are from the National Health and Nutrition Survey Examination Surveys (NHANES). Source of table: National Center for Health Statistics. (January, 2007). *Prevalence of overweight and obesity among children and adolescents: United States, 2003-2004.* Retrieved January 24, 2007, from www.cdc.gov/nchs/products/pubs/pubd/hestats/overweight/overwght_child_03.htm

Causes of Overweight and Obesity

Overweight and obesity rates are climbing throughout developed countries. This is believed to be due to several factors: (1) food, especially high-calorie, high-fat types, has become plentiful and inexpensive; (2) technological advances have reduced the need for physical activity; (3) modern forms of entertainment tend to focus on sedentary activities; and (4) the overall design of urban and suburban built environments discourages walking and other uses of the outdoors. Table 10.5 contains a summary of various factors that influence the increase in excess weight.

Studies comparing the lifestyles of people around the world reveal strong links between environment and excess weight. For example, the traditional hunter-gatherer lifestyle of Australian Aborigines combined a high level of physical activity with low-calorie and high-fiber foods. After transitioning to a Western lifestyle, the Aborigines began to report high rates of obesity, hypertension, and type 2 diabetes (American Obesity Association, 2005,

TABLE 10.5 FACTORS THAT INFLUENCE INCREASING RATES OF OBESITY

LOCATION OR TYPE OF ACTIVITY	EFFECT OF MODERNIZATION	INFLUENCE ON OBESITY
Transportation	Rise in car ownership. Increase in driving shorter distances.	Decrease in walking and cycling.
At Home	Increase in use of modern appliances. Increase in ready-made foods and ingredients for cooking. Increase in television viewing and computer and video game use.	Decrease in manual labor. Increase in consumption of convenience foods that contribute to obesity. Decrease in time spent on more active recreational pursuits.
In the Workplace	Increase in sedentary occupational lifestyles due to technology; increase in computerization.	Decrease in physically demanding labor.
Public Places	Increase in the use of elevators and escalators.	Decrease in walking and use of stairs.
Urban Residency	Increase in crime in urban areas.	Decrease in numbers of women, children, and the elderly going out alone.

Adapted from: American Obesity Association. (May, 2005). *AOA fact sheets: Obesity — a global epidemic.* Retrieved January 24, 2007, from http://obesity1.tempdomainname.com/subs/fastfacts/obesity_global_epidemic.shtml

BOX 10.2   EXAMPLES OF GOVERNMENT TOOLS, INITIATIVES, AND PROGRAMS TO ADDRESS OVERWEIGHT AND OBESITY

- Healthy People 2010 Toolkit: helps groups develop and sustain plans of action to achieve Healthy People goals in their communities (U.S. Department of Health and Human Services)
- Hearts 'N' Parks: initiative to implement activities that encourage healthy eating and physical activity (National Institutes of Health and the National Recreation and Park Association)
- Girls and Obesity Initiative: identify existing government programs and adapt them to gender-specific guidance for girls (Office on Women's Health)
- WIN the Rockies (Wellness in the Rockies): improve attitudes and behavior about food, physical activity, and body image among rural residents of Idaho, Montana, and Wyoming (U.S. Department of Agriculture's Cooperative State Research, Education, and Extension Service)
- Wisdom Steps Health Promotion Program for Elders: promote health awareness among Native American elders (Office for American Indian, Alaska Native, and Native Hawaiian Programs)
- Blueprint for Action on Breastfeeding: provide action steps to focus attention on the importance of breastfeeding (U.S. Department of Health and Human Services)

"Obesity—A Global"). On the other hand, native Hawaiians have reduced obesity rates by returning to a traditional diet (American Obesity Association, 2005, "Obesity—A Global").

Changes in social structure are also credited with affecting how people eat and subsequently gain weight. For example, many more mothers are working today than in the past, thus cutting the time they have available for cooking meals. In addition, more families are now headed by a single mother who may have less money and time to spend on nutritious foods and cooking. This has been borne out by studies that demonstrate that children who live with single mothers are significantly more likely to become obese (Strauss and Knight, 1999).

Another factor is access to healthy foods. Government nutritional guidelines recommend eating at least five fruits and vegetables each day. Unfortunately, many foods with the highest nutritional value, such as fresh fruits, vegetables, and fish, are also among the most expensive. This may be one reason why rates of obesity are positively correlated with lower

income and lower educational levels (Strauss and Knight, 1999; American Obesity Association, 2005, "Obesity in the U.S.; U.S. Department of Health and Human Services, 2001). For example, women in lower socioeconomic groups are 50 percent more likely to be obese than those with higher socioeconomic status (U.S. Department of Health and Human Services, 2001).

Implications for Designers

The magnitude of weight-related health problems has caught the attention of health professionals as well as individuals at all levels of government. A 2001 report issued by the U.S. Surgeon General, "Call to Action to Prevent and Decrease Overweight and Obesity," includes as a goal the encouragement of "environmental changes that help prevent overweight and obesity" (U.S. Department of Health and Human Services, 2001). As a result, numerous federally funded studies and programs have been established to explore the causes of and find solutions to this problem. The role of the built environment has been targeted as an area of interest, as evidenced by the allocation of $5 million in 2004 to fund projects that "delineate the significance and impact of the built environment on overweight and obesity" (U.S. Department of Health and Human Services, 2004). Many programs, such as the examples in Box 10.2, have been developed by a wide variety of government agencies to fight overweight and obesity.

The reasons for the current overweight and obesity epidemic are extremely complex and include not only environmental but also social, cultural, genetic, physiologic, metabolic, behavioral, and psychological components (American Obesity Association, 2005, "Obesity in the U.S."; U.S. Department of Health and Human Services, 2001; Rosenbloom et al., 2000). Nevertheless, because various elements of the built environment have been linked to increases in weight gain, it makes sense for professionals such as interior designers to have some understanding of the problem. At the macro level, the growth of suburban neighborhoods that encourage heavy use of automobiles has been associated with increasing rates of obesity and decreasing levels of physical fitness (Savich, 2003). In many urban neighborhoods, perceived or real issues of safety, along with the lack of clean, barrier-free walking pathways, are possible reasons for the decrease in walking for health, recreation, or as a means of transportation (Alfonzo, 2005). This may also be one of the causal factors in the high correlation between low income and high obesity rates in females: lower-income neighborhoods are less likely to be perceived as safe for walking and other outdoor activities. At the micro level, as in residences and buildings, the large number of sedentary-encouraging features, such as television sets and computers, has a positive correlation with inactivity and excess weight.

Possibilities for action on the part of designers exist because they have the means to modify environments to promote and support healthy eating and increased physical activity. This is not to say that interior designers are in a position to dictate lifestyles, but they can suggest environmental changes that encourage healthy habits, as seen in the following sections.

Encouraging Good Nutrition

A major component of good nutrition involves achieving an **energy balance.** This means that the energy taken in from foods, in the form of calories, is equivalent to the amount of energy used by the body. When there is excess energy—too many calories—it is stored in the body as fat to be available for later use. A second component of good nutrition is supplying the body with needed nutrients such as vitamins, minerals, and proteins.

Two significant contributors to nutritional problems and the prevalence of overweight individuals in the United States are price and convenience. The lowest-priced foods tend to contain the most calories and the smallest amounts of nutrients. So-called fast foods, for example, are typically high in fats and contain few, if any, vegetables and fruits. The same is true for many snack foods, which are popular because they are filling and they appeal to developed tastes for fats and salt. By contrast, the foods recommended for weight control and good health tend to be more expensive. Examples include fresh vegetables, fruits, and fish.

Creative responses are being developed to resolve this problem. One example is the creation of the Access to Healthy Foods Coalition in the state of Washington. This coalition includes schools, grocery stores, worksites, food growers, and trucking companies that produce, transport, and distribute fresh, nutritious foods to those who need them, such as by supplying food banks (Centers for Disease Control and Prevention, 2005). One way that designers might become involved in these efforts is to suggest the establishment of gardens by communities, neighborhoods, and individuals. Community gardens, in particular, provide a variety of benefits: a source of fresh produce, a venue for getting outdoor exercise working the garden, and a support system for people who are working together to improve their health (see Figure 10.2).

FIGURE 10.2 Community gardens in urban settings offer the availability of healthy fresh foods, opportunities for physical activity, and the chance to socialize with neighbors.

FIGURE 10.3 Adequate storage areas, such as this stand-alone pantry, make cooking at home more convenient. It also allows the purchase of large, more economically priced containers of often-used items.

In some cases, the lack of neighborhood grocery stores results in limited access to fresh, healthy foods. This situation tends to be more prevalent in lower-income areas and has been identified as one reason for the disproportionately high rates of obesity and related health problems among minorities and lower-income individuals. A study that examined changes in diet after the construction of a supermarket in an area that did not have one found that 60 to 75 percent of the individuals who previously had a poor diet now began eating more fruits and vegetables (Wrigley et al., 2003). Thus, built-environment professionals involved with community planning should consider ways to increase food access in communities where it is lacking.

Designing Supportive Kitchens

The multibillion-dollar convenience food industry is the second major contributor to unhealthy eating habits. In spite of their high popularity among children and busy adults, convenience foods tend to combine the worst characteristics of foods: high fat, calories, sodium, and low nutrient value, especially the nutrients needed by growing children. To help decrease overreliance on convenience foods, designers can consider ways to make meal preparation easier when they plan kitchens and storage spaces. As discussed in previous chapters, adequate spaces for washing fresh foods; convenient-to-access and easy-to-clean cutting boards; and safe and convenient storage areas for cooking knives and cooking utensils are a few ideas. Many newer kitchens feature islands with small sinks that make cleaning and cutting fresh foods easier. In addition, designers can plan for the storage of fresh fruits and vegetables, whether in refrigerator drawers, on pantry shelves, or even in outdoor areas (in cool climates). Whole grains are another component of a healthy diet, but these can become infested with insects if not stored properly. Therefore, designers should plan adequate space for large containers with tight-fitting lids should be provided. (See Figure 10.3.)

Other features that encourage cooking with fresh ingredients include shelves for storing cookbooks in view and a small desk or counter area for such tasks as reviewing recipes and making shopping lists. Also, designers should consider storage for pots and pans, especially the large pots required for cooking beans and pasta. These frequently become buried under piles and difficult to extract from the cupboard. Another common problem is the storage of lids for pots and pans, making finding the right one a frustrating task. In short, designers should consider every aspect for making cooking as convenient and pleasurable as possible (see Figure 10.4). (Chapter 7 contains more kitchen planning ideas.)

Special consideration should be given when designing kitchens for the elderly or those with physical disabilities. Older adults tend to suffer nutritional deficiencies, and they are the population most likely to gain excess weight. In fact, older adults have the highest prevalence of overweight and obesity, especially men ages 65 to 74 and women ages 55 to 64 (American Obesity Association, 2005, "Obesity in the U.S."). This is due in part to the difficulties encountered in meal preparation, the cost considerations, and for some, a lack of interest in preparing food for one person and then eating alone. Older adults are more likely to prepare meals in kitchens in which needed items can be grasped without undue reaching and bending and in which appliances are easy to access and use. There are kitchen designs and products available for individuals in wheelchairs or who use walkers, and these should be investigated for clients who can benefit from them. In addition, kitchen and dining areas can be cheerfully decorated so they are pleasant places in which to spend time and invite others to share a meal.

Many older adults enjoy eating at least one meal a day in a public setting. Restaurants should have easily accessible spaces for the elderly (as well as for the disabled of any age). Community centers and senior centers, which may be stand-alone facilities or located in buildings such as churches, can provide hot meals for older adults. (See Figure 10.5.) Designers should include cooking and meal-preparation facilities in the original design of such structures or add to existing ones to provide communities with the means to ensure the nutrition of older adults, as well as giving them a chance for social interaction.

Discouraging Overeating

When overeating is a problem, there are ways that designers can adjust the eating environment in the home (as well as in restaurants) to help prevent high food intakes. This is especially important because children form their eating habits at home, and these habits will help determine their health for the rest of their lives. As mentioned previously, some studies have

shown that obesity in mothers is the most significant risk factor for obesity in children. This is why health professionals stress that encouraging healthy eating habits for all family members is important (Rosenbloom et al., 2000). In addition to suggestions regarding cooking and meal preparation, there are a number of strategies designers can suggest for eating areas. For example, because the color blue is an appetite suppressant, some experts suggest that blue should be used for plates, napkins, placemats, or dining room walls. The colors red, yellow, and orange should be avoided in kitchen and eating areas because they tend to stimulate the appetite. As an aside, many fast-food restaurants use red in their logos and decor to encourage potential customers to think about food.

The size of plates can influence how much people eat. Growing portion sizes have been cited as contributing to weight problems because people tend to eat what is placed in front of them. In homes, restaurants, and institutional

FIGURE 10.4 Pots and pans can pile up in cupboards, making them difficult to access and put away. Consider ways to create storage to make using these items more convenient. Ideas include drawers and pullout shelves.

FIGURE 10.5 Attractive dining areas in community centers offer older Americans the chance to eat nutritious meals and socialize with others. These areas should be bright, cheerful, and accessible to walkers and wheelchairs.

facilities, designers can recommend that dinner plates be downsized. Luncheon-sized or large salad plates are often the right size for holding an appropriate amount of food. Smaller beverage glasses are also suggested as alternatives to the now-common twelve-ounce and even quart-sized drinks.

Much of overeating is done mindlessly, so strategies to keep eaters in the present can be helpful. For example, because overeating is more likely to take place in dimly lit areas, adequate lighting in eating areas is recommended because it increases awareness. Another suggestion is to place a mirror where people can see themselves eating. A study that involved 1,300 people showed that when given a choice between obviously low- and high-calorie options, a higher percentage of those who were dining in front of a mirror choose the lower-calorie option than those who were not eating in front of a mirror. In the home, mirrors should be incorporated into the decor.

The number and location of television sets in a household is correlated to overweight in both children and adults. There are a variety of factors at work here: television viewing often substitutes for physical activity and sports; eating and drinking high-calorie snacks and beverages frequently accompanies television viewing; and eating is often featured in commercials, especially those aimed at children. In addition, when the television is on during meals, attention is drawn away from the eating experience, increasing the tendency to overeat.

Workplace Issues

More than 100 million Americans spend the majority of their day at a worksite (U.S. Department of Health and Human Services, 2001). Employers in the United States are the principal suppliers of health insurance, and the dramatically rising cost of this benefit is becoming burdensome for some and impossible for others. As such, more employers are becoming involved in their employees' health as an economic factor in their business operations.

An important design consideration for the workplace is the creation of eating spaces that are pleasant and conducive to healthy eating. For example, there should be refrigerators large enough for employees to store lunches brought from home, sinks for washing fruits and cleaning up after meals, and sufficient numbers of microwaves and toaster ovens for heating foods. Vending machines should carry healthy options, such as fruits and juices, rather than the typical high-calorie, low-nutrient choices. Designers can make eating spaces more appealing by suggesting wooden dining furniture instead of the commonly used folding tables and metal chairs. The decor should invite workers to eat sit-down meals instead of grab-and-run snacks.

Accommodating Breastfeeding

Breastfeeding infants has been encouraged by many programs, including some sponsored by the federal government, as a way to reduce obesity as children age. Some studies report that breastfeeding lowers the prevalence of obesity, although others show a small correlation between the two (Butte, 2001; Owen et al., 2005). Other benefits linked to breastfeeding include improved neural and psychosocial development; protection against allergy-related diseases; and lowering cholesterol levels in later life (Owen et al., 2005). There is also some evidence that mothers who breastfeed may return to their prepregnancy weight more quickly (U.S. Department of Health and Human Services, 2001). For these reasons, combined with the possibility that some protection against obesity is indeed provided, it makes sense to encourage mothers to breastfeed their babies. Although breastfeeding can be done in public, many mothers prefer privacy. Thus, designers should create appropriate spaces for breastfeeding in workplaces, public facilities, schools, retail outlets, and other locations frequented by mothers and infants. These areas should be warm and dimly lit; they should be large enough so that strollers can be pushed inside and parked; and they should be furnished with comfortable seating and a changing table.

Encouraging Good Nutrition in Schools

Schools are to children what workplaces are to adults: the place where they spend a large portion of their time. Most children eat at least one meal a day at school, but millions of children eat both breakfast and lunch there. This makes the issue of nutrition one of concern to schools as well as families. There have been calls to remove vending machines from schools, especially primary and elementary schools, unless they contain healthy snacks and foods, as well as removing high-calorie, low-nutrition snacks from student stores. In addition, school kitchens must be designed for the preparation of meals that not only meet nutrition standards, such as the inclusion of fruits and vegetables, but are appetizing as well. As in homes, this means providing adequate refrigeration, sinks, storage, and food preparation areas.

FIGURE 10.6 School cafeterias should be designated to provide inviting places that encourage healthy eating.

Because families are eating out more than in the past, students of all ages have higher expectations of school cafeteria services and environments. In response, some schools are developing creative ways to present foods. For example, Aramark, a contractor of school lunch services, developed the Cart Park: a bright red and yellow mobile unit that contains a variety of foods from which students can choose (Crosby, 1999). In Portland, Oregon, the U-Chews program features a cart with empty lunch boxes that students can fill by selecting among the foods displayed (Crosby, 1999).

In addition to good presentation of foods, eating areas for both students and staff should be comfortable and pleasant. Many school buildings are old and have outdated cafeterias. Walls and furnishings are often bland, institutional colors, garbage cans are located throughout the eating areas, and overcrowding is common. Combined with flooring and walls made of hard finishes, the result can be a noisy, smelly environment that is not very conducive to eating. A trend that designers might consider is revamping cafeterias to look more like commercial eating establishments; using bright colors, such as the school colors; replacing the traditional long, impersonal tables with groupings of smaller ones; adding booths; installing adequate windows; and installing brighter lights. The goal is to create a fun, pleasant place that encourages children and teens to make nutritious food choices and then take the time to eat them. Designers should also suggest providing refrigerators and microwaves for children who bring their lunches from home. (See Figure 10.6.)

Designing for a Larger America

Although the ideal is to create surroundings that discourage overweight, the reality is that designers are confronted with creating environments that accommodate larger people. Additional space, larger furnishings, and stronger floors are just some of the features necessary to meet the needs of people who weigh hundreds of pounds and cannot use standard-sized items. One ergonomist reports that his most common client request is for office chairs that can hold more than the standard 300 pounds (Janis, 2007).

Public areas must include seating for large individuals. It is recommended that these be blended in among standard-size seating for both aesthetic and personal consideration. A design challenge is to provide safe and comfortable furnishings without drawing attention to what is for many an embarrassing condition. In environments commonly frequented by obese individuals, such as health-care facilities, bathrooms must be designed to accommodate extra weight. Bathrooms should include toilets and grab bars that will not give under extreme weight and pressure and larger shower units, for example.

In addition to creating appropriate spaces, furnishings that meet the needs of overweight and obese individuals are available.

PHYSICAL ACTIVITY

Physical activity provides a multitude of health benefits, as shown in Box 10.3. In fact, it has been said that if exercise could be put into a bottle, it would constitute the world's first true miracle drug. On the other hand, a lack of physical activity accounts for up to 10 percent of the deaths in the United States (Wener and Evans, 2007).

Physical activity influences body weight in at least three ways. The first is that it increases the number of calories burned each day over and above the amount of energy used simply to maintain body functions. Muscles require energy to contract and relax, so the more movement, the more calories burned. Even **moderate activity,** defined as the amount needed to use about 150 calories each day or 1,000 calories each week, is beneficial to health. (See Box 10.4 for examples of moderate activities.) The second way is that regular exercise increases the body's consumption of energy even when it is at rest. The reverse may also be true: sedentary behavior may promote low energy requirements, thus making the extra calories consumed by most Americans, including children, more likely to be converted to fat, rather than burned as energy (Maffeis, 1999). And the third way is that muscle tissue uses more energy to maintain itself than does fat tissue. Thus, the more muscle in the body, the faster calories are burned.

In spite of the many proven benefits of exercise, fewer than half of all Americans get the recommended amounts of at least 30 minutes of moderate activity five days a week or 20 minutes of **vigorous activity** three days a week. In fact, results from the 2000 National Health Interview Survey show that only 19.0 percent of adults regularly engaged in a high level of physical activity, with 23.5 percent engaging in medium-level activity (Barnes and Schoenborn, 2003). Even children and adolescents are getting less exercise than the recommended 60 minutes per day for their age groups. Only about 50 percent of young people ages 12–21 regularly engage in vigorous physical activity, with about 25 percent engaging in no vigorous physical activity at all. This is especially problematic because it has been shown that participation in physical activity declines significantly with increase in age, so those who do little as youngsters are not likely to improve their habits (National Center for Chronic Disease Prevention and Health Promotion, 1999).

Adequate physical activity is especially important for children for several reasons. As discussed in Chapter 8, physical movement promotes healthy physical and mental development. For example, poor bone strength in childhood can increase the risk of osteoporosis later in life (Stratton, 2000). In addition, a lack of physical activity often results in excess weight, which, in turn, predisposes children to overweight and obesity as adults.

The decline in physical activity levels among young people has many causes. One is the reduction or elimination of physical education classes in schools. This is unfortunate because many children spend the majority of their time at school; in addition, this is where many learn the physical activity habits that will last throughout their lives. Some

schools have made these cuts in response to the recently mandated emphasis on academics and required standardized testing; however, at least one study has shown that regular physical activity can favorably influence academic performance (Sallis et al., 1999). This is not surprising when we consider that exercise increases blood circulation and the distribution of oxygen to the brain.

BOX 10.3 BENEFITS OF REGULAR PHYSICAL ACTIVITY

- Reduces risk for heart attack and colon cancer
- Helps body use insulin properly, thus decreasing risk for diabetes
- Helps lower high blood pressure
- May reduce risk for stroke
- Helps control weight by increasing the amount of energy used
- Contributes to healthy bones, muscles, and joints
- Reduces falls among older adults
- Helps relieve the pain of arthritis
- Reduces symptoms of anxiety and depression
- Promotes psychological well-being
- Prevents functional limitations and improves physical function
- Is associated with fewer hospitalizations, physician visits, and medications

Adapted from: Centers for Disease Control and Prevention. (2006). *Physical activity and good nutrition: Essential elements to prevent chronic diseases and obesity.* [Brochure]. Atlanta, GA: Author.

National Institute of Diabetes and Digestive and Kidney Diseases. (2006). *Am I at risk for type 2 diabetes? Taking steps to reduce your risk of getting diabetes* (NIH Publication No. 07-4805). Bethesda, MD: Author.

U.S. Department of Health and Human Services. (June 20, 2002). *Physical activity fundamental to preventing disease.* Retrieved December 3, 2006, from http://aspe.hhs.gov/health/reports/physicalactivity/physicalactivity.pdf

BOX 10.4 EXAMPLES OF MODERATE-LEVEL PHYSICAL ACTIVITIES

- Washing and waxing a car for 45 minutes
- Gardening for 30–45 minutes
- Washing windows or floors for 45–60 minutes
- Wheeling self in wheelchair for 30–40 minutes
- Raking leaves for 30 minutes
- Playing touch football for 45 minutes
- Dancing (fast, social) for 30 minutes
- Running one mile in 10 minutes

Source: National Heart, Lung, and Blood Institute. (n.d.) *Moderate-level physical activities.* Retrieved December 3, 2007, from www.nhlbi.nih.gov/hbp/prevent/p_active/m_l_phys.htm

FIGURE 10.7 Incorporating exercise into daily life is an efficient way to increase physical activity. Attractive, well-lit stairs are more likely to be used than the bland, isolated stairwells that exist in many buildings.

place, some large companies are designing their campuses to encourage walking. Parking lots are located at a distance from buildings, pathways between buildings are made inviting, and facilities such as cafeterias are placed some distance from offices. (Provisions must be made, of course, for disabled workers.) Designers must consider weather conditions and perhaps include covers over walkways or install tunnels in areas where the weather is extreme.

Stairs offer another way of incorporating exercise into daily life. Climbing stairs both increases the heart rate and exercises the leg muscles. The benefits of stair use were borne out by a study of 11,000 Harvard alumni, which found that climbing at least twenty floors each week lowered the risk of stroke or death by 20 percent (Paffenbarger et al., 1986). Although artificial stairs (stair climbers or steppers) have become commonplace in public and home gyms, the real stairs in most buildings discourage use. They are inconveniently located in out-of-the-way corners, appear drab and unattractive, and feel unsafe. Elevators and escalators, on the other hand, are generally centrally located and inviting. This is true even in settings where the goal is to promote health, such as hospitals and clinics. Designers can encourage the use of stairs in existing buildings in a number of ways: providing adequate signs that indicate their location, posting signs that promote the healthfulness of climbing stairs, painting stairwells attractive colors, providing adequate lighting, and adding piped-in music. (See Figure 10.7.)

Promoting Walking Among Adults

In the past, walking was a natural part of most people's everyday life. People walked to school, to the store, to the post office, and to visit their neighbors. Current land-use patterns in the United States discourage walking and other forms of exercise (Frank et al., 2006; Savich, 2003). Zoning ordinances separate residential and commercial areas, and street designs such as cul-de-sacs interrupt direct connections between streets. Studies have found that less walking takes place among people who live in these suburban-type designs than among those

The Surgeon General has identified schools as "a key setting for public health strategies to prevent and decrease the prevalence of overweight and obesity" (U.S. Department of Health and Human Services, 2001). Reversing the cuts in physical education can be a starting point. Designers can become involved in promoting such initiatives in their communities. From a professional standpoint, their work might involve planning appropriate areas for exercise and activities and locker rooms built with easy-to-clean, nonslip surfaces and proper ventilation.

Physical Activity in Daily Life

Physical activity can be integrated into the everyday lives of people of all ages. In the work-who live in more traditional urban neighborhoods. A 1999 survey conducted in Seattle, a city of many suburbs, found that 85.5 percent of all work trips and 86 percent of all nonwork trips were made in private vehicles (Frank et al., 2006). Walking today is widely viewed as recreation rather than transportation (Evans-Cowley, 2006).

Implications for Designers

Creating safe and appealing walking paths in both urban and suburban neighborhoods would benefit all age groups and particularly older adults, who report that walking is their favorite physical activity (Joseph and Zimring, 2007). As with other age groups, older adults' perception of an environment influences how much they walk (Joseph and Zimring, 2007). Positive factors for this age group include enjoyable scenery, convenient locations, and walking accessibility to recreational facilities and retail establishments. Other desirable characteristics for recreational walking include long, uninterrupted stretches and hills and inclines. Thus, designing appealing and useful walkways is especially important when planning all types of residential communities and facilities for older adults. Box 10.5 contains suggestions for increasing the walkability of various settings in the built environment.

Urban settings with safe, pleasant walkways that connect businesses, parks, restaurants, and other destinations encourage walking as a means of transportation. Such places also reduce the use of fossil fuels and harmful emissions from cars.

Walking and Cycling for Children

Walking and cycling are excellent physical activities for young people because they fulfill the utilitarian purpose of providing transportation. Youths who use foot or pedal power are developing habits that may extend into adulthood. This is significant, because many adults cite lack of time as the reason they fail to get enough exercise. Thus, making a practice of incorporating physical activity into daily activities such as transportation is an excellent

---

BOX 10.5 INCREASING WALKABILITY

- Revise land-use policies to enable increased mixed-use development.
- Emphasize the centrality of resources.
- Increase pedestrian accessibility to commercial establishments.
- Protect green space through land trust funds and zoning ordinances that protect undeveloped land.
- Renovate urban centers.
- Create walking and cycling pathways with safety features such as marked crosswalks and good lighting.
- Encourage the building of high-density neighborhoods with physical and visual access to green space, public buildings, and mixed-use facilities.
- Locate neighborhoods adjacent to existing urban infrastructure.
- Create a variety of pathways and walking surfaces to give potential walkers multiple options.
- Provide the means, such as bridges and medians, to overcome pedestrian barriers.
- Maintain cleanliness and upkeep of streets, sidewalks, and pathways.
- Encourage street components to increase comfort and attractiveness, such as canopies, arcades, benches, and fountains.

Adapted from: Savich, H. V. (2003). How suburban sprawl shapes human well-being. *Journal of Urban Health, 80,* 590–607.

Jackson, L. E. The relationship of urban design to human health and condition. *Landscape and Urban Planning, 64,* 191–200.

Alfonzo, M. A. (2005). To walk or not to walk? The hierarchy of walking needs. *Environment and Behavior, 37,* 808–836.

---

start to lifelong healthy habits. It has also been found that adults who walk during their daily activities are more likely to engage in leisure-time physical exercise than those who sit during most of the day (Barnes and Schoenborn, 2003).

BOX 10.6 THE SUSTAINABILITY CONNECTION

Children's play requirements change as they grow older. Outdoor home play areas and equipment should encourage open-ended activities that are not bound by age limitations or specific activities. For example, a sandbox can be large enough to accommodate small children digging and playing and older children building elaborate castles and villages. Teens might enjoy creating elaborate sculptures. Forts and tree houses can serve as private getaways or as clubhouses when friends come to play. Children's gardens can increase in size and complexity as children grow older and are more able to care for them. And structures can be designed to be convertible for other uses. A wooden picnic table, for example, might be temporarily converted into a fort with an oversized tablecloth.

Adapted from: Sunset Publishing Corporation. (2004). *Kids' places to play.* Menlo Park, CA: Author.

FIGURE 10.8 Appealing parks that attract public use are clean and safe, as well as providing any number of amenities such as museums, gardens, pathways, and week-end entertainment.

Implications for Designers

A major reason for driving children to school and other activities is safety. Parents worry about crime, fast-moving traffic, and the lack of judgment of small children. To reverse this trend, programs are being developed to promote walking and biking to school. For example, Safe Routes to School in Denmark and the United Kingdom includes the creation of safe walking paths, secured bicycle storage areas in schools, and safety training for children (Osborne, 2005). In the United States, the Centers for Disease Control and Prevention's Nutrition and Physical Activity Program has developed the KidsWalk-to-School program to encourage and assist communities in creating safe environments that support walking and cycling to school (Centers for Disease Control and Prevention, 2006, "Kids"). Designers should investigate these initiatives for ideas and possible funding sources when planning facilities that house children, such as schools and day-care centers.

Parks and Public Places

Parks have great potential to provide green space and opportunities for physical activity for people of all ages; however, safety has become an issue in many public spaces, including parks and wilderness areas. In cities, for example, some public spaces serve as gathering places for groups that intimidate other members of the public. Teenagers may congregate in parks and display behaviors, such as smoking, swearing, and drinking, that prevent park use by younger children whose parents do not want them exposed to such activities. Women and older adults likewise tend to feel uncomfortable where these kinds of activities occur.

In addition to teens, illegal drug users are sometimes attracted to public spaces. These individuals are bad examples, and their behavior can pose a danger to other park users; moreover, they sometimes leave harmful paraphernalia, such as needles, in play areas. Homeless populations, which have increased since the release of many mentally ill patients from facilities in the 1980s, frequently use public parks for shelter. Their presence also deters people from using public areas for physical activity.

Implications for Designers

Although public safety is under the jurisdiction of public officials, designers can become involved in helping create public policy and suggesting ways to improve the quality and safety of public places. For example, it is believed that boredom motivates some teens to engage in unacceptable activities. Thus, creating meeting places with interesting, age-appropriate activities for teens could contribute to their health, as well as the health of community members who wish to use outdoor areas free of intimidation. Facilities for teens might include spaces in schools that are accessible after school; community centers with access to computers, video games, and homework tutors; sports facilities such as basketball courts and playing fields (in addition to those used by teams at practice); skateboard parks; climbing walls; and gathering places for listening to music, talking, and dancing.

In addition to working as a community to solve social problems such as homelessness, immediate measures can be taken to make spaces safer. For example, San Diego's Balboa Park is patrolled by police officers on horseback, a practice that actually adds to the pleasant ambience of the park. Amenities that attract large numbers of people to the park include cafes, art exhibits and sales, vendors, and entertainment. (See Figure 10.8.) As more people use parks, they become less attractive to individuals who engage in antisocial behaviors. Additional security measures that parks can include are security cameras, adequate lighting, and citizen patrols.

In addition to safety, people of all ages benefit from convenience features such as clean restrooms, drinking water, lighting, shade, picnic tables, and places to sit. Walking paths should vary in difficulty, with resting places at frequent intervals to enable individuals of all fitness levels to benefit from them. Fitness trails in many parks incorporate exercise stations to add other types of physical movement to the walking or running experience. (See Figure 10.9.)

Finally, access to parks and open spaces determines their level of use, especially by children and older adults who wish to walk or cycle. Busy streets and highways often act as barriers to the public. When parents must transport children to parks and playgrounds the frequency of visits becomes limited, especially among working parents. Providing unobstructed walking and cycling paths, along with conveniently located bus stops, increases park use.

Playgrounds

Some schools encourage outdoor activities, but the areas set aside for play activities are often far from optimal. One reason is that children's playscapes, whether in school yards, day-care centers, or public parks, are usually designed by adults. For decades the most important concern has been safety, a natural and responsible response to the many accidents that occur in playgrounds. (See Chapter 9 for more information about playground safety.) Other factors that influence playground design include the need for easy maintenance and surveillance by adults and the desire for a neat and tidy look; an unintended result is that many, if not most,

FIGURE 10.9 Many parks have built fitness equipment, spaced at intervals along walkways and paths, to challenge those who wish to incorporate more exercise into their walks.

planned play areas are rather sterile and boring (Veitch et al., 2006; Lindholm, 1995), offering little benefit to children (Malone and Trantor, 2003).

Even when efforts are made to provide interesting play areas, adults often miss the mark. It has been suggested that much of the research conducted about children's environments lacks insight into how children view the world and about their play preferences (Burke, 2005). This is an important point because designing outdoor spaces that appeal to children is especially important today due to the amount

BOX 10.7   A UNIQUE APPROACH TO DETERMINING YOUNG CLIENTS' NEEDS

A study conducted in Leeds, England, involved having children, ages seven to eleven, photograph play areas for one week. The criterion was that the areas evoke either positive or negative emotions. During follow-up interviews, the children were shown the developed images they had taken and asked to choose and discuss one. The interviewer then selected a photo that countered the child's first choice in some way and invited the child's comments about it. Most of the photos were of outdoor spaces, with many featuring natural materials such as grasses. Open spaces were also mentioned frequently in the interviews.

Adapted from: Burke, C. (2005). Play in focus: Children researching their own spaces and places for play. *Children, Youth, and Environments*, 15, 27–53.

of competition from indoor activities—television, computers, and video games—vying for their attention.

Implications for Designers

An approach to playground design that has been tried in England and elsewhere is to solicit children's opinions and ideas, as described in Boxes 10.7 and 10.8.

As these boxes suggest, children are drawn to natural outdoor environments, a preference supported by many studies (Titman, 1994). A

BOX 10.8   SUGGESTIONS FROM CHILDREN

When children in Canada were asked what they felt they needed in their school play areas, they offered the following suggestions:
• Nature trails
• Gardens
• Shade trees and bushes
• Flowers
• Peaceful sounds
• Shelters from wind, rain, sun, noise, and rough play
• Social places with seats and tables
• Seating for outdoor classrooms
• Murals
• Colorful pavement markings for games
• Mazes
• Places for music, dance, drama, and arts and crafts
• Wildlife habitat such as bird feeders and ponds

Adapted from: Coffey, A. (2006). *A guide to transforming school grounds:* Canadian Biodiversity Institute. Ottawa: Marquardt Printing Ltd.

correlated finding is that physical activity is greater among young children during times of free play than during structured activities (Bailey et al., 1994). Children's activities are highly related to their environment, an example of the theory of **affordance,** which states that the form of a space influences the activities that occur in it (Cosco and Moore, 1999). For example, closed-in spaces, such as those created by shrubs, large rocks, and built structures, are seen as potential forts, dens, and hiding places; hills are structures for climbing and sliding; and open areas are for running and chasing.

Natural environments also provide the elements that young children use to explore their world: colors, temperatures, smells, textures, and sounds (Skantze, 1995). Children interact with things around them by touching, digging, and collecting. This is one reason why they find items they can manipulate—dirt, leaves, pinecones, and grasses—appealing. Another is that children enjoy using natural materials to create their own play areas, something they cannot do with play equipment that is cemented into the ground. Creating their own spaces, such as planting a garden, adds a "special layer of meaning to the place" (Cosco and Moore, 1999).

Of course, playgrounds, especially in urban areas, cannot always take advantage of natural landscapes. In most cases, the natural landscape has already been paved over. Thus, redesigning may be necessary to bring in some of the characteristics that make natural landscapes desirable. Successful projects transforming barren, nondescript playgrounds have been carried out successfully in several countries, and models exist to help designers move forward (Coffey, 2006). Examples of design actions include providing varied ground covers, such as grass, paving stones, and sand; building adventure play features, such as tunnels, into the landscape; planting trees, shrubs, and other greenery; and providing loose materials that children can manipulate. (See Figure 10.10.)

In addition to adding natural elements to playgrounds, it is suggested that they be divided into spaces suitable for small groups to meet and play (Malone and Tranter, 2003). Many

FIGURE 10.10 Children enjoy variety in their playscapes, such as different levels and textures. In this example, the rocks and trees provide hiding places, the structures offer climbing and crawling opportunities, and the open area can be used for running or games.

playgrounds offer few or no opportunities for children who are not athletic to comfortably develop their skills. Wide-open hardscapes encourage chasing and games that involve kicking balls around. These designs also favor competitive games in which less athletic children either cannot or prefer not to participate (Barbour, 1999). Moreover, in well-intentioned attempts to use the space available, teachers may encourage such games, with the result that some children are intimidated and develop an aversion to physical activity. Areas in which children can engage in cooperative rather than competitive activities are more likely to promote enjoyment of physical activity.

Another argument against wide-open hardscapes is the issue of bullying. Some researchers believe that a major reason for bullying in school yards is the competition for territory prompted by large, flat expanses of hard surface that children stake out and defend (Coffey, 2006). Other contributing factors to bullying are the boredom that results from such designs and the lack of private areas where children can get away from bullies (Malone and Tranter, 2003; Lambert, 1999). When dividing play areas, however, care must be taken to balance the equipment and opportunities for play in the various areas because research indicates that hostility over space and equipment allocations perceived as unfair can also be a factor in bullying (Malone and Tranter, 2003; Rivkin, 1995).

Safety must continue to be a factor when designing and choosing play equipment. At the same time, various age and ability levels should be considered. In an Australian study, parents complained that the equipment in a typical playground was designed for very young children. Older children found it uninteresting and unchallenging and did not enjoy visiting parks and playgrounds as they grew older (Veitch et al., 2005).

BOX 10.9 THE SUSTAINABILITY CONNECTION

Walking and cycling as means of transportation could cut energy consumption and reduce emissions from vehicles, thus cutting our dependence on oil resources and improving our air quality. Even more significant is the belief by many scientists that the heavy use of fossil fuels is a major cause of global warming. Thus, decreasing their use could mean helping to sustain the earth as we know it.

Physical Activity and the Workplace

Adults spend a large number of their waking hours working. In the past, this often meant long hours of physical labor, but as we have moved from an agrarian to an industrial and now to a knowledge- and service-based economy, more workers now spend more time at desks and computers. As a result, we have become increasingly sedentary at work.

In view of the many health benefits of exercise, many employers are encouraging their employees to exercise by providing environments in which they can do so. Employees who engage in physical exercise improve their alertness, mental concentration, stamina, reaction time, and memory. The Health Canada Population Health Survey reports additional benefits, including increased morale, reduced injury rates, better employee relations, and improved job satisfaction (Toronto Public Health, 2007). Also, as with the population at large who are physically active, they enjoy better overall health, have lower average medical expenses (Pratt et al., 2000), and use between 6 and 32 percent less short-term sick leave (National Center for Chronic Disease Prevention and Health Promotion, 1999). Because employers suffer from lost productivity during sick leave and pay the majority of health insurance costs in the United States, they have a bottom-line interest in medical expense savings.

Many employers, therefore, are heeding the section of the Surgeon General's *Call to Action* that encourages them to "establish worksite exercise facilities or create incentives for employees to join local fitness centers" (U.S. Department of Health and Human Services, 2001). One response has been the creation of employee wellness programs. As many as 81 percent of businesses with more than 50 employees reportedly have some type of health program (Krieger, 2005). Large companies that have calculated the financial benefits from such programs include the following:

- General Electric: Fitness program members reduced their health-care costs by 38 percent during an 18-month period.

- DuPont: Each dollar invested in workplace health promotion yielded $1.42 over two years in lower absenteeism costs.
- Traveler's Corporation: Each dollar invested yields a return of $3.40 (Krieger, 2005).

Implications for Designers

An important part of many wellness programs is an exercise facility. These range from hallways designated as walking paths to complete gyms with sophisticated exercise equipment. Designers can assist employers by ensuring that gyms and other exercise areas have appropriate flooring (see Chapter 3), surfaces that are easy to clean and disinfect, adequate ventilation, and temperature controls separate from other areas of the building. (See Chapter 5 for information on indoor climate.) To inspire effective workouts, designers can use attractive colors; safely affix mirrors to walls so they won't crack with accidental impact; and provide outlets for music. Some exercise facilities have flat-screen television sets attached to the walls facing treadmills, stationary bicycles, and stair climbers. Changing rooms with lockers and showers make exercise during the lunch hour or before or after work more convenient for employees.

STRESS

When we experience stress, whether physical or mental, the brain initiates a chain of physical reactions in the body. Recall from Chapter 2 that if these reactions are experienced over time they can damage the body, suppress the immune system, and cause both acute and chronic illnesses. In fact, it is widely believed that many visits to a physician's office are prompted by stress-related symptoms.

Workplace Stress

For thousands of years, the stress of work was mainly physical. Stress today tends to be mental, the effects of pushing to produce more, at lower costs, in an environment that allows little physical activity and movement.

BOX 10.10 EXPERT SPOTLIGHT: Wellness and Fitness Centers

David A. Hall, Ed.D, CRSS
Director of Campus Recreation
Springfield College
Springfield, MA

There are a combination of reasons that are prompting corporations, housing/apartment developments, adult communities, municipalities, and colleges and universities nationwide to build wellness and fitness facilities. They include the proactive intention of promoting healthy lifestyles; the financial impetus of having healthier and more productive employees; and the advantage of offering an employee benefit for recruiting and retention.

There are competing and conflicting data regarding health and wellness. We see pronouncements such as "Americans are fatter than ever;" ". . . health care costs due to hypokinetic diseases are skyrocketing because of inactivity;" ". . . the average American workday is now the longest in the world;" ". . . more Americans are exercising than ever;" and ". . . fitness and wellness centers are seeing their largest increases in membership."

Strange as it may seem, all of these pronouncements may be true. There are 300 million Americans: many of these folks are attempting to achieve a healthier lifestyle, while many are not. The health and wellness industry is growing and doing a better job of doing scholarly research and communicating their findings to the general public.

Regardless of the impetus for creating a fitness facility, the main result is relatively simple: people who exercise see many benefits to their overall health by simply exercising three to five times per week for just 30 minutes a session. These benefits include increased cardiovascular fitness, increased flexibility, improved body composition, increased muscular strength and endurance, improved energy levels, elevated mood, and a better self-image.

Today's physical facilities have come a long way from the square box dungeons of the 1950s, 1960s, and 1970s. Many are spectacular in their architectural design and offer inviting, safe, and open activity spaces. The best designs also allow for the privacy and comfort of each individual user. Optimal flooring such as cushioned, suspended wood or padded synthetic surfaces with vibrant color schemes offer injury prevention, as well as being easy to maintain. Biomechanically correct weight and cardiovascular equipment is now offered by many reputable vendors and learning to use them correctly is easier than ever.

Wellness and fitness facilities and amenities are now more readily available than ever, as are qualified professionals. Our biggest task now is to get these nonexercising Americans to set aside the needed 30 minutes per day, three to five times a week on a consistent basis. If those of us in the industry can do that, we will all benefit from the results.

Although workplace conditions have improved and the number of hours worked declined with the rise of worker unions in the early part of the last century, in recent years the average number of hours spent working increased steadily for many people. This is especially true for professional careers, such as law and management, in which individuals are expected to "pay their dues" by working long hours. In addition, technology that was originally intended to make life easier may actually be adding to our stress as cell phones and laptop computers make it possible for us to be continually in touch and on the job. This may be one reason why surveys show that between 29 and 40 percent of workers believe their jobs are very or extremely stressful (Sauter et al., n.d.). Studies have also revealed the following employee perceptions of workplace stress:

- Twenty-five percent feel that their number one stressor in life is their job.
- Seventy-five percent believe they have more job stress than employees of the last generation.
- Many believe that workplace problems are more strongly associated with health problems than any other stressor (Sauter et al., n.d.).

Many employers are recognizing the human and financial costs of stress among their employees. For example, health-care expenditures are reportedly 50 percent greater for workers who report high levels of stress (Sauter et al., n.d.). Research has also found that workplace stress is associated with increased absenteeism, tardiness, and thoughts about leaving the job. Common specific reactions to stress are listed

BOX 10.11 EARLY SIGNS OF JOB STRESS

- Headache
- Sleep disturbances
- Difficulty in concentrating
- Short temper
- Upset stomach
- Job dissatisfaction
- Low morale

Adapted from: Sauter, S., Murphy, L., Colligan, M., Swanson, N., Hurrell, J. Jr., Scharf, F. Jr., et al. (n.d.). Stress . . . at work. (DHHS NIOSH Publication No. 99–101). Washington, DC: National Institute for Occupational Safety and Health.

in Box 10.11, all of which interfere with employee performance and productivity (Sauter et al., n.d.). This is why, in addition to providing the means to engage in physical exercise, up to half of large corporations are including stress management in their employee wellness programs, ranging from offering stress-release and time-management workshops to providing extensive relaxation centers (Sauter et al., n.d.).

Implications for Designers

Employees find it particularly difficult to cope with environmental factors over which they have no control, including uncomfortable temperatures, inappropriate workstations, and noise. Interior designers can suggest the application of ergonomic considerations in the workplace, as described in Chapter 7.

Designers also can assist in stress-reduction efforts by planning areas within the workplace where employees can escape from everyday duties and engage in stress-reducing activities. For example, the goal in designing eating areas should be to create an atmosphere that encourages relaxation during lunch and breaks. As such, they might incorporate the following characteristics and features:

- Clean and comfortable and away from noisy work areas
- Tables that accommodate small groups.
- Comfortable chairs
- Attractively decorated with color, plants, and calming artifacts
- Windows that allow the entry of natural light or lighting that replicates natural light as closely as possible
- Outdoor dining areas for use during warm weather

A common cause of workplace stress is lack of communication among employees, so designers should consider creating spaces in which employees can meet and share ideas. These can include conference rooms, small break rooms with adequate furniture for small groups, and benches in outdoor areas where informal and impromptu meetings can take place. In other words, create an environment that encourages and enables interpersonal connections while, at the same time, provides spaces for doing private work.

For optimal rest and renewal, workplaces should include quiet locations for reflection, meditation, or simply escaping from noise and activity. Such places can be simple, perhaps involving an unused or small storage area. The furnishings should be comfortable, such as lounge-type chairs, recliners, rocking chairs, or large floor pillows. Small outdoor areas can also be designed using plants, a small water feature, and seating (see Figure 10.11).

FIGURE 10.11 This is an example of a well-designed outdoor area in which employees can relax, visit, and recharge before returning to work.

Large companies such as Google are providing amenities such as day-care and laundry facilities to relieve the stress of balancing long hours at work with personal responsibilities. Provisions are also made that allow employees to bring pets to work. While these provisions are likely outside the capabilities of many employers, designers can still add convenience and homelike touches to workplaces that help employees lower their stress and become more productive.

Reducing Stress with Physical Activity

Physical exercise helps reduce stress in a number of ways:

- More oxygen and nutrients are distributed to the cells throughout the body, including to the brain.
- The neurotransmitters serotonin and norepinephrine, helpful in relieving depression, are activated and balanced.
- Endorphins, neurotransmitters that facilitate feelings of well-being and aid in relaxation, are produced (Mayo Clinic, 2005, "Exercise").

In addition to initiating physical responses, physical activity can increase levels of self-confidence and accomplishment, provide distraction from dwelling on bad feelings, and provide opportunities to decrease isolation by interacting with others (Mayo Clinic, 2005, "Depression"). Physical activity has been shown to improve self-esteem and reduce levels of anxiety in teens (National Center for Chronic Disease Prevention and Health Promotion, 1999).

Exercise is a positive coping mechanism that can be substituted for commonly used but generally unhelpful "stress relievers," such as overeating and drinking alcohol. In fact, the positive effects of physical activity can be powerful, as evidenced by studies showing it to reduce rates of illness and death from mental health disorders (U.S. Preventive Services Task Force, 1996). Even for people of average health, many experts believe that physical

---

BOX 10.12 VIEW TO THE FUTURE

Components of an "Ideal" Workplace Stress Management Center
- Library of stress and relaxation resources
- Biofeedback equipment to teach muscle relaxation
- Light-sound machines to drive brainwave activity and facilitate a state of relaxation
- Restricted environmental stimulation technique (shallow, high-density floating pool)
- Lounging furniture
- Yoga, meditation, and relaxation classes
- Massage table or chair
- Professional, qualified staff

Adapted from: Randolfi, E. A. (1997). Developing a stress management and relaxation center for the worksite. *Worksite Health*, 4(3), 40–44.

---

activity has a direct correlation to happiness and satisfaction with one's life and may be a better predictor of satisfaction than health and income (Kopec, 2006). Thus, we can see that in addition to the many benefits discussed in the previous sections, physical activity should be promoted as a means of reducing stress and preventing the physical problems to which stress can lead.

Stress-Reducing Environments

Relaxing spaces have a sense of harmony and simplicity. They are uncluttered, meaning that the contents of a structure have a purpose or are meaningful to the people who use them. Many homes and offices become filled with items that are outdated or are being saved "just in case" they might be needed in the future. Such environments can be distracting rather than restful, because the presence of clutter reminds people of things they have to do or should do and prevents escape from everyday concerns. This is why freedom from clutter is especially important in bedrooms, which should be conducive to rest and sleep. Designers can increase their value to clients by helping them choose and organize their belongings to create more harmonious surroundings. (It should be noted, however, that not everyone's definition of clutter is the same. For example, some people find comfort surrounding themselves with items they have collected from their travels, creating an environment that would be too busy for others. As with all facets of design, getting to know your clients and their preferences can help you determine what is appropriate.)

Good organization is another key to achieving a low-stress environment. Essential items such as mail and bills to be paid should be conveniently located and easy to find. Nothing increases stress like rummaging through piles on the dining room table to find a needed document. Explore the needs of clients to ensure that their surroundings support their daily activities. For example, a family with school-age children should have a convenient place to set out lunches, backpacks, sports equipment, and anything else they will need during the day. A large calendar and bulletin board can serve as the family organizer. In an office setting, the staff mailboxes should be organized with easy-to-reach cubbyholes and a counter for setting purses and sorting mail. Knowing your clients and their daily activities is necessary for creating stress-free designs.

Sleeping Spaces

Sleep deprivation has been cited as a major problem in the United States, with more than half of adults sleeping less than seven hours most nights and having difficulty sleeping a few nights a week (Winerman, 2004). Inadequate sleep reduces alertness, attention span, and reaction time (Winerman, 2004), thus interfering with tasks such as driving. Difficulty sleeping is also a common problem among teens, as discussed in Chapter 8.

Implications for Designers

Designers can contribute to solving the sleep deficit by creating sleeping areas that promote sleep and rest. A good start is to eliminate clutter, as mentioned previously, as well as items that contribute to allergies, as discussed in Chapters 3 and 4. Second, colors can influence rest, with soft hues generally being the best. Some color specialists believe that colors have special properties and suggest the following as

good choices for a bedroom or space designated for relaxation:

- Pale green: relieves anxiety; stimulates the immune system; and promotes feelings of harmony, hope, and serenity
- Powder blue: lowers blood pressure, decreases heart rate, and encourages sleep
- Violet: suggests calm and spirituality
- Mauve and pink: encourage love and romance (Craven, 2003)

Special Spaces

Special spaces, sometimes called sacred spaces, provide the opportunity to get away from one's usual environment. This "getting away" is the first step in attention restoration therapy, a recognized process for relieving stress (Kaplan and Kaplan, 1989). This theory is based on observations that when we become fatigued, it becomes difficult to pay sustained attention, even to our daily tasks. In a sense, our minds become overwhelmed and fatigued and need rest, just like our physical bodies.

Implications for Designers

When helping clients design sacred spaces, it is essential for the designer to fully understand their needs and preferences because these can vary greatly among individuals, even within a single household. The space may serve as a place for prayer, yoga, meditation, reading, or simply enjoying silence. The contents might include sacred books; family mementos; handcrafted pieces; items from nature, such as rocks and shells; and spiritual symbols or sculptures. Some people find meaning in setting up small altars.

Special spaces need not take up much room and may be created in areas such as an attic, walk-in closet, bedroom corner, cellar, or an outdoor space such as a gazebo. Furnishings can be simple but should be comfortable. Examples include a rocking chair, floor cushions or pillows, prayer mat, and meditation chair (low to the floor). Low tables can provide surfaces for books or small displays. Because listening to as well as making music has therapeutic properties, the room may be equipped for these activities. (See Figure 10.12.)

Meditation

Research has shown that **meditation,** which involves focusing the mind, can be effective in healing both physical and mental health problems, including the following:

- Anxiety
- Pain
- Depression
- Mood and self-esteem problems
- Stress
- Insomnia
- Physical or emotional systems related to chronic diseases such as heart disease, HIV/AIDS, and cancer (National Center for Complementary and Alternative Medicine, 2006)

Research about how meditation affects bodily changes is ongoing. Recall from Chapter 2 that activities in the sympathetic nervous system prepare the body to handle emergencies, in other words, to experience stress. On the other hand, the parasympathetic nervous system calms the body after the perceived danger has passed. It may be that meditation relieves stress by reducing the action of the sympathetic nervous system while increasing activity in the parasympathetic system (National Center for Complementary and Alternative Medicine, 2006).

Implications for Designers

Designers can create areas for meditation in a small room or even the corner of another room, such as a bedroom. Or it may be the same as the special space, discussed in the previous section. It is best if the area is protected from outside noise. This can be achieved by using soft fabrics and wool carpets to absorb sounds or by covering the walls with a sound-absorbing material such as cork. Tall leafy plants also serve to absorb sound. Masking sounds is another method and can be achieved with wind chimes, recordings of natural sounds, or the bubble of an indoor fountain (Craven, 2003).

FIGURE 10.12 Spaces for relaxation or meditation at home can be simple. Here, a comfortable chair set in a garden room provides an inviting setting.

Nature as a Restorative Agent

Nature has long been known for its restorative properties. The gentle sounds of wind and water, soft edges and curves of cliffs and lakes, and fresh fragrances of pine trees have the ability to take us on a mental vacation, away from the stresses of everyday life. As discussed previously, children prefer natural play areas. These childhood preferences persist into adulthood. For example, one study found that when asked to recall their most playful areas as children, most adults mentioned natural environments such as beaches, woods, streams, and trees (Cosco and Moore, 1999). Escape from reality is vital to play for individuals of all ages.

In addition to adding pleasure to life, contact with nature appears to aid in healing. In one study, postsurgical patients in Pennsylvania who were assigned to rooms with windows looking out at natural scenes had shorter hospital stays and took fewer pain-relieving medications than matched patients who viewed a brick wall (Ulrich, 1984). Another study, conducted in a children's hospital, found that creating a garden area reduced the young patients' stress and enhanced the healing process

(Whitehouse et al., 2001). Even the vital signs of healthy individuals can be influenced by the presence of natural elements. For example, a study on reactions to views seen when walking showed that subjects who saw trees had a more rapid decrease in blood pressure than those who walked among manmade structures (Hartig et al., 2003).

Implications for Designers

As the built environment replaces nature, paving over what were once forests and meadows, designers need to consider ways of reincorporating nature into our lives. This can be done in many ways, including landscaping and gardens; placing windows so they face natural views; planning atriums as part of a building; including live plants inside buildings; and constructing and furnishing with natural materials, such as wood and stone. Shapes can be borrowed from nature, such as an asymmetrical, rounded-edge coffee table in the living room or a curved walkway approaching the front door. Some people enjoy themed nature decor, such as rooms incorporating a day at the beach by using blues and whites, shells and driftwood, furnishings of rattan, and sculptures of seagulls.

Even photographs and paintings of nature can have restorative influences. This is because of the associations and memories of past experiences in nature that are brought to mind when viewing these images (Ohta, 2001). Bringing nature indoors or adjacent to a building is especially important for environments from which residents are less likely to leave with any frequency, such as hospitals, nursing homes, and assisted-living facilities.

Water as a Restorative Agent

The soothing and healing properties of water have been recognized for thousands of years. Ancient Egyptians bathed with essential oils and flowers, and the Romans constructed communal public baths for their citizens. Today, hydrotherapy is used both for relaxation and to treat arthritis, burns, spasticity, musculoskeletal disorders, spinal cord injuries, and the paralysis associated with stroke. The heat and movement of water increase blood circulation, which then assists in moving fluids and inflammatory particles, the causes of pain, away from the joints. Heat and gentle movement also help relax muscle contractions, thus relieving tightness in the neck, shoulders, and back and tension headaches.

Implications for Designers

Hydrotherapy can be provided by jetted bathtubs and hot tubs. Some benefits can be gained from showerheads that deliver pulsating streams of water. Soaking tubs, such as those used in Japan for centuries, can be installed in homes. To further enhance the relaxation experience, chromotherapy tubs are now available that have colored lights in healing hues.

Saunas use steam and heat, at temperatures between 104 and 122°F, to cleanse and relax the body. Originating in Scandinavia as wooden cabins with fires and hot rocks on which water was poured to produce steam, they are now available in many health clubs. Small saunas can be installed in homes.

Any source of hydrotherapy must be maintained properly or it can become a source of mold and bacteria. Indoor tubs must be easy to drain, clean, and disinfect. Some large tubs have lips to prevent overflow and wet floors. Hot tubs must be monitored for proper chemical balance, with chlorine added as needed, because the high temperature of the water, up to 104°, causes the chlorine to dissipate quickly. One solution to this problem is to install automatic chlorine dispensing devices. The most important factor in maintaining pool water quality is its **pH** (measure of acidity and alkalinity). The ideal pH range is between 7.4 and 7.6 (Morgan, 2003). If pH levels are too low, the water irritates the eyes, ears, and mucous membranes, as well as corroding the pool's metal surfaces. If levels are too high, iron and calcium can precipitate and cause the water to become cloudy and scale to form on the filter and other components. It is especially important that the water in hot tubs be recirculated quickly to ensure purity because of the tubs' small size in relation to the number of bathers that may be present (Morgan, 2003).

Following these guidelines helps ensure that water provides stress reduction without presenting health hazards.

GLOSSARY TERMS

Affordance

Energy balance

Meditation

Moderate activity

Morbidity

Morbid obesity

pH

Type 2 diabetes

Vigorous activity

LEARNING ACTIVITIES

1. Start a resource file of kitchen designs and products to increase the efficiency of kitchens to make them more "cook-friendly." Use your findings to design a convenient kitchen that is easy to use and clean. Write a description of the features you have included.

2. Spend a few hours observing the physical characteristics of your community. Your goal is to identify features that encourage and discourage physical activity. Create a written list and suggestions for how the barriers to activity might be removed.

3. Visit multistoried buildings, such as department stores and hospitals, and look for the stairs. Are they easy to find? Are the stairwells appealing? Do they feel safe? How many people appear to be using them? Choose one example and suggest how it could be improved to encourage more use.

4. Develop a description of an ideal public park that accommodates people of all ages. Then create a rating sheet (checklist) and use it to evaluate a park in your area. Write a report of your findings, including suggestions for how the park could be improved.

5. Interview a friend or classmate about how he or she likes to relax at home. Use what you learn to design a room or space that accommodates those preferences.

BOX 10.13 EXPERT SPOTLIGHT: Designing for Comfort

Gigi Davis Brown, IDEC, Allied ASID. M.ED
Author of: *Guidelines for Creating Sanctuary At Home and Work*
Program Director Interior Design
Tucson, AZ

I design for comfort. It seems like comfort is needed more than ever before. This is probably because there seems to be a lot more stress in our everyday lives and more need to be released from this stress. So where do we get this release? I believe the best place to start is with our living and working environments. Although it would be hard to imagine our entire home and workplace as sanctuaries, we can designate some smaller area, such as part of a table, shelf, or desk, to place something that symbolizes happiness or peace to you. This can then remind you of the need to take a moment and breathe. A focus area can be as simple as a chair or rug, even a pillow to sit on. (I think about all the pillows I have lost, or left behind, on traveling trips!) Whenever you are in this space, it is a reminder to let yourself go, relax, and take the mind, body, and spirit into a gentle and calmer place.

There are people who go to great lengths to create a sanctuary space. They may build a chapel on their property or have a yoga studio next to their bedroom. But it actually takes very little to create stress-free environments. You need to like how it feels through all the senses, touch (one of my favorites), smell, sight, and taste. Yes, you can taste a space, or place. Think chocolate walls! Depending on your clients' space allotments and finances, you can help them create a space that is "just right" to help eliminate stress.

SUGGESTED WEB SITES

1. The Surgeon General's Call to Action to Prevent and Decrease Obesity and Overweight 2001 www.surgeongeneral.gov/topics/obesity/calltoaction/CalltoAction.pdf
This article, written for the general public, discusses this major public health problem. The report also suggests ways that everyone, including built-environment professionals, can contribute to resolving the problem.

2. Mayo Clinic
www.mayoclinic.com
The Mayo Clinic's Web site has articles and videos for the general public on the topics discussed in this chapter: fitness, food and nutrition, meditation, relaxation, sleep, stress, and weight loss.

3. National Program for Playground Safety
www.playgroundsafety.org
This organization disseminates information about safe play areas, including suggested standards, safety tips, and a directory of manufacturers of playground surfaces and equipment.

4. KidsWalk to School
www.cdc.gov/nccdphp/dnpa/kidswalk/index.htm
The CDC has developed the KidsWalk-to-School program to encourage a return to walking rather than being driven to school. The program encourages partnerships between various segments of the community, including schools, police, public works, parents, and local politicians.

5. Transforming School Grounds
www.schoolgrounds.ca/
The Canadian Biodiversity Institute helps schools create "healthy enjoyable play and social spaces." Their Web site contains a wealth of information about how to improve play spaces, including site design, plant lists, and before and after photos of completed projects.

6. Project for Public Spaces
www.pps.org
Project for Public Spaces (PPS) is a nonprofit organization dedicated to creating and sustaining public places that build communities. Its Web site contains articles about and examples of people-friendly spaces.

7. Developing a Stress Management and Relaxation Program for the Worksite
www.imt.net/~randolfi/WorkStress.html
Dr. Randolfi's article describes an ideal stress management program, including suggestions for equipment and supplies.

8. National Center for Alternative and Complementary Medicine
Meditation for Health
http://nccam.nih.gov/health/meditation
Meditation has gained popularity in the United States. This Web site offers basic information that can be useful for designers whose clients practice meditation and are interested in dedicating an area in their homes or offices to this practice.

REFERENCES

Alfonzo, M. A., (2005). To walk or not to walk? The hierachy of walking needs. *Environment and Behavior, 37*(6), 808-836.

American Obesity Association. (May, 2005). *Obesity – a global epidemic.* Retrieved December 3, 2007, from http://obesity1.tempdomainname.com/subs/fastfacts/obesity_global_epidemic.shtml

American Obesity Association. (May, 2005). *Obesity in the U.S.* Retrieved September 14, 2006, from www.obesity.org/subs/fastfacts/obesity_US.shtml

Bailey, R., Olson, J., Pepper, J., Barstow, T., & Cooper, D. (1994). The level and tempo of children's physical activities: An observational study. *Medicine & Science in Sports & Exercise, 95,* 1033-1041.

Barbour, A. C. (1999). The impact of playground design on the play behaviors of children with differing levels of physical competence. *Early Childhood Research Quarterly, 14*(1), 75-98.

Barnes, P. M. and Schoenborn, C. A. (May 14, 2003). Physical activity among adults: United States, 2000. *Advance data from vital and health statistics,* no. 333. Hyattsville, MD: National Center for Health Statistics.

Burke, C. (2005). Play in focus: Children researching their own spaces and places for play. *Children, Youth, and Environments, 15*(2), 27-53.

Butte, N. F. (2001). The role of breastfeeding in obesity. *Pediatric Clinics of North America, 48*(1), 189-198.

Centers for Disease Control and Prevention. (Modified November, 2005). *Preventing chronic diseases: Investing wisely in health: Preventing obesity and chronic diseases through good nutrition and physical activity.* Retrieved December 3, 2007, from http://www.cdc.gov/nccdphp/publications/factsheets/Prevention/obesity.htm

Centers for Disease Control and Prevention. (2006). *KidsWalk-to-school.* Retrieved January 31, 2007, from www.cdc.gov/nccdphp/dnpa/kidswalk

Coffey, A. (2006). *A guide to transforming school grounds: Canadian Biodiversity Institute.* Ottawa, Canada: Marquardt Printing Ltd.

Cosco, N. & Moore, R.. (1999, January). *Playing in place: Why the physical environment is important in playwork.* Paper presented at the 14th Playeducation Annual Play and Human Development Meeting: Theoretical Playwork. Ely, Cambridgeshire, UK.

Craven, J. (2003). *The healthy home: Beautiful interiors that enhance the environment and your well-being.* Gloucester, MA: Rockport Publishers.

Crosby, M. A. (October, 1999). Pleasing students isn't child's play: Dining in the school cafeteria. *Restaurants USA Online.* Retrieved January 28, 2007, from www.restaurant.org/rusa/magArticle.cfm?ArticleID=450

Encinosa, W. E., Bernard, D. M., Steiner, C. A., & Chen, C., (2005). Use and costs of bariatric surgery and prescription weight-loss medications. *Health Affairs, 24*(4), 1039-1046.

Evans-Cowley, J. (2006). Sidewalk planning and policies in small cities. *Journal of Urban Planning and Development, 132*(2), 71-75.

Frank, L. D., Sallis, J. F., Conway, T. L., Chapman, J. E., Saelens, B. E., & Bachman, W. (2006). Associations between neighborhood walkability and active transportation, body mass index, and air quality. *Journal of the American Planning Association, 72*(1), 75-87.

Hartig, T., Evans, G. W., Jamner, L. D., Davis, D. S., & Gärling, T. (2003). Tracking restoration in natural and urban field settings. *Journal of Environmental Psychology, 23*(2), 109-123.

Janis, P. (2007). Is bigger better? *ASID ICON.* [Electronic version.] Retrieved July 10, 2007, from www.fsidesigner.com/pdf/supersizearticlemarchaprilicon1.pdf

Joseph, A., & Zimring, C. (2007). Where active older adults walk: Understanding the factors related to path choice for walking among active retirement community residents. *Environment & Behavior, 39,* 75-105.

Kaplan, R., & Kaplan, S. (1989). *The experience of nature: A psychological perspective.* New York: Cambridge University Press.

Kopec, DAK. (2006). *Designing for the elderly population: The Americans with Disabilities Act and its implications for an aging America.* Washington, DC: American Society of Interior Designers.

Krieger, E. B. (2005) Working out at work. *WebMD.* Retrieved January 29, 2007, from www.medicinenet.com/script/main/art.asp?articlekey=50932

Lambert, E. B. (1999). Do school playgrounds trigger playground bullying? *Canadian Children, 24*(1), 25-31.

Lindholm, G. (1995). Schoolyards: The significance of place properties to outdoor activities in schools. *Environment and Behavior, 27*(3), 259-293.

Maffeis, C. (1999) Childhood obesity: The genetic-environmental interface. *Baillere's Clinical Endocrinology and Metabolism, 13*(1) 31-46.

Malone, K., & Tranter, P. (2003). Children's environmental learning and the use, design and management of schoolgrounds. *Children, Youth and Environments, 13,* 2.

Mayo Clinic. (July 26, 2005). *Exercise: 7 benefits of regular physical activity.* Retrieved February 10, 2007, from www.mayoclinic.com/health/exercise/HQ01676

Mayo Clinic. (November 9, 2005). *Depression and anxiety: Exercise eases symptoms.* Retrieved February 10, 2007, from www.mayoclinic.com/health/depression-and-exercise/MH00043

Morgan, M. (2003). *Environmental health* (3rd ed.). Belmont, CA: Wadsworth.

National Center for Chronic Disease Prevention and Health Promotion. (1999). *Physical activity and health: A report of the surgeon general.* Atlanta: Author.

National Center for Complementary and Alternative Medicine. (Last modified May 16, 2006). *Backgrounder: Meditation for health purposes.* Retrieved February 11, 2007, from http://nccam.nih.gov/health/meditation

National Center for Health Statistics. (January, 2007). *Prevalence of overweight and obesity among adults: United States, 2003-2004.*

Retrieved December 2, 2007, from www.cdc.gov/nchs/products/pubs/pubd/hestats/overweight/overwght_adult_03.htm

Office of the Actuary at the Centers for Medicare and Medicaid Services. (n.d.). *Estimations of national spending on health care goods and services.* Retrieved January 29, 2007, from www.cms.hhs.gov/NationalHealthExpend-Data/downloads/highlights.pdf

Ohta, H. (2001). A phenomenological approach to natural landscape cognition. *Journal of Environmental Psychology, 21*(4), 387-403.

Osborne, P. (2005). Safe routes for children: What they want and what works. *Children, Youth, and Environments, 15*(1), 234-239.

Owen, C. G., Martin, R. M., Whincup, P. N., et al. (2005). Effect of infant feeding on the risk of obesity across the life course: a quantitative review of published evidence. *Pediatrics, 115,* 1367-77.

Paffenbarger, R. S., Jr., Hyde, R. T., Wing, A. L., and Hsieh, C. C.. (1986). Physical activity, all-cause mortality, and longevity of college alumni. *New England Journal of Medicine,* 288(8), 1728-1732.

Pratt, M., Macera, C. A., & Wang, G. (2000). Higher direct medical costs associated with physical inactivity. *The Physician and Sports Medicine, 28,* 10, 63-70.

Rivkin, M., (1995). *The great outdoors: Restoring children's right to play outside.* Washington, DC: National Association for the Education of Young Children.

Rosenbloom, A., Arslanian, S., Brink, S., Conschafter, K., Jones, K. L., Klingensmith, G., et al. (2000). Type 2 diabetes in children and adolescents. *Diabetes Care, 23*(3), 381-389.

Sallis, J. F., McKenzie, T. L., Kolody, B., Lewis, M., Marxhall, S., & Rosengard, P. (1999). Effects of health-related physical education on academic achievement: Project SPARK. *Research Quarterly for Exercise and Sport, 70,* 127-134.

Sauter, S., Murphy, L., Colligan, M., Swanson, N., Hurrell, J. Jr., Scharf, F. Jr., et al. (n.d.). *Stress at work.* (DHHS NIOSH Publication No. 99-101). Washington, DC: National Institute for Occupational Safety and Health.

Retrieved December 3, 2007, from www.cdc.gov/niosh/stresswk.html

Savich, H. V. (2003). How suburban sprawl shapes human well-being. *Journal of Urban Health, 80*(4), 590-607.

Skantze, A. (1995). Experiencing and interpreting city architecture. *Architecture and Behaviour, 11*(1), 5-10.

Stratton, G. (2000). Promoting children's physical activity in primary school: An intervention study using playground markings. *Ergonomics, 43,* 1538-1546.

Strauss, R. S. and Knight, J. (1999). Influence of the home environment on the development of obesity in children. *Pediatrics, 103*(6), E85.

Titman, W. (1994). *Special places, special people: The hidden curriculum of school grounds.* Surrey, UK: World Wide Fund for Nature/Learning Through Landscapes.

Toronto Public Health. (2007). *Physical activity in the workplace.* Retrieved February 5, 2007, from www.toronto.ca/health/wc_index.htm

Ulrich, R. S. (1984). View through a window may influence recovery from surgery. *Science, 224*(4647), 420-421.

U.S. Department of Health & Human Services. (2004). *Obesity and the built environment.* Retrieved February 1, 2007 from http://grants.nih.gov/grants/guide/rfa-files/RFA-ES-04-003.html

U.S. Department of Health & Human Services. (February, 2003). News Release: *Study shows sharp rise in the cost of diabetes nationwide.* Retrieved January 25, 2007 from www.dhhs.gov/news/press/2003pres/20030227a.html

U.S. Department of Health and Human Services. (2001). *The Surgeon General's call to action to prevent and decrease overweight and obesity.* [Rockville, MD]: U.S. GPO, Washington, DC: Author.

U.S. Preventive Services Task Force. (1996). *Guide to clinical preventive services* (2nd ed.). Baltimore: Williams and Wilkins.

Veitch, J., Bagley, S., Ball, K., & Salmon, J. (2006). Where do children usually play? A qualitative study of parents' perceptions of influences on children's active free play. *Health & Place, 12,* 383-393.

Wener, R. E. & Evans, G. W. (2007). A morning stroll: Levels of physical activity in car and mass transit commuting. *Environment & Behavior, 39*(1), 62-74.

Whitehouse, S., Varni, J. W., Seid, M., Cooper-Marcus, C., Ensberg, M. J., Jacobs, J. R., et al. (2001). Evaluating a children's hospital environment: Utilization and customer satisfac-tion. *Journal of Environmental Psychology, 21*(3), 301-314.

Winerman, L. (2004). Sleep deprivation threatens public health, says research award winner. *Monitor on Psychology, 35*(7), 61.

Wrigley, N., Warm, D., and Margetts, B., (2003). Deprivation, diet and food retail access: Findings from the Leeds "food deserts" study. *Environment and Planning A, 35,* 1, 151-188.

Glossary

A

Abrasion A type of wound where the top layer of skin is removed, usually with very little bleeding. This type of wound is usually quite painful, and can easily be infected since dirt and germs can become embedded in it.

Absorption Process by which a substance or particle is drawn into the structure of another.

Absorption coefficient Percent of sound absorbed by a material.

Accessibility The degree that the built environment can be accessed by all people with a varying degree of abilities.

Acid rain Rain that collects pollutants from the air, especially those with a high acidic content, as it falls to the earth.

Activities of daily living (ADL) The things we normally do in daily living including any activity we perform for self-care (such as feeding ourselves, bathing, dressing, grooming), work, homemaking, and leisure.

Acoustics The sense of hearing or the science of sound often used to describe the sound quality of the environment.

Adult day-care center Also known as adult day services, this type of facility provides supervised care for individuals who need assistance during the day, such as elderly and disabled persons.

Affordance A theory suggesting that the physical form of a space influences the activities that individuals perform within it.

Age-related changes Changes that occur in the human body as a result of the normal aging process.

Aging in place Planning and altering residences to make them more compatible to the needs of people as they age.

Air exchange rate The rate of airflow moving through a space, usually expressed in terms of room volume units per unit of time, such as room air changes per hour.

Albedo The measure of a material's ability to reflect solar radiation.

Allergen A substance that does not bother most individuals but causes an exaggerated response in others. Responses range from rashes and itching to a closed airway and death.

Allergy A condition in which the body has an exaggerated response to a foreign substance. Also known as hypersensitivity.

Alteration (Americans with Disabilities Act of 1990) Any change, addition, or modification in construction or occupancy.

Alzheimer's disease A progressive, neurodegenerative disease that causes the loss of function and death of nerve cells in several areas of the brain and leads to the loss of mental functions such as memory and learning.

Americans with Disabilities Act Accessibility Guidelines (ADAAG) Provides the scope and technical specifications for new construction and alterations undertaken by entities covered by the ADA.

Americans with Disabilities Act of 1990 (ADA) A federal law providing civil rights protections to individuals with disabilities, requiring accessible public transportation services and/or facilities along highways, trails, sidewalks, and other public settings.

Anatomy A branch of biology concerned with the structure and organization of living things.

Anthropometrics Refers to the different measurements of body sizes and proportions of people belonging to different populations.

Arc-fault circuit-interrupters (AFCIs) Electrical circuit-interrupters that continuously monitor for unintended arcs (discharge of electricity across a circuit), which they can distinguish from the normal arching that occurs when a switch is operated.

Articulation class A single number rating used for comparing acoustical ceilings and acoustical screens for speech privacy purposes; or, the listener's ability to understand the spoken word within a space.

Articulation index A measure of speech intelligibility within a room, which influences the acoustical environment.

Antioxidant Any substance that reduces oxidation, a process that results in the release of free radicals that can damage the chemical structures of the body's cells.

Arsenic A very poisonous chemical element used as an ingredient in pesticides and rodenticides.

Asbestos A naturally occurring fibrous silicate mineral that has been popular in manufacturing and industry because of its strength, and chemical and fire resistance.

Assisted-living residence These residential facilities provide care for persons who need some help with activities of daily living yet wish to remain as independent as possible.

Asthma A condition marked by labored breathing and wheezing, chest constriction, and/or coughing or gasping.

Attentional fatigue Mental fatigue experienced when individuals have to pay sustained attention to their environment.

B

Bacteria A large group of single-cell micro-organisms, some of which cause infections and disease in humans.

Barrier removal Removal, rearrangement, or modification of objects positioned or structured in a manner that impedes access.

Behavior zoning Assigning specific, separate locations in a structure, mode of transportation, etc., for cigarette smoking.

Bioaccumulation The process by which the concentrations of some toxic chemicals gradually increase in living tissue, such as in plants, fish, or people as they breathe contaminated air, drink contaminated water, or eat contaminated food.

Biomass A renewable fuel composed of grown or discarded organic matter.

Biophilia A theory proposing that people have a deep need to experience the natural environment.

Blepharitis An inflammation of the edge of the eyelid, caused by bacterial infection or allergic reactions to smoke, dust or chemicals.

Brain stem The part of the brain that connects the brain to the spinal cord and controls involuntary functions such as breathing and heart rate.

Bronchi Tubes that branch from the trachea into the lobes of the lungs, where they further branch into bronchial tubes.

Bronchioles Small tubes that extend from the two branches of the windpipe and end in small air sacs called alveoli.

Building America A U.S. Department of Energy program developed to help private builders construct cost-effective, zero-energy houses.

Building-integrated photovoltaic (BIPV) technologies The incorporation of photovoltaics (large numbers of cells to capture solar energy) into building components such windows, skylights, and siding shingles.

Building-related illnesses (BRI) Diagnosable illnesses with a known cause that often results from deficiencies in: design, operation, or maintenance of heating, ventilating, and air-conditioning (HVAC) systems, structural defects, and interior surface problems.

C

Candela The unit of measure for the intensity of light at the source roughly equal to the amount of light in any direction from the flame of a candle.

Carbon footprint The total impact of human activities as measured by the amount of carbon dioxide produced by human activities such as building, heating, and driving cars.

Carbon monoxide A colorless, odorless, poisonous gas, produced by incomplete burning of carbon-based fuels, including gasoline, oil, wood, and cigarette smoke.

Carbon neutral Maintaining a balance between the amount of carbon produced and used up, especially carbon-dioxide emissions.

Carcinogen Any substance known to cause cancer.

Carpal tunnel syndrome A condition in which the median nerve, which passes through the wrist, becomes compressed.

Cataract A disease that causes the lens or its capsule to become cloudy and can result in partially or severely decreased vision.

Cell The structural and functional unit of all living organisms, sometimes called the building blocks of life.

Cellular migration A complex phenomenon that requires the coordination of numerous cellular processes.

Chronic A condition or disease that lasts for a long time or is permanent.

Chronic obstructive pulmonary disease (COPD) A progressive lung disease process characterized by difficulty breathing, wheezing, and a chronic cough.

Circadian rhythms Name given to the "internal body clock" that regulates the 24-hour cycle of biological processes within life.

Clean air delivery rate (CADR) A method for expressing the efficiency of an air cleaner, it is obtained by multiplying a cleaning unit's efficiency by its airflow rate.

Cognitive Refers to the mental processes of knowing, perceiving, learning, being aware, and judging.

Color blindness A genetic disorder carried by females, but transmitted only to male children. The cone cells in the retina are unable to distinguish colors, especially red, green, blue, or mixtures of these colors.

Color rendering index Also known as CRI, is a measurement of the effect a light source has on the perceived color of objects and surfaces. High CRI light makes virtually all colors look natural and vibrant. Low CRI causes some colors to appear washed out or even to take on a completely different hue.

Congenital A condition or defect that is present at birth.

Conjunctivitis An inflammation of the membrane that lines the inner eyelids. Symptoms include redness, pain, swelling, and the discharge of mucous. It is caused by irritants or pathogens; the bacterial form is highly contagious.

Continuous sound level The average sound energy over a given time.

Contaminant A physical, chemical, biological, or radiological substance or matter that has an adverse effect on air, water, or soil.

Continuing-care community Residential community for older people to spend the remainder of one's life. These communities often offer a choice of services and living situations.

Convection The exchange of body heat, with the surrounding air.

Coronary artery disease The narrowing of the coronary arteries, usually caused by atherosclerosis, and may progress to heart damage due to lack of blood supply.

Cumulative trauma disorder (CTD) An injury to the musculoskeletal system that is a result of a gradual wear and tear process, or an accumulation of microtrauma, that eventually causes pain, inflammation, and loss of function.

D

Daylight harvesting The use of photosensors to determine the amount of natural light entering a room and then adjust the level of artificial light needed to maintain predetermined levels of illumination.

Daylighting The use of natural light as a source of interior illumination.

Decay To break down into smaller parts.

Decibel (dB) A unit used to convey the intensity of sound.

Decomposition Wasting away or otherwise disintegration or decay of materials.

Dehumidifier A device that removes moisture from the air.

Dementia Chronic intellectual impairment with organic origins that affects a person's ability to function in a social or occupational setting.

Dendritic trimming The natural occurrence of reducing the number of dendrite connections.

Deoxyribonucleic acid (DNA) The complex molecules inside cells that contain and pass on genetic information to the next generation of cells.

Dermatitis An inflammation of the skin caused by an allergic reaction or contact with an irritant. It can also be caused by extreme temperatures and infections.

Differentiation The normal process through which cells mature so they can carry out the jobs they were meant to do.

Dioxin A highly poisonous chemical produced in certain chemical manufacturing and disposal processes.

Disability A physical or mental incapacity, either congenital or resulting from an injury or illness, etc.

Dose A general term denoting a specific quantity.

E

Effective temperature The temperature that considers both ambient air and radiant surfaces.

Electricity grid The system of equipment and wiring that produces and transmits electrical power to customers.

Electrostatic precipitator Air cleaners that electrically charge airborne particles and then capture them on metal plates.

Embodied energy The total energy required to produce a finished product, including the energy used to grow, extract, manufacture, and transport it to the point of use.

Emphysema A lung disease in which the air sacs are enlarged and damaged, resulting in increased air retention and reduced exchange of gases.

ENERGY STAR A federal program created to rate and promote the use of energy-efficient computers, appliances, and building techniques.

Energy balance A state of equilibrium in which the number of calories consumed is equal to the amount of energy used by the body.

Ergonomic design An approach to design that applies ergonomic principles to ensure the best fit between humans and their environment.

Ergonomics The science of adapting all aspects of the environment, including equipment and furnishings, to increase the health, safety, and productivity of humans.

F

Fetal alcohol syndrome A pattern of mental and physical birth abnormalities found in some children of mothers who drank alcohol excessively during pregnancy.

Fiberglass A composite material that relies on small glass fibers for its strength.

Fibromyalgia A chronic disorder characterized by widespread musculoskeletal pain, fatigue, and multiple tender points that occurs in precise, localized areas, particularly in the neck, spine, shoulders, and hips; also may cause sleep disturbances, morning stiffness, irritable bowel syndrome, anxiety, and other symptoms.

Floor suspension system A type of flooring that reduces pressure and tension on joints.

Footcandle The amount of light that falls on the surface within a one-foot radius of its source.

Formaldehyde A chemical used in manufacturing and chemical industries that may increase the risk of developing leukemia and brain cancer.

Fossil fuels Fuels based on hydrocarbon. These include oil, natural gas, and coal.

Frequency The number of occurrences within a given time period. When applied to sound, frequency is the number of vibrations made by a sound wave and determines the pitch of a sound.

Fungi Organisms that lack chlorophyll, including molds, mildews, mushrooms, and yeast. A few types of fungi cause infections and allergies and damage the immune system.

G

Gestation The nine-month period of human pregnancy from conception to birth.

Glare Light that is brighter than the level to which the eyes are adapted.

Glaucoma Disorder of the eye characterized by an increase of pressure within the eyeball.

Global warming The phenomenon of the increase in temperature of the air near the earth and the ocean waters. Some scientists believe this may be caused by the release of greenhouse gases into the atmosphere.

Green building materials Raw construction materials deemed to fulfill green requirements such as being renewable.

Green building products Products that are safer for human health and/or the environment than traditional alternatives.

Green design An alternate term for sustainable design.

Green Seal An independent, nonprofit environmental testing program.

Greenhouse gases Gases that trap the sun's heat so that it can't be reflected back into the atmosphere.

Ground-fault circuit-interrupters (GFCIs) Electrical circuit-interrupters that shut off a circuit when an unintentional electrical path is established between a source of current and a grounded surface. An example is when a person comes into contact with an energized part and his body becomes part of the circuitry.

Gun safe or cabinet A storage device with security measures to prevent general access.

H

Heat pump Device that circulates a refrigerant to absorb heat or coolness from the earth, air, or water to use to efficiently heat and cool buildings and provide hot water.

HEPA filters High-efficiency particulate air filters.

Herniated disk A condition where the outer fibrous ring is torn, resulting in the central part of the intervertebral disc to protrude into the spinal canal.

Hertz (Hz) A measurement of frequency in cycles per second.

Homeostasis A term used to describe the maintenance of physiological and psychological stability.

Human factors An alternative term for *ergonomics.*

Humidifier A device that adds moisture to the air.

Humidity The concentration of water vapor in the air, which can make the temperature of the surrounding air feel warmer than actuality because the cooling effect of evaporation from the skin is reduced.

Hydrocarbons Molecules that contain hydrogen and carbon atoms. These form the basis for fossil fuels.

Hypertension Blood pressure above the normal range.

I

Illuminance The total amount of light falling on a surface as measured in footcandles or lux.

Immune deficiency disorders Disorders in which part of the body's immune system is missing or does not function properly.

Immune system The organs and processes that work together to protect the body against infection.

Immune-system sensitizer Components ingested, inhaled, or absorbed into the body that cause the immune system to become more sensitive.

Infiltration Air leakage, which can escape through cracks between the glass assembly and the window frame or cracks between wall joints, resulting in heat loss.

Insensible perspiration Naturally occurring perspiration under normal circumstances.

K

Keratitis An inflammation of the cornea, usually caused by trauma or infections.

L

Lead A soft, heavy, toxic, and malleable metal, used in building construction and materials.

Lead poisoning The result of lead accumulating in the body, through either inhalation or ingestion (eating). Although some lead is excreted in the urine, most of it goes into the red blood cells where it can interfere with the production of hemoglobin, the component of blood that carries oxygen from the lungs to the tissues.

LEED Leadership for Energy and Environmental Design. A group that has developed a well-respected rating system for green buildings.

Legionnaires' disease Bacterial infection of the lungs.

Leukemia A type of cancer that affects the blood or blood-forming organs.

Life quality Opportunity to live as independently and purposefully as possible.

Light shelf Reflective structure installed either inside or outside windows that increases the amount of light that enters the window.

Light tube Pipe-shaped openings that transport light from the outside to the inside of a building.

Liquefaction The process of liquifying.

Long-term care facility A facility that provides a range of health, personal care, social, and housing services to people who are unable to care for themselves independently as a result of chronic illness or mental/physical disabilities.

Lumen Measurement of light output from a source.

Lux The amount of visible light per square meter incident on a surface.

M

Macular degeneration A chronic disease of the eyes caused by the deterioration of the central portion of the retina, known as the macula, which is responsible for focusing central vision in the eye.

Malignant melanoma A serious, sometimes fatal type of skin cancer, in which a mole changes shape, darkens, becomes painful, and/or bleeds easily.

Mechanical ventilation Controlled, purposeful introduction of outdoor air to the conditioned space.

Meditation The practice of focusing the mind on an image or word with the purpose of calming the mind and relaxing the body.

Melatonin A hormone released during darkness that is responsible for drowsiness.

Metabolism The chemical and physiological processes by which the body builds and maintains itself and by which it breaks down food and nutrients to produce energy.

Microbial volatile organic compound (mVOC) Compounds produced by molds that evaporate and enter the air. These cause the odors we associate with mold.

Mitosis The replication of a cell to form two daughter cells with identical sets of chromosomes.

Moderate activity The amount of physical activity needed to use about 150 calories each day or 1000 calories each week.

Mold A form of fungus that can cause illness and disease in humans.

Morbid obesity A level of obesity considered dangerous to health.

Morbidity The condition of being diseased or in poor health.

Motor skills Skills using the small and large muscles of the body; includes fine and gross movements.

Muscle strain Overexertion of a single or group of muscles.

Mutate In genetics, a change in the DNA sequence that results in a new character or trait not found in the original cell.

Myelin sheath The fat and protein-containing material that surrounds and protects some nerves.

Myelination The second of two changes during brain development after birth. During this process, neurons and dendrites become coated with a fatty substance (myelin) to enable neural impulses to travel faster.

Mycotoxin A toxic substance produced by mold.

N

National Safety Council A not-for-profit safety organization that was chartered by the U.S. government in 1913 to protect the safety of Americans at home, on the roads, and at work.

Natural ventilation A type of air movement that depends on natural means for bringing outdoor air indoors.

Net-zero energy Refers to a balance of zero when measuring the amount of energy used by a building. An example is planting trees to compensate for using a fossil-fuel energy source.

Neurotransmitter A specialized chemical messenger that sends a message from one nerve cell to another.

New construction (Americans with Disabilities Act of 1990) A new building, work done to fill in a gutted building, or the addition of tenant space in an existing building.

Noise-induced hearing loss (NIHL) The slow loss of hearing caused by too much noise.

Noise isolation class A single number rating of the degree of speech privacy achieved through the use of an acoustical ceiling and sound-absorbing screens in an open office.

Noise load The total level of noise within a room.

Noise reduction coefficient (NRC) A measure of sound absorbed by a material.

O

Off-gassing The release of gases or vapors by a material over time. (Also called *outgassing.*)

Organ A group of tissues in a living organism that have been adapted to perform a specific function.

Organophosphates Any of several organic compounds containing phosphorus, some of which are used as fertilizers and pesticides.

Osteoarthritis A condition caused by wear and tear that causes inflammation of the joint, causing swelling, pain, and stiffness.

Osteoporosis A decrease in bone mass and bone density and an increased risk and/or incidence of fracture.

Outgassing The release of gases or vapors by a material over time. (Also called *off-gassing.*)

Ozone Extremely reactive form of oxygen, normally occurring around electrical discharges and present in the atmosphere in small but active quantities.

P

Pacemaker Device that sends electric impulses to the cardiac (heart) muscles signaling them to contract and relax in order to push blood through the circulatory system. (Also refers to specialized muscle tissue in the body that performs this function.)

Parkinson's disease A slowly progressive neurodegenerative disease characterized by tremors and muscle weakness.

Passive design Defined by Randy Croxton, a pioneer of ecological design, as allowing a building to "default to nature." It requires a holistic, comprehensive approach that considers how a building might be constructed to take advantage of every available natural resource, such as sunlight, wind, vegetation, and land forms, to supply its heating, cooling, ventilating, and lighting needs.

Persistent organic pollutant (POP) A class of chemicals that persist in the environment, are capable of long-range transport, bioaccumulate in human and animal tissue, and have significant impacts on human health and the environment.

Percentage efficiency rate The measure of how well an air filter collects pollutants from the air.

pH Measure of acidity and alkalinity.

Photovoltaics Solar cells that convert sunlight into electrical energy.

Physiology A branch of biology that deals with the functions and activities of life or of living matter (as organs, tissues, or cells) and of the physical and chemical phenomena involved.

Places of accommodation Privately run facilities whose operations affect commerce and are open to the public.

Pollutant Any substance that causes harm to the environment when it mixes with soil, water, or air.

Precautionary Principle The concept that if something might harm human health, it is wise to take precautions even if the harm has not been fully proven scientifically.

Proprioceptors Receptors located in the muscles, tendons, joints, and the inner ear that send signals to the brain regarding the body's position.

R

Radiation The heat or cold that surfaces such as walls and windows give off. The difference in temperature between ambient air and radiant surfaces should be small, not more than 2 to 3°C higher or lower

Radon A radioactive gas that is released by uranium, a substance found in soil and rock, which can damage lung cells and lead to lung cancer if inhaled.

Range of motion The range, measured in degrees of a circle, through which a joint may be moved.

Reasonable accommodation Modifications or adjustments to a program, work environment, or job description that make it easier for a person with a disability to equally participate in an activity.

Reflex sweating The sweating that takes place when an individual is exposed to uncomfortably high temperatures.

Refractive errors Conditions in which the eyeball is misshapen so that light rays do not hit the retina properly to create a clear image.

Relative humidity The amount of water vapor in the air, compared to the amount the air could hold if it was totally saturated.

S

Seasonal affective disorder (SAD) A form of depression associated with a lack of daylight.

Septicemia Also called blood poisoning; this is a disease that affects many organ systems due to toxins in the blood, which are released by bacteria or other microorganisms.

Sick building syndrome (SBS) A set of symptoms that affect multiple occupants of a building; often related to the duration spent in the building, and go away once out of the building.

Sink effect A reaction that takes place when materials that may not outgas volatile organic compounds themselves absorb the chemicals outgassed by other materials and later release them into the air.

Smoke detector A device that utilizes optical, optical/thermal, or ionization techniques to detect smoke particles.

Solar heat gain coefficient (SHGC) The fraction of solar energy that enters a window and becomes heat, expressed as a value between 0 and 1.

Solar reflectance index (SRI) A rating system to indicate a roof's ability to reflect heat.

Sound masking A low-level, broadband sound precisely contoured to mask (cover up) unwanted background noise and distracting speech.

Sound transmission class (STC) A numeric representation of how much noise is stopped by some item or barrier.

Source management Minimizing or eliminating pollutants.

Spores The seeds of mold or fungi.

Sprain A sudden or violent twist or wrench of a joint leading to the stretching or twisting of ligaments.

Spring-load floor A type of flooring system that reduces impact pressure on the skeletal system. Often used in recreation areas where high-impact activities occur.

Static effort The body maintaining one position over a period of time, resulting in a prolonged state of muscle contraction and compression of the blood vessels.

Stroke Temporary or permanent loss of the blood supply to the brain, or sudden and severe bleeding in the brain.

Sty A bacterial infection of an oil gland in the eyelid.

Summated frequency level The percentage of time that a designated decibel was reached or exceeded during a given period of time.

Sustainability All those elements that comprise the design, development, and construction of the built environment that have the potential of permanently altering the physical environment and/or the human condition.

Sustainable design A design approach that emphasizes energy conservation, healthy indoor environments, and overall structural durability.

Sympathetic nervous system The branch of the involuntary nervous system that prepares the body for fight or flight by speeding up heartbeat and breathing, and at the same time shutting down digestive functions.

Synapse The junction where a signal is transmitted from one nerve cell to another, usually by a neurotransmitter.

Synaptogenesis The process during which the brain cells form most of their interconnections. This takes place from about the sixth month of pregnancy to a child's second birthday.

Syndrome A set of symptoms or conditions that occur together and suggest the presence of a certain disease or an increased chance of developing the disease.

Synergism The interaction of actions, chemicals, etc., such that the total effect is greater than the sum of the individual effects.

System (human body) Groups of organs that work together to perform specific body functions, such as the digestive system.

Systemic illness Illnesses that affect multiple systems concurrently or progressively.

T

Tetanus A disease-causing bacteria that produces painful, rigid muscle contractions, especially in the neck and jaw.

Thermal comfort Describes a person's psychological state of mind and usually refers to whether a person is feeling too hot or too cold.

Thermal conduction The transmission of heat across matter such as windows, walls, and floors.

Thermal regulation The ability to maintain temperature within certain boundaries, even when the surrounding temperature is different.

Thermoregulatory The ability to maintain a constant internal body temperature independent from the environmental temperature.

Threshold limit values (TLVs) A numeric representation of the exposure limits a person can tolerate.

Tinnitus The sensation of ringing or buzzing in the ears. It has various causes, including loud noise.

Tissue A group of similar cells that perform certain specialized functions in the body.

Toxicity The ability of a substance to cause harmful health effects.

Traumatic brain injury (TBI) Refers to any injury to the brain resulting from the application of external forces to the skull.

Trichinosis A disease caused by eating undercooked meat that contains trichinae, which develop as adults in the intestines and as larvae in the muscles, causing intestinal disorders, fever, nausea, muscular pain, and edema of the face.

Type 2 diabetes A chronic condition in which the body does not pass glucose into the cells where it can be used as fuel. The resulting high levels of glucose in the blood can damage various essential body parts.

U

Underwriters Laboratories An organization that classifies, tests, and inspects electronic devices, fire protection equipment and assemblies, and specific construction materials for life-safety performance.

Universal design The creation of built environments that are suitable for people of all ages, sizes, and abilities.

V

Ventilation The process of supplying or removing air by natural or mechanical means to or from any space.

Vertical storage The use of wall space to provide storage areas.

Vigorous activity Physical activities that cause hard breathing and sweating and are performed for at least 20 minutes a minimum of 3 days out of 7.

Visible transmittance The visible spectrum, or daylight, that is allowed through a window.

Vitamin D A fat-soluble vitamin needed for bones and teeth structure and formed in the skin as a result of exposure to sunlight.

Viruses Clusters of genetic material surrounded by chemicals that can cause many of the most serious diseases.

Volatile organic compounds (VOC) Compounds that can come from many products, such as office equipment, adhesives, carpeting, upholstery, paints, solvents, and cleaning products. They evaporate easily at room temperature and can cause cancer when concentrated indoors.

W

Watt A measure of electrical power, such as the amount of light produced by a bulb.

Z

Zero-Energy Homes A U.S. Department of Energy program developed to help private builders construct cost-effective, zero-energy homes.

Credits

Index

Note: figures and tables indicated with *f* and *t*